A

C000048870

101 ROUTES IN FRANCE

CONTENTS

Produced by the Publications Division of the Automobile
Association.

Typeset by Armitage Rand.
Printed by RD Litho.

ISBN 0 86145 2712

AA Ref: 58719

Published by the Automobile Association, Basingstoke,
Hampshire RG21 2EA.

USING THIS BOOK
Touring Information

Roads and travel
Throughout France main and secondary roads are normally good, although sometimes not finished to our standards. Wide strips on the edge may be uneven and surfaces are sometimes allowed to deteriorate beyond the customary limits before being repaired. However, comfortable motoring is the general rule.

On most of the motorways in France tolls are charged and you may feel they are expensive. No doubt you will weigh the cost against time and convenience, particularly as the alternative roads are often fast. A leaflet detailing tolls is available from the AA on request.

Motoring in winter
Motoring during the winter months is not severely restricted except in the high Alps and Pyrénées. Elsewhere in the mountains, snow is usually quickly swept away from the main roads. General touring in the Massif Central is not recommended in winter. The notes heading the relevant itineraries contain any necessary comment on winter closures: see also *Winter conditions* and the details of the *principal mountain passes* in the publication *Travellers' Guide to Europe*.

Getting around Paris
For many years it has been the long-standing practice to avoid Paris, but with the construction of motorways to the capital, and with the completion of the dual-carriageway ring road, many recommended routes are now via Paris. The ring road is signposted as the Boulevard Périphérique. It is described in Itinerary 101. Itineraries radiating from Paris cross the ring road at the 'Portes' (gateways) indicated. To avoid Paris centre follow that part of the ring road between your approach 'Porte' and your exit 'Porte'.

On approaching the Boulevard Périphérique the following signs are used to divert the traffic streams: 'Paris-Nord', 'Paris-Est', 'Paris-Sud', and 'Paris-Ouest'. Once on the ring road, the main direction signs are: 'Aeroport Charles de Gaulle' and 'Lille, Bruxelles' for Autoroute A1; 'Metz, Nancy, Strasbourg' for A4; 'Lyon' for A6; 'Chartres, Orléans' for A10/A11; and 'Rouen' for A13.

Transit traffic between Autoroute A1 (from Lille) and either the A6 (for Lyon), or A10 (for Orléans), and A11 (for Chartres) can save 3 miles by following Autoroute A3.

Travelling north to south, leave the A1 shortly after Charles de Gaulle Airport and follow signs 'Paris Est', 'Bordeaux, Nantes and Lyon'. On reaching Porte de Bagnolet follow signs 'Paris Sud' to join the Boulevard Périphérique, then signs 'Lyon' and 'Autoroute A6'. In the opposite direction follow signs 'Paris Est' then 'Autoroute A3', 'Aeroport Charles de Gaulle', and 'Lille, Bruxelles'.

Calais and Boulogne to Paris
There is a toll motorway route (using Autoroutes A26 and A1) between Nordausques, Arras and Paris. From Calais to Paris it is now quicker, therefore, to motor this way. From Boulogne, however, there is little advantage in time, and N1 is recommended. This is also the road to use from Calais if the motorway is not favoured.

Le Havre and Dieppe to Paris
From Le Havre the toll motorway, Autoroute A13, can be used from just south of the Pont de Tancarville (toll bridge across the River Seine).

Continued overleaf

Town plans
Plans of the ferry ports and the environs of Paris are shown on pages 6-11. The plans are primarily intended as a guide through or around the town.

TOWN PLAN LEGEND

Motorway	Pedestrians	Post Office (PO)
Throughroute	Information Office (i)	Airport ✈
Throughroute dual carriageway	Hospital (H)	Port Agent AA|PA
Main road		
Other road	Police Station (POL)	Port and Recovery Agent AA|PA/RA

This motorway leads past Mantes and St-Germain, to the Boulevard Périphérique (Paris ring road) and this is the recommended entry to the city. Instead of the toll motorway, route N15 can be used from Le Havre via Rouen to Mantes, from whence the toll free section of the motorway can be followed to Paris. From Dieppe the usual route is via toll motorway, Autoroute A13, which is joined 10km beyond Rouen.

To Biarritz
From Calais and Boulogne to Paris, then to Tours via toll motorway, Autoroute A10. Routes from Dieppe and Le Havre converge here, then continue via Bordeaux.

To Perpignan (for eastern Spain)
The shortest route from Paris via N7 to Moulins and N9 via Clermont-Ferrand, St-Flour and Millau is **not** the recommended route for a quick journey. Between Clermont-Ferrand and Lodève it passes through mountainous country and is very slow. The alternatives lie to the west or east of the Massif Central. The western route follows N20 via Orléans, Limoges, Toulouse and Narbonne. It is generally a fast road except for the stretch between Brive and Cahors, which is hilly and winding but not particularly restrictive. The eastern route employs motorways: Autoroute A6 between Paris and Lyon, A7 on to Orange near Avignon, and A9 from Orange via Nîmes, Montpellier and Beziers to Narbonne and Perpignan. By travelling from Calais via Autoroutes A26 and A1 to Paris and then by the ring road to A6, most of this route between Calais and Perpignan can be covered by motorway. It is now, therefore, the recommended and faster approach to the eastern Spanish border.

To Geneva and Mont Blanc Tunnel (for Italy)
The fastest approach is via Paris ring road (see above) and the A6 Autoroute du Soleil to Mâcon Junc, then via Bourg-en-Bresse to Geneva. Geneva can be bypassed by continuing on Autoroute A40 to Chamonix for the Mont Blanc Tunnel and northern Italy.

To the Riviera (Côte d'Azur)
The fastest approach to the Mediterranean coast is by the Rhône Valley from Lyon to Avignon, using Autoroute A7 and then A8. The alternative via Grenoble is the lower *Route des Alpes* over the mountains; it is a good but comparatively slow road. To reach Lyon the fastest approach is now via Paris (see above) and A6. The alternative via Arras, Soissons, Troyes, and Dijon is, however, a fairly fast road and could be used instead of motorways, but it is hilly, and caravans should go via St-Quentin, Reims, and Chaumont to Dijon following the Marne valley.

HOW TO USE THE ITINERARIES
Choosing your route

First refer to the key map (pages 12-15) which shows all the itineraries listed in this book. From this map choose the itineraries needed to make up your route. Each itinerary is numbered on the key map; these numbers relate to the appropriate itinerary in this book. They are not road numbers or page numbers.

The itineraries

Each itinerary gives a description of the road, scenery, and route details for a journey between two points. The description makes special mention of hills steeper than 10 per cent, and includes comparative notes to help you choose between alternative routes where applicable. Itineraries can be used in either direction. The strip maps alongside the itineraries are not drawn to scale.

Abbreviations:

The following abbreviations are used in the itineraries:

Bd	boulevard
Br	bridge
ft	feet
Iter	itinerary
Junc	road junction
km	kilometres
max grad	maximum gradient
R	river
rly sta	railway station
SP	sign post
unclass, uncl.	unclassified road
X-rds	crossroads

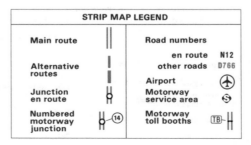

STRIP MAP LEGEND			
Main route	‖	Road numbers	
		en route	N12
Alternative routes		other roads	D766
		Airport	✈
Junction en route		Motorway service area	⑤
Numbered motorway junction	⑭	Motorway toll booths	TB

Example:

An example of an itinerary is given below:

33 Dieppe – Rouen
(61 km = 38 miles)
Through a series of valleys set between low hills, passing by apple orchards and meadows. SP 'Paris' & 'Rouen'. In the opposite direction SP 'Dieppe' & 'Le Havre' out of Rouen.

N27			Dieppe	61
	3	3	Junc with D915	58
	6	3	St-Aubin-sur-Scie	55
	8	2	Sauqueville	53
	18	10	Belmesnil	43
	29	11	Tôtes	32
	38.5	9.5	Le Boulay	22.5
			(Clères 5.5km by D6)	
N315	43	4.5	Junc N27/N315	18
			(Rouen 15km by N27)	
A15	49.5	6.5	Motorway fork	11.5
			(Junc N315/A15)	
	51	1.5	Service area	10
			(northbound only)	
	54.5	3.5	Canteleu/Maromme Junc	6.5
			(exit for northbound	
			traffic only)	
N15	58.5	4	Motorway terminus	2.5
	61	2.5	**Rouen**	
1	**2**	**3**	**4**	**5**

Explanation:

1 Road numbers. Each road number applies from the place against which it is printed to the point where another number is shown. When using the itinerary in the opposite direction, each road number applies as far as the place against which it is printed.

2 The distance in kilometres from the starting point to each place in the itinerary, the last distance being the total for the whole journey.

3 The distance between one place and the next in the itinerary.

4 Placenames, landmarks, and road junctions on the route. If in square brackets, for example [Mornas], it means that either there is a bypass or the place is to the left or right of the road. A place printed in red means that it is described in the gazetteer. Itinerary numbers appearing in brackets, for example (Iter 25, 90) after a placename or road junction indicate a link to another itinerary.

5 The distance in kilometres from the finishing point to all places in the itinerary. The mileage conversion of the total distance is given in the heading of the itinerary; there is a conversion table on the inside back cover. You can calculate the approximate travelling time for each itinerary by considering the kilometre distance as minutes – eg, 60km (37.5 miles) takes about 60 minutes; make allowances for travel on motorways and for delays in larger towns and cities.

The Channel Ports: Boulogne/Calais

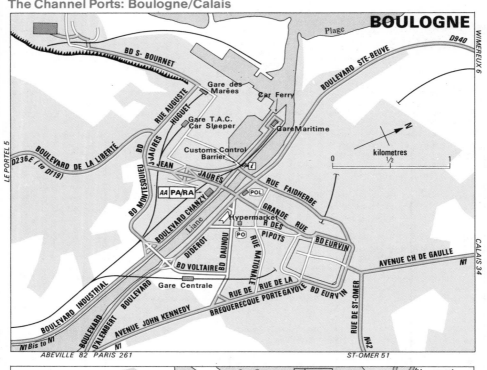

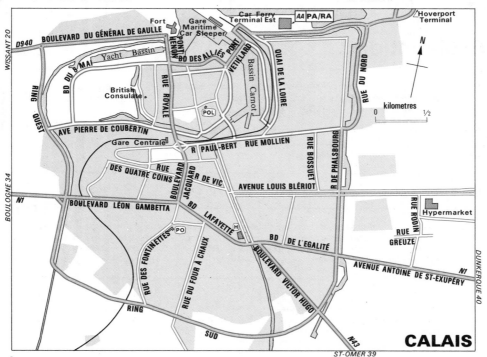

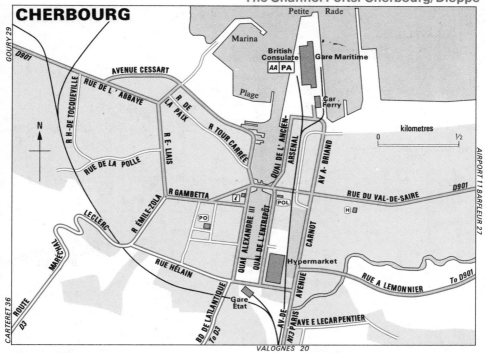

CHERBOURG

Petite Rade

Marina

Plage

British Consulate
AA PA

Gare Maritime

Car Ferry

GOURY 29
D901

AVENUE CESSART

RUE DE L' ABBAYE

R H-DE TOCQUEVILLE

R DE LA PAIX

R TOUR CARRÉE

R E. LIAIS

RUE DE LA POLLE

QUAI DE L' ANCIEN- ARSENAL

AV A- BRIAND

kilometres
0   ½

N

AIRPORT 11 BARFLEUR 27

R GAMBETTA

R ÉMILE-ZOLA

i

POL

RUE DU VAL-DE-SAIRE   D901

H

LECLERC

PO

QUAI ALEXANDRE III

QUAI DE L'ENTREPÔT

CARNOT

MARÉCHAL

RUE HÉLAIN

Hypermarket

AVENUE

RUE A. LEMONNIER   To D901

CARTERET 36
ROUTE
D3

BD DE L'ATLANTIQUE
To D3

Gare
État

AV. DE

N3 PARIS

AVE E LECARPENTIER

VALOGNES 20

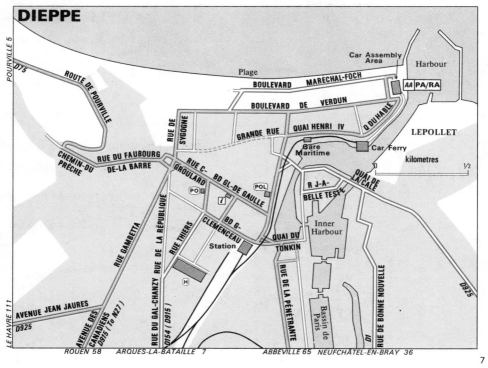

DIEPPE

Car Assembly
Area

Harbour

Plage

BOULEVARD   MARECHAL-FOCH

AA PA/RA

POURVILLE 5
D75

ROUTE DE POURVILLE

BOULEVARD   DE   VERDUN

RUE DE SYGOGNE

GRANDE RUE

QUAI HENRI IV

Q. DU HÂBLE

LEPOLLET

CHEMIN-DU
PRÊCHE

RUE DU FAUBOURG
DE-LA-BARRE

RUE C-
GROULARD

BD GL-DE GAULLE

PO

i

POL

Gare
Maritime

Car Ferry

QUAI DE
LA CALE

R J-A-
BELLE TESTE

RUE GAMBETTA

RUE DE LA RÉPUBLIQUE

RUE DU GAL-CHANZY

RUE THIERS

BD G-
CLEMENCEAU

Station

QUAI DU
TONKIN

Inner
Harbour

H

RUE DE LA PÉNÉTRANTE

Bassin de
Paris

RUE DE BONNE NOUVELLE

D925

LE HAVRE 111

AVENUE JEAN JAURES

AVENUE DES
CANADIENS

D925

D154 (D915)

D915 (To N27)

D1

ROUEN 58   ARQUES-LA-BATAILLE 7   ABBEVILLE 65 NEUFCHÂTEL-EN-BRAY 36

The Channel Ports: Dunkerque/Le Havre

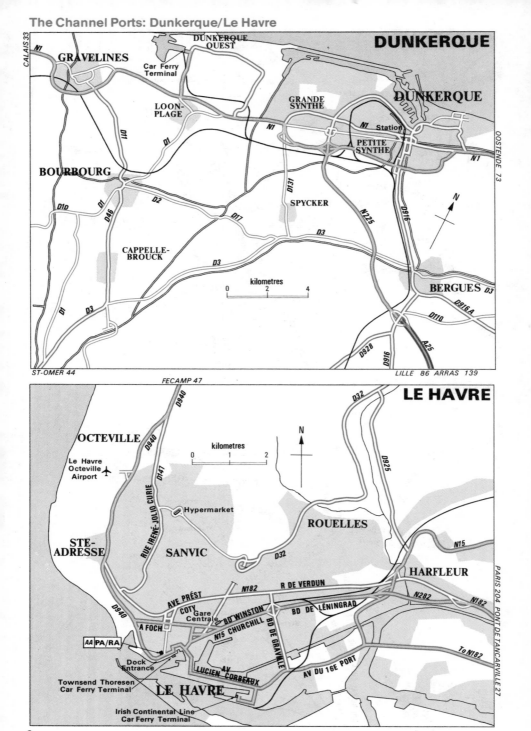

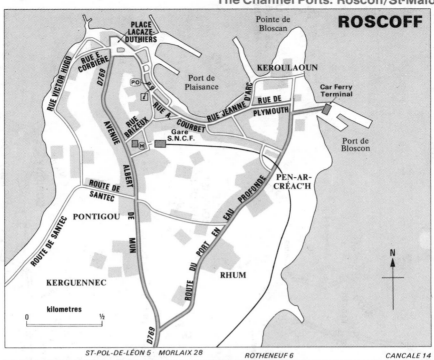

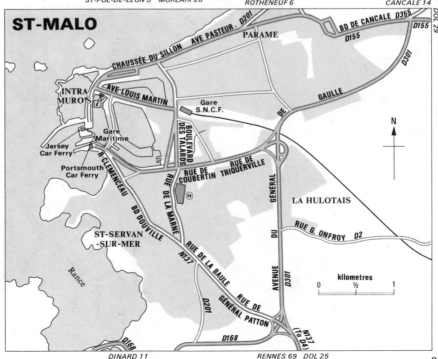

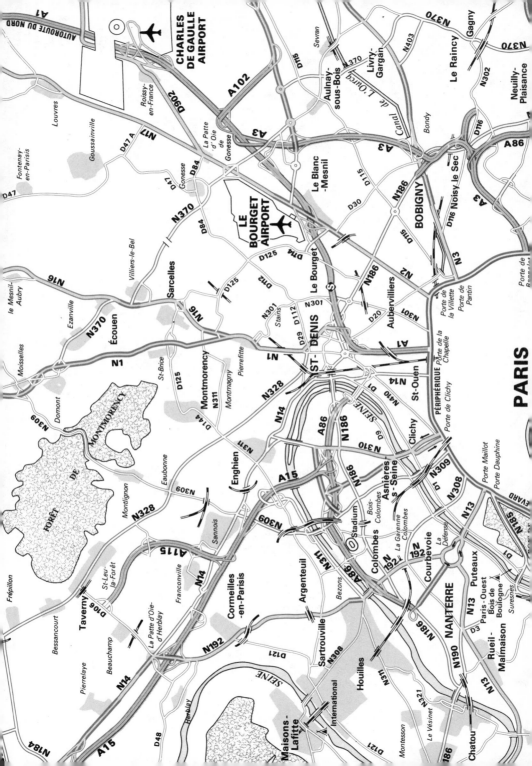

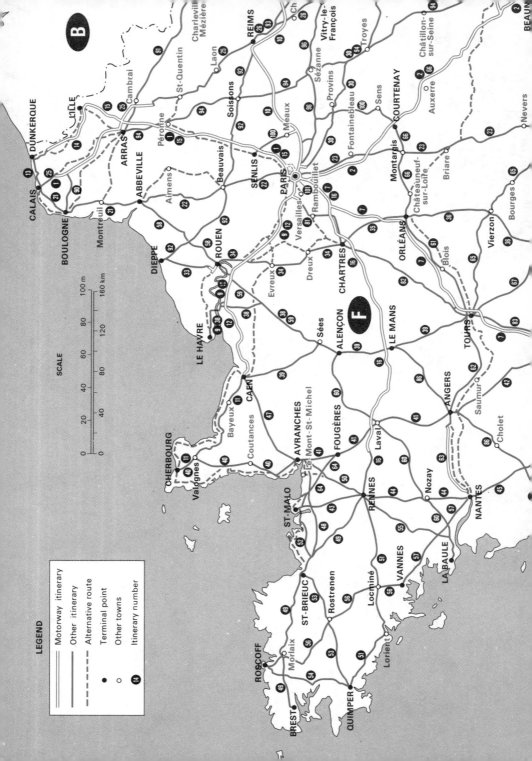

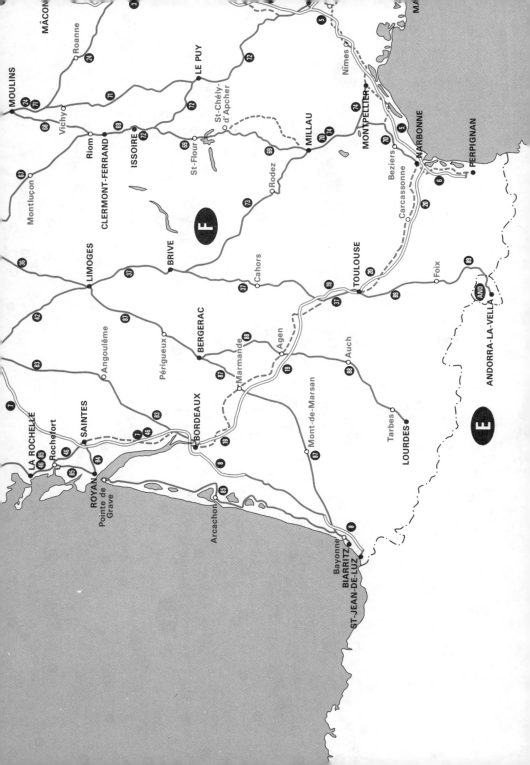

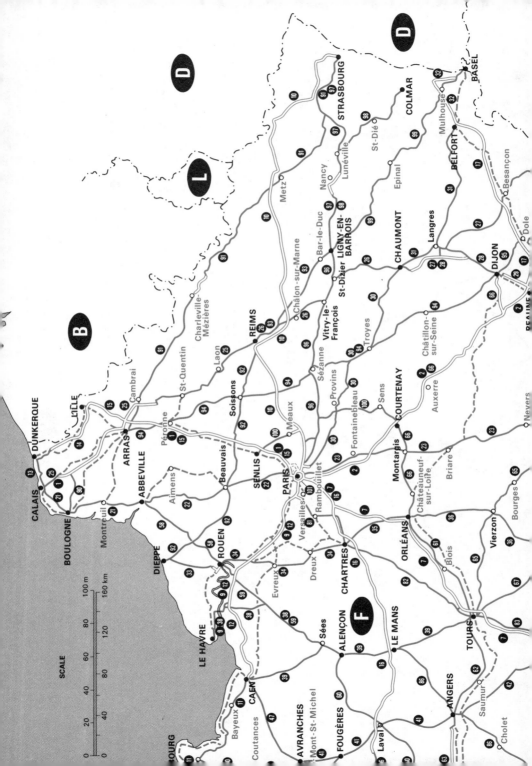

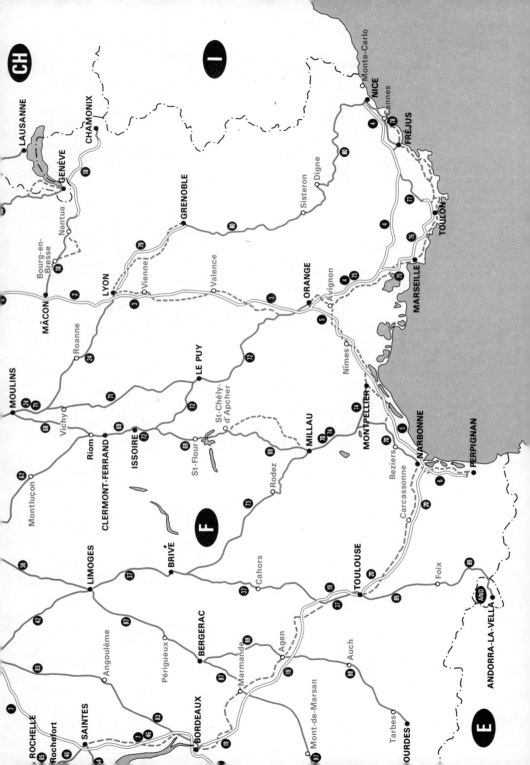

1 Calais – Paris

(290km = 180 miles)

Mainly straight tree-lined road across flat country to Ardres, then pleasant and undulating; after Nordausques the route follows toll motorways A26 and A1, the *Autoroute du Nord.*

Not all junctions are listed. Moderate scenery to Roye then pleasant rolling countryside. Through Forest of Ermenonville after Senlis. SP 'St-Omer' out of Calais, then 'Paris'. In the opposite direction SP 'Lille' and then 'Calais' onto A26.

For non-motorway route Calais – Paris follow Iter 21-22. If proceeding to A6 (for Lyon), A10 (for Orléans), or A11 (for Chartres) follow Autoroute A3 SP *'Paris-Est',* then *'Paris-Sud', 'Lyon'* and *'Autoroute A6'.* In the opposite direction SP *'Paris-Est',* then *'Autoroute A3'* and *'Lille, Bruxelles'.*

N43		Calais	290
	8	8	Les Attaques	282
	11	3	Le Pont d'Ardres	279
	16	5	Ardres	274
A26	23	7	Nordausques Junc with Autoroute A26	267
	37	14	St-Omer Junc (no. 3) (Iter 90) (Toll booths)	253
	68	31	Lillers Junc (no. 5)	222
	80	12	Béthune Junc	210
	91.5	11.5	Aix-Noulette Junc (Junc with Autoroute A21, Lens 9km)	198.5
	96	4.5	Service area	194
	104	8	Arras Nord Junc (no. 7) (Iter 25, 90)	186
A1	113	9	Motorway X-rds (Junc A26/A1) (Arras/Fresnes Junc, on Iter 15, 3km)	177
	119	6	Arras-Est Junc (Iter 91)	171
	130	11	Service area	160
	137	7	Bapaume Junc	153
	146	9	Motorway fork (Junc with A2; exit for northbound traffic only)	144
	161	15	Asservillers service area	129
	162	1	Péronne Junc	128
	182	20	Roye Junc	108
	203	21	Ressons Junc & service area	87
	217	14	Compiègne Junc (Iter 92)	73
	241	24	Senlis/Meaux Junc (Iter 100) (Toll booths)	49
	256	15	Survilliers/ Ermenonville Junc	34
	258	2	Vémars service area	32
	267	9	Aéroport Charles de Gaulle Junc	23
	270	3	Junc with Autoroute A102	20
	271	1	Motorway fork (Junc A1/A3; *see heading*)	19

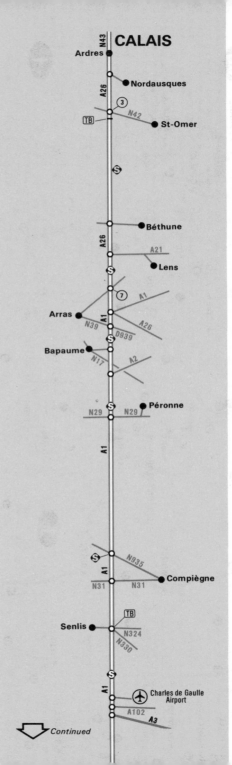

Continued

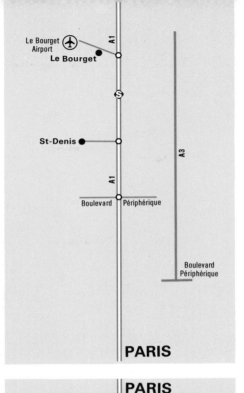

275	4	Le Bourget Airport Junc	15
278	3	La Courneuve service area	12
280	2	St-Denis/Enghien Junc	10
281.5	1.5	Pierrefitte/St-Denis/La Courneuve Junc	8.5
284	2.5	Junc A1/Bd Périphérique (Porte de la Chapelle) (Iter 101)	6
290	6	Paris	

or by Autoroute A3

A3		Motorway fork (Junc A1/A3)	15
2	2	Aulnay (Zone Industrielle) Junc	13
4.5	2.5	Aulnay Junc	10.5
7.5	3	Bobigny/Bondy Junc	7.5
10	2.5	Motorway fork	5
10.5	0.5	Motorway fork (Junc with A86)	4.5
13	2.5	Romainville/Montreuil Junc	2
15	2	Junc A3/Bd Périphérique (Porte de Bagnolet) (Iter 101)	

2 Paris – Lyon

(465km = 289 miles)

This route follows toll motorway *Autoroute du Soleil;* **not all** junctions are listed. Throughout the scenery rarely fails to be attractive as the route first touches the Forest of Fontainebleau then continues through farming country, woods and vineyards. After Chalon the route passes through the wide undulating and wooded valley of the R Saône, including the wine growing country after Mâcon. SP 'Autoroute du Sud' and 'Lyon'.
In the opposite direction SP 'Paris'.
For non-motorway route Paris – Lyon follow Iter 23 & 24.

N20		Paris	465
	5.5	5.5	Junc N20/Bd Périphérique (Porte d'Orléans) (Iter 101)	459.5
A6	6.5	1	Junc Bd Périphérique/ A6	458.5
	12.5	6	Motorway fork for Orly Airport	452.5
	14.5	2	Junc with N186 (Versailles/Fresnes Junc; exit for northbound traffic only)	450.5
	17.5	3	Motorway fork (Junc with A10)	447.5
	22	4.5	Chilly-Mazarin Junc	443
	25	3	Savigny/Epinay Junc	440
	31.5	6.5	Evry/Ris Orangis Junc	433.5
	37.5	6	Service area	427.
	42.5	5	Corbeil Sud Junc	422.5
	43	0.5	Melun Junc	422

53	10	Fontainebleau-Nord/Cely Junc	412
58	5	Toll booths	407
67	9	Achères service area	398
70	3	Ury Junc	395
79	9	Fontainebleau-Sud Junc	386
82	3	Nemours Junc	383
84	2	Service area	381
90	6	Motorway fork (Junc with A70) (Dordives, on Iter 23, 9km)	375
120	30	Courtenay/Sens Junc (Iter 66, 100)	345
132	12	Service area	333
137	5	Joigny/Toucy Junc	328
163	26	Auxerre Nord Junc	302
174	11	Auxerre Sud/Chablis Junc	291
176.5	2.5	Venoy service area	288.5
198	21.5	Nitry Junc	267
219	21	Avallon/Saulieu Junc	246
223	4	Service area	242
244	21	Bierre-lès-Semur Junc	221
265	21	Service area	200
274	9	Dijon motorway fork (Junc with A38; Iter 66)	191
296	22	Service area	169
299	3	Col de Bessey en Chaume (1,854 ft)	166
311	12	Beaune motorway fork (Junc with A31; Iter 17, 29)	154
315	4	Beaune/Chagny Junc	150
319	4	Beaune service area	146
338	19	Chalon-Nord Junc (Chalon-sur-Saône, 3.5km)	127
344	6	Chalon-Sud Junc	121
351	7	Service area	114
365	14	Tournus Junc (Tournus, 2km)	100
384	19	Mâcon service area	81
390	6	Mâcon-Nord Junc (Iter 18)	75
403	13	Mâcon-Sud Junc	62
416	13	Service area	49
421	5	Belleville Junc	44
436	15	Villefranche Junc (Toll booths)	29
441	5	Anse Junc	24
444.5	3.5	Les Chères service area	20.5
454	9.5	Limonest Junc	11
455.5	1.5	Service area	9.5
459	3.5	Ecully Junc	6
461	2	Lyon-Vaise/Tassin Junc	4
465	4	Lyon	

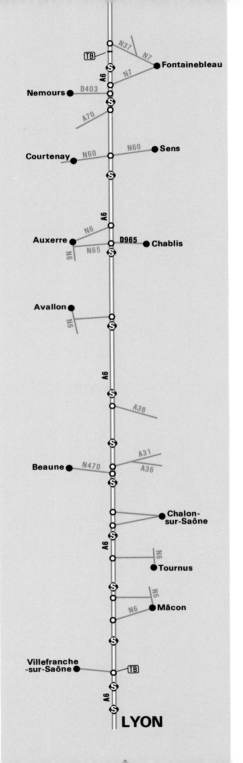

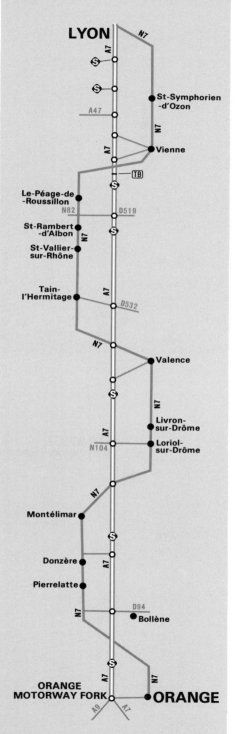

3 Lyon – Orange

(198km = 123 miles via A7)
(198.5km = 123.5 miles via N7)

The first route follows the A7 toll motorway – *Autoroute du Soleil*. The second is by the parallel all-purpose road N7, and once clear of the suburbs it is a fast road with several attractive stretches.

Both routes follow the wide valley of the R Rhône.

There are occasional views of the river and to the east of the foothills of the distant Alps, and to the west of the Central Plateau.

The first route is SP 'Marseille'; the second is SP 'Vienne' & 'Valence' out of Lyon. In the opposite direction both routes are SP 'Lyon' ('Péage' for the motorway, or 'par RN' for the all-purpose road).

A7				
			Lyon	198
	2	2	La Mulatière/Oullins Junc	196
	6.5	4.5	Pierre-Bénite Junc & service area	191.5
	7.5	1	St-Fons Junc	190.5
	8.5	1	Feyzin Junc	189.5
	15	6.5	Solaize Junc & service area	183
	21.5	6.5	Givors/St-Etienne Junc (with A47)	176.5
	28	6.5	Vienne Nord Junc (exit for southbound traffic only)	170
	34	6	Condrieu/Ampuis Junc	164
	35	1	Vienne Sud Junc (exit for northbound traffic only)	163
	36	1	Toll booths	162
	37	1	Reventin service area	161
	55	18	Chanas/St-Rambert-d-Albon/Annonay Junc	143
	60	5	St-Rambert-d'Albon service area	138
	86	26	Tain-l'Hermitage/Tournon/Romans Junc	112
	97	11	Valence – Nord Junc	101
	105	8	Valence – Sud Junc	93
	109	4	Portes-lès-Valence service area	89
	124	15	Loriol/Privas/Crest Junc	74
	133	9	Montélimar Nord/Le Teil Junc	65
	151	18	Montélimar service area	47
	155	4	Montélimar Sud/Pierrelatte Junc	43
	177	22	Bollène/Pont-St-Esprit Junc	21
	189	12	Mornas service area	9
	198	9	Orange motorway fork (Junc A7/A9)	

or avoiding toll motorway

N7				
		Lyon	198.5	
6	6	St-Fons	192.5	
11	5	Feyzin	187.5	
14.5	3.5	[St-Symphorien-d'Ozon]	184	
27.5	13	Vienne	171	
40.5	13	Auberives-sur-Varèze	158	
46.5	6	Le-Péage-de-Roussillon	152	
56	9.5	St-Rambert-d'Albon	142.5	
68.5	12.5	[St-Vallier-sur-Rhône]	130	
76	7.5	Erôme	122.5	
82.5	6.5	Tain-l'Hermitage	116	
		(Tournon over river)		
91.5	9	Pont-de-l'Isère	107	
100.5	9	Valence-sur-Rhône	98	
119	18.5	Livron-sur-Drôme	79.5	
122	3	[Loriol-sur-Drôme]	76.5	
129.5	7.5	Les Reys-de-Saulce	69	
132.5	3	Le Logis Neuf	66	
141	8.5	L'Homme-d'Armes	57.5	
145.5	4.5	[Montélimar]	53	
154.5	9	[Pierrelatte/Montélimar	44	
		Sud Junc of		
		A7 Autoroute]		
160.5	6	[Donzère]	38	
167.5	7	[Pierrelatte]	31	
179.5	12	[La Croisière]	19	
		(Pont-St-Esprit		
		4km by D994)		
183.5	4	[Mondragon]	15	
188	4.5	[Mornas]	10.5	
192	4	Piolenc	6.5	
198.5	6.5	Orange		

4 Orange – Nice

(274km = 170.5 miles)

Following toll motorways *Autoroute du Soleil* (A7) and *Autoroute La Provençale* (A8) throughout.

The A7 passes through mostly arid landscape typical of Provence gradually improving as one approaches Avignon. After passing along R Durance Valley the landscape once again becomes barren and rocky. Vine growing districts are bypassed as the A8 moves along the Côte d'Azur with its many famous towns and resorts stretched along the coastline. **Not all** junctions are listed. SP 'Marseille', 'Nice'. In the opposite direction. SP 'Lyon'.

A7				
		Orange motorway fork	274	
		(Junc A7/A9)		
17	17	Sorgues service area	257	
		(northbound only)		
21	4	Avignon – Nord/	253	
		Carpentras-Junc		
28	7	Morières service area	246	
		(southbound only)		
31	3	Avignon-Sud Junc	243	
44	13	Cavaillon/Nîmes Junc	230	
54	10	Sénas Junc	220	
59.5	5.5	Toll booths	214.5	
61	1.5	Salon Nord Junc	213	
		(exit for southbound		
		traffic only)		
68	7	Salon Sud Junc	206	
74	6	Toll booths	200	
75	1	Lançon service area	199	

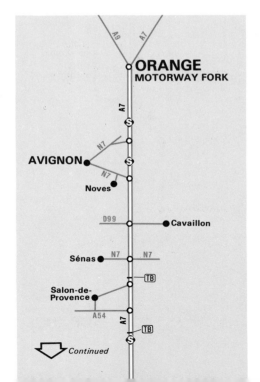

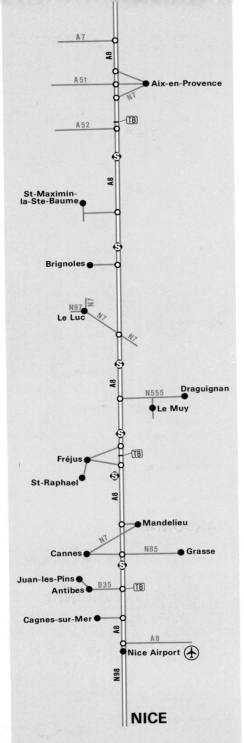

A8	81	6	Motorway fork (Junc A7/A8) (Iter 75)	193
	95.5	14.5	Aix Ouest Junc (Aix-en-Provence 4km)	178.5
	98	2.5	Junc with *Autoroute* A51	176
	101.5	3.5	Aix Est Junc	172.5
	106.5	5	Le Canet Junc	167.5
	108.5	2	Gardanne Junc	165.5
	109	0.5	Toll booths	165
	110.5	1.5	Motorway fork (Junc with A52)	163.5
	118.5	8	Service area	155.5
	137.5	19	St-Maximin/Marseille Junc	136.5
	147.5	10	Brignoles service area	126.5
	153.5	6	Brignoles Junc	120.5
	178.5	25	Le Luc/Toulon Junc	95.5
	187.5	9	Vidauban service area	86.5
	197.5	10	Le Muy/Draguignan/ St-Tropez/Ste-Maxime Junc	76.5
	207.5	10	Le Canaver service area (westbound only)	66.5
	209.5	2	Puget-s-Argens/Fréjus/ St-Raphael Junc	64.5
	211.5	2	Toll booths	62.5
	214.5	3	Fréjus/St-Raphael Junc (exit for westbound traffic only)	59.5
	215	0.5	Fréjus service area (eastbound only)	59
	225.5	10.5	Les Adrets Junc	48.5
	237.5	12	Cannes Airport/ Mandelieu/La Napoule Junc	36.5
	245.5	8	Cannes/Grasse Junc	28.5
	249	3.5	Les Bréguières service area	25
	253	4	Antibes/Juan-les- Pins/Golfe Juan Junc (Toll booths)	21
	258.5	5.5	Villeneuve-Loubet/ Bouches du Loup Junc (exit for eastbound traffic only)	15.5
	260	1.5	Cagnes-s-Mer Junc	14
	266	6	St-Laurent-du-Var-Junc	8
N202	267	1	Junc for Nice centre and Airport (via Promenade des Anglais)	7
N98	267.8	0.8	Junc N202/N98	6.2
	268	0.2	[Nice Airport]	6
	274	6	**Nice**	

5 Orange – Narbonne

(193km = 120 miles by toll motorway)
(221.6km = 137.5 miles by all-purpose road)
Alternative routes, by toll motorway *Autoroute la Languedocienne,* or by fairly fast all-purpose road. Both routes cross the rocky hills and plateaux of Provence to the vineyards of Languedoc. The R Gard is crossed at Remoulins, note excursion to Pont-du-Gard. After Montpellier across a windswept plain between the sea and distant mountains. The first route is SP 'Narbonne'; the second is SP 'Avignon' out of Orange. In the opposite direction SP 'A9 Montpellier' for the first route, or SP 'Béziers' for the second route out of Narbonne.

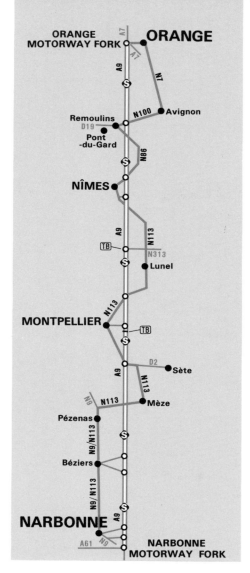

A9				
			Orange motorway fork	193
			(Junc A7/A9)	
	18	18	Tavel service area	175
	29	11	Remoulins/Avignon Junc	164
	44	15	Nîmes-Marguerittes service area	149
	47	3	Nîmes – Est Junc	146
	55	8	Nîmes – Ouest/Garons Airport Junc	138
	73	18	Gallargues Junc	120
			(Toll booth)	
	77	4	Vidourle service area	116
	90	13	Vendargues Junc	103
	97	7	Montpellier-Est/ Fréjorgues Airport/ Les Plages Junc	96
	101	4	Montpellier-Sud Junc	92
	106.5	5.5	Montpellier-Ouest Junc	86.5
	107.5	1	Toll booths	85.5
	111	3.5	Montpellier-Fabrègues service area	82
	122.5	11.5	Sète Junc	70.5
	147.5	25	Agde/Pézenas Junc	45.5
	155	7.5	Béziers-Montblanc service area	38
	159.5	4.5	Béziers-Est Junc	33.5
	166	6.5	Béziers-Ouest Junc	27
	182	16	Narbonne-Vinassan service area	11
	188	6	Narbonne Est Junc (Narbonne 2km)	5
	192	4	Narbonne Sud Junc	1
	193	1	**Narbonne** motorway fork (Junc A9/A61)	

or avoiding motorway

N7				
			Orange	221.6
	9	9	[Courthézon]	212.6
	18.5	9.5	Sorgues	203.1
	24.5	6	Le Pontet	197.1
N100	29	4.5	Avignon	192.6
	39.5	10.5	La Bégude-de-Saze	182.1
	47.5	8	Junc with Autoroute A9 (Remoulins/Avignon Junc)	174.1
N86	51	3.5	Remoulins (Pont-du-Gard 3km)	170.6

Continued

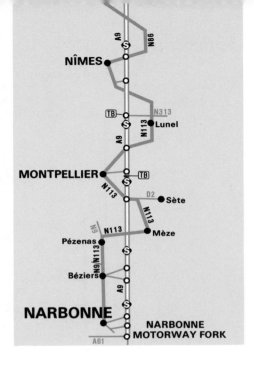

	52.8	1.8	St-Bonnet-du-Gard	168.8
	59.8	7	Bezouce	161.8
	61.5	1.7	St-Gervasy	160.1
N113	71	9.5	[Nîmes]	150.6
	78	7	Milhaud	143.6
	83	5	Uchaud	138.6
	88	5	Codognan	133.6
	92	4	Junc with N313	129.6
	98	6	Lunel	123.6
	109	11	Baillargues	112.6
	111	2	Junc with Autoroute A9 (Vendargues Junc)	110.6
	113	2	Vendargues	108.6
	122	9	Montpellier	99.6
	125.6	3.6	Junc with N112	96
	127.2	1.6	Junc with link rd to Montpellier-Ouest Junc of Autoroute A9	94.4
	132.4	5.2	Fabrègues	89.2
	140.4	8	Gigean	81.2
	148.6	8.2	[Bouzigues]	73
	153.6	5	Mèze	68
	165.6	12	Montagnac	56
N9/ N113	169.6	4	Junc N113/N9	52
	172	2.4	Pézenas	49.6
	179.3	7.3	Valros	42.3
	194.6	15.3	Béziers	27
	204.6	10	[Nissan-lez-Ensérune]	17
	214.8	10.2	Coursan	6.8
	221.6	6.8	Narbonne	

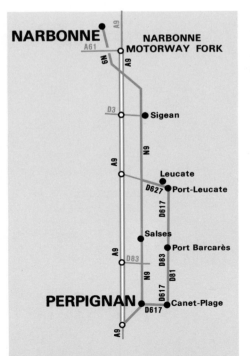

6 Narbonne – Perpignan

(58km = 36 miles by toll motorway)
(61km = 38 miles by all-purpose road)
(75.5km = 47 miles by touring route)

The first route is by toll motorway throughout, following the *Autoroute La Catalane*. The second route, by N9, is a fast but sometimes crowded road, which by-passes most of the villages. Both routes cross the windswept, desolate, coastal plain with occasional views of inshore lagoons and distant mountains. The third route passes between an inland lagoon (Etang de Leucate ou de Salses) and the sea, and includes the coastal resorts of Port-Leucate, Port-Barcarès and Canet-Plage.

Note: If bound for Le Boulou and Spain, Perpignan can be bypassed by continuing on the motorway.

A9			Narbonne motorway Fork (Junc A9/A61) (town 6km north)	58
	14	14	Sigean/Port-la-Nouvelle Junc	44
	23	9	Lapalme service area	35
	25	2	Leucate Junc	33
D83	47	22	Perpignan Nord Junc (Perpignan Sud Junc, 14km by A9)	11
N9	48	1	Junc D83/N9	10
	58	10	Perpignan	

or avoiding toll motorway

N9			Narbonne	61
	3	3	Junc with N213 (Narbonne Sud Junc of Autoroute A9 1 km)	58
	8.7	5.7	Prat-de-Cest	52.3
	13	4.3	[Peyriac-de-Mer]	48
	21	8	[Sigean]	40
	29	8	Les Cabanes-de-Lapalme	32
	32.5	3.5	Junc with D627	28.5
	37	4.5	Les Cabanes-de-Fitou	24
	46	9	[Salses]	15
	51	5	Junc with D83	10
	61	10	Perpignan	

or by touring route

N9			Narbonne	75.5
			as above	
D627	32.5	32.5	Junc with D627	43
	37.5	5	[Leucate]	38
	40.5	3	[Leucate-Plage]	35
	46.5	6	[Port-Leucate]	29
D83	48	1.5	Road number change	27.5
	50	2	[Port Barcarès]	25.5
	53.5	3.5	Junc for Le Barcarès	22
D81	54.5	1	Junc D83/D81	21
	60.5	6	[Ste-Marie]	15
D617	64.5	4	Junc D81/D617 (Canet-Plage 2 km)	11
	65.5	1	[Canet]	10
	75.5	10	Perpignan	

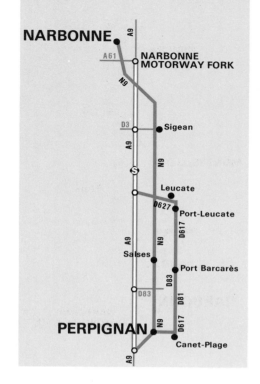

7 Paris – Bordeaux

(588 km = 365.5 miles)

This route follows toll motorway *Autoroute l'Aquitaine;* **not all** junctions are listed. After extensive suburbs, through pleasant undulating countryside at first then a rather monotonous plain to the wooded country near Orléans. After the city, by the broad Loire valley although little is seen of the river. After Tours across an open plain to Ste-Maure but more attractive to Poitiers and beyond. Then follows a stretch of more open, fairly flat farming country to St-Jean-d'Angély, on the R Boutonne. The route then continues through undulating, sometimes well-wooded country and concludes with a run across the wine growing district near the rivers Dordogne and Garonne.

SP 'Lyon' out of Paris, then 'Chartres' and 'Orléans', and then 'Tours', 'Poitiers' and finally 'Bordeaux'. In the opposite direction SP 'Paris'.

For the non-motorway route Paris-Bordeaux follow Iter 81-83.

N20			Paris	588
	5.5	5.5	Junc N20/Bd Périphérique (Iter 101) (Porte d'Orléans)	582.5
A6	6.5	1	Junc Bd Périphérique/A6	581.5
	12.5	6	Motorway fork for Orly Airport	575.5

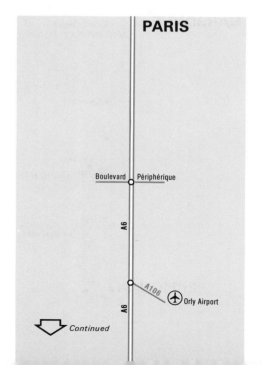

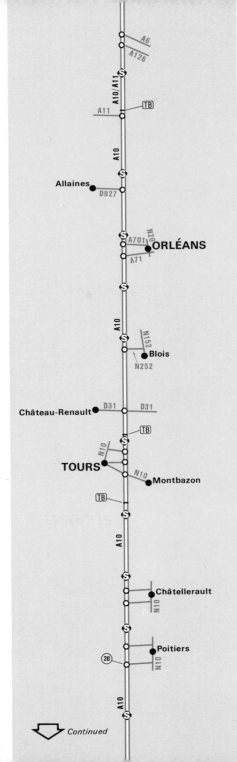

	14.5	2	Junc with N186 (Versailles/Fresnes Junc; exit for northbound traffic only)	573.5
A10	17.5	3	Motorway fork (Junc A6/A10)	570.5
	19.5	2	Longjumeau Junc	568.5
	21.5	2	Motorway fork (Junc with A126)	566.5
	23	1.5	Palaiseau/Massy Junc	565
	23.5	0.5	Motorway fork	564.5
	32	8.5	Les Ulis/Paris Ouest Junc (exit for northbound traffic only)	556
	34	2	Lyon/Montlhéry/Evry Junc	554
	37	3	Limours service area	551
	52	15	Dourdan Junc	536
	57	5	Toll booths	531
	58	1	Motorway fork (Junc A10/A11)	530
	68	10	Allainville/Étampes Junc	520
	89	21	Service area	499
	97	8	Allaines/Chartres Junc (Iter 35)	491
	122	25	Orléans service area	466
	125	3	Orléans Nord Junc (Orléans, 9km)	463
	131	6	Orléans Ouest Junc (Junc with A71)	457
	147	16	Meung Junc	441
	149	2	Service area	439
	175	26	Blois service area	413
	181	6	Blois Junc	407
	211	30	Amboise/Château-Renault Junc	377
	225	14	Toll booths	363
	227	2	Tours service area	361
	232	5	Tours Nord/Airport Junc	356
	239	7	Tours Centre Junc (Tours, 2km)	349
	244	5	Chambray Junc	344
	245	1	Tours Sud/Montbazon Junc	343
	260	15	Toll booths	328
	266	6	Service area	322
	274	8	Ste-Maure Junc	314
	298	24	Châtellerault service area	290
	306	8	Châtellerault Nord Junc	282
	312	6	Châtellerault Sud Junc	276
	325	13	Poitiers service area	263
	334	9	Poitiers Nord Junc (Poitiers 6km)	254
	344	10	Poitiers Sud Junc (no. 20) (Poitiers 7km)	244
	371	27	Rouillé-Pamproux service area	217
	377	6	St-Maixent/Lusignan Junc (no. 21)	211 / 211

Continued

397	20	Niort Nord Junc (no. 22) (Niort 15km)	191
405	8	Service area	183
413	8	Surgères/Niort Sud Junc (no. 23) (Niort 11km) (Epannes 12.5km)	175
446	33	St-Jean-d'Angely Junc (no. 24)	142
455.5	9.5	Fenioux service area	132.5
465	9.5	Br over R Charente	123
473	8	Saintes Junc (no. 25)	115
490	17	St-Léger service area	98
495	5	Pons Junc (no. 26)	93
518	23	Mirambeau Junc (no. 27)	70
531	13	Blaye Junc (no. 28)	57
540	9	Saugon service area	48
560	20	Toll booths	28
561	1	St-André-de-Cubzac Nord N10/Libourne Junc (no. 29 a/b; exit for southbound traffic only)	27
563	2	Junc with N137 (no. 30b; exit for northbound traffic only)	25
563.5	0.5	St-André-de-Cubzac Sud Junc (no. 30a; exit for northbound traffic only)	24.5
568.5	5	Br over R Dordogne	19.5
569.5	1	Ambarès/St-Loubès Junc (no. 31; southbound only)	18.5
572	2.5	Ambarès/St-Loubès Junc (no. 32; northbound only)	16
575.5	3.5	Carbon-Blanc Junc (no. 33)	12.5
577	1.5	Bordeaux-St-Jean Junc (no. 34)	11
579.5	2.5	Lormont Junc (no. 3)	8.5
uncl. 580.5	1	Br over R Garonne	7.5
582.5	2	Junc with Bordeaux ring road (no. 4)	5.5
588	5.5	Bordeaux	

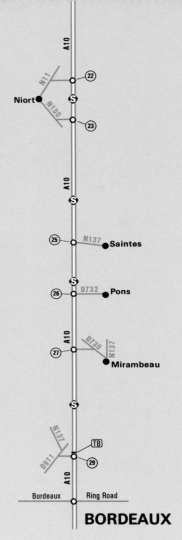

8 Bordeaux – St-Jean-de-Luz
(206km = 128 miles)

Leave Bordeaux by the toll-free section of Autoroute A63. The first few miles through open farming country, then a fast dual-carriageway road through the dense pine forest and heather-clad moorland of Les Landes. The distant Pyrénées come into view beyond Castets. Then continue by toll motorway (Autoroute de la Côte Basque) passing through pleasant, well-wooded country on the extreme

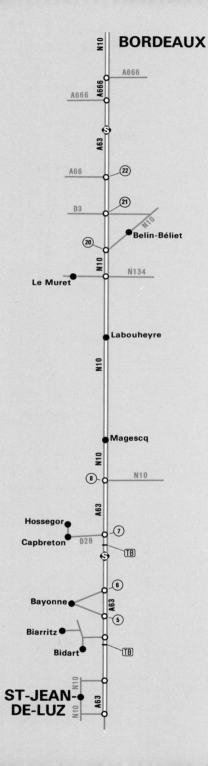

west of the Pyrénées Mountains.
SP 'Bayonne' and 'Espagne' out of Bordeaux. In the
opposite direction SP 'Bayonne' and then 'Bordeaux'.
Note: If bound for Hendaye, Irun and Spain (Espagne), St-Jean-de-Luz can be bypassed by continuing on the motorway.

N10			Bordeaux	206
A666	6.5	6.5	Junc with Bordeaux ring road	199.5
A63	8.5	2	Motorway terminus	197.5
	10.5	2	Pessac/Bersol Junc	195.5
	13	2.5	Cestas/Canéjean Junc	193
	17	4	Bordeaux Cestas service area	189
	20.5	3.5	Pierroton Junc	185.5
	29.5	9	Marcheprime/Le Barp Junc	176.5
	33.5	4	Arcachon Junc (no. 22)	172.5
	44.5	11	Salles/Belin-Béliet Junc (no. 21)	161.5
N10	55.5	11	Motorway terminus (exit no. 20)	150.5
	58.5	3	Le Muret Junc (no. 19; exit for southbound traffic only)	147.5
	60.5	2	Junc with N134 (for Le Muret & Mont de M)	145.5
	71.5	11	[Liposthey]	134.5
	83.5	12	[Labouheyre]	122.5
	91.5	8	Junc with D44 (for Sabres)	114.5
	102.5	11	[Laharie]	103.5
	113	10.5	Junc with D41 (for Rion)	93
	124	11	Junc for Castets (exit for southbound traffic only)	82
	126.5	2.5	Junc with D947 (for Dax & Castets)	79.5
	138.5	12	[Magescq]	67.5
	147	8.5	Junc for Soustons (exit for northbound traffic only)	59
A63	148.5	1.5	Junc with Autoroute A63 (St-Geours-de-Maremne Junc, no. 8)	57.5
	165.5	17	Capbreton/Hossegor Junc (no. 7)	40.5
	166	0.5	Toll booths	40
	170.7	4.7	Labenne service area	35.3
	182.5	11.8	Bayonne Nord Junc (no. 6) (Bayonne 2km)	23.5
	188.5	6	Bayonne Sud Junc (no. 5) (Bayonne 4.5km)	17.5
	193.5	5	Biarritz/Bidart Junc (no. 4)	12.5
	194	0.5	Toll booths	12
	198.5	4.5	Bidart service area	7.5
uncl.	202.5	4	St-Jean-de-Luz Nord Junc (St-Jean-de-Luz Sud Junc, 5.5km by A63)	3.5
N10	203	0.5	Junc motorway slip road/N10	3
	206	3	St-Jean-de-Luz	

9 Le Havre – Paris

(200km = 124.5 miles by toll motorway)
(218km = 135.5 miles by all-purpose road)

Both routes are SP 'Rouen' & 'Paris' out of Le Havre; blue signs with the added word 'Péage' for the toll route via Pont de Tancarville, or white signs for the all-purpose road N15. The first route, via the toll motorway, is level at first with the flat marshes of the Seine estuary on one side and wooded cliffs on the other. From the Tancarville suspension toll bridge the route skirts the *Marais Vernier* (reclaimed marshland), then joins the toll motorway, *Autoroute de Normandie*, for Paris. A pleasant run through wooded country, with occasional views of the River Seine.

The second route avoids the toll motorway, and goes through undulating country to Rouen, then follows the valley of the River Seine and in parts is very attractive, particularly as it passes through the Forêt de Louviers beyond Pont de l'Arche, and as it skirts the south bank of the river after Vernon.

From St-Germain-en-Laye the route is through a built-up area. In the opposite direction the first route is SP 'Rouen' & 'Caen', then 'Pont de Tancarville' & 'Le Havre'; the second is SP 'St-Germain' out of Paris.

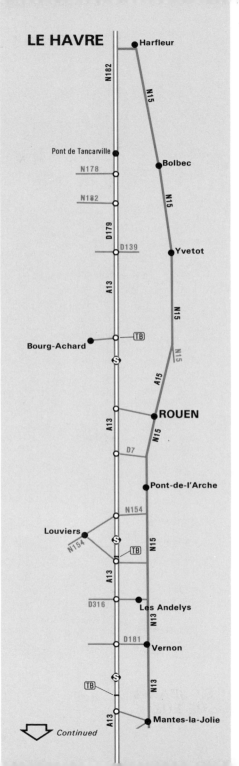

N182			Le Havre	200
	7	7	[Harfleur]	193
	26	19	Junc with D982	174
			(Lillebonne 10km)	
	27.5	1.5	Pont de Tancarville	172.5
	29	1.5	Junc with N178	171
D179	35	6	Junc N182/D179	165
			(Pont Audemer 12km)	
	42.5	7.5	Junc with D139	157.5
			(Bourneville 1.5km)	
A13	44	1.5	Autoroute entrance	156
			(Pont de Tancarville/ Le Havre exit for westbound traffic)	
	45	1	Pont Audemer/Bourne-ville Junc (exit for westbound traffic only)	155
	59	14	Bourg-Achard Junc (Toll booths)	141
	62	3	Bosgouet service area	138
	68	6	Maison-Brûlee/Alençon Junc	132
	72	4	Rouen Junc	128
	81	9	Elbeuf/Rouen Junc	119
	93	12	Louviers Nord/Evreux Junc (Iter 34)	107
	97	4	Vironvay service area	103
	99.5	2.5	Toll booths	100.5
	100	0.5	Louviers Sud Junc (exit for westbound traffic only)	100
	109	9	Gaillon/Les Andelys Junc (exit for westbound traffic only)	91
	120	11	Vernon Junc	80
	128	8	Chaufour/Bonnières Junc	72
	138	10	Rosny-s-Seine service area	62
	141	3	Toll booths	59
	143	2	Mantes-Sud Junc	57

Continued

PARIS

145	2	Mantes-Est Junc	55
156	11	Flins/Renault Junc	44
164	8	Morainvilliers service area	36
168	4	Poissy/St-Germain Junc	32
180.5	12.5	Motorway fork (Junc with A12)	19.5
181.5	1	Versailles-Ouest/ St-Germain Junc	18.5
184.5	3	Versailles-Nord/ Vaucresson Junc	15.5
193	8.5	Junc A13/Bd Périphérique (Iter 101) (Porte d'Auteuil)	7
200	7	Paris	

or avoiding toll motorway

N182			Le Havre	218
N15	7	7	[Harfleur]	211
	12	5	Gainneville	206
	17	5	St-Aubin	201
	19.5	2.5	St-Romain-de-Colbosc	198.5
	29.5	10	[Bolbec]	188.5
	45	15.5	Junc with D33 (Pont de Brotonne 14km)	173
	51.5	6.5	[Yvetot]	166.5
	55	3.5	Junc with N29	163
	59.5	4.5	Croix Mare	158.5
	69.5	10	[Barentin]	148.5
A15	71	1.5	Junc N15/A15 (Rouen 15.5km by N15)	147
	75.5	4.5	Motorway fork (Junc with N315)	142.5
	77	1.5	Service area (northbound only)	141
	80.5	3.5	Canteleu/Maromme Junc (exit for northbound traffic only)	137.5
N15	84.5	4	Motorway terminus	133.5
	87	2.5	Rouen	131
	92	5	Amfreville-la-Mi-Voie	126
	97.5	5.5	Le Port-St-Ouen (Elbeuf Junc on Autoroute A13, 4.5km)	120.5
	105	7.5	Pont-de-l'Arche	113
	112	7	Junc with N154 (Louviers/Evreux Junc of A13, 0.5km)	106
	117.3	5.3	Vironvay	100.7
	128.3	11	[Gaillon]	89.7
	141.7	13.4	Vernon	76.3
N13	151.2	9.5	Junc N15/N13	66.8
	153.2	2	Bonnières-sur-Seine	64.8
	156.8	3.6	Rolleboise	61.2
	160	3.2	Rosny-sur-Seine	58
D113	167	7	Mantes-la-Jolie	51
	173.5	6.5	[Mézières]	44.5
	178	4.5	[Aubergenville]	40
	184	6	[Ecquevilly]	34
	188.5	4.5	[Orgeval]	29.5
N13	190	1.5	[Poissy/St-Germain Junc of Autoroute A13]	28
	197	7	[St-Germain-en-Laye]	21

LE HAVRE

Harfleur · N182 · N15 · Pont de Tancarville · N178 · N182 · Bolbec · D179 · D139 · Yvetot · N15 · A13 · Bourg-Achard · A15 · N15 · ROUEN · D7 · N15 · Pont-de-l'Arche · N154 · N15 · Louviers · N154 · D139 · Les Andelys · A13 · N13 · Vernon · TB · N13 · Mantes-la-Jolie · D113 · Orgeval · D113 · A13 · N13 · St-Germain-en-Laye

Continued

200	3	Port-Marly (for Marly-le-Roi)	18
203	3	Bougival	15
204.7	1.7	La Malmaison	13.3
206.5	1.8	Rueil-Malmaison	11.5
210	3.5	Rond Point des Bergères	8
211.3	1.3	La Défense	6.7
212.3	1	Pont de Neuilly (Br over R Seine)	5.7
214.7	2.4	Junc Bd Périphérique/N13 (Porte Maillot) (Iter 101)	3.3
218	3.3	Paris	

10 Paris – Strasbourg

(488km = 303 miles)

This route follows toll motorways *Autoroute de L'Est*; **not all** junctions are listed; initially route passes through congested suburbs of Paris, later emerging into well wooded country. Views are picturesque following the Marne Valley, and across the vine growing Champagne district until Reims. The chalk downland scenery following is rather monotonous, but becomes more pleasant as one approaches Metz and continues on into Strasbourg. SP 'Metz' 'Strasbourg' . in the opposite direction SP 'Paris'. *For non-motorway route follow Iter 96 & 97.*

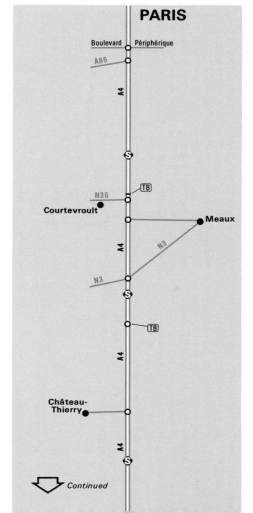

		Paris	488	
A4	6	6	Junc A4/Bd Périphérique (Porte de Bercy)	482
	7	1	Ivry sur Seine Junc (exit for westbound traffic only)	481
	10	3	Junc with A86	478
	10.5	0.5	Joinville Junc	477.5
	14.5	4	Pont de Nogent Junc	473.5
	18.5	4	Noisy-le-Grand Junc	469.5
	24	5.5	Val Maubuée Junc	464
	27.5	3.5	Melun/Lagny Junc	460.5
	33	5.5	Service area	455
	41.5	8.5	Toll booths	446.5
	42	0.5	Coutevrault Junc (exit for westbound traffic only) (Iter 100)	446
	44.5	2.5	Crecy Junc (exit for eastbound traffic only)	443.5
	46.5	2	Meaux Junc (exit for eastbound traffic only)	441.5
	60.5	14	St-Jean/La Ferté s/s Jouarre Junc	427.5
	63	2.5	Service area	425
	70.5	7.5	Montreuil-aux-Lions Junc (Toll booths)	417.5
	91.5	21	Château-Thierry Junc (Iter 94)	396.5
	103.5	12	Le Tardenois service area	384.5

Continued

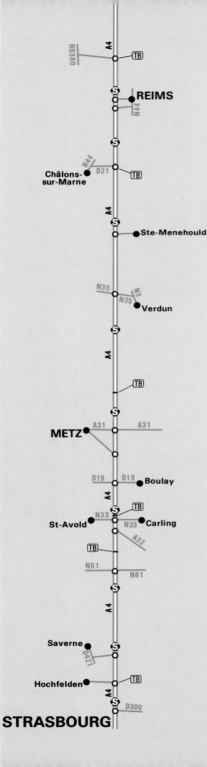

117.5	14	Dormans Junc (Toll booths)	370.5
136	18.5	Service area	352
140.5	4.5	Reims-Tinqueux Junc	347.5
143.5	3	Reims-Centre Junc	344.5
145	1.5	Reims-Cathédrale Junc	343
146.5	1.5	Reims-St-Rémi Junc	341.5
148.5	2	Reims-Cormontreuil Junc (Iter 26)	339.5
166	17.5	Reims-Champagne service area	322
177.5	11.5	Châlons-s-Marne Junc (Toll booths) (Iter 26)	310.5
212	34.5	Valmy service area	276
218.5	6.5	Ste-Menehould Junc	269.5
249.5	31	Voie Sacrée/Verdun Junc	238.5
267.5	18	Verdun-St-Nicolas service area	220.5
276.5	9	Fresnes-en-Woëvre Junc	211.5
298.5	22	Jarny/Briey Junc	189.5
301	2.5	Toll booths	187
305.5	4.5	Auboué/Briey Junc	182.5
311	5.5	Metz-St-Privat service area	177
319	8	Semécourt Junc	169
321.5	2.5	Motorway X-rds (Junc A4/A31) (Metz 10km)	166.5
324	2.5	Argancy Junc	164
334	10	Metz Est Junc (exit for westbound traffic only) Metz 8km)	154
349	15	Boulay Junc	139
363	14	Longeville service area	125
366.5	3.5	Toll booths	121.5
367	0.5	St-Avold/Carling Junc	121
374	7	Motorway fork (Junc with A32)	114
379	5	Farebersviller Junc	109
384.5	5.5	Toll booths	103.5
395	10.5	Sarrreguemines Junc	93
405	10	Keskastel service area	83
413	8	Sarre Union Junc	75
433	20	Phalsbourg Junc	55
442	9	Saverne service area	46
444	2	Saverne Junc	44
461	17	Hochfelden Junc & Toll booths (exit for westbound traffic only)	27
467.5	6.5	Brumath Nord/ Haguenau Junc	20.5
470	2.5	Brumath service area	18
473	3	Vendenheim/Brumath Sud Junc	15
477	4	Hoerdt/Karlsruhe Junc	11
480	3	Mundolsheim/ Reichstett Junc	8
484	4	Bischheim Junc	4
486	2	Strasbourg Nord Junc	2
488	2	Strasbourg	

11 Cherbourg – Caen

(120km = 74.5 miles direct)
(189km = 117.5 miles touring)
Scenically rather featureless; the towns provide the main
interest. The touring route follows the coast of the Cotentin
Peninsula, with some stretches by the sea. Utah Beach
(D421), Omaha Beach (Vierville to Colleville) and
Arromanches were points of landing in the Normandy
invasion of June 1944. Note links with Caen's northern
bypass.

N13			Cherbourg	120
	20	20	[Valognes]	100
			(Iter 40)	
	27	7	Montebourg	93
			(Quinéville on touring	
			route 7.5km by D42)	
	37	10	[Ste-Mère-Eglise]	83
	50.5	13.5	Carentan	69.5
	54.5	4	La Fourchette	65.5
	61.5	7	Isigny-sur-Mer	58.5
	77.5	16	Formigny	42.5
	92.5	15	[Bayeux]	27.5
	115.5	23	Junc with Caen bypass	4.5
	120	4.5	Caen	

alternative route

D116			Cherbourg	189
	7.5	7.5	Bretteville	181.5
D210	15.5	8	[Fermanville]	173.5
D901	20.2	4.7	St-Pierre-Eglise	168.8
	24.8	4.6	Tocqueville	164.2
D1	30	5.2	Barfleur	159
	38	8	Réville	151
	41	3	St-Vaast-la-Hougue	148
D14	43.5	2.5	Quettehou	145.5
	49.5	6	Aumeville-Lestre	139.5
D42	55	5.5	Junc D14/D42	134
D421	58	3	Quinéville	131
	61	3	Les Gougins	128
	64	3	Ravenoville-Plage	125
	68.5	4.5	Les Dunes-de-	120.5
			Varreville Monument	
			(Utah Beach)	
D913	72.5	4	La Madeleine	116.5
			Monument	
	77	4.5	Ste-Marie-du-Mont	112
	79.5	2.5	Vierville	109.5
N13	84	4.5	Junc D913/N13	105
	87.5	3.5	Carentan	101.5
	91.5	4	La Fourchette	97.5
	98.5	7	Isigny-sur-Mer	90.5
D514	100.5	2	Junc N13/D514	88.5
	108.5	8	Grandcamp-Maisy	80.5
	119.5	11	Vierville-sur-Mer	69.5
			(Omaha Beach)	
	122.5	3	St-Laurent-sur-Mer	66.5
	125	2.5	Colleville-sur-Mer	64
	128.5	3.5	Ste-Honorine-des-	60.5
			Pertes	
	132.5	4	Port-en-Bessin	56.5
			(Bayeux 9km by D6)	
	137.5	5	Abbaye-Ste-Marie	51.5
	143.5	6	Arromanches-les-Bains	45.5
	152	8.5	[Ver-sur-Mer]	37

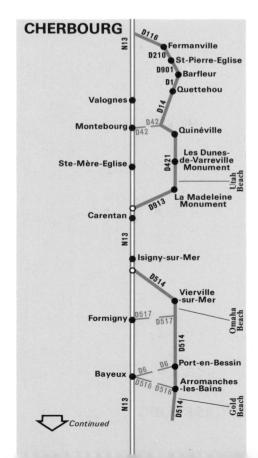

Continued

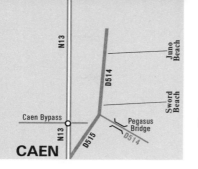

	157	5	Courseulles-sur-Mer	32
	160	3	Bernières-sur-Mer	29
	162	2	St Aubin-sur-Mer	27
	164	2	Langrune-sur-Mer	25
	165	1	Luc-sur-Mer	24
	169	4	Lion-sur-Mer	20
	174	5	Riva-Bella	15
	175	1	Ouistreham	14
D515	179	4	Junc D514/D515	10
	179.5	0.5	Bénouville	9.5
	185	5.5	[Hénouville-St-Clair]	4
	187	2	Junc with Caen bypass	2
	189	2	**Caen**	

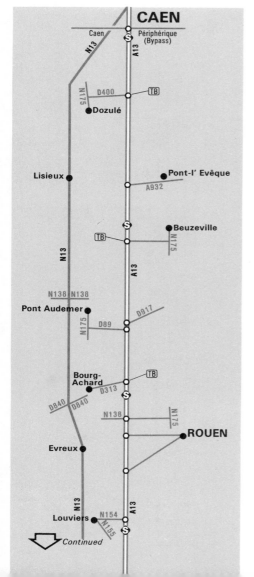

12 Caen – Paris

(237km = 147.5 miles by toll motorway)
(217.8km = 135.5 miles by all-purpose road)
Alternative routes by toll motorway or by all-purpose road.
The first route follows the toll motorway *Autoroute de Normandie*.

From the open countryside around Caen through the orchards of the Auge region to the generally level Roumois plateau. After Pont Audemer a pleasant run through wooded country, with occasional views of the River Seine. The second route is by a fairly fast all-purpose road, and is rather dull at first, later improving with several woods and orchards. Beyond Lisieux the descent into the Eure Valley is followed by an ascent and a wide stretch of level country. A further descent into the Risle valley is followed by a drive across the plain of Neubourg. Then an easy undulating road through attractive country, descending into the valley of the River Seine at Bonnières. From St-Germain-en-Laye the route is through a built-up area. Both routes are SP 'Paris' ('Péage' for the motorway, or 'par RN' for the all-purpose road N13). In the opposite direction the first route is SP 'Rouen' & 'Caen'; the second is SP 'St-Germain' out of Paris.

A13				
			Caen	237
	6	6	Caen Périphérique Sud Junc	231
	8	2	Giberville service area	229
	23	15	Dozulé/Cabourg Junc (Toll booths)	214
	46	23	Pont-l'Evêque Junc	191
	56	10	Beuzeville service area	181
	60	4	Beuzeville/Le Havre Junc (Toll booths)	177
	81	21	Pont de Tancarville/Le Havre Junc (exit for westbound traffic only)	156
	82	1	Pont Audemer/ Bourneville Junc (exit for west- bound traffic only)	155
	96	14	Bourg-Achard Junc (Toll booths)	141
	99	3	Bosgouet service area	138
	105	6	Maison-Brûlée/Alençon Junc (Iter 59)	132
	109	4	Rouen Junc	128
	118	9	Elbeuf/Rouen Junc	119
	130	12	Louviers Nord/Evreux Junc (Iter 34)	107
	134	4	Vironvay service area	103

136.5	2.5	Toll booths	100.5
137	0.5	Louviers Sud Junc (exit for westbound traffic only)	100
146	9	Gaillon/Les Andelys Junc (exit for westbound traffic only)	91
157	11	Vernon Junc	80
165	8	Chaufour/Bonnières Junc	72
175	10	Rosny-s-Seine service area	62
178	3	Toll booths	59
180	2	Mantes-Sud Junc	57
182	2	Mantes-Est Junc	55
193	11	Flins/Renault Junc	44
201	8	Morainvilliers service area	36
205	4	Poissy/St-Germain Junc	32
217.5	12.5	Motorway fork (Junc with A12)	19.5
218.5	1	Versailles-Ouest/St-Germain Junc	18.5
221.5	3	Versailles-Nord/Vaucresson Junc	15.5
230	8.5	Junc A13/Bd Périphérique (Iter 101) Porte d'Auteuil)	7
237	7	Paris	

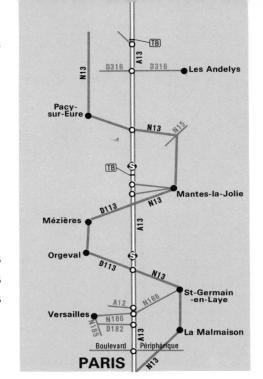

or avoiding toll motorway

N13		Caen	217.8
	9	9	Cagny	208.8
	13	4	Bellengreville	204.8
	16	3	Moult	201.8
	32	16	Crèvecoeur-en-Auge	185.8
	41.5	9.5	La Boissière	176.3
	49	7.5	Lisieux	168.8
	63	14	L'Hôtellerie	154.8
	66.5	3.5	[Thiberville]	151.3
	75.5	9	La Bretagne	142.3
	83	7.5	X-rds (N138)	134.8
	100.5	17.5	X-rds (D840)	117.3
	116.5	16	Parville	101.3
	120.5	4	Evreux (Iter 34)	97.3
	137.5	17	[Pacy-sur-Eure]	80.3
	145	7.5	Chaufour	72.8
	146.5	1.5	Chaufour/Bonnières Junc of Autoroute A13	71.3
	151	4.5	Junc with N15	66.8
	153	2	Bonnières-sur-Seine	64.8
	156.6	3.6	Rolleboise	61.2
	159.8	3.2	Rosny-sur-Seine	58
D113	166.8	7	Mantes-la-Jolie	51
	173.3	6.5	[Mézières]	44.5
	177.8	4.5	[Aubergenville]	40
	183.8	6	[Ecquevilly]	34
	188.3	4.5	[Orgeval]	29.5
N13	189.8	1.5	[Poissy/St-Germain Junc of Autoroute A13]	28
	196.8	7	[St-Germain-en-Laye]	21

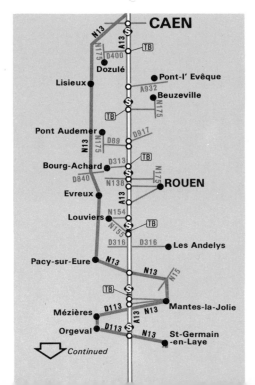

Continued

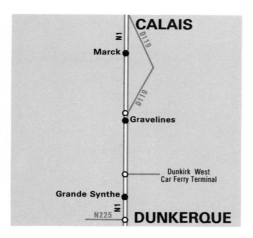

199.8	3	Port-Marly (for Marly-le-Roi)	18
202.8	3	Bougival	15
204.5	1.7	La Malmaison	13.3
206.3	1.8	Rueil-Malmaison	11.5
209.8	3.5	Rond Point des Bergères	8
211.1	1.3	La Défense	6.7
212.1	1	Pont de Neuilly (Br over R Seine)	5.7
214.5	2.4	Junc Bd Périphérique/ N13 (Porte Maillot) (Iter 101)	3.3
217.8	3.3	Paris	

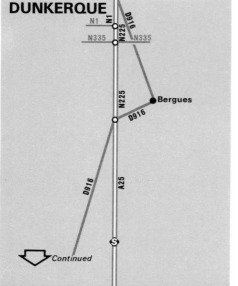

13 Calais – Dunkerque (Dunkirk)

(43km = 26.5 miles)

A fairly fast route, crossing flat rather uninteresting country with sand dunes between the road and the sea.

Note: The Dunkirk West Car Ferry Terminal is situated at Dunkerque Port Ouest, 16km west of the town centre.

N1		**Calais**	43
	8	8	Marck (for Calais Airport)	35
	15	7	Oye-Plage	28
	20	5	Road Junc (Gravelines 2km)	23
	26	6	[Gravelines-les-Huttes]	17
	29.5	3.5	Road Junc (Dunkirk West Car Ferry Terminal 3km; Loon – Plage 1.5km)	13.5
	35.5	6	[Grande-Synthe]	7.5
	39	3.5	Junc with Expressway	4
	43	4	**Dunkerque** (Dunkirk)	

14 Dunkerque (Dunkirk) – Lille

(79km = 49 miles by motorway)
(77km = 48 miles by all-purpose road)

Alternative routes, by toll-free motorway or all purpose road, across generally flat, agricultural countryside. The first route is signposted 'Calais' out of Dunkirk, then 'Lille'; the second is signposted 'Amiens', 'Lille' and 'Paris' along D916.

From Dunkirk West Car Ferry Terminal (16km W of town centre) follow SP 'Dunkerque', then on outskirts of town follow SP 'Lille' to join 'Expressway' (N225) to Bergues Junc (13km) then as below. In reverse direction, in Dunkerque, SP 'Calais' then 'Car Ferry' and 'Port Ouest'.

N1			**Dunkerque** (Dunkirk)	79
N225	4	4	Junc N1/Expressway N225	75
	6	2	Junc with N335	73
A25	17	11	Bergues Junc	62
	33	16	Winnezeele Junc (exit for northbound traffic only)	46
	34.5	1.5	Service area	44.5
	37	2.5	Steenvoorde/Ypres (Ieper) Junc	42

Continued

46	9	Méteren/Bailleul Junc	33
48	2	Hazebrouck Junc (exit for westbound traffic only)	31
52	4	Bailleul Junc (exit for westbound traffic only)	27
60	8	Armentières Ouest Junc	19
64.5	4.5	Armentières Est Junc	14.5
70.5	6	Lomme Junc	8.5
72	1.5	Junc with N41 (Béthune Junc; exit for westbound traffic only)	7
uncl. 76	4	Lille-Ouest/Centre Ville Junc	3
79	3	Lille	

or avoiding motorway

D916		**Dunkerque** (Dunkirk)	77
9	9	[Bergues]	68
11	2	Bergues Junc with Autoroute A25	66
19.7	8.7	Wormhout	57.3
29.5	9.8	[Cassel]	47.5
D933 35.7	6.2	l'Hazewinde	41.3
39.2	3.5	Caëstre	37.8
42.2	3	Flêtre	34.8
44.5	2.3	Meteren/Bailleul Junc with Autoroute A25	32.5
48.5	4	Bailleul	28.5
54	5.5	Le Seau	23
61	7	Armentières	16
64	3	La Chapelle	13
69.5	5.5	Lomme	7.5
77	7.5	Lille	

15 Lille–Paris

(221km = 137.5 miles by toll motorway)
(228km = 141.5 miles by all-purpose road)
Alternative routes, by toll motorway or by all-purpose
road. The first route follows the 'Paris' toll motorway
Autoroute du Nord. The second route leaves Lille by
the 'Seclin' road and runs more or less parallel to the
motorway, and includes Lens and Vimy, of First World
War associations.
Both routes pass initially through agricultural scenery
of little interest. There are coal mines in the
Carvin/Hénin area.
Later moderate scenery to Roye, then pleasant rolling
country. Through Forêt d'Ermenonville after Senlis.
Finally along busy streets of Paris.
If proceeding to A6 (for Lyon), A10 (for Orléans), or
A11 (for Chartres) follow Autoroute A3 SP *'Paris-Est'*,
then *'Paris-Sud', 'Lyon'* and *'Autoroute A6'.* In the
opposite direction SP *'Paris—Est',* then *'Autoroute A3'*
and *'Lille, Bruxelles'.*

		Lille	221
A1	3	3	Lille-Est/Centre Ville Junc	218
	5	2	Motorway fork (Junc with A22)	216

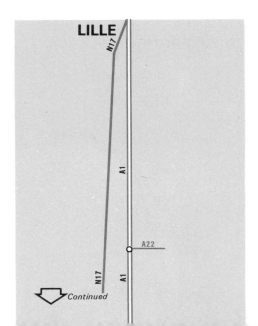

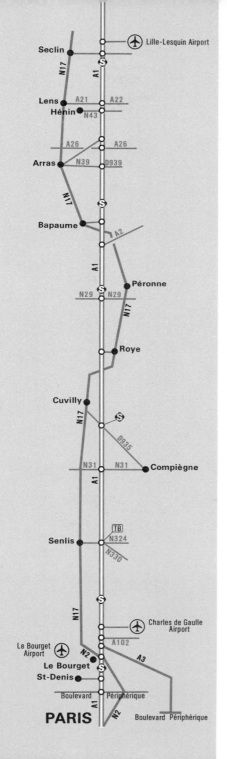

7	2	Lesquin/Aéroport de Lille Junc	214
12	5	Seclin Junc	209
14	2	Phalempin service area	207
21	7	Carvin/Lens Junc	200
28	7	Junc with Autoroute A21	193
30	2	Hénin/Douai Junc	191
41	11	Arras/Fresnes Junc	180
44	3	Motorway X-rds (Junc A26/A1) (Iter 25)	177
50	6	Arras-Est Junc (Iter 91)	171
61	11	Service area	160
68	7	Bapaume Junc	153
77	9	Motorway fork (Junc with A2; exit for northbound traffic only)	144
92	15	Assevillers service area	129
93	1	Péronne Junc	128
113	20	Roye Junc	108
134	21	Ressons Junc & service area	87
148	14	Compiègne Junc (Iter 92)	73
172	24	Senlis/Meaux Junc (Iter 100) (Toll booths)	49
187	15	Survilliers/ Ermenonville Junc	34
189	2	Vémars service area	32
198	9	Aéroport Charles de Gaulle Junc	23
201	3	Junc with Autoroute A102	20
202	1	Motorway fork (Junc A1/A3; see heading)	19

(For Autoroute A3 see details below)

206	4	Le Bourget Airport junc	15
209	3	La Courneuve service area	12
211	2	St-Denis/Enghien Junc	10
212.5	1.5	Pierrefitte/St-Denis/La Courneuve Junc	8.5
215	2.5	Junc A1/Bd Périphérique (Porte de la Chapelle) (Iter 101)	6
221	6	Paris	

or by Autoroute A3

A3			Motorway fork (Junc A1/A3)	15
	2	2	Aulnay (Zone Industrielle) Junc	13
	4.5	2.5	Aulnay Junc	10.5
	7.5	3	Bobigny/Bondy Junc	7.5
	10	2.5	Motorway fork	5
	10.5	0.5	Motorway fork (Junc with A86)	4.5
	13	2.5	Romainville/Montreuil Junc	2

	15	2	Junc A3/Bd Périphérique (Porte de Bagnolet) (Iter 101)	

alternative route

D549			Lille	228
D925	11	11	Seclin	217
N17	20	9	Carvin	208
	32	12	[Lens]	196
	39.5	7.5	[Vimy]	188.5
	44.5	5	Junc with Autoroute A26 (Iter 1, 25)	183.5
	50.5	6	Arras	177.5
	53.5	3	Beaurains	174.5
	65.9	12.4	Ervillers	162.1
	72.8	6.9	Bapaume (Iter 94)	155.2
	76.8	4	Beaulencourt	151.2
	78.8	2	Le Transloy	149.2
	82.6	3.8	Sailly-Saillisel	145.4
	85.8	3.2	Rancourt	142.2
	88.3	2.5	Bouchavesnes-Bergen	139.7
	95.2	6.9	Péronne	132.8
	102.2	7	Villers-Carbonnel	125.8
	107.7	5.5	Marchélepot	120.3
	110.7	3	Omiécourt	117.3
	124.2	13.5	Roye	103.8
	128.2	4	Junc with D930	99.8
	140.2	12	Orvillers-Sorel	87.8
	142.7	2.5	Cuvilly	85.3
	143.7	1	Junc with D938	84.3
	145.7	2	Junc with D935	82.3
	157.7	12	Estrées St-Denis	70.3
	160.5	2.8	X-rds (N31)	67.5
	167.2	6.7	St-Martin-Longeau	60.8
	171.7	4.5	Pont Ste-Maxence	56.3
	177.2	5.5	Fleurines	50.8
	183.7	6.5	Senlis	44.3
	193.4	9.7	La Chapelle en-Serval	34.6
	202.4	9	[Louvres]	25.6
	210.4	8	Junc with D902	17.6
N2	214.4	4	Le Bourget Airport	13.6
	215.4	1	Junc with Autoroute A1	12.6
	216.2	0.8	Le Bourget	11.8
	221.7	5.5	Junc with Bd Périphérique (Iter 101) (Porte de la Villette)	6.3
	228	6.3	Paris	

16 Paris–Rennes

(351km = 218 miles)
This route follows the toll motorway, *Autoroute-l'Océ*ane, A11 and A81 to the motorway terminus' near La Gravelle, then continues by *Voie Express* (dual carriageway) to Rennes; **not all** junctions are listed. After extensive suburbs, through agricultural country pleasantly wooded in places. SP 'Lyon' out of Paris, then 'Orléans' and 'Chartres', and then 'Le Mans' and 'Rennes'. In the opposite directions SP 'Paris'.

N20			Paris	351
	5.5	5.5	Junc N20/Bd Périphérique	345.5

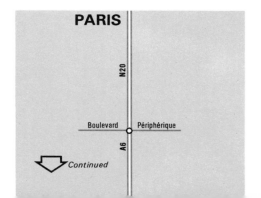

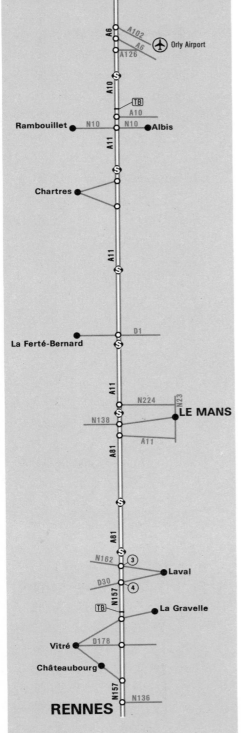

			(Iter 101)	
			(Porte d'Orléans)	
A6	6.5	1	Junc Bd Périphérique/ A6	344.5
	12.5	6	Motorway fork for Orly Airport	338.5
	14.5	2	Junc with N186 (Versailles/Fresnes Junc; exit for northbound traffic only)	336.5
A10	17.5	3	Motorway fork (Junc A6/A10)	333.5
	19.5	2	Longjumeau Junc	331.5
	21.5	.2	Motorway fork (Junc with A126)	329.5
	23	1.5	Palaiseau/Massy Junc	328
	23.5	0.5	Motorway fork	327.5
	32	8.5	Les Ulis/Paris Ouest Junc (exit for northbound traffic only)	319
	34	2	Lyon/Montlhéry/ Evry Junc	317
	37	3	Limours service area	314
	52	15	Dourdan Junc	299
	57	5	Toll booths	294
A11	58	1	Motorway fork (Junc A10/A11)	293
	64	6	Ablis/Rambouillet Junc	287
	84	20	Chartres service area	267
	87	3	Chartres Est Junc (Chartres, 4.5km)	264 264
	100	13	Thivars/Chartres Sud Junc (Iter 82)	251
	131	31	Brou service area	220
	135	4	Luigny Junc	216
	163	28	La Ferté-Bernard Junc	188
	168	5	Service area	183
	195	27	Le Mans Est Junc (Le Mans, 12.5km)	156
	199	4	Service area	152
	204	5	Le Mans Nord Junc	147
A81	208	4	Motorway fork (Junc A11/A81) (Le Mans, 9km)	143
	235	27	Joué-en-Charnie Junc (no.1)	116
	244	9	Service area	107
	257	13	Vaiges Junc (no.2)	94
	272	15	Laval service area	79
	277	5	Laval Est Junc (no.3)	74
	284	7	Laval Ouest Junc (no.4) (Iter 41)	67
N157	301	17	La Gravelle/Vitré Junc (no.5) (Toll booths) (Vitré 14km)	50
	313.5	12.5	Junc with D178	37.5
	331	17.5	Junc with D857 (Châteaubourg 1.5km; Vitré 17km)	20
	343	12	Junc with Rennes bypass (N136)	8
	346	3	[Cesson Sévigné]	5
	351	5	Rennes	

17 Beaune–Belfort

(188km = 117 miles by toll motorway)
(199km = 123.5 miles by all purpose road)
Alternative routes, by toll motorway or by all purpose road. The first route initially follows a short section of the 'Dijon' motorway, then along the 'La Comtoise', the Beaune–Mulhouse Autoroute A36. Very pleasant scenery, passing through many forests, generally hilly and well-wooded country bordering the very attractive valley of the R Doubs.

The second route, by the parallel all-purpose road, is through open country and forest to Seurre, where the R Saône is crossed, then straight and level across the Doubs-Saône plain towards Dole.

After the Dole bypass a very pleasant run by the attractive valley of the River Doubs, followed to St-Vit, and from Besançon to L'Isle-sur-le-Doubs. Finally across wooded country to Belfort. SP 'Dijon' & then 'Mulhouse' along the motorway; or SP 'Dole' for the all-purpose road out of Beaune. In the opposite direction SP 'Montbéliard', 'Besançon' & 'Lyon' ('Péage') for the first route, or SP 'Besançon par RN' for the second route out of Belfort.

A31			Beaune motorway fork (Junc A6/A31) (town 7km southwest)	188
A36	4	4	Motorway fork (Junc A31/A36)	184
	21	17	Service area	167
	25	4	Seurre Junc (no.1)	163
	55	30	Dole Junc (no.3)	133
	61	6	Dole service area	127
	87	26	Besançon-Ouest Junc	101
	96	9	Besançon (6km) – Centre Junc	92
	109	13	Besançon service area	79
	130	21	Baume-les-Dames Junc	58
	155	25	Toll booths	33
	161	6	Service area	27
	168	7	Montbéliard-Sud Junc	20
	170	2	Montbéliard Junc	18
	172	2	Souchaux/Exincourt Junc	16
	186	14	Belfort-Sud Junc (Belfort–Nord Junc, on Iter 32, 5km by A36)	2
N19	188	2	Belfort	

or avoiding toll motorway

D973			Beaune	199
	12	12	Corberon	187
	22	10	[Pouilly-sur-Saône]	177
	25	3	Seurre	174
N73	30	5	Junc D973/N73	169
	42	12	Chemin	157
	51	9	Tavaux	148
N5	55	4	Junc N73/N5	144
N73	61.5	6.5	[Dole] (Iter 95)	137.5
	76.5	15	Orchamps	122.5
	83.2	6.7	Dampierre	115.8
	89.2	6	St-Vit	109.8
	101.7	12.5	Château-Farine	97.3

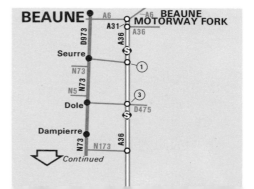

N83	108	6.3	Besançon	91
			(Iter 27)	
	117	9	Roche-lez-Beaupré	82
	127.5	10.5	Roulans	71.5
	138.5	11	Baume-les-Dames	60.5
	153.5	15	Clerval	45.5
	160.5	7	Rang	38.5
	165.5	5	L'Isle-sur-le-Doubs	33.5
	167.5	2	Médière	31.5
	177.5	10	Arcey	21.5
	187.5	10	Héricourt	11.5
	196	8.5	Bavilliers	3
	199	3	Belfort	

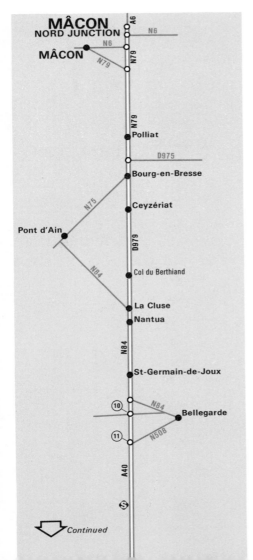

18 Mâcon–Chamonix

(223km = 138.5 miles)
A fast run over the Plain of Bresse to Bourg-en-Bresse, then hilly and winding to Nantua (max grad 15%) passing through pleasant scenery. After Nantua and the gorge and lake scenery of the Jura the route is by toll motorway (Autoroute A40). Across cultivated country to the valley of the R Arve, which is followed from Annemasse to Chamonix. At Le Fayet the gorges of the Arve begin and the road passes below Mont Blanc. The valley road continues into Chamonix but the approach to the Mont Blanc tunnel leads off to the right.
An alternative route between Bourg-en-Bresse and Nantua, which is fast to Pont d'Ain (N75) then winding but well engineered to Nantua (N84) is often preferred though 9 miles longer, and is more suitable for caravans.

unclass			Mâcon-Nord Junc of	223
			Autoroute A6	
			(town 7.5km south)	
N6	1.5	1.5	Junc motorway slip	221.5
			road/N6	
N179	3.5	2	Junc N6/N179	219.5
			(Mâcon bypass)	
N79	10	6.5	Junc N179/N79	213.5
	16.5	6.5	St-Cyr-sur-Menthon	206.5
	28.5	12	Polliat	194.5
	34.5	6	Junc with D975	188.5
D979	39	4.5	Bourg-en-Bresse	184
	44.2	5.2	St-Just	178.8
	47.9	3.7	Ceyzériat	175.1
	57.9	10	Hautecourt	165.1
	68.5	10.6	Col du Berthiand	154.5
			(2,559ft)	
N84	77.5	9	La Cluse	145.5
	81	3.5	Nantua	142
	83.8	2.8	Les Neyrolles	139.2
	94.3	10.5	[St-Germain-de-Joux]	128.7
A40	100.5	6.2	Junc with Autoroute	122.5
			A40	
	104.5	4	Bellegarde Junc	118.5
			(no.10)	
	107.5	3	Bellegarde viaduct	115.5
	112	4.5	Frangy Junc (no.11)	111
	118.5	6.5	Vuache tunnel (1.4km)	104.5
	122	3.5	Valleiry service area	101
			(eastbound only)	

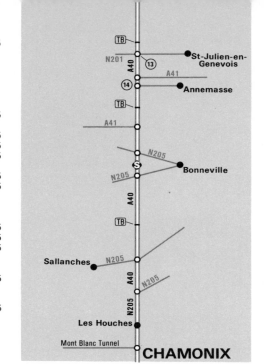

126.5	4.5	Toll booths	96.5
134	7.5	St-Julien Junc (no.13) (Genève, Geneva, 11km)	89
146	12	Junc with A411 (Genève, Geneva, 7km)	77
146.5	0.5	Annemasse Junc (no.14)	76.5
152.5	6	Toll booths	70.5
154.5	2	Findrol Junc (no.15)	68.5
157.5	3	Motorway fork (Junc with A41)	65.5
164.5	7	Bonneville Junc	58.5
166.5	2	Pontchy service area	56.5
169	2.5	Bonneville Est Junc (exit for westbound traffic only)	54
182.5	13.5	Cluses Junc	40.5
183.5	1	Toll booths	39.5
192.5	9	Sallanches Junc (exit for southbound traffic only)	30.5
200.5	8	Le Fayet Junc (exit for eastbound traffic only)	22.5
N205 202.5	2	Junc A40/N205	20.5
215	12.5	[Les Houches]	8
N506 220	5	Junc N205/N506 (Tunnel du Mont Blanc 4km)	3
223	3	Chamonix (3,412ft)	

19 Bordeaux–Toulouse

(243km = 151 miles by toll motorway)
(249km = 154.5 miles by N113 & N20)
The first route follows the A62 toll motorway—
Autoroute des Deux Mers. The second route follows
the parallel, all purpose road. Both pass at first
through a district famous for white wines, but after
Langon the cultivated country is only of moderate
interest. Both routes follow the wide valley of the R
Garonne all the way. On the second route, the R
Garonne is crossed at Langon, the R Lot at Aiguillon,
and the R Tarn, an important tributary is being
crossed at Moissac.
SP 'Toulouse'. In the opposite direction SP 'Bordeaux'.

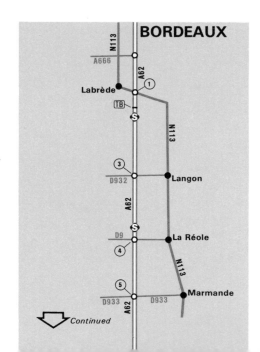

		Bordeaux	243
A62	9	9	Motorway terminus (Junc with Bordeaux ring road)	234
	20	11	Labrède Junc (no.1)	223
	25	5	Toll booths	218
	27	2	Les Landes service area	216
	34	7	Podensac Junc (no.2)	209
	45	11	Langon Junc (no.3)	198
	61	16	Le Bazadais service area	182
	64	3	La Réole Junc (no.4)	179
	81	17	Marmande Junc (no.5)	162

Continued

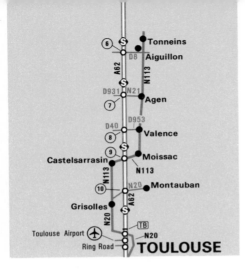

95	14	Le Queyran service area	148
103	8	Aiguillon Junc (no.6)	140
125	22	Agen-Porte d'Aquitaine service area	118
134	9	Agen (6km) Junc (no.7)	109
159	25	Valence Junc (no.8)	84
172	13	Garonne service area	71
179	7	Castelsarrasin/Moissac Junc (no.9)	64
202	23	Montauban Junc (no.10) (Iter 37)	41
217	15	Frontonnais service area	26
228	11	St-Jory Junc (no.11)	15
235	7	Toll booths	8
A624 236	1	Toulouse-Nord Junc	7
239	3	Junc for Toulouse Airport	4
uncl. 240	1	Motorway terminus (Toulouse ring road)	3
243	3	Toulouse	

or avoiding toll motorway

Route	km	dist	Place	rem
N113			Bordeaux	249
	6	6	Le Pont-de-la-Maye	243
	7	1	Junc with Bordeaux ring road	242
	17	10	La Prade	232
	18.5	1.5	Junc with Autoroute A62	230.5
	23	4.5	Castres-Gironde	226
	30	7	Virelade	219
	32	2.5	Podensac	216.5
	35.5	3	Cérons	213.5
	38.5	3	Barsac	210.5
	41.5	3	Preignac	207.5
	46.5	5	Langon	202.5
	48.5	2	[St-Macaire]	200.5
	59.5	11	Gironde-sur-Dropt	189.5
	64	4.5	La Réole	185
	72	8	Lamothe-Landerron	177
	83	11	Marmande	166
	100	17	Tonneins	149
	109	9	Nicole	140
	111	2	[Aiguillon]	138
	120	9	[Port-Ste-Marie]	129
	130	10	St-Hilaire-de-Lusignan	119
	139.5	9.5	Agen	109.5
	144.5	5	Bon-Encontre	104.5
	159.5	15	[Lamagistère]	89.5
	165.5	6	Valence	83.5
	172.5	7	Malause	76.5
	183	10.5	Moissac	66
	191	8	Castelsarrasin	58
	198.5	7.5	St-Porquier	50.5
	204	5.5	X-rds with D928	45
	209	5	Finhan	40
N20	218.5	9.5	Junc N113/N20	30.5
	220	1.5	[Grisolles]	29
	232	12	St-Jory	17
	241	9	Lacourtensourt	8
	249	8	Toulouse	

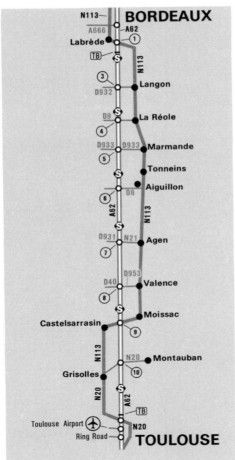

20 Toulouse–Narbonne

(146km = 90.5 miles via A61)
(151.9km = 94.5 miles via N113)
The first route is via the A61 toll motorway
(Autoroute des Deux-Mers). The second route is fast
and gently undulating through agricultural country
with vineyards. After Carcassonne (view of ancient
Cité from bridge) across a countryside of low rocky
hills.

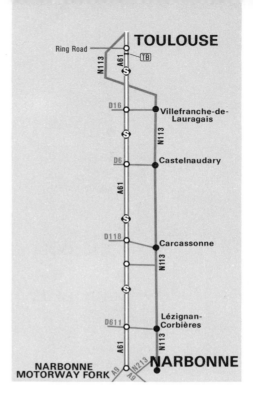

			Toulouse	146
A61	6	6	Toulouse-Sud/ Ramonville Junc of A61 Autoroute	140
	7	1	Toll booths	139
	15.5	8.5	Toulouse-Sud service area	130.5
	31	15.5	Villefranche-de- Lauragais Junc	115
	41.5	10.5	Lauragais service area	104.5
	55	13.5	Castelnaudary Junc	91
	79.5	24.5	Carcassonne-Arzens service area	66.5
	87	7.5	Carcassonne–Ouest Junc	59
	97	10	Carcassonne-Est Junc	49
	107.5	10.5	Les Corbières service area	38.5
	125	17.5	Lézignan–Corbières Junc	21
	146	21	Narbonne motorway fork (Junc A61/A9) (**Narbonne** 6km north)	

**or avoiding toll
motorway**

N113			Toulouse	151.9
	7.5	7.5	[Ramonville-St-Agne]	144.4
	11	3.5	Castanet	140.9
	34.5	23.5	Villefranche-de- Lauragais	117.4
	57	22.5	[Castelnaudary]	94.9
	77.5	20.5	Alzonne	74.4
	85.5	8	Pezens	66.4
	94.5	9	Carcassonne	57.4
	101.3	6.8	Trèbes les Capucins	50.6
	109.6	8.3	Barbaira	42.3
	113.2	3.6	Capendu	38.7
	131.4	18.2	Lézignan–Corbières	20.5
	139.4	8	Villedaigne	12.5
	146.4	7	Junc with D613	5.5
	149.4	3	Junc with N213	2.5
	151.9	2.5	**Narbonne**	

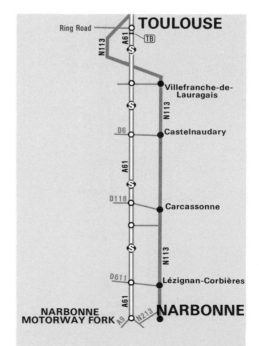

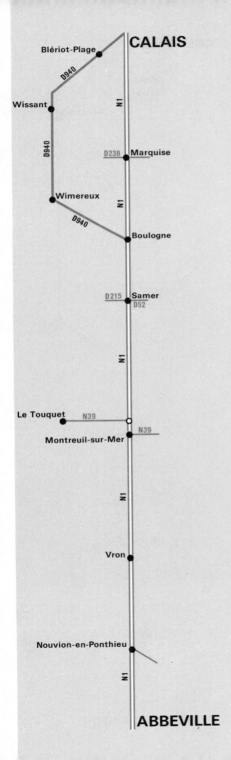

21 Calais–Boulogne–Abbeville

(115.7km = 72 miles direct)
(124.5km = 77.5 miles via the coast to Boulogne)

(a) Calais – Boulogne-sur-Mer

(34.2km = 21 miles direct)
(43km = 26.5 miles via the coast)
Pleasant and undulating passing through pastoral
country. SP 'Paris', 'Boulogne' and 'Abbeville' out of
Calais (from port 'Toutes Directions' through town).
The alternative (SP 'Boulogne par la côte') is very
pleasant, winding with easy rise and fall offering wide
views from the cliffs of the sea and downland.
In the opposite direction SP 'Calais' by N1; or SP
'Calais par la côte' by D940.

N1		Calais	34.2
	3	3	[Fort Nieulay]	31.2
5.5	2.5	Coquelles	28.7
20	14.5	Marquise	14.2
24.6	4.6	Wacquinghen	9.6
31	6.4	[Colonne-de-la-Grande Armée]	3.2
34.2	3.2	**Boulogne-sur-Mer**	

alternative route

D940		Calais	43
3	3	Blériot Plage	40
9.5	6.5	Sangatte	33.5
13.5	4	Escalles	29.5
19.7	6.2	Wissant	23.3
22.9	3.2	Tardinghen	20.1
25.4	2.5	Audinghen	17.6
		(Cap Gris-Nez 3km)	
29.4	4	Audresselles	13.6
31.4	2	Ambleteuse	11.6
37.2	5.8	Wimereux	5.8
43	5.8	**Boulogne-sur-Mer**	

(b) Boulogne-sur-Mer – Abbeville

(81.5km = 50.5 miles)
Moderately fast, but in parts winding and undulating.
The Forest of Crécy is skirted for some distance after
Bernay, otherwise mainly open agricultural country.
SP 'Paris' out of Boulogne (from port SP 'Sortie/Exit'
and then 'Toutes Directions'). In the opposite direction
SP 'Calais' and 'Boulogne'.

N1		Boulogne-sur-Mer	81.5
5	5	Pont-de-Briques	76.5
15	10	[Samer]	66.5
35	20	Junc with N39	46.5
		(Le Touquet 15km)	
37	2	[Montreuil-sur-Mer]	44.5
43.8	6.8	Wailly-Beaucamp	37.7
48.8	5	Nempont-St-Firmin	32.7
50.8	2	Nampont-St-Martin	30.7
55.1	4.3	Vron	26.4
60.1	5	Bernay	21.4
68.3	8.2	Nouvion-en-Ponthieu	13.2
73.7	5.4	Hautvillers	7.8
81.5	7.8	**Abbeville**	

22 Abbeville–Paris

(162.1km = 100.5 miles via D901)
(180.6km = 112 miles via Amiens)

The first and recommended route, via D901 to Beauvais, is by a moderately fast, undulating, and slightly winding road mainly across open agricultural country; later partly wooded but scenically of little special merit. Parts of the road south of Beauvais carry heavy traffic, and the streets of Paris are particularly congested.

SP 'Beauvais' and 'Paris' out of Abbeville. In the opposite direction SP 'Beauvais' on leaving the A1 near St-Denis, and later SP 'Calais', 'Boulogne' and 'Abbeville' on leaving Beauvais. The second route follows the N1 via Amiens, mostly fairly fast and undulating, but 18.5km longer.

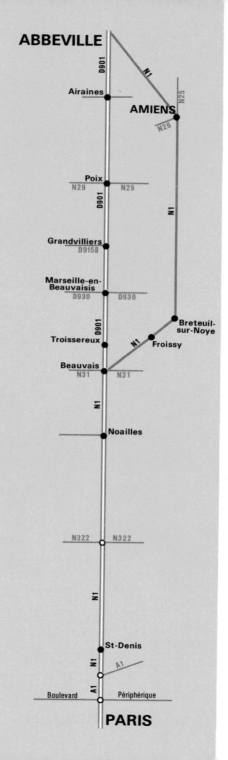

D901		Abbeville	162.1
	3.5	3.5 Epagnette	158.6
	8	4.5 Pont Remy	154.1
	13.2	5.2 Sorel-en-Vimeu	148.9
	20.2	7 Airaines	141.9
	29.5	9.3 Camps-en-Amiénois	132.6
	32	2.5 [Lincheux]	130.1
	42.5	10.5 Poix	119.6
	47.7	5.2 Equennes	114.4
	57.2	9.5 Grandvilliers	104.9
	67.9	10.7 Marseille-en-Beauvaisis	94.2
	73.1	5.2 St-Omer-en-Chaussée	89
	80.1	7 Troissereux	82
N1	86.6	6.5 Beauvais (Iter 92)	75.5
	90.1	3.5 Allonne	72
	93.1	3 Warluis	69
	101.6	8.5 Noailles	60.5
	110.3	8.7 La Mare-d'Ovillers	51.8
	125.8	15.5 R Oise br	36.3
	126.3	0.5 Junc with N322	35.8
		(Beaumont-sur-Oise 3km; l'Isle-Adam 3km)	
	138.3	12 [Moisselles]	23.8
	147.8	9.5 Pierrefitte	14.3
	150.6	2.8 [St-Denis]	11.5
A1	152.6	2 Junc N1/A1	9.5
	156.1	3.5 Junc with Bd Périphérique (Iter 101) (Porte de la Chapelle)	6
	162.1	6 Paris	

alternative route

N1		Abbeville	180.6
	6	6 [Bellancourt]	174.6
	13	7 Ailly-le-Haut-Clocher	167.6
	22.6	9.6 Flixecourt	158
	26.6	4 Junc with N235	154
	41.1	14.5 Junc N1/D933	139.5
	45.1	4 Amiens	135.5
	50.6	5.5 Dury	130
	57.1	6.5 St-Sauflieu	123.5
	62.1	5 Essertaux	118.5
	63.1	1 Flers-sur-Noye	117.5
	73.6	10.5 Esquennoy	107
	77.1	3.5 [Breteuil]	103.5
	87.1	10 Froissy	93.5
	105.1	18 Beauvais	75.5
		as above	
	180.6	75.5 Paris	

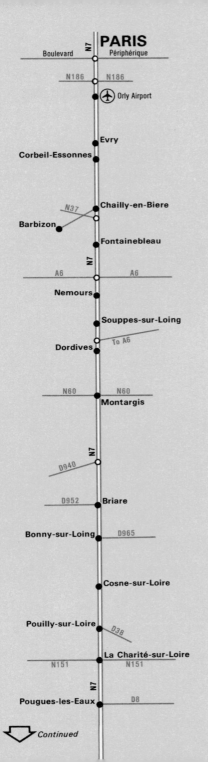

23 Paris–Moulins

(295.8km = 184 miles)

Once clear of the built-up suburbs of Paris this, on the whole, fairly fast and straight route passes through the agricultural country of the Seine valley, and later through the magnificent forest of Fontainebleau. From Nemours along the pleasant Loing valley to Montargis, then through well-wooded country to Briare, on the R Loire. Onwards to Nevers wide and straight following the broad valley of the middle Loire through rich, agricultural country with occasional woods. Then by the broad fertile valley of the distant R Allier.

SP 'Fontainebleau par RN7' out of Paris, then 'Nemours', 'Nevers', and finally 'Moulins'. In the opposite direction SP 'Paris'. *For route by toll motorway, Autoroute du Soleil A6, to Nemours, see Iter 2.*

unclass			Paris	295.8
N7	8	8	Junc with Bd Périphérique (Porte d'Italie; Iter 101)	287.8
	11.5	3.5	Villejuif	284.3
	15.5	4	Junc with N186 (La Belle Épine)	280.3
	18.2	2.7	[Orly Airport]	277.6
	19.7	1.5	Paray-Vieille-Post	276.1
	22.5	2.8	Juvisy-sur-Orge	273.3
	24.5	2	Viry-Châtillon	271.3
	28.2	3.7	Ris-Orangis	267.6
	31.2	3	[Evry]	264.6
	35.5	4.3	Corbeil-Essonnes	260.3
	39.8	4.3	Le Plessis-Chênet	256
	46.8	7	Ponthierry	249
	55.3	8.5	Chailly-en-Biere (Barbizon 2km)	240.5
	56.8	1.5	Junc with N37	239
	65.3	8.5	[Fontainebleau]	230.5
	71.3	6	Bourron	224.5
	76.8	5.5	Fontainebleau Sud Junc of Autoroute A6 (Iter 2)	219
	80.8	4	Nemours	215
	87.8	7	Glandelles	208
	91.8	4	Souppes-sur-Loing	204
	96.3	4.5	Junc with motorway spur to A6	199.5
	96.8	0.5	Dordives	199
	114.8	18	Montargis (Iter 66)	181
	119.8	5	[Mormant-sur-Vernisson]	176
	131.8	12	[Nogent-sur-Vernisson]	164
	136.8	5	Les Bézards	159
	138.8	2	Junc with D940	157
	143.3	4.5	[La Bussière]	152.5
	155.8	12.5	[Briare]	140
	167.8	12	[Bonny-sur-Loire]	128
	172.8	5	[Neuvy-sur-Loire]	123
	179.8	7	La Celle-sur-Loire	116
	182.8	3	Myennes	113
	186.3	3.5	[Cosne-sur-Loire]	109.5
	194.3	8	Maltaverne	101.5
	201.3	7	[Pouilly-sur-Loire]	94.5
	214.3	13	La Charité-sur-Loire	81.5
	218.3	4	La Marche	77.5
	228.3	10	Pougues-les-Eaux	67.5

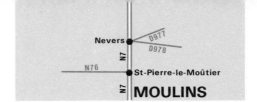

239.3	11	Nevers	56.5
242.3	3	St-Antoine	53.5
252.8	10.5	[Magny-Cours]	43
263.8	11	St-Pierre-le-Moûtier	32
282.8	19	Villeneuve-sur-Allier	13
295.8	13	**Moulins**	

24 Moulins–Lyon

(185km = 115 miles)

At first the route offers extensive views over the wide plain of the Allier, then follows a picturesque and fairly fast road across the low foothills of the Mountains of La Madeleine. Beyond Roanne it is an attractive run with moderate gradients over the Monts du Lyonnais with wide views to the south of the distant Central Plateau.

The route is SP 'Lyon'. In the opposite direction SP 'Paris RN7' and 'Vichy' out of Lyon. *Note:* Junc with A6; this motorway can be used to bypass Lyon if continuing by Iter 3.

N7		**Moulins**	185
	5.5	5.5 Toulon-sur-Allier	179.5
	25	19.5 St-Loup	160
	27.5	2.5 Chazeuil	157.5
	30	2.5 Varennes-sur-Allier	155
	40.6	10.6 St-Gérand-le-Puy	144.4
	50.6	10 Lapalisse	134.4
	52.9	2.3 St-Prix	132.1
	67.9	15 St-Martin-d'Estréaux	117.1
	75.3	7.4 La Pacaudière	109.7
	87	11.7 St-Germain-Lespinasse	98
	99	12 Roanne	86
	108	9 [L'Hôpital-sur-Rhins]	77
	109	1 Junc with N82	76
	116.4	7.4 St-Symphorien-de-Lay	68.6
	130.8	14.4 Col du Pin-Bouchain	54.2
		(2,493ft)	
	141.2	10.4 Tarare	43.8
	146.9	5.7 Pontchara-sur-Turdine	38.1
	159.6	12.7 [L'Arbresle] (Eveux	25.4
		1.5km by D19)	
	170.6	11 La Tour-de-Salvagny	14.4
D407	179	8.4 Tassin	6
		(Junc with A6	
		Autoroute, 1km)	
	185	6 **Lyon**	

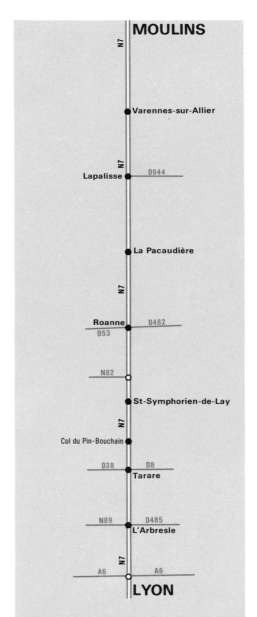

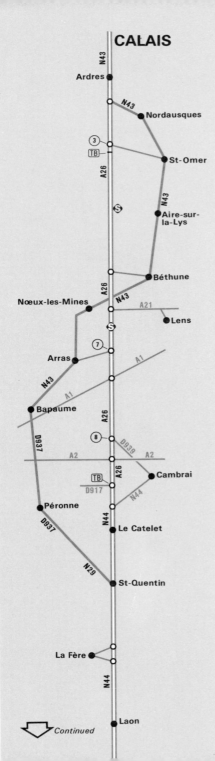

CALAIS

25 Calais–Reims

(276km = 171.5 miles by toll motorway)
(282.5km = 175.5 miles by all-purpose road)
Alternative routes, by toll motorway or by all-purpose road. Both routes are SP 'St-Omer' and follow the same road from Calais to Nordausques, and again from St-Quentin to Reims. Initially a mainly straight, tree-lined road across flat country from Calais to Ardres, then generally pleasant and undulating. After Nordausques the first route follows the 'Paris' & 'Reims' toll motorway, Autoroute A26, through gently undulating farming country to its present end south of Cambrai. The route then continues by all-purpose road, a fast run through the cultivated valley of the upper Escaut to Le Catelet, and on over hills to the R Somme at St-Quentin. Onwards to Reims mainly a fast tree-lined road across open country of little particular interest, apart from its World War 1 associations. Slightly more wooded beyond La Fère. The first route is SP 'St-Omer' out of Calais, then 'Paris' as far as Arras, and then 'Reims'. In the opposite direction SP 'Laon', 'St-Quentin', then 'Cambrai', and finally 'Calais'.
The second route avoids the motorway, and passes through similar country, but is industrial around and after Béthune.

N43			Calais	276
	8	8	Les Attaques	268
	11	3	Le Pont d'Ardres	265
	16	5	Ardres	260
A26	23	7	Nordausques Junc with Autoroute A26	253
	37	14	St-Omer Junc (no.3) (Iter 90) (Toll booths)	239
	68	31	Lillers Junc (no.5)	208
	80	12	Béthune Junc	196
	91.5	11.5	Aix-Noulette Junc (Junc with Autoroute A21, Lens 9km)	184.5
	96	4.5	Service area	180
	104	8	Arras Nord Junc (no.7) (Iter 90)	172
	113	9	Motorway X-rds (Junc with A1) (Iter 15)	163
	134	21	Marquion Junc (no.8) (Cambrai 10km)	142
	141	7	Motorway X-rds (Junc with A2)	135
	150	9	Masnières Junc (Cambrai Sud motorway terminus & toll booths)	126
D917	150.5	0.5	Junc motorway slip road/D917	125.5
N44	152.7	2.2	Junc D917/N44 (Cambrai 10.5km)	123.3
	162.2	9.5	Le Catelet	113.8
	167.2	5	Bellicourt	108.8
	169.7	2.5	Junc with D932	106.3
	180.7	11	St-Quentin	95.3
	195.9	15.2	[Vendeuil]	80.1
	200.9	5	Junc with N32 (La Fere 2km)	75.1
	225.7	24.8	[Laon]	50.3

Continued

49

248	22.3	Corbeny	28
252	4	[La Ville-aux-Bois] British Military Cemetery	24
256	4	Berry-au-Bac	20
276	20	**Reims**	

or avoiding toll motorway

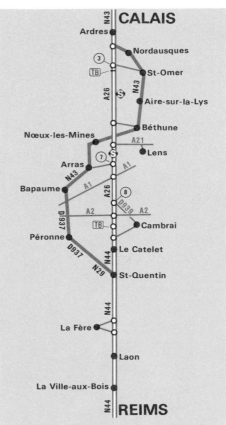

N43			Calais	282.5
	8	8	Les Attaques	274.5
	11	3	Le Pont d'Ardres	271.5
	16	5	Ardres	266.5
	23	7	Junc with Autoroute A26	259.5
	24	1	Nordausques	258.5
N42	37.5	13.5	St-Martin-au-Laërt	245
N43	39	1.5	St-Omer	243.5
	53.5	14.5	Wittes	229
	57.3	3.8	[Aire-sur-la-Lys]	225.2
	64.3	7	Norrent Fontes	218.2
	71.8	7.5	[Lillers]	210.7
	79.3	7.5	[Chocques]	203.2
D937	84.5	5.2	Béthune	198
	90.5	6	Noeux-les-Mines	192
	94.5	4	Sains-en-Gohelle	188
	97	2.5	Aix Noulette	185.5
	102	5	Souchez	180.5
	106.5	4.5	La Targette	176
N17	113.5	7	Arras	169
	116.5	3	Beaurains	166
	132.2	15.7	Sapignies	150.3
	135.8	3.6	Bapaume	146.7
			(Bapaume Junc of A1 Autoroute 2km; Iter 1)	
	139.8	4	Beaulencourt	142.7
	151.3	11.5	Bouchavesnes-Bergen	131.2
	155.2	3.9	Mont-St-Quentin	127.3
D937	158.2	3	[Péronne]	124.3
D944	161.2	3	Junc D937/D944	121.3
N29	168.2	7	Junc D944/N29	114.3
	173	4.8	Poeuilly	109.5
	176.6	3.6	Vermand	105.9
	187.2	10.6	St-Quentin	95.3

as above

282.5	95.3	**Reims**

26 Reims–Chaumont

(181km = 112.5 miles)
Fast, straight and undulating, joining the broad, cultivated Marne plain at Châlons. Later the Marne-Saône canal is followed across good farming country to St-Dizier, then very attractive keeping close to the R Marne between thickly wooded heights.
SP 'Châlons', then 'Vitry' & then 'Chaumont'. In the

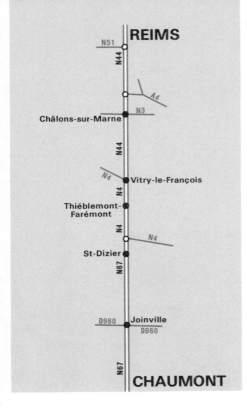

opposite direction SP 'St-Dizier', then 'Reims'.
For alternative route by toll motorway, Autoroute A4, to Châlons-sur-Marne, see Iter 10.

N44			**Reims**	181
	4	4	Junc with link rd for Reims/Cormontreuil Junc of A4 Autoroute (Iter 10)	177
	8.5	4.5	[Fort-de-la Pompelle]	172.5
	16	7.5	Beaumont-sur-Vesle	165
	21	5	[Les Petites-Loges]	160
	35.2	14.2	[Le Veuve] (Châlons-sur-Marne junc of A4 Autoroute 1km by D21) (Iter 10)	145.8
	43.8	8.6	[Châlons-sur-Marne]	137.2
	53	9.2	Chepy	128
	62.7	9.7	La Chaussée-sur-Marne	118.3
N4	77.4	14.7	Vitry-le-François	103.6
	80.6	3.2	Marolles	100.4
	88	7.4	[Thiéblemont-Farémont]	93
	97	9	Perthes	84
N67	104.5	7.5	Junc N4/N67	76.5
	106.5	2	St-Dizier (Iter 96)	74.5
	111	4.5	Marnaval	70
	126.5	15.5	Rachecourt-sur-Marne	54.5
	135.5	9	Vecqueville	45.5
	138.5	3	Joinville	42.5
	140.9	2.4	Rupt	40.1
	143.5	2.6	Fronville	37.5
	152	8.5	Gudmont	29
	157	5	Provenchères	24
	164.3	7.3	Soncourt	16.7
	170.3	6	[Bologne]	10.7
	175.6	5.3	Brethenay	5.4
	181	5.4	**Chaumont**	

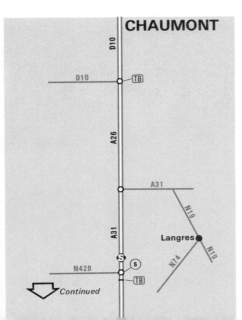

27 Chaumont–Besançon–Lausanne
(274.5km = 170.5 miles)

(a) Chaumont–Besançon

(152km = 94.5 miles)
A very pleasant run. Initially following the 'Dijon' toll-motorway through undulating and well-wooded farming country. Later descending from the Plateau de Langres into the basin of the R Saône, crossed at Gray, and continuing through the wooded country of Franche-Comté to the R Doubs at Besançon.
SP 'Dijon' & 'Besançon' to junction no.6, then 'Gray' & 'Besançon'. In the opposite direction SP 'Chaumont'.
For the non-motorway route via Langres to Longeau see Iter 28.

D10			**Chaumont**	152
A26	12	12	Chaumont Junc of Autoroute A26 (toll booths)	140
A31	31	19	Junc A26/A31 (Langres 16km)	121
	44	13	Langres service area	108
	46	2	Langres Sud Junc (no.6)	106
	46.5	0.5	Toll booths	105.5

D428	46.8	0.3	Junc motorway slip	105.2
			road/D428	
N74	55	8.2	Junc D428/N74	97
			(Langres **4.5km**)	
D67	62	7	Longeau	90
	63	1	Percey-le-Pautel	89
	70	7	Chassigny	82
	86	16	Champlitte	66
	101	15	Chargey-lès-Gray	51
	106	5	Gray	46
	114	8	Cresancey	38
	118	4	Venère	34
	121	3	Bonboillon	31
	129.5	8.5	[Marnay]	22.5
	131	1.5	Junc with D109	21
	135	4	[Recologne]	17
	139	4	Audeux	13
	144	5	Pouilley-les-Vignes	8
	152	8	Besançon	

(b) Besançon – Lausanne

(122.5km = 75.5 miles)

Fine view of the Doubs Valley on leaving Besançon.
Across fine hilly countryside of the Jura foothills,
partially wooded, although desolate rocky stretch
before Pontarlier. Thereafter pleasant wooded scenery
to the frontier, then cultivated and of moderate
interest.

*A parallel motorway is now available from Oulens-
sous-Echallens, east of La Sarraz, to Lausanne. This
is a section of the N1 motorway from Lausanne to
Yverdon, which has a direct link with the Lausanne
motorway bypass.*

N57			Besançon	122.5
	4.5	4.5	Morre	118
	9.5	5	Junc with D67	113
	14	4.5	Mamirolle	108.5
	20.5	6.5	L'Hôpital-du-Grosbois	102
	23.5	3	Junc with D461	99
	35	11.5	Nods	87.5
	44	9	[St-Gorgon-Main]	78.5
	49	5	La Vrine	73.5
	57	8	Pontarlier (2,746ft)	65.5
	60.5	3.5	La Cluse-et-Mijoux	62
	61	0.5	Junc with D67bis	61.5
	62.5	1.5	La Gauffre	60
	74	11.5	Les Hôpitaux–Neufs	48.5
	76	2	[Jougne]	46.5
9	80	4	*French Customs* of	42.5
			Ferrière-sous-Jougne	
			and *Swiss Customs* of	
			Vallorbe-Route	
	83.5	3.5	Vallorbe (2,506ft)	39
	99.5	16	Pompaples	23
	100.5	1	La Sarraz (1,640ft)	22
	106	5.5	Cossonay	16.5
	116	10	Crissier	6.5
			(Crissier Junc of	
			Motorway N1, 0.5km)	
	122.5	6.5	**Lausanne** (1,591 ft)	

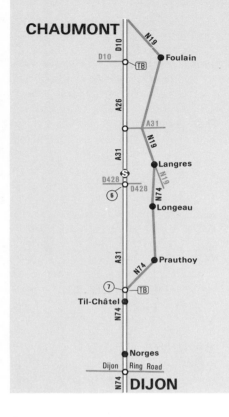

28 Chaumont–Dijon

(106km = 66 miles)
(102.5km = 63.5 miles)
Alternative routes, by toll motorway or all-purpose road. The first route, by toll motorway, passes through undulating and well-wooded farming country to its present end near Til-Châtel. The alternative route follows the attractive valley of the R Marne to Langres (but little is seen of the river). The road is slightly winding and undulating, passing through grazing country with well-wooded hillsides. After Langres a fast, straight run across farming country to the vineyards of the Côte d'Or.
The first route is SP 'Dijon'; the second is SP 'Langres' & then 'Dijon'.
In the opposite direction both routes are SP 'Chaumont'.

D10			Chaumont	106
A26	12	12	Chaumont Junc of Autotoute A26 (toll booths)	94
A31	31	19	Junc A261/A31 (Langres 16km)	75
	44	13	Langres service area	62
	46	2	Langres Sud Junc (no.6)	60
	77	31	Til-Châtel Junc (no.7) (motorway terminus & toll booths)	29
N74	77.5	0.5	Junc motorway slip road/N74	28.5
	80	2.5	Til-Châtel	26
	95	15	Norges	11
	101	6	Junc with D996 and Dijon ring road	5
	106	5	Dijon	

alternative route

N19			Chaumont	102.5
	7	7	[Luzy-sur-Marne]	95.5
	11	4	Foulain	91.5
	15	4	[Marnay-sur-Marne]	87.5
	25.5	10.5	Junc with Autoroute A31	77
	29.5	4	Humes	73
N74	35.5	6	Langres	67
	39.5	4	[Sts-Geosmes]	63
	40	0.5	Junc with D428 (Iter 27)	62.5
	47	7	Longeau	55.5
	52	5	[St-Michel]	50.5
	57	5	Prauthoy	45.5
	59.5	2.5	Vaux-sous-Aubigny	43
	70.5	11	Orville	32
	74	3.5	Junc with Autoroute A31	28.5
	76.5	2.5	Til-Châtel *as above*	26
	102.5	26	Dijon	

29 Dijon—Beaune

(42km = 26 miles via motorway)
(38km = 23.5 miles via N74)
The recommended route is via toll motorway,
Autoroute A31 and A6. The alternative route passes
through the famous vineyards of the Côte d'Or,
reading like a wine list, for so many villages have
given their name to famous vintages. SP 'Lyon par
l'Autoroute' from Dijon.

			Dijon	42
A31	7.5	7.5	Dijon motorway	34.5
			terminus	
	9	1.5	Toll booths	33
	14	5	Gevrey service area	28
	25	11	Nuits-St-Georges Junc	17
	34	9	Motorway fork	8
			(Junc with A36) (Iter 17)	
A6	38	4	Beaune motorway fork	4
			(Junc A31/A6) (Iter 2)	
	42	4	Beaune/Chagny Junc	
			(Beaune 3km)	

			alternative route	
N74			Dijon	38
	11.5	11.5	Gevrey-Chambertin	26.5
	17	5.5	Vougeot	21
	19.5	2.5	Vosne-Romanée	18.5
	22	2.5	Nuits-St-Georges	16
	38	16	**Beaune**	

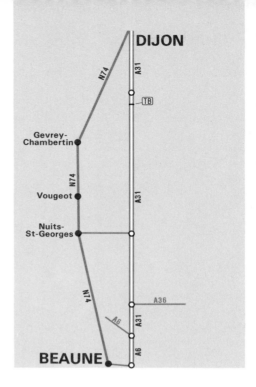

30 Paris–Troyes–Chaumont

(253km = 157 miles)

(a) Paris – Troyes

(157km = 97.5 miles)
Suburban route to Boissy-St-Leger. Then fast across
the cultivated plain between the Rivers Marne and
Seine. The latter is crossed at Nogent and the rim of
the plateau followed above the marshy valley all the
way to Troyes.

			Paris	157
A4	6	6	Junc Bd Périphérique/	151
			A4 (Porte de Bercy)	
			(Iter 101)	
	7	1	Ivry s/Seine Junc (exit	150
			for westbound traffic	
			only)	
A86	10	3	Motorway fork	147
			(Junc A4/A86)	
N19	11.5	1.5	Créteil Junc	145.5
	12	0.5	Créteil	145
	15.5	3.5	Les Petits Carreux,	141.5
			Junc with D60	
	18	2.5	Boissy-St-Léger	139
	28	10	Brie-Comte-Robert	129
	35	7	Coubert	122
	43	8	Guignes	114
	51	8	Mormant	106
	62	11	Nangis	95

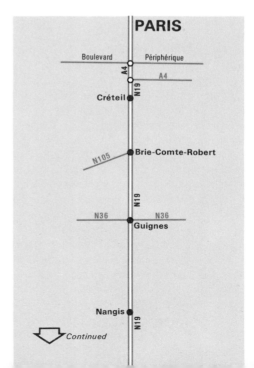

Continued

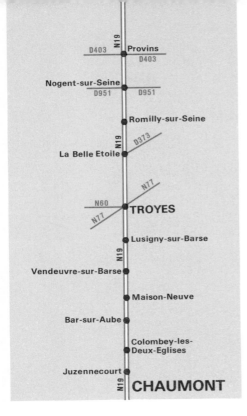

73	11	Maison-Rouge	84
84	11	[Provins]	73
89	5	Sourdun	68
96	7	Le Meriot	61
101	5	[Nogent-s-Seine]	56
111.5	10.5	St-Hilaire-sous-Romilly	45.5
119	7.5	Romilly-sur-Seine	38
123.5	4.5	Les Granges	33.5
132	8.5	La Belle Etoile (Iter 94)	25
138.5	6.5	Fontaine-les-Grès	18.5
146	7.5	La Malmaison	11
157	11	**Troyes**	

(b) Troyes – Chaumont

(96km = 59.5 miles)
Crosses from the R Seine to the valley of the Aube,
and later to the R Marne at Chaumont; rather
monotonous and undulating through farming country.
*A parallel toll motorway (Autoroute A26) is planned
to duplicate the whole of this route.*

N19		Troyes	96
	3.5	3.5	St-Parres-aux-Tertres	92.5
	15.3	11.8	Lusigny-sur-Barse	80.7
	31.1	15.8	Vendeuvre-sur-Barse	64.9
	36.6	5.5	Magny-Fouchard	59.4
	44.4	7.8	Maison-Neuve	51.6
	46.4	2	Arsonval	49.6
	53.8	7.4	Bar-sur-Aube	42.2
	62.3	8.5	Lignol-le-Château	33.7
	68.8	6.5	Colombey-les-Deux-Eglises	27.2
	77.4	8.6	Juzennecourt	18.6
	88.8	11.4	Jonchery	7.2
	96	7.2	**Chaumont**	

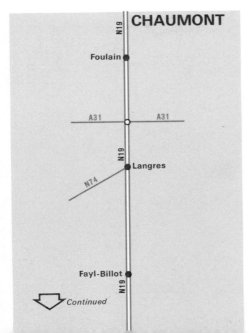

31 Chaumont—Belfort

(177km = 110 miles)
A very pleasant run. Initially following the attractive
valley of the R Marne (but little is seen of the river).
The road is slightly winding and undulating, passing
through grazing country with well-wooded hillsides.
After Langres a fairly fast road with constant rise and
fall across a vast, undulating, partly wooded plain
stretching from the R Marne to the R Saône. The
open country continues to beyond Lure, where the
road enters the 'Belfort Gap' between the Vosges
Mountains to the north and the Jura Mountains to
the south.
SP 'Langres', then 'Vesoul' & then 'Belfort'. In the
opposite direction SP 'Paris' & 'Chaumont'.
*For alternative route by toll motorway, Autoroute
A26, to Langres, see Iter 28.*

N19		Chaumont	177
	7	7	[Luzy-sur-Marne]	170
	11	4	Foulain	166
	15	4	[Marnay-sur-Marne]	162
	25.5	10.5	Junc with Autoroute A31	151.5
	29.5	4	Humes	147.5
	35.5	6	Langres	141.5
	60	24.5	Fayl-Billot	117

Continued

85.5	25.5	Combeaufontaine	91.5
97.5	12	Port-sur-Saône	79.5
104	6.5	Charmoille	73
106.2	2.2	Pusey	70.8
111	4.8	[Vesoul]	66
123.4	12.4	[Calmoutier]	53.6
136.4	13	Amblans	40.6
143.9	7.5	[Lure]	33.1
150.9	7	La Côte	26.1
156.4	5.5	Ronchamp	20.6
159.4	3	Le Bas des Côtes	17.6
162.7	3.3	Le Ban-de-Champagney	14.3
173.5	10.8	Essert	3.5
177	3.5	Belfort	

32 Belfort – Basel

(82km = 51 miles by toll motorway)
(66km = 41 miles by all-purpose road)
Alternative routes, by toll motorway or all-purpose road
through undulating, wooded country of the 'Belfort Gap',
between the Vosges Mountains to the north and the Jura
Mountains to the south. The first route follows part of the
Beaune-Mulhouse Autoroute A36, later joining the toll free
A35 from Colmar for the final run across the cultivated
Rhine valley to Basel.
The second route is winding and undulating with a
maximum gradient of 11%.
SP 'Mulhouse' & 'Bâle' along the motorway; or SP 'Altkirch'
& 'Bâle par CD' for the all-purpose road. Finally SP 'Bâle
Tourisme', for entry by Burgfelderstrasse. In the opposite
direction SP 'France' out of Basel by a different frontier
crossing then continue by SP 'Mulhouse' for the first route
or SP 'Altkirch' & 'Belfort' for the second route.

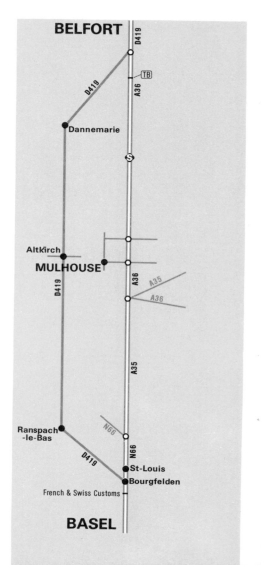

D419			Belfort	82
	3.5	3.5	Perouse	78.5
	5.5	2	Junc D419/motorway approach road	76.5
A36	6	0.5	Belfort-Nord Junc	76
	12	6	Toll booths	70
	25	13	La Porte d'Alsace service area	57
	28	3	Burnhaupt Junc	54
	36.5	8.5	Lutterbach/Dornach Junc	45.5
	38.5	2	Mulhouse-Ouest Junc	43.5
	42	3.5	Mulhouse – Centre Junc	40
	45	3	Ile Napoléon Junc	37
A35	47	2	Motorway X-rds (Junc A36/A35)	35
	52	5	Rixheim Junc	30
	66	14	Bartenheim Junc	16
D12	70	4	St-Louis/Bâle motorway terminus	12
N66	71	1	St-Louis-la-Chaussée	11
	75	4	St-Louis	7
	77	2	Bourgfelden	5
	77.5	0.5	French and Swiss Customs	4.5
	82	4.5	**Basel (Bâle)** (Basle)	

**or avoiding toll
motorway**

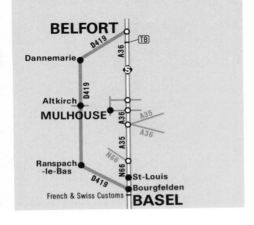

D419			Belfort	66
	3.5	3.5	Pérouse	62.5
	5.5	2	[Belfort-Nord Junc of Autoroute A36]	60.5
	7	1.5	Bessoncourt	59
	11.5	4.5	Frais	54.5
	14	2.5	Foussemagne	52
	24	10	Dannemarie	42
	27.5	3.5	Ballersdorf	38.5
	34.5	7	Altkirch	31.5
	37.5	3	Wittersdorf	28.5
	39.5	2	Tagsdorf	26.5
	52	12.5	Ranspach-le-Bas	14
	58.5	6.5	Hésingue	7.5
	61	2.5	Bourgfelden	5
	61.5	0.5	*French and Swiss Customs*	4.5
	66	4.5	**Basel (Bâle)** (Basle)	

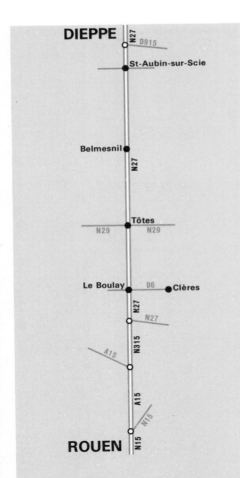

33 Dieppe – Rouen

(61km = 38 miles)
Through a series of valleys set between low hills passing by apple orchards and meadows.
SP 'Paris' & 'Rouen'. In the opposite direction SP 'Dieppe' & 'Le Havre' out of Rouen.

N27			Dieppe	61
	3	3	Junc with D915	58
	6	3	St-Aubin-sur-Scie	55
	8	2	Sauqueville	53
	18	10	Belmesnil	43
	29	11	Tôtes	32
	38.5	9.5	Le Boulay (Clères 5.5km by D6)	22.5
N315	43	4.5	Junc N27/N315 (Rouen 15km by N27)	18
A15	49.5	6.5	Motorway fork (Junc N315/A15)	11.5
	51	1.5	Service area (northbound only)	10
	54.5	3.5	Canteleu/Maromme Junc (exit for northbound traffic only)	6.5
N15	58.5	4	Motorway terminus	2.5
	61	2.5	Rouen	

34 Rouen – Chartres

(128km = 79.5 miles direct route)
(140.5km = 87 miles touring route)

By the valley of the Seine, crossed at Pont-de-l'Arche, then rising through forest to Louviers. For the next few kilometres the R Eure is in sight, then the road rises through wooded country to Evreux then straight and fast across an open plain. SP 'Mantes' and 'Paris' out of Rouen. The alternative, which follows the Eure valley, is far more attractive, but it is slower.

An alternative route by Autoroute A13 to Louviers is available. Follow signs 'Paris par l'Autoroute' to Louviers/Evreux junction.

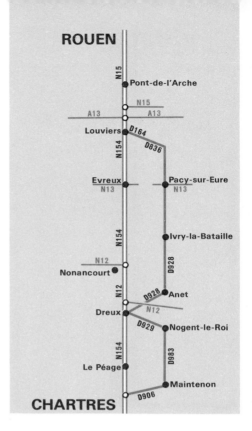

N15			Rouen	128
	5	5	Amfreville-la-Mi-Voie	123
	10.5	5.5	Le Port St-Ouen	117.5
	18	7.5	Pont-de-l'Arche	110
N154	25	7	Junc N15/N154	103
	25.5	0.5	Louviers/Evreux Junc of A13 Autoroute (Iter 9.12)	102.5
	29.5	4	[Louviers]	98.5
	44.5	15	Le Boulay-Morin	83.5
	48	3.5	Gravigny	80
	51	3	Evreux	77
	59	8	Seugey	69
	64	5	Thomer-la-Sôgne	64
	77.5	13.5	Buray	50.5
N12	79	1.5	Junc N154/N12 (Nonancourt 1km)	49
	83	4	St-Rémy-sur-Avre	45
N154	90.5	7.5	Junc N12/N154	37.5
	93	2.5	Dreux	35
	100	7	Marville-Moultier-Brule	28
	111	11	Le Péage	17
	124	13	Lèves	4
	128	4	Chartres	

alternative route

N15			Rouen	128
	5	5	Amfreville-la-Mi-Voie	123
	10.5	5.5	Le Port St-Ouen	117.5
	18	7.5	Pont-de-l'Arche	110
N154	25	7	Junc N15/N154	103
	25.5	0.5	Louviers/Evreux Junc of A13 Autoroute (Iter 9.12)	102.5
	29.5	29.5	[Louviers]	111
D164	30	0.5	Junc N155/D164	110.5
D836	33.5	3.5	Junc D164/D836	107
	39.3	5.8	Fontaine-Heudebourg	101.2
	45.3	6	Autheuil	95.2
	58.3	13	Pacy-sur-Eure	82.2
	65.5	7.2	Breuilpont	75
	69	3.5	Bueil	71.5
D62	69.5	0.5	Junc D836/D62	71
D16	71	1.5	Rd No. change	69.5
D933	75.5	4.5	[Ivry-la-Bataille]	65
D928	77.5	2	Oulins	63
	80.5	3	Anet	60
	92.5	12	Fermaincourt	48
D929	96.5	4	Dreux	44
	107	10.5	Villemeux-sur-Eure	33.5
D983	113.5	6.5	Nogent-le-Roi	27
D906	121.5	8	Maintenon	19
N154	134.5	13	Junc D906/N154	6
	136.5	2	Lèves	4
58	140.5	4	Chartres	

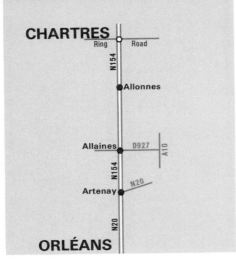

35 Chartres – Orléans

(73km = 45.5 miles)
Fast, straight and level, crossing the cultivated but featureless plain of La Beauce. SP 'Orléans; in the opposite direction 'Paris' on N20.
A parallel toll motorway, Autoroute A10, is available between Allaines and Orléans (see Iter 7).

N154			Chartres	73
	3.5	3.5	Junc with Chartres ring road	69.5
	5.5	2	Bonville	67.5
	18.5	13	Allonnes	54.5
	29	10.5	Ymonville	44
	37.5	8.5	Allaines (Allaines/Chartres (Junc of A10 Autoroute 2km by D927; Iter 7)	35.5
N20	52.5	15	[Artenay]	20.5
	58.2	5.7	Chevilly	14.8
	63	4.8	Cercottes	10
	73	10	Orléans	

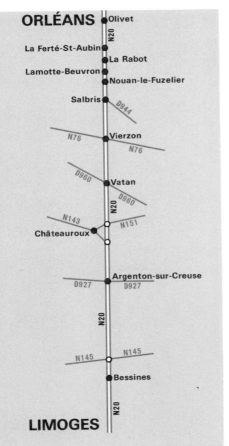

36 Orléans – Limoges

(262.2km = 163 miles)
A fairly fast and picturesque run, to beyond Salbris through the woods of Sologne, a drained marsh famous for game. The R Cher is crossed at Vierzon and the level road continues across farming country, also well-wooded after Châteauroux, to Argenton-sur-Creuse. Onwards the road is undulating (max grad 10%).
The route is SP 'Vierzon' out of Orléans. In the opposite direction follow SP 'Châteauroux' and 'Paris'.
A parallel toll motorway (Autoroute A71) is planned to duplicate the route between Orléans and Vierzon. A 7km long section west of Orléans is already open, and the section from Olivet to Salbris is under construction.

N20			Orléans	262.2
	5.3	5.3	[Olivet]	256.9
	23	17.7	La Ferté-St-Aubin	239.2
	31	8	Le Rabot	231.2
	38	7	Lamotte-Beuvron	224.2
	44.2	6.2	Nouan-le-Fuzelier	218
	56.7	12.5	Salbris	205.5
	79.7	23	[Vierzon] (Iter 65)	182.5
	90.2	10.5	Massay	172
	107.2	17	Vatan	155
	130.7	23.5	Céré	131.5
	137.2	6.5	[Châteauroux] (Iter 67)	125
	152.7	15.5	[Lothiers]	109.5
	159.7	7	Tendu	102.5
	167.7	8	Argenton-sur-Creuse	94.5
	177.2	9.5	Celon	85
	197.2	20	Rhodes	65
	201.2	4	Bois-Mandé	61
	215.2	14	Junc with N145	47
	221.7	6.5	Morterolles-sur-Semme	40.5
	226.7	5	Bessines	35.5
	233.7	7	Chanteloube	28.5
	242.7	9	La Crouzille	19.5
	253.7	11	Grossereix	8.5
	262.2	8:5	Limoges	

37 Limoges – Toulouse

(311km = 193 miles)

A pleasant, undulating and winding road across the picturesque Department of Corrèze, crossing the River Vézère at Uzerche, and the R. Corrèze at Brive. After Brive the road is winding, hilly and slow as it crosses attractive moorland, and at Souillac, the famous valley of the Dordogne. (Note the excursion to Rocamadour). After Cahors, on the R Lot, the road is less winding, passing vineyards, and from Caussade generally straight, fast, and rather monotonous as it first crosses the R Tarn at Montauban then joins the Garonne valley near Grisolles. The route is SP 'Brive' and 'Toulouse'.

A parallel toll motorway, Autoroute A62, is available for the final section between Montauban and Toulouse (see Iter 19).

N20			
		Limoges	311
5	5	Junc with D704	306
11.5	6.5	[Boisseuil]	299.5
18.5	7	[Pierre-Buffiere]	292.5
29.5	11	Magnac-Bourg	281.5
41.5	12	Masseret	269.5
56.5	15	Uzerche	254.5
58	1.5	Junc with N120	253
66.5	8.5	La Bariolet	244.5
78	11.5	Junc for Donzenac	233
96	18	Brive-la-Gaillarde	215
105	9	[Noailles]	206
116	11	Cressensac	195
133	17	Souillac	178
135.8	2.8	Lanzac	175.2
149.5	13.7	Payrac (Rocamadour 22km by D673)	161.5
166.5	17	Pont de Rhodes	144.5
167.5	1	Frayssinet	143.5
184	16.5	Pelacoy	127
189	5	St-Pierre-Lafeuille	122
193	4	St-Henri	118
197	4	Junc with D911	114
200	3	Cahors	111
237	37	[Caussade]	74
248	11	Albias	63
259	11	Montauban	52
270	11	[Montauban Junc (no. 10) of A62 Autoroute, 1km]	41
282	12	[Grisolles]	29
294	12	St-Jory	17
311	17	Toulouse	

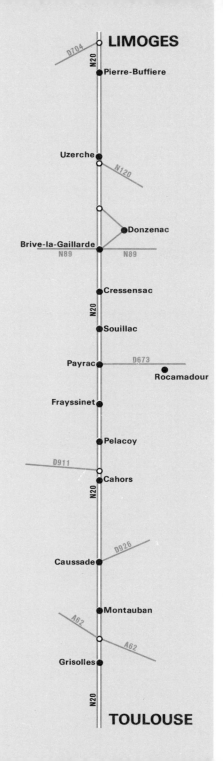

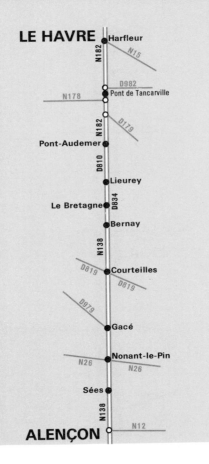

38 Le Havre – Alençon

(169.5km = 105.5 miles)

Level at first with the flat marshes of the Seine estuary on one side and wooded cliffs on the other. From modern Tancarville suspension toll br, route skirts Marais Vernier (reclaimed marshland), then crosses attractive valley of R Risle, bridged at Pont Audemer, and continues through pleasant farmlands.

After Bernay, fast straight stretches across stock-raising, fruit-growing, farmland. Chaumont forest is crossed after Monnai.

The route is SP 'Pont de Tancarville' & 'Paris' out of Le Havre. In the opposite direction SP 'Bernay' & 'Rouen' on N138, then SP 'Pont Audemer', 'Tancarville' and 'Le Havre'.

N182			Le Havre	169.5
	7	7	[Harfleur]	162.5
	26	19	Junc with D982	143.5
			(Lillebonne 10km)	
	27.5	1.5	Pont de Tancarville	142
	29	1.5	Junc with N178	140.5
			(for Lisieux & Caen)	
	35	6	Junc with D179	134.5
			(for Rouen & Paris)	
	39	4	Ste-Opportune-le-Mare	130.5
D810	47	8	Pont-Audemer	122.5
	58.5	11.5	La Noë-Poulain	111
D834	62.5	4	Lieurey	107
	72	9.5	La Bretagne	97.5
			(X-rds with N13)	
N138	80	8	Bernay	89.5
	91.5	11.5	Broglie	78
	99.5	8	Courteilles	70
	108.5	9	Monnai	61
	122.5	14	Gacé	47
	135	12.5	Nonant-le-Pin	34.5
	147	12	[Sées]	22.5
	158	11	Vingt-Hanaps	11.5
	166.5	8.5	Junc with N12	3
	169.5	3	Alençon	

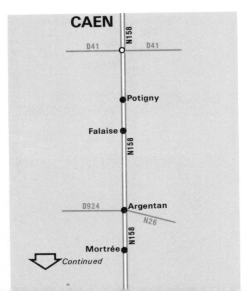

39 Caen – Tours

(235.5km = 146.5 miles)

A fairly fast road throughout, initially straight, but undulating crossing an agricultural plain.

Scenically a rather featureless road to Le Mans, the towns providing the main interest. Note in particular the view of the castle at Falaise. After Le Mans, where the River Sarthe is crossed, the countryside of dense pine forests and later the vineyards of Touraine, are far more attractive.

From Km4 (south of Le Mans) to a point 7km later, the road forms part of the course of the Le Mans 24-hour race.

The route is SP 'Alençon' out of Caen. In the opposite direction SP 'Le Mans' out of Tours, and SP 'Rouen' along the N138 out of Alençon.

N158			Caen	235.5
	11	11	X-rds with D41	224.5
	25	14	Potigny	210.5
	31.5	6.5	Aubigny	204
	34.5	3	Falaise	201
	38	3.5	St-Clair	197.5
	57.5	19.5	Argentan	178
	72.5	15	Mortrée	163

N138	80	7.5	[Sées]	155.5
	91	11	Vingt-Hanaps	144.5
	99.5	8.5	Junc with N12	136
	102.5	3	Alençon	133
	111.5	9	Oisseau-le-Petit	124
	116.5	5	La Hutte	119
	125.5	9	Beaumont-sur-Sarthe	110
	131.5	6	St-Marceau	104
	140.5	9	La Bazoge	95
	146.5	6	[Le Mans-Nord Junc of A11 Autoroute] (Iter 16)	89
	152	5.5	Le Mans	83.5
	164	12	Mulsanne	71.5
	173.6	9.6	Ecommoy	61.9
	193.8	20.2	Château-du-Loir	41.7
	199.1	5.3	Dissay-sous-Courcillon	36.4
	214.4	15.3	Neuillé-Pont-Pierre	21.1
	224.9	10.5	[Charentilly]	10.6
	228.7	3.8	[La Membrolle-sur-Choisille]	6.8
N10	233.5	4.8	Junc N138/N10	2
	235.5	2	**Tours**	

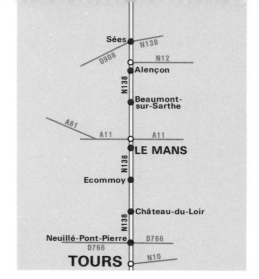

40 Cherbourg – Avranches

(127.7km = 79 miles direct)
(164.5km = 102 miles touring)
The direct route is fairly fast across undulating grazing
country of the Cotentin Peninsula. The touring route keeps
close to the coast, which at many points can be reached by
byroads; these excursions are particularly recommended
up to Carteret.

N13			Cherbourg	127.7
D2	20	20	[Valognes] (Iter 11)	107.7
	24.3	4.3	Lieusaint	103.4
D900	35.4	11.1	St-Sauveur-le-Vicomte	92.3
	45.4	10	Le Haye-du-Puits	82.3
	53.6	8.2	Lessay	74.1
D2	54.6	1	Junc D900/D2	73.1
	65.7	11.1	Montsurvent	62
D971	74.7	9	Coutances	53
	76.2	1.5	Junc with D7	51.5
	83.7	7.5	Quettreville	44
	87.9	4.2	Muneville-sur-Mer	39.8
	92.2	4.3	Bréhal	35.5
D973	102.7	10.5	Granville	25
	116.7	14	Sartilly	11
	125.7	9	Pont Gilbert	2
	127.7	2	**Avranches**	

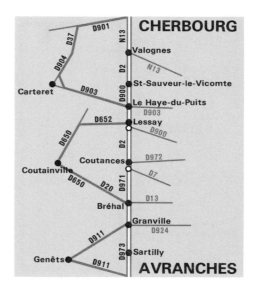

alternative route

D901			Cherbourg	164.5
	4.2	4.2	Hameau-de-la-Mer	159.3
D37	14.2	10	Junc D901/D37	149.3
	21.2	7	Vasteville	142.3
D904	29.7	7.5	Junc D37/D904	134.8
	30.2	0.5	Benoîtville	134.3
	33.2	3	[Les Pieux]	131.3
D903	49.4	16.2	[Carteret]	115.1
	50.4	1	[Barneville-Carteret]	114.1

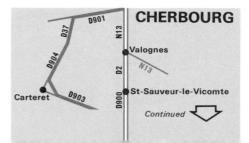

Continued

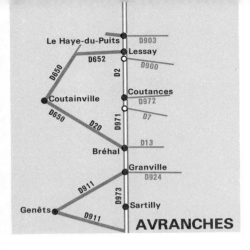

D900	69.4	19	La Haye-du-Puits	95.1
D652	77.6	8.2	Lessay	86.9
D650	80.6	3	Junc D652/D650	83.9
	84.1	3.5	[Pirou]	80.4
D651	94.1	10	Junc D650/D651	70.4
D44	99.6	5.5	Coutainville	64.9
D650	101.1	1.5	Junc D44/D650	63.4
D20	105.6	4.5	[Pont-de-la-Roque]	58.9
	109.6	4	Montmartin-sur-Mer	54.9
	112.1	2.5	Annoville	52.4
D971	120.6	8.5	Bréhal	43.9
D911	131.1	10.5	Granville	33.4
			(Avranches 25km by D973)	
	134.3	3.2	St-Pair-sur-Mer	30.2
	139	4.7	Jullouville	25.5
	142	3	Carolles	22.5
	147	5	St-Jean-le-Thomas	17.5
	153.8	6.8	Genêts	10.7
	164.5	10.7	**Avranches**	

41 Avranches – Angers

(162km = 100.5 miles)

An undulating road winding at times, chiefly through agricultural districts with orchards but often more intensively wooded. Maximum gradient is 10%. After Dompierre-du-Chemin note 'Rochers du Saut du Roland', a picturesque natural feature. The valley of the R Mayenne is followed from Laval to the confluence with the River Loire at Angers.

SP 'Fougères' and 'Le Mont St-Michel' out of Avranches.

N175			**Avranches**	162
	3	3	Junc with D104 (Avranches bypass)	159
	4	1	Road Junc (Pont aubault 3km)	158
N176	7	3	Junc N175/N176 (for 'Alençon' and 'Fougères')	155
D998	7.5	0.5	Junc N176/D998	154.5
	18.5	11	St James	143.5
D798	21.5	3	Road no. change	140.5
	22.5	1	La Ferré	139.5
D155	39	16.5	Junc D798/D155	123
D798	40.5	1.5	Fougères	121.5
	52	11.5	Dompierre-du-Chemin	110
D30	59.8	7.8	Rd number change	102.2
	61.8	2	La Croixille	100.2
	70.5	8.7	Le Bourgneuf la Forêt	91.5
	77	6.5	St-Ouen-des-Toits	85
	84	7	[Laval Ouest Junc (no. 4) of A81 Autoroute] (Iter 16)	78
N162	89.5	5.5	Laval	72.5
	99	9.5	Entrammes	63
	118.5	19.5	Château-Gontier	43.5
	140.5	22	Le Lion-d'Angers	21.5
	148	7.5	La Membrolle-sur-Longuenée	14
	157	9	Avrillé	5
	162	5	**Angers**	

42 Angers – Limoges

(253km = 157 miles)

Leave Angers by the 'Niort' & 'Poitiers' road to the SE, crossing the rivers Authion, the Loire and the Louet, then continue by a pleasant and fairly fast road through agricultural country.

Pleasant woodland either side of Noyant, and through the Forest of Cizay approaching Montreuil.

From Loudun a generally undulating, pleasantly wooded road, with fast, straight stretches through agricultural country. To the south of the road 10km from Poitiers, at Nouaillé, is the site of the famous battle fought by the Black Prince in 1356.

N160			Angers	253
N260	4	4	Junc N160/N260	249
N748	11	7	Junc N260/D748	242
	11.5	0.5	Haute Perche	241.5
	17	5.5	[Brissac-Quincé]	236
D761	20	3	Junc D748/D761	233
	23	3	Les Alleuds	230
	29	6	Noyant-la-Plaine	224
	41	12	Doué-la-Fontaine	212
N147	53	12	Montreuil-Bellay	200
	69	16	Les Trois-Moutiers	184
	77	8	[Loudun]	176
	85	8	[Angliers]	168
	104	19	Mirebeau	149
	114	10	Etables	139
	125	11	Migné-Auxances	128
	133	8	Poitiers (Iter 83)	120
	151.5	18.5	Fleuré	101.5
	159.5	8	Lhommaizé	93.5
	169.5	10	Lussac-les-Châteaux	83.5
	192.5	23	Junc with D942	60.5
	202	9.5	St-Bonnet-de-Bellac	51
	207.5	5.5	Junc with D951	45.5
	212.5	5	Bellac	40.5
	220.5	8	Berneuil	32.5
	246	25.5	Couzeix	7
	253	7	Limoges	

43 St-Malo – Rennes

(69km = 43 miles)

Uninteresting at first, later pleasantly wooded.

N137			St-Malo	69
	4.5	4.5	Junc with D168 (R Rance barrage 3km; Iter 52)	64.5
	7	2.5	Junc with D4	62
	13	6	[Châteauneuf-d'Ile-et-Vilaine]	56
	20	7	Le Vieux-Bourg	49
	28.5	8.5	La Coudraye (Dinan 11km by D794)	40.5
	32	3.5	Pleugueneuc	37
	41	9	Tinténiac	28
	46.5	5.5	Junc with D795 (Héde, 1km)	22.5
	55.5	9	La Mézière	13.5
	58	2.5	Montgerval	11
	67	9	Junc with Rennes bypass	2
	69	2	Rennes	

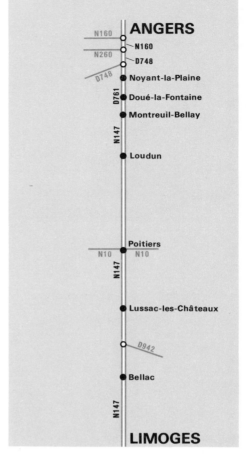

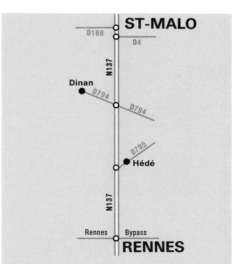

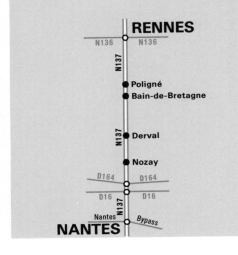

44 Rennes – Nantes

(106km = 66 miles)
A fairly fast road with sections of dual-carriageway. Hilly at first affording views of the wooded La Vilaine valley; later undulating agricultural country. SP 'Nantes'. In the opposite direction SP 'Rennes'.

N137				
			Rennes	106
	4	4	Junc with Rennes bypass (N136)	102
	9	5	La Chaussairie	97
	26.5	17.5	Poligné	79.5
	32.5	6	Bain-de-Bretagne	73.5
	53.5	21	Derval	52.5
	66.5	13	[Nozay] (Iter 60)	39.5
	78.5	12	Junc with D164	27.5
	82	3.5	Junc with D16	24
	94.5	12.5	La Ménardais	11.5
	100	5.5	Junc with Nantes bypass	6
	106	6	**Nantes**	

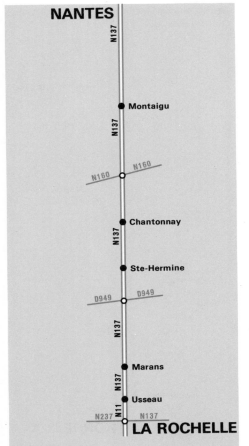

45 Nantes – La Rochelle

(149.5km = 93 miles)
At first woods of the Bocage Vendée, particularly attractive by Aigrefeuille and along the valley to Montaigu. Otherwise to La Rochelle broad, drained marshlands ('Marais'), with, after Ste Gemme, drainage canals criss-crossing the land. SP 'La Rochelle'.

N137			Nantes	149.5
	9	9	Les Soriniéres	140.5
	22	13	Aigrefeuille-sur-Maine	127.5
	35.5	13.5	Montaigu	114
	54.5	19	St-Fulgent	95
	57.5	3	La Brossière	92
	60	2.5	X-rds (N160) (Iter 86)	89.5
	61.5	1.5	L'Oie	88
	68.5	7	St-Vincent-Sterlanges	81
	75	6.5	[Chantonnay]	74.5
	92	17	Ste-Hermine	57.5
	101	9	Ste-Gemme-la-Plaine	48.5
	103	2	X-rds (D949)	46.5
	115.5	12.5	Chaillé-les-Marais	34
	126.5	11	Marans	23
N11	138.5	12	Usseau	11
	141.5	3	[Dompierre-sur-Mer]	8
	146.5	5	Junc with La Rochelle bypass	3
	149.5	3	**La Rochelle** *(ferry connection with Ile de Ré)*	

46 La Rochelle – Bordeaux

(186 km = 115.5 miles by toll motorway)
(187 km = 116 miles by all-purpose road)
Both routes are signposted 'Rochefort', 'Saintes' &
'Bordeaux' out of La Rochelle, and follow the same road to
Saintes bypass. Rather dull to Rochefort, although the coast
is within easy reach. Later pleasantly wooded. After Saintes
a choice of routes, the first by toll motorway (Autoroute
A10), the second by all-purpose road. Both routes pass
through undulating, sometimes well-wooded country and
conclude with a run across the wine growing district near
the rivers Dordogne and Garonne.

In the opposite direction both routes are SP 'Paris' out of
Bordeaux.

D937			La Rochelle	186
N137	5.5	5.5	Junc with La Rochelle bypass	180.5
	10.5	5	Loin du Bruit (Châtelaillon-Plage 1.5km)	175.5
	22	11.5	Junc with D937 (Fouras 5km)	164
	31	9	[Rochefort] (Iter 85)	155
	36	5	[Tonnay-Charente]	150
	39	3	Junc with D739	147
	51.5	12.5	Beurlay	134.5
	57	5.5	St-Porchaire	129
	69.5	12.5	[Saintes] (town 2km)	116.5
uncl.	70	0.5	Junc N137/motorway slip road	116
A10	71	1	Saintes Junc (no. 25) of Autoroute A10	115
	88	17	St-Léger service area	98
	93	5	Pons Junc (no. 26)	93
	116	23	Mirambeau Junc (no. 27)	70
	129	13	Blaye Junc (no. 28)	57
	138	9	Saugon service area	48
	158	20	Toll booths	28
	159	1	St-André-de-Cubzac Nord N10/Libourne Junc (no. 29 a/b; exit for southbound traffic only)	27
	161	2	Junc with N137 (no. 30b; exit for northbound traffic only)	25
	161.5	0.5	St-André-de-Cubzac Sud Junc (no. 30a; exit for northbound traffic only)	24.5
	166.5	5	Br over R Dordogne	19.5
	167.5	1	Ambarès/St-Loubès Junc (no. 31; southbound only)	18.5
	170	2.5	Ambarès/St-Loubès Junc (no. 32; northbound only)	16
	173.5	3.5	Carbon-Blanc Junc (no. 33)	12.5
	175	1.5	Bordeaux-St-Jean Junc (no. 34)	11
	177.5	2.5	Lormont Junc (no. 3)	8.5
uncl.	178.5	1	Br over R Garonne	7.5
	180.5	2	Junc with Bordeaux ring road (no. 4)	5.5
	186	5.5	Bordeaux	

or avoiding toll motorway

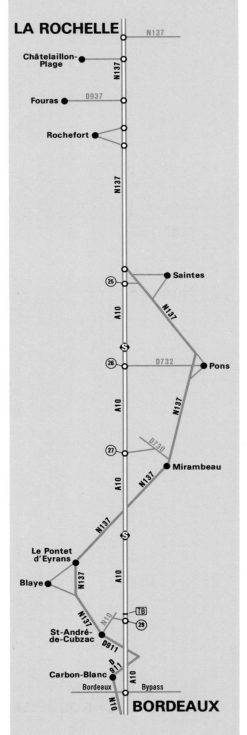

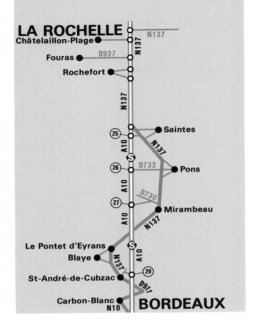

			La Rochelle	187
			as above	
N137	69.5	69.5	[Saintes] (town 2km)	117.5
	70	0.5	[Junc with Autoroute A10]	117
	74	4	Road Junc (Saintes 3km)	113
	82.6	8.6	La Jard	104.4
	92	9.4	[Pons]	95
	103	11	St-Genis-de-Saintonge	84
	115	12	Mirambeau	72
	116.5	1.5	Petit Niort	70.5
	120.5	4	Pleine-Selve	66.5
	127.5	7	St-Aubin-de-Blaye	59.5
	132	4.5	Etauliers	55
	136	4	Le Pontet d'Eyrans (Blaye 9km)	51
	144	8	Junc with D937 (Blaye 6km)	43
	153.5	9.5	[Pugnac]	33.5
D911	162	8.5	Junc N137/N10/D911 (Junc for Autoroute A10)	25
	164	2	St-André-de-Cubzac	23
	169.5	5.5	St-Vincent-de-Paul	17.5
	172.5	3	La Grave-d'Ambarès	14.5
	177.5	5	Carbon-Blanc	9.5
N10	179	1.5	Junc with Autoroute A10	8
	187	8	**Bordeaux**	

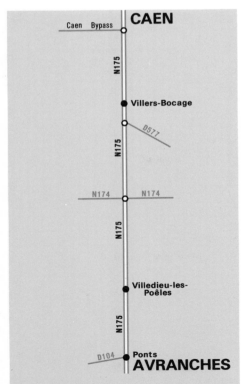

47 Caen – Avranches

(101 km = 63 miles)

Through the hedgerows of the Bocage plateau, the scene of fierce fighting in 1944; views of hilly wooded country after Villedieu-les-Poêles.

			Caen	101
N175				
	6	6	Junc with Caen ring road	95
	26	20	Villers-Bocage	75
	31	5	Junc with D577	70
	42.5	11.5	St-Martin-des-Besaces	58.5
	52	9.5	X-rds with N174	49
	60	8	[Pont-Farcy]	41
	79	19	[Villedieu-les-Poêles]	22
	90	11	Ste-Pience-Le Parc	11
	98.5	8.5	Ponts (Junc with Avranches bypass)	2.5
	101	2.5	**Avranches**	

48 Avranches – St-Brieuc

(124km = 77 miles)

To Dinan a moderately fast road, generally straight, and in parts hilly, with good cross-country views. A pleasant view of the River Rance on entering Dinan.

Later fast, wide and undulating over a tableland of meadows, wild moorland covered by gorse, a few stunted trees and occasional pinewoods.

Between Pontaubault and Pontorson note the excursion to Mont-St-Michel.

The route is SP 'Fougères' and 'Le Mont-St-Michel' out of Avranches, later SP 'Dinan' and then SP 'St-Brieuc'.

In the opposite direction SP 'Dinan' and 'Rennes' on N12, then SP 'Dol', and then 'Pontorson' and finally 'Avranches'.

Note: If proceeding by Iter 49, St-Brieuc can be bypassed by continuing on the N12; SP 'Morlaix' and 'Brest'. If proceeding by Iter 53 note short cut via D10 to Quintin.

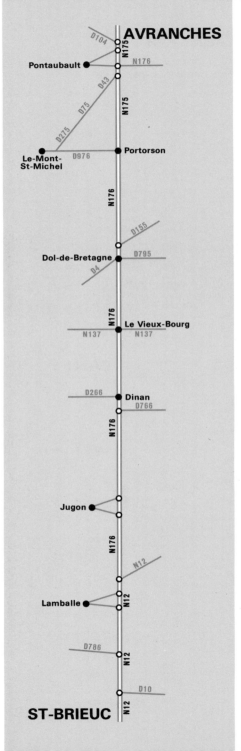

N175		**Avranches**	124
	3	3	Junc with D104	121
			(Avranches bypass)	
	4	1	Road Junc	120
			(Pontaubault 3km)	
	7	3	Junc with N176	117
			(for 'Alençon & Fougères')	
	8.5	1.5	Junc with D43	115.5
			(Mont-St-Michel 13.6km)	
	10.5	2	Précey	113.5
	16.8	6.3	Brée	107.2
N176	22	5.2	Pontorson	102
			(Mont-St-Michel 9km)	
	37	15	Baguer-Pican	87
	39	2	Junc with D155	85
	41	2	Dol-de-Bretagne	83
			(Iter 64)	
	53	12	La Butte	71
	54	1	[Le Vieux-Bourg]	70
			(Iter 43)	
	65	11	[Lanvallay]	59
	67	2	Dinan	57
	69	2	Junc with D766	55
	76.2	7.2	[Vildé-Guingalan]	47.8
	89	12.8	[Jugon]	35
N12	102	13	Junc N176/N12 (Iter 49)	22
	105	3	[Lamballe]	19
	115	10	Junc with D786	9
			(Iter 52)	
	119	4	Junc with D10	5
			(Quintin, on Iter 53, 20km by D10 & D790)	
	124	5	St-Brieuc Junc	5
			(**St-Brieuc,** 2km)	

49 Rennes–Brest

(243.7km = 151.5 miles)

A fast run, mainly by dual-carriageway. At first gently undulating through meadows and orchards, particularly attractive where the route crosses the Rance valley after Quédillac.

Later long and straight stretches, particularly after Guingamp, with easy rise and fall across open country. SP 'St-Brieuc', then SP 'Morlaix' and 'Brest'. In the opposite direction SP 'Morlaix' and 'St-Brieuc', and then SP 'Rennes'. From Landivisiau the alternative D712 follows the attractive Elorn valley to Landerneau, then via Guipavas to Brest.

N12		**Rennes**	243.7
	3	3	Junc with Rennes bypass (N136)	240.7
	22	19	[Bédée]	221.7
	31	9	[Montauban]	212.7
	33	2	Junc with N164	210.7
	40	7	[Quédillac]	203.7
	42.7	2.7	[St-Jouan-de-l'Isle]	201
	52.7	10	[Broons]	191
	64.2	11.5	[Langouhèdre]	179.5
	72.2	8	Plestan	171.5
	75.7	3.5	Junc with N176 (Iter 48)	168
	78.7	3	[Lamballe]	165
	88.7	10	Junc with D786 (Iter 52)	155
	92.7	4	Junc with D10	151
	97.7	5	St-Brieuc Junc (St-Brieuc, 2km)	146
	103.7	6	Junc with D786	140
	107.2	3.5	Junc with D6	136.5
	117.7	10.5	Junc with D7 (Châtelaudren 2km)	126
	131.7	14	[Guingamp]	112
	135.7	4	Junc with D767 (Lannion 28km)	108
	145.7	10	[Louargat]	98
	154.7	9	Plounévez-Moëdec	89
	162.2	7.5	Junc for Plounérin	81.5
	175.7	13.5	Junc for Plouigneau	68
	183.7	8	Junc with D786 (Morlaix 3km)	60
	187.7	4	Junc with D58 (Roscoff 25km by Iter 56)	56
	188.7	1	Junc with D712 (Morlaix 3.5km)	55
	191.2	2.5	Junc with D785	52.5
	199.7	8.5	Junc with D31 (Guimiliau 4km)	44
	204.7	5	[Landivisiau]	39
	222.7	18	Junc with D770 (Landerneau 5km)	21
D788	237.7	15	Junc N12/D788	6
	243.7	6	**Brest**	

50 Avranches–Rennes

(75km = 46.5 miles direct)
(87.6km = 54.5 miles touring)
The first route is generally straight and in parts hilly, with scenery of only moderate interest.
The touring route includes the famous island Abbey of Mont-St-Michel. SP 'Fougères' and 'Le Mont-St-Michel' out of Avranches, and then 'Rennes' for the first route or 'Le Mont-St-Michel' for the second.
In the opposite direction both routes are SP 'Caen' and 'Le Mont-St-Michel' out of Rennes, and later 'Avranches'.

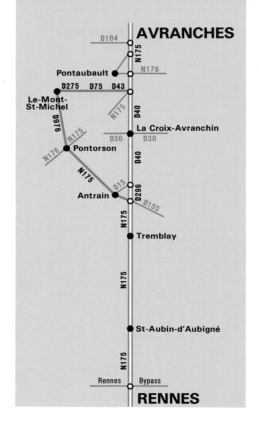

N175			Avranches	75
	3	3	Junc with D104	72
			(Avranches bypass)	
	4	1	Road Junc	71
			(Pontaubault 3km)	
	7	3	Junc with N176	68
			(for 'Alençon' and	
			'Fougères')	
D43	8.5	1.5	Junc N175/D43	66.5
			(SP 'Rennes')	
D40	9	0.5	Roundabout	66
	17.5	8.5	La Croix-Avranchin	57.5
	24	6.5	Montanel	51
D296	27	3	Road no. change	48
	28.5	1.5	Junc with D15	46.5
			(Antrain 3km)	
N175	31	2.5	Junc D296/N175	44
			(Antrain 1.5km)	
	34	3	Tremblay	41
	39.5	5.5	Romazy	35.5
	56.5	17	St-Aubin-d'Aubigné	18.5
	70	13.5	Maison-Blanche	5
	72	2	Junc with Rennes	3
			bypass	
	75	3	Rennes	

or by touring route

			Avranches	87.6
			as above	
D43	8.5	8.5	Junc N175/D43	79.1
			(for 'Rennes')	
	11.7	3.2	Courtils	75.9
D75	13.7	2	Bas Courtils	73.9
D275	15.1	1.4	Junc D75/D275	72.5
D976	20.1	5	Junc D275/D976	67.5
	22.1	2	Mont-St-Michel	65.5
N175	31.1	9	Pontorson	56.5
	42.1	11	Antrain	45.5
	43.6	1.5	Junc with D296	44
	46.6	3	Tremblay	41

as above

87.6	41	Rennes	

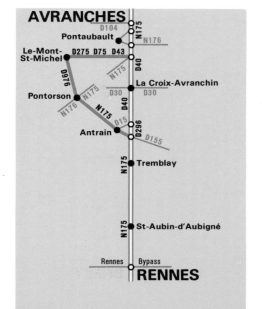

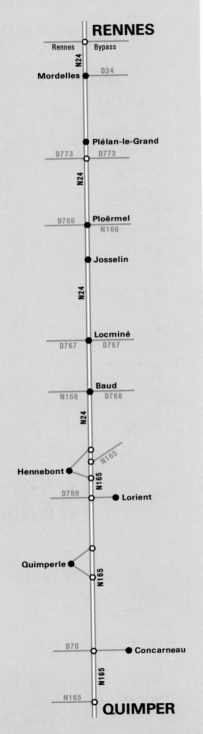

RENNES

Rennes | Bypass
N24
Mordelles • | D34

• Plélan-le-Grand
D773 | D773
N24

D766 | **Ploërmel**
N166

• Josselin
N24

Locminé
D767 | D767

Baud
N168 | D768
N24

Hennebont •
N165
D769 | • Lorient
N165

Quimperle •
N165

D70 | • Concarneau
N165

N165
QUIMPER

51 Rennes–Quimper

(205.5km = 127.5 miles)

To Ploërmel it is a fairly fast road of moderate interest. The military zone between Beignon and Campénéac is sometimes closed in which case turn right at the end of Plélan-le-Grand and follow D38 to Paimpont then turn left and right for D40 and D312 to Campénéac. Beyond Ploërmel at first an attractive, hilly and winding road, then by expressway, a fast road with long sections of dual-carriageway to Quimper.

			Rennes	205.5
N24	3	3	Junc with Rennes bypass	202.5
	13.5	10.5	Mordelles	192
	34.5	21	Plélan-le-Grand	171
	40	5.5	Junc with D773	165.5
	41.5	1.5	Beignon	164
	50.5	9	Campénéac	155
	56.5	6	Gourhel	149
	58	1.5	Junc with Ploërmel bypass	147.5
	59.5	1.5	Ploërmel	146
	61.5	2	Junc with Ploërmel bypass	144
	71.5	10	[Josselin]	134
	83	11.5	Mégris	122.5
	96	13	[Locminé] (Iter 56)	109.5
	111.5	15.5	Baud	94
	113	1.5	Tenuel	92.5
	123.5	10.5	Junc for Languidic	82
	129	5.5	Exit for Hennebont	76.5
N165	132.5	3.5	Junc N24/N165	73
	134.5	2	Hennebont Sud Junc (exit for westbound traffic only)	71
	137.5	3	Hennebont Ouest Junc	68
	139.5	2	Lanester Junc	66
	142.5	3	Lorient Junc	63
	145.5	3	Quéven Junc	60
	150.5	5	Guidel/Moëlan-s-Mer Junc	55
	156.5	6	Quimperlé Est Junc (Quimperlé 4km)	49
	162.5	6	Quimperlé Ouest Junc	43
	172	9.5	Junc with D4	33.5
	179.5	7.5	Junc with D24	26
	187.5	8	Junc with D70 (Concarneau 6km) (Fouesnant 11km)	18
	198.5	11	Junc with D765	7
	203.8	5.3	Road Junc (roundabout) (Quimper Nord, on Iter 54; 4.4km by N165)	1.7
	205.5	1.7	Quimper	

52 St-Malo–St-Brieuc

(73km = 45.5 miles direct)
(115km = 71.5 miles touring)

The R Rance is crossed by the modern hydro-electric dam. The direct route then continues by a mainly winding and undulating road across pleasantly wooded country. The section along the N12 is by dual-carriageway.

The touring route passes within easy reach of the sea and includes many popular resorts and beautiful stretches of coastline. The scenery inland is varied and of little interest, but numerous coves and quaint fishing villages lie only a short distance from the main route. The best coastal scenery can only be reached on foot. The direct and touring routes link with each other between Ploubalay and Tregon. SP Dinard out of St-Malo. In the opposite direction SP 'Dinan' and 'Rennes' on N12

Note: If proceeding by Iter 49, St-Brieuc can be bypassed by continuing on the N12, SP 'Morlaix' and 'Brest'. If proceeding by Iter 53 note short cut via D10 to Quintin.

N137			St-Malo	73
D201	3	3	Junc N137/D201	70
D168	4	1	Junc D201/D168	69
	6	2	R Rance barrage	67
	7.5	1.5	Junc with D114 (Dinard 3.5km)	65.5
	9	1.5	Junc with D266 (Dinard 3km)	64
D768	14.5	5.5	Road no. change	58.5
D786	16.5	2	Plobalay	56.5
	19	2.5	Junc with D26 (St-Jacut-de-la-Mer 5km)	54
	20	1	Trégon	53
D768	20.5	0.5	Junc D786/D768	52.5
	27.5	7	Plancoët	45.5
	29	1.5	Junc with D794	44
	41	12	St-Denoual	32
	53.5	12.5	Lamballe	19.5
N12	55.5	2	Junc D768/N12 (Iter 49)	17.5
	64	8.5	Junc with D786	9
	68	4	Junc with D10 (Quintin, on Iter 53, 20km by D10 & D790)	5
	73	5	St-Brieuc Junc (St-Brieuc, 2km)	

or by touring route

			St-Malo	115
			as above	
D168	6	6	R Rance barrage	109
D114	7.5	1.5	Junc D168/D114	107.5
D786	11	3.5	Dinard	104
	15.5	4.5	St-Lunaire	99.5
	19.5	4	St-Briac-sur-Mer	95.5
	21.5	2	Lancieux	93.5
	25	3.5	[Ploubalay]	90
	27.5	2.5	Junc with D26 (St-Jacut-de-la-Mer 5km)	87.5
	28.5	1	Trégon	86.5
	29	0.5	Junc with D768	86
	32.5	3.5	Notre-Dame-du-Guildo	82.5

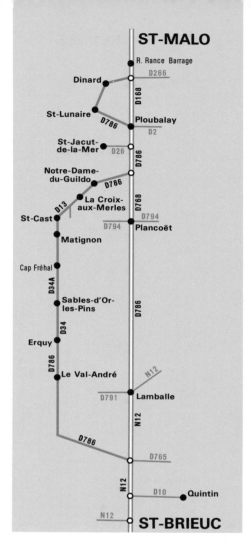

Continued ⟱

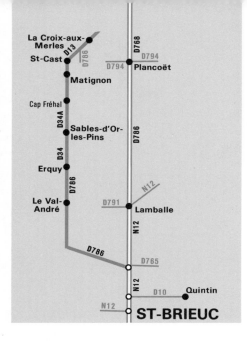

	33.5	1	La Croix-aux-Merles	81.5
D13	35	1.5	Junc D786/D13 (Matignon, 3km direct)	80
	41	6	St-Cast	74
D786	47	6	Matignon	68
D16	53.5	6.5	St-Aide	61.5
	58.5	5	Plévenon	56.5
D34A	62	3.5	Cap Fréhel	53
	67	5	[Pléhérel Plage] (Vieux-Bourg)	48
D34	70.5	3.5	Sables-d'Or-les-Pins	44.5
D786	74.5	4	Junc D34/D786	40.5
	78	3.5	Erquy	37
	84.5	6.5	Junc with D17A (Le Poirier, 5.5km direct)	30.5
	87	2.5	Pléneuf-Val-André	28
	89	2	Le Val-André	26
	94	5	Le Poirier	21
	97.5	3.5	Planguenoual	17.5
	102	4.5	Les Ponts-Neuf	13
	105.5	3.5	St-René	9.5
N12	106	0.5	Junc D786/N12 (Iter 49)	9
	110	4	Junc with D10 (see above)	5
	115	5	St-Brieuc Junc (St-Brieuc, 2km)	

53 St-Brieuc–Quimper

(129km = 80 miles)

Pleasant road through hilly country passing picturesque Quintin and the horse-breeding region around Corlay. Note the excursion to the Gorges de Toul Goulic of the R Blavet. 5km after Rostrenen crosses the Nantes-Brest canal. Onwards the road skirts the Montagnes Noires.

N168			St-Brieuc	129
	8	8	St-Julien	121
D790	11	3	Junc N168/D790	118
	19	8	Quintin	110
	36	17	Corlay	103
	43.4	7.4	St-Nicolas-du-Pélem	85.6
	48.4	5	Junc with D8 (Gorges de Toul-Goulic 5km)	80.6
	49.6	1.2	Plounévez-Quintin	79.4
N164	59	9.4	[Rostrenen] (Iter 56)	70
D3	62.5	3.5	Junc N164/D3	66.5
	66.5	4	Glomel	62.5
	76.5	10	Tréogan	52.5
D769	80	3.5	Junc D3/D769	49
D1	85.5	5.5	Gourin	43.5
D15	94.5	9	Roudouallec	34.5
	106	11.5	Coray	23
N165	126	20	Junc D15/N165	3
	129	3	Quimper	

54 Roscoff–Quimper

(102km = 63.5 miles)

Follow SP 'Morlaix' out of Roscoff, bypassing St-Pol-de-Léon. The route then continues with SP 'Lesneven' and 'Brest', and then 'Landivisiau', a mainly quiet and fairly picturesque run. Initially flat country, later hilly with slight undulations. The section along the N165 is very fast, mainly by dual-carriageway. In the opposite direction follow SP 'Brest' out of Quimper.

D769			Roscoff	102
D788	2.5	2.5	Road Junc (St-Pol-de-Léon 2.5km)	99.5
	6	3.5	Junc with D10	96
	7	1	Junc with D58	95
D69	12	5	Junc D788/D69	90
	19.5	7.5	[Plouvorn]	82.5
D30	27.5	8	[Landivisiau]	74.5
D764	39.5	12	Junc D30/D764	62.5
D18	42.5	3	Sizun	59.5
	49	6.5	Junc with D35	53
	54.5	5.5	Hanvec	47.5
N165	58.5	4	Junc D18/N165 (SP 'Roscoff Car Ferry' for northbound traffic)	43.5
	60.5	2	Junc with D791 (Le Faou 1km)	41.5
	72.5	12	[Port-Launay]	29.5
	75	2.5	Junc with N164 (Châteaulin 4km)	27
	88	13	Junc with D61 (Briec 2km)	14
	97.6	9.6	Quimper Nord Junc	4.4
	102	4.4	Quimper	

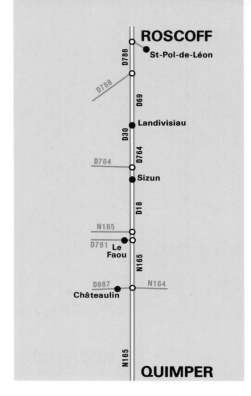

55 Rennes–La Baule

(130km = 81 miles)

Interesting drive, crossing the R Vilaine at Pont Réan and Redon, through attractive country; past pinewoods before reaching St-Gildas-des-Bois, then across a marshy plain.

In the opposite direction SP 'St-Nazaire' out of La Baule, then SP 'Nantes' as far as the junction with the D773, and then SP 'Pontchâteau' & 'Redon'.

D177			Rennes	130
	3	3	Junc with Rennes bypass	127
	5.8	2.8	[St-Jacques-de-la-Lande]	124.2
	7.8	2	X-rds with D34	122.2
	15.3	7.5	Pont-Réan	114.7
	15.8	0.5	Le Boël	114.2
	19.6	3.8	Guichen	110.4
	27.3	7.7	[Guignen]	102.7
	33.6	6.3	[Lohéac]	96.4
	39.6	6	Junc with D777	90.4
	53.6	14	[Renac]	76.4
D775	66	12.4	Redon	64
D164	67.5	1.5	St-Nicolas-de-Redon	62.5
D773	72	4.5	Junc D164/D773	58
	83	11	St-Gildas-des Bois	47
	88	5	Drefféac	42

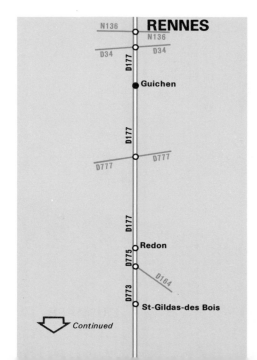

Continued

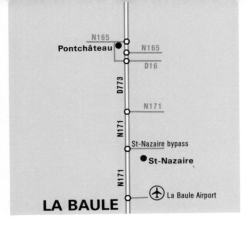

N165	92	4	Junc D773/N165 (Iter 57) (Pontchâteau 1km)	38
D773	94	2	Junc N165/D773	36
	95	1	Junc with D16 (Pontchâteau 1km)	35
	99	4	Besné	31
N171	106	7	Junc D773/N171	24
	109.5	3.5	[Montoir-de-Bretagne]	20.5
	112	2.5	Junc for Trignac	18
	114	2	Junc with St-Nazaire bypass (St-Nazaire 4km)	16
	118	4	Junc with D492	12
	125.5	7.5	Junc for La Baule airport	4.5
	127	1.5	Escoublac	3
	130	3	La Baule	

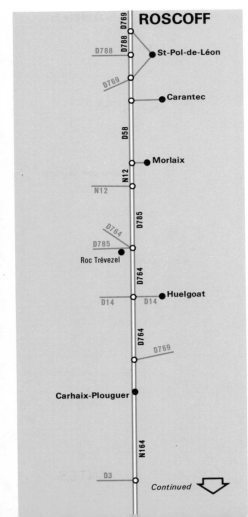

56 Roscoff–Vannes

(184km = 114.5 miles)

A fast road throught coastal farming country to Morlaix bypass, then going inland across the peat moors of the Monts d'Arrée and passing close to the Roc Trévezel. SP 'Morlaix' for the first 25km, then SP 'Brest' for the short section along N12 and then branch right at SP 'Quimper' & 'Carhaix' to join D785. At X-rds (nr Roc Trévezel) turn left at SP 'Carhaix', 'Huelgoat' & 'Lorient'.

Beyond Carhaix a hilly road with several attractive stretches to Pontivy on the R Blavet. After Locminé over the desolate Landes de Lanvaux; later through a military training camp and on to Vannes.

D769			Roscoff	184
D788	2.5	2.5	Road Junc (St-Pol-de-Léon 2.5km)	181.5
	6	3.5	Junc with D10	178
D58	7	1	Junc D788/D58	177
	10	3	Junc with D769	174
	10.1	0.1	Road Junc (St-Pol-de-Léon 2.5km)	173.9
	13.4	3.3	Pont de la Corde	170.6
	13.5	0.1	Junc with D173 (Carantec 4km)	170.5
	15.4	1.9	Junc for Henvic	168.6
	21	5.1	Junc with D769	163.5
	23.3	2.8	Junc with D19	160.7
N12	25	1.7	Junc with N12 (Iter 49) (Morlaix bypass)	159
	26	1	Junc with D712	158
D785	28.5	2.5	Junc N12/D785 (Iter 49)	155.5
	34	5.5	Pleyber-Christ	150
	41.5	7.5	[Plounéour—Ménez]	142.5
D764	45	3.5	X-rds (nr Roc Trévezel)	139
	49.5	4.5	[La Feuillée]	134.5
	59	9.5	Junc with D14 (Huelgoat 2km)	125
	72.5	13.5	Junc with D769	111.5
N164	75	2.5	Carhaix–Plouguer	109
	81	6	Le Moustoir	103
	85	4	La Pie	99
	91.5	6.5	Junc with D3	92.5

Continued

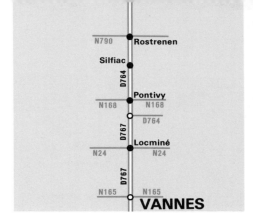

D764	95	3.5	Rostrenen (Iter 53)	89
	112.5	17.5	Silfiac	71.5
	118	5.5	X-rds with D18	66
	122	4	[Kerbédic]	59.5
	128.5	6.5	Stival	55.5
	132	3.5	Pontivy	52
D767	135	3	Junc D764/D767	49
	141	6	[Moustoir-Remungol]	43
	152	11	Guernic	32
	156	4	[Locminé] (Iter 51)	28
	165	9	Colpo	19
	169	4	Pont-du-Loc	15
	176.5	7.5	Junc with D778	7.5
	177.5	1	Meucon	6.5
	183	5.5	Junc with N165	1
			(Vannes bypass)	
	184	1	Vannes	

57 Vannes–Nantes

(110km = 68.5 miles)
A fairly fast road. The wide R Vilaine is crossed at La-Roche-Bernard. Forested before junc with D2 but otherwise mainly open country, partly along the low crest of the Sizzon de Bretagne hills.

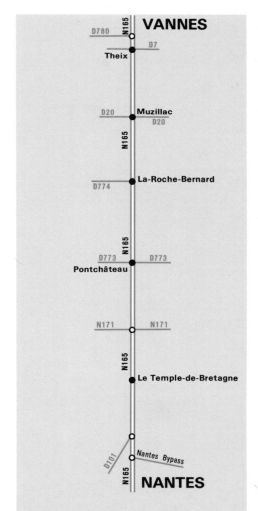

N165			[Vannes]	110
	5.5	5.5	Junc with D780	104.5
			(Sarzeau 17km)	
	9	3.5	[Theix]	101
	14.5	5.5	[La Trinité-Surzur]	95.5
	25	10.5	[Muzillac]	85
	39	14	Pont la Vilaine	71
	40	1	[La-Roche-Bernard]	70
	51	11	Junc with D2 for	59
			Château-de-la-	
			Bretesche (1km)	
	59	8	[Pontchâteau]	51
			(Iter 55)	
	75	16	Junc with N171	35
			(Iter 60)	
	86	11	[Le Temple-de-	24
			Bretagne]	
	97.5	11.5	Junc with D101	12.5
			(Nantes, 12km by	
			D101)	
	101	3.5	Junc with Nantes bypass	9
			(Nantes Est Junc, on	
			Iter 63, 13km)	
	110	9	Nantes	

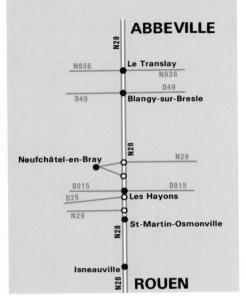

58 Abbeville–Rouen

(96km = 59.5 miles)
Cultivated country to Bouttencourt, then undulating
and wooded to beyond Les Hayons, then again
generally level and of little scenic interest. SP 'Rouen'.

N28			Abbeville	96
	5.5	5.5	Villers-sur-Mareuil	90.5
	14	8.5	St-Maxent	82
	19	5	Le Translay	77
	23.5	4.5	Bouttencourt	72.5
	24	1	Blangy-sur-Bresle	71.5
	35.5	11	Fourcarmont	60.5
	45.5	10	Ménonval	50.5
	49	3.5	Junc with N29	47
			(Neufchâtel-en-Bray 4km)	
	53.5	4.5	Road Junc	42.5
			(Neufchâtel-en-Bray 2km)	
	59	5.5	Les Hayons (Iter 92)	37
	66	7	Junc with N29	30
	67	1	St-Martin-Osmonville	29
	86.5	19.5	Isneauville	9.5
	91.5	5	Bois-Guillaume	4.5
	96	4.5	Rouen	

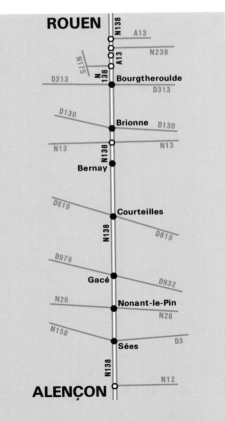

59 Rouen–Alençon

(147.3km = 91.5 miles)
Initially running behind the industrial villages of the
Seine, then following part of the *Autoroute de
Normandie* (motorway) for a short while. The route is
well wooded to Bourgtheroulde, and very pleasant
descending to and rising from R Risle at Brionne.
Later fast, straight stretches across stock-raising,
fruit-growing, farmland. Chaumont Forest is crossed
after Monnai.
The route is SP 'Paris par l'Autoroute' and 'Elbeuf' out
of Rouen, SP 'Caen' on A13 and then 'Alençon'.
In the opposite direction SP 'Bernay' and 'Rouen'.

N138			Rouen	147.3
	10	10	Junc with A13 to Paris	137.3
	13	3	Junc with N238	134.3
			(Elbeuf 7km)	
A13	15	2	Junc N138/Rouen Junc	132.3
			of Autoroute A13	
			(Iter 9, 12)	
N138	19.5	4.5	La Maison Brûlée/	127.8
			Alençon Junc	
	25.5	6	Bourgtheroulde	121.8
	43	17.5	Brionne	104.3
	49	6	X-rds with N13	98.3
	57.8	8.8	Bernay	89.5
	69.3	11.5	Broglie	78
	77.3	8	Courteilles	70
	86.3	9	Monnai	61
	100.3	14	Gacé	47
	112.8	12.5	Nonant-le-Pin	34.5
	124.8	12	[Sées]	22.5
	135.8	11	Vingt-Hanaps	11.5
	144.3	8.5	Junc with N12	3
	147.3	3	Alençon	

60 Alençon–La Baule

(259.2km = 161 miles)

A pleasant run through pretty and well-wooded country. South of Lalacelle and Pré-en-Pail rises the Mont des Avaloirs, the highest point (1,370ft) of this region.

After Laval a generally fast road across undulating pastoral country with orchards, occasionally well wooded.

The route is SP 'Rennes' on N12, and then SP 'Nantes' out of Laval. In the opposite direction, SP 'St-Nazaire' out of La Baule, then SP 'Nantes' as far as La Moëre, and then SP 'Châteaubriant' and 'Laval' and finally SP 'Paris' on N12.

N12		Alençon	259.2
	11.5	11.5 St-Denis-sur-Sarthon	247.7
	18.5	7 Lalacelle	240.7
	24.5	6 Pré-en-Pail	234.7
	36.5	12 Javron	222.7
N162	61.5	25 Mayenne	197.7
	66.2	4.7 Moulay	193
	85.2	19 Louverné	174
	87.2	2 [Junc (no.3) of	172
		Autoroute A81]	
		(Iter 16)	
N171	92.2	5 Laval	167
	110.2	18 Cossé-le-Vivien	149
	122.2	12 Craon	137
	132.2	10 Renazé	127
	143.2	11 Pouancé	116
	153.2	10 Soudan	106
	159.2	6 Châteaubriant	100
	169.2	10 La Croix-Laurent	90
	176.7	7.5 Treffieux	82.5
N137	185.7	9 Junc N171/N137	73.5
	188.2	2.5 [Nozay] (Iter 44)	71
N171	189.7	1.5 Junc N137/N171	69.5
	192.7	3 La Grigonnais	66.5
	202.2	9.5 Blain	57
	211.2	9 Bouvron	48
	219.2	8 La Moëre (X-rds N165)	40
		(Iter 57)	
	222.2	3 Junc with D17 (Savenay	37
		1km)	
	235.2	13 Junc with D773	24
	238.7	3.5 [Montoir-de-Bretagne]	20.5
	241.2	2.5 Junc for Trignac	18
	243.2	2 Junc with St-Nazaire	16
		bypass	
		(St-Nazaire 4km)	
	247.2	4 Junc with D492	12
	254.7	7.5 Junc for La Baule airport	4.5
	256.2	1.5 Escoublac	3
	259.2	3 La Baule	

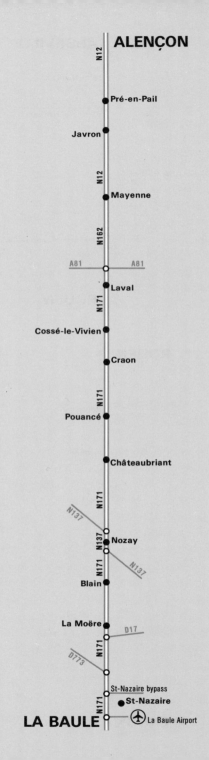

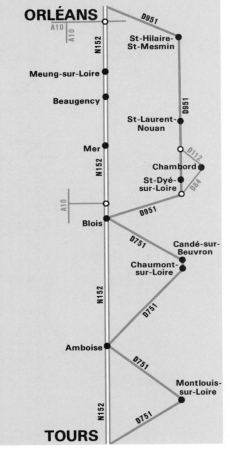

61 Orléans–Tours

(118.4km = 73.5 miles north side)
(118.5km = 73.5 miles south side)
Two attractive, straight and level drives along the wide valley of the Loire, passing through the very attractive wooded country of Touraine, popularly known as the Châteaux country.
Little is seen of the river until Blois, and then, the better views of the river are from the north side. The first, or north side, route is usually followed but carries heavier traffic and is built up to Beaugency. The second route is more leisurely, and the highlight of the south side is the visit to the Château of Chambord.

For parallel toll motorway route see Iter 7.

N152			Orléans	118.4
	4	4	Junc with motorway approach road (Orléans Ouest Junc of Auto-route A10 1km; Iter 7)	114.4
	5.2	1.2	La Chapelle-St-Mesmin	113.2
	12.5	7.3	St-Ay	105.9
	14	1.5	Cropet	104.4
	18.2	4.2	Meung-sur-Loire	100.2
	25.5	7.3	Beaugency	92.9
	38.5	13	Mer (Château of Talcy 10km by D15)	79.9
	43.8	5.3	Suèvres	74.6
	48.9	5.1	Ménars	69.5
	53.6	4.7	La Chaussée-St-Victor	64.8
	54.6	1	Junc with motorway approach road (Blois Junc of Autoroute A10 3.5km; Iter7)	63.8
	57.4	2.8	Blois	61
	68	10.6	[Chouzy-sur-Cisse]	50.4
	79.4	11.4	Veuves	39
	92.6	13.2	Amboise	25.8
	105.1	12.5	La Frillière	13.3
	108.4	3.3	[Vouvray]	10
	111.4	3	Rochecorbon	7
	118.4	7	**Tours**	

alternative via south side

D951			Orléans	118.5
	2.3	2.3	St-Pryvé-St-Mesmin	116.2
	7	4.7	St-Hilaire-St-Mesmin	111.5
	9.8	2.8	Mareau-aux-Prés	108.7
	23.5	13.7	Les Trois Cheminées	95
	30.2	6.7	St-Laurent-Nouan	88.3
	35.4	5.2	Nouan-sur-Loire	83.1
	36.4	1	Junc with D112 (Chambord 8.5km)	82.1
	38.7	2.3	Muides-sur-Loire	79.8
	41.7	3	St-Dyé-sur-Loire	76.8
	45.7	4	Junc with D84 (Chambord 8km)	72.8
D751	56	10.3	Blois	62.5
	62	6	Chailles	56.5
	65	3	Villelouet	53.5
	69.5	4.5	Candé-sur-Beuvron	49
	76	6.5	Chaumont-sur-Loire	42.5
	80	4	Rilly-sur-Loire	38.5
	83	3	Mosnes	35.5
	93	10	Amboise	25.5
	106.5	13.5	Montlouis-sur-Loire	12
	118.5	12	**Tours**	

62 Tours–Angers

(111.8km = 69.5 miles direct)
(137.3km = 85.5 miles touring)

Alternative routes north and south of the R Loire, through Touraine into Anjou. Many fine views of the river. The first route runs close to the picturesque north side of the river but carries heavier traffic. The second route is recommended for visiting the celebrated châteaux. It runs through very attractive scenery to the south of the R Loire, but only within sight of the river from Montsoreau to Gennes. After Azay-le-Rideau the touring route follows a short section of the Indre valley, and the Vienne valley is followed from Chinon to Candes-St-Martin.

Note: If continuing towards Nantes by the south side follow Iter 63 from Erigné.

N152		**Tours**	111.8
	3.5	3.5 St-Cyr-sur-Loire	108.3
	11.5	8 La Port-de-Luynes	100.3
		(Luynes 1.7km	
		by D49)	
	20	8.5 Cinq-Mars-la-Pile	91.8
	25	5 Langeais	86.8
	42	17 La Chapelle-sur-Loire	69.8
	46.5	4.5 Le Port-Boulet	65.3
	49.5	3 Chouzé-sur-Loire	62.3
	63	13.5 Villebernier	48.8
D952	67.5	4.5 Saumur	44.3
	75	7.5 [St-Martin-de-la-Place]	36.8
	78	3 St-Clément-des-Levées	33.8
	82	4 Les Rosiers	29.8
	92.4	10.4 St-Mathurin-sur-Loire	19.4
	98.9	6.5 La Bohalle	12.9
	101.2	2.3 La Daguenière	10.6
	106.8	5.6 La Pyramide	5
	111.8	5 Angers	

or by touring route

D7		**Tours**	137.3
	12.5	12.5 Savonnières	124.8
	15	2.5 Villandry	122.3
D39	18.5	3.5 Le Moulinet	118.8
		(Rigny Ussé 17km	
		by D7; see below)	
	20.5	2 Vallères	116.8
D751	25.5	5 Junc D39/D751	111.8
	26.5	1 Azay-le-Rideau	110.8
D17	28	1.5 La Chapelle-St-Blaise	109.3
D7	35.2	7.2 Junc D17/D7	102.1
	41.7	6.5 Rigny Ussé	95.6
D16	45.5	3.8 Junc D7/D16	91.8
	46.5	1 Huismes	90.8
D751	53.5	7 Junc D16/D751	83.8
D749	55.5	2 Chinon	81.8
D751	57.5	2 St-Lazare	79.8
	65.5	8 Thizay	71.8
	72.5	7 Candes-St-Martin	64.8
D947	74.5	2 Montsoreau	62.8
		(Fontevraud-l'Abbaye	
		4.5km by D947)	
	80	5.5 Souzay	57.3
D161	85.5	5.5 Saumur	51.8
D751	88	2.5 St-Hilaire-St-Florent	49.3
	95.4	7.4 Chênehutte-les-Tuffeaux	41.9
	100.8	5.4 Gennes	36.5

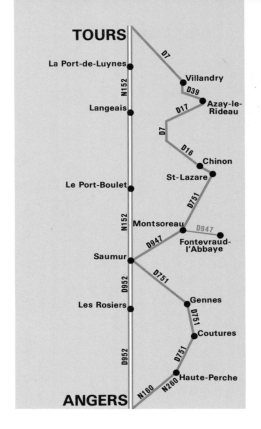

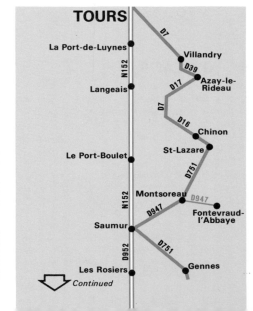

Continued

	111.8	11	Coutures	25.5
	119.3	7.5	St-Saturnin-sur-Loire	18
	121.5	2.2	St-Jean-des-Mauvrets	15.8
	123.3	1.8	Juigne-sur-Loire	14
D748	125.8	2.5	Haute Perche	11.5
			(Erigné on Iter 63, 1.5km)	
N260	126.3	0.5	Junc D748/N260	11
N160	133.3	7	Junc N260/N160	4
	137.3	4	Angers	

63 Angers–Nantes

(89km = 55.5 miles by toll motorway)
(87.5km = 54.5 miles by all-purpose road)
(105.2km = 65.5 miles by touring route)
Three routes are now available. The first route is by
toll motorway (Autoroute l'Océane). The second route,
by N23, is fairly fast and follows the northern side of
the wide valley of the R Loire, but little is seen of the
river. The third route is a touring route along the
southern side of the Loire, passing closer to the river;
it is particularly attractive along the Corniche
Angevine between Rochefort and Chalonnes.

N23			Angers	89
A11	6.5	6.5	Junc N23/A11	82.5
	10	3.5	Angers Ouest Junc (no.1)	79
	36	26	Varades service area	53
	50	14	Ancenis Junc (no.2) (Toll booths)	39
	79	29	Nantes Est Junc (Junc for northern bypass; Nantes 9km by N23)	10
	89	10	Nantes	

or avoiding
toll motorway

N23			Angers	87.5
	6.5	6.5	Junc with Autoroute A11	81
	8	1.5	St-Jean-de-Linières	79.5
	17	9	[Château de Serrant]	70.5
	18	1	St-Georges-sur-Loire	69.5
	26	8	Champtocé	61.5
	39	13	Varades	48.5
	51	12	[Ancenis]	36.5
	74.5	23.5	Le Chemin-Nantais	13
	78.5	4	Junc with Autoroute A11	9
	82	3.5	Junc with Nantes northern bypass	5.5
	87.5	5.5	Nantes	

or by
touring route

N160			Angers	105.2
	6	6	Les Ponts de Cé	99.2
D751	8.5	2.5	Erigné	96.7
	16	7.5	Béhuard	89.2
	20.5	4.5	Rochefort-sur-Loire	84.7

Continued

30.5	10	Chalonnes	74.7
38.9	8.4	[Montjean-sur-Loire]	66.3
45.3	6.4	Vaugirault	59.9
52.3	7	St-Florent-le-Vieil	52.9
56.8	4.5	Le Marillais	48.4
58.5	1.7	[Château-de-la Bourgonnière]	46.7
60.5	2	Bouzillé	44.7
65.2	4.7	Liré (Ancenis 3km by D763)	40
74.2	9	Champtoceaux	31
79.2	5	La Varenne	26
85.9	6.7	La Pierre Percée	19.3
105.2	19.3	Nantes	

64 St-Malo–Fougères

(75.5km = 47 miles via D4 to Dol)
(79.5km = 49.5 miles via D155 to Dol)
To Dol both routes cross level country with scenery of
only moderate interest, though the second route
includes a stretch along the Bay of Mont-St-Michel,
which presents at low tide a remarkable, if somewhat
desolate appearance. After Dol-de-Bretagne an
undulating road (max grad 11%) through forested
country.
Note: Traffic out of St-Malo usually follows the first
route to Dol (via D4), whereas traffic into St-Malo
follows road D155.

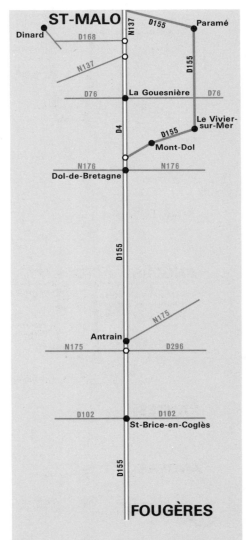

N137			**St-Malo**	75.5
	4.5	4.5	Junc with D168 (R Rance barrage 3km) (Iter 52)	71
D4	7	2.5	Junc N137/D4	68.5
	13	6	La Gouesnière	62.5
D4/ D155	23.5	10.5	Junc D4/D155	52
D155	25	1.5	[Dol-de-Bretagne] (Iter 48)	50.5
	34	9	La Boussac	41.5
	40	6	Trans	35.5
N175	50	10	Antrain	25.5
D155	51.5	1.5	Junc N175/D155	24
	61	9.5	St-Brice-en-Coglès	14.5
	64.5	3.5	St-Étienne-en-Coglès	11
	75.5	11	**Fougères**	

			alternative route	
D155			**St-Malo**	79.5
	3.5	3.5	Paramé (Rothéneuf 4km)	76
	5	1.5	Junc with D355 (Cancale 9km)	74.5
	11	6	X-rds with D76 (Cancale 5km)	68.5
	15	4	St-Benoît-des-Ondes	64.5
	21	6	Le Vivier-sur-Mer	58.5
	26	5	[Mont Dol]	53.5
D4/ D155	27.5	1.5	Junc D155/D4	52
D155	29	1.5	[Dol-de-Bretagne] (Iter 48)	50.5
			as above	
	79.5	50.5	**Fougères**	

65 Tours–Moulins

(252km = 156.5 miles)

An attractive run through the valley of the River Cher,
followed to Vierzon, and the vineyards of Touraine;
several cave cellars upon the neighbouring hill sides.
For a while the valley is left between Selles-sur-Cher
and Villefranche then the road closely follows the
canal, running with the river. From Vierzon by the
broad Yèvre valley to Bourges. Then straight and fast
across the Berry plateau to the broad Allier valley. SP
'Vierzon' out of Tours and in the opposite direction
out of Bourges. Also SP 'Nevers' and 'Paris' in the
opposite direction on the N7.

N10		Tours	252
N76	3	3	Junc N10/N76	249
	5.8	2.8	St-Avertin	246.2
	11.8	6	Véretz	240.2
	27.8	16	Bléré	224.2
	35.3	7.5	Junc with D80	216.7
			(Chenonceaux 2.5km)	
	38.3	3	[St-Georges-sur-Cher]	213.7
	43.3	5	Junc with D764	208.7
			(Montrichard 1km)	
	60.5	17.2	[St-Aignan]	191.5
	62.5	2	Noyers-sur-Cher	189.5
	75	12.5	Selles-sur-Cher	177
	93.3	18.3	Villefranche-sur-Cher	158.7
	101.6	8.3	Mennetou-sur-Cher	150.4
	104.6	3	Châtres-sur-Cher	147.4
	118.5	13.9	Vierzon (Iter 36)	133.5
	127	8.5	Vignoux-sur-Barangeon	125
	134.5	7.5	Mehun-sur-Yèvre	117.5
	152	17.5	Bourges	100
	165	13	[St-Just]	87
	186.4	21.4	Blet	65.6
	203.3	16.9	[Sancoins]	48.7
	211.8	8.5	Mornay-sur-Allier	40.2
N7	220	8.2	St-Pierre-le-Moûtier	32
	239	19	Villeneuve-sur-Allier	13
	252	13	Moulins	

66 Orléans–Dijon

(297.6km = 185 miles by recommended route)
(290.3km = 180.5 miles by touring route)
The first route follows the Loire valley to Châteauneuf-sur-Loire, then an undulating road through the Forest of Orléans and, after crossing the River Loing at Montargis, past the Forest of Montargis. After Courtenay by toll motorway, following part of the 'Paris-Lyon' *Autoroute du Soleil* A6, and later A38 to Dijon. Generally through farming country, woods and vineyards. The touring route follows the middle Loire to Neuvy-sur-Loire. This stretch of the river valley is cultivated and of no great scenic interest, in contrast with the lower and upper reaches. Between Châteauneuf-sur-Loire and Ouzouer-sur-Loire it increases in interest and it is only 3km longer to follow D60 and D119, running close to the river and by-passing Sully-sur-Loire. After Neuvy-sur-Loire the scenery improves and in parts, particularly between Clamecy on the River Yonne and Avallon, is very fine. The final stretch through the Côte d'Or hills and along the River Ouche is also very attractive.

N152			Orléans	297.6
N60	8	8	Junc N152/N60	289.6
	19	11	Junc with D921	278.6
	28	9	Junc with D952	269.6
			(Châteauneuf-sur-Loire 2km)	
	41	13	Junc with D948	256.6
	48	7	Bellegarde	249.6
	55.5	7.5	Ladon	242.1
	62.5	7	St-Maurice-sur-Fessard	235.1
	71.5	9	Montargis (Iter 23)	226.1
	80.8	9.3	La Chapelle-St-Sépulcre	216.8
	97.6	16.8	Courtenay	200
A6	101.6	4	Courtenay/Sens Junc of Autoroute A6 (Iter 2)	196
	113.6	12	Service area	184
	118.6	5	Joigny/Toucy Junc	179
	144.6	26	Auxerre Nord Junc	153
	155.6	11	Auxerre Sud/Chablis Junc	142
	158.1	2.5	Venoy service area	139.5
	179.6	21.5	Nitry Junc	118
	200.6	21	Avallon/Saulieu Junc	97
	204.6	4	Service area	93
	225.6	21	Bierre-lès-Semur Junc	72
	246.6	21	Service area	51
A38	255.6	9	Dijon motorway fork (Junc A6/A38 (Iter 2)	42
	256.6	1	Pouilly-en-Auxois Junc	41
	262.1	5.5	Civry-en-Montagne Junc	35.5
	264.6	2.5	Aubigny-les-Sombernon Junc	33
	267.6	3	Sombernon Junc	30
	277.6	10	Pont de Pany Junc	20
	281.6	4	Fleury-sur-Ouche Junc	16
	286.6	5	Velars-sur-Ouche Junc	11
N5	292.1	5.5	Plombières lès Dijon	5.5
	297.6	5.5	Dijon	

or by touring route

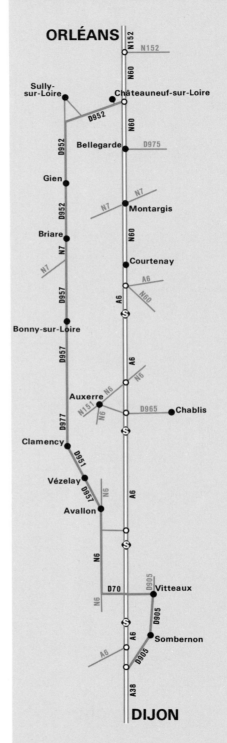

ORLÉANS

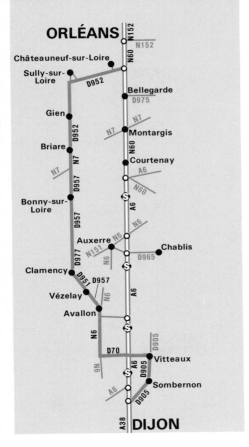

DIJON

N152			Orléans	290.3
N60	8	8	Junc N152/N60	282.3
	19	11	Junc with D921	271.3
D952	28	9	Junc N60/D952	262.3
			(Châteauneuf-sur-Loire 2km)	
	41	13	Junc with D948	249.3
			(Sully-s-Loire 7km)	
	43	2	Les Bordes	247.3
	51	8	Ouzouer-sur-Loire	239.3
	67	16	Gien	223.3
N7	77	10	Briare	213.3
	89	12	[Bonny-sur-Loire]	201.3
D957	94	5	Neuvy-sur-Loire	196.3
	103	9	Arquian	187.3
	110	7	St Amand-en-Puisaye	180.3
	118	8	Bouhy	172.3
	125	7	Entrains-sur-Nohain	165.3
	136.5	11.5	Billy-sur-Oisy	153.8
D977	141.5	5	Junc D957/D977	148.8
D951	147	5.5	Clamecy	143.3
	149.5	2.5	Armes	140.8
	155	5.5	Dornecy	135.3
D957	170	15	Vézelay	120.3
	173	3	St-Père	117.3
	182	9	Pontaubert	108.3
N6	186	4	Avallon	104.3
	193	7	Junc with N146	97.3
	196	3	[Cussy-les-Forges]	94.3
D70	209.5	13.5	Junc N6/D70	80.8
	223.9	14.4	Précy-sous-Thil	66.4
	233.3	9.4	Junc with D970	57
	234.3	1	Junc with D970	56
D905	241.9	7.9	Vitteaux	48.4
	261.3	19.4	Sombernon	29
A38	264.3	3	Junc D905/A38	26
	270.3	6	Pont de Pany Junc	20
			as above	
	290.3	20	Dijon	

TOURS

67 Tours–Clermont-Ferrand

(305.5km = 190 miles)
To Cormery the route crosses the pastures and woods of the Champeigne plateau (the land between the Rivers Indre and Cher) then by the Indre valley; somewhat monotonous agricultural country. Between Cormery and Chambourg-sur-Indre D17 offers a pleasant digression by the river. The district between Châteauroux and La Châtre is associated with George Sand. Straight and fast over the sparsely populated Berry plateaux to Montluçon then rise and fall through hilly country: from Montaigut onwards, very attractive, with fine views, until the long descent to the plain. Finally a fast road from Riom into Clermont-Ferrand, with views of the approaching Dômes mountains of the Central Plateau.

N10			Tours	305.5
N143	5	5	Junc N10/N143	300.5
			(Chambray Junc of A10 Autoroute 0.5km)	
	19.2	14.2	Cormery	286.3
	34.7	15.5	[Chambourg-sur-Indre]	270.8

⬇ Continued

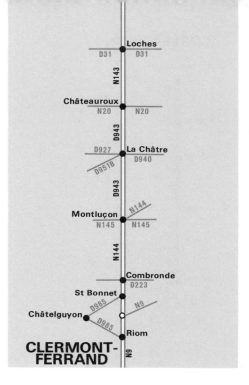

	40.7	6	Loches	264.8
	56.5	15.8	Fléré-la-Rivière	249
	63	6.5	Châtillon-sur-Indre	242.5
	71	8	Clion	234.5
	87	16	Buzançais	218.5
	97.5	10.5	Villedieu-sur-Indre	208
D943	111.5	14	Châteauroux (Iter 36)	194
	115	3.5	Junc with Châteauroux bypass	190.5
	120.3	5.3	Etrechet	185.2
	125.6	5.5	Ardentes	179.7
	141.8	16	Vic	163.7
	143.8	2	Nohant	161.7
	149.3	5.5	La Châtre	156.2
	160.3	11	Champillet	145.2
	167.3	7	Châteaumeillant	138.2
	179.8	12.5	Culan	125.7
	201	21.2	La Chapelaude	104.5
N144	213	12	Montluçon	92.5
	220.5	7.5	Néris-les-Bains	85
	238.8	18.3	Montaigut	66.7
	241.8	3	St-Eloy-les-Mines	63.7
	255.1	13.3	Pont-de-Menat	50.4
	265.8	10.7	St-Pardoux	39.7
	278.5	12.7	Combronde	27
	285.5	7	St-Bonnet (Châtelguyon 4km)	20
N9	288	2.5	Junc N144/N9	17.5
	289.5	1.5	Riom (Châtelguyon 5km)	16
	302.5	13	Montferrand	3
	305.5	3	Clermont-Ferrand	

68 Moulins–Clermont-Ferrand

(96.5km = 60 miles)
By the pleasant Allier and Sioule valleys to Gannat, then across the Limagne plain. Fast into Clermont-Ferrand.

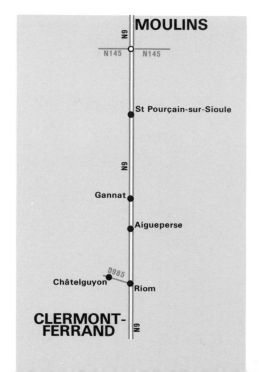

			Moulins	96.5
N9	9	9	Chemilly	87.5
	10	1	Junc with N145	86.5
	18.3	8.3	Châtel-de-Neuvre	78.2
	30.3	12	St Pourçain-sur-Sioule	66.2
	47.5	17.2	Le Mayet-d'Ecole	49
	55.5	8	Gannat	41
	64.3	8.8	Aigueperse	32.2
	71.5	7.2	Le Cheix	25
	80.5	9	Riom (Châtelguyon 5km)	16
	93.5	13	Montferrand	3
	96.5	3	Clermont-Ferrand	

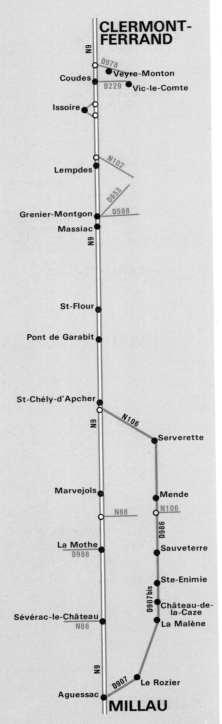

69 Clermont-Ferrand–Millau

(251.7km = 156.5 miles direct)
(276.2km = 171.5 miles touring)
Through the hills and mountains of Auvergne.
Between Coudes and Issoire there is a delightful
stretch alongside the R Allier. After Issoire an
extremely picturesque drive; between Lempdes and
Grenier-Montgon through the Gorges de l'Allagnon.
From St-Flour generally winding and slow through the
high Auvergne. At Pont de Garabit note the Gorge de
Truyère and the Garabit railway viaduct, 400ft above
the river. Shortly after Le Monastier-en-Geraudan join
the verdant Lot valley and follow the river closely to
La Mothe, then ascend to the open, somewhat
desolate Causse de Sauveterre. A pleasant run follows
from the old town of Séverac-le-Château down to
Millau, on the Tarn.
The touring route leaves the main route at St-Chély-
d'Apcher, and is generally slow, hilly and winding
across a high plateau to Mende. After a short stretch
alongside the River Lot, the road then crosses the
desolate Causse de Sauveterre and descends in
unguarded hairpin bends to Ste-Enimie, on the River
Tarn. For the next 50km the road winds through the
spectacular Gorges du Tarn, usually riding high
above the shallow stream with cliffs towering on both
sides. *The highest parts of this route may be closed in
severe winter weather.*

N9			Clermont-Ferrand	251.7
	7.5	7.5	[Pérignat-lès-Sarliève]	244.2
	18	10.5	Junc with D978	233.7
			(Veyre-Monton 2.5km)	
	24	6	[Coudes]	227.7
			(Vic-le-Comte 5km)	
	34.5	10.5	[Issoire] (1,266ft)	217.2
			(Iter 72)	
	44.5	10	[St-Germain-Lembron]	207.2
	51.5	7	Junc with N102	200.2
	53.5	2	Lempdes (1,440ft)	198.2
	72.4	18.9	[Grenier-Montgon]	179.3
	76.9	4.5	Massiac (1,762ft)	174.8
	97.2	20.3	Col de la Fageolle	154.5
			(3,691ft)	
	107.7	10.5	St-Flour (2,904ft)	144
	118.7	11	Pont de Garabit	133
	133.2	14.5	La Garde	118.5
	142.2	9	[St-Chély-d'Apcher]	109.5
			(3,280ft)	
	143.7	1.5	Junc with N106	108
	151.7	8	Aumont-Aubrac	100
	161.7	10	Col des Issartes	90
			(3,707ft)	
	174.7	13	Marvejols	77
	180.7	6	Le Monastier	71
	183.2	2.5	Junc with N88	68.5
	194.7	11.5	La Mothe	57
	219.7	25	Séverac-le-Château	32
	244.7	25	Aguessac	7
	251.7	7	Millau (1,243ft)	

or by touring route

			Clermont-Ferrand *as above*	276.2
N9	142.2	142.2	[St-Chély-d'Apcher] (3,280ft)	134
N106	143.7	1.5	Junc N9/N106	132.5
	149.2	5.5	Rimeize	127
	160.2	11	Serverette	116
	172.5	12.3	[Rieutort-de-Randon] (3,730ft)	103.7
N88	190.2	17.7	Mende (2,398ft)	86
N106	197.2	7	Balsièges (2,284ft)	79
D986	197.7	0.5	Junc N106/D986	78.5
	208.7	11	[Sauveterre] (3,110ft)	67.5
D907 bis	218.7	10	Ste-Enimie (1,541ft)	57.5
	223.7	5	[St-Chély-du-Tarn]	52.5
	226.9	3.2	Château-de-la-Caze	49.3
	231.9	5	La Malène	44.3
	243.9	12	Les Vignes	32.3
D907	248.9	5	Road no. change	27.3
	254.4	5.5	[Le Rozier] (1,280ft)	21.8
	260.2	5.8	Boyne	16
	264.4	4.2	Rivière-sur-Tarn	11.8
N9	269.2	4.8	Aguessac	7
	276.2	7	Millau (1,243ft)	

70 Millau–Narbonne

(148.7km = 92.5 miles)

Views over the Tarn and Doubie valleys on the ascent to the vast barren Causse de Larzac. On this plateau graze the herds of sheep, providing the milk for 'Roquefort' cheese. Then down by the impressive Pas de l'Escalette into vine-growing Languedoc, and along the Hérault valley to Pézenas. Wild sections of plateau follow. The famous Canal du Midi is crossed at Béziers and there is a fine view point 5km beyond Nissan-lez-Ensérune before the long descent to the plain of the R Aude, crossed at Coursan. *A parallel toll motorway (Autoroute A9) is available for the final section between Pézenas and Narbonne (see Iter 5).*

N9			Millau (1,243ft)	148.7
	19	19	La Cavalerie (2,625ft)	129.7
	41	22	Le Caylar (2,401ft)	107.7
	45.5	4.5	Pas de l'Escalette (2,044ft)	103.2
	61	15.5	[Lodeve] (531ft)	87.7
	78.3	17.3	[Clermont-l'Hérault]	70.4
	89.1	10.8	Paulhan	59.6
	95.1	6	Lésignan-la-Cèbe	53.6
N9/ N113	96.7	1.6	Junc N113/N9	52
	99.1	2.4	Pézenas	49.6
	100.1	1	Junc with D13 (Agde/Pézenas Junc of Autoroute A9, 10km; Iter 5)	48.6
	106.4	6.3	Valros	42.3
	121.7	15.3	Béziers	27
	131.7	10	[Nissan-lez-Ensérune]	17
	141.9	10.2	Coursan	6.8
	148.7	6.8	Narbonne	

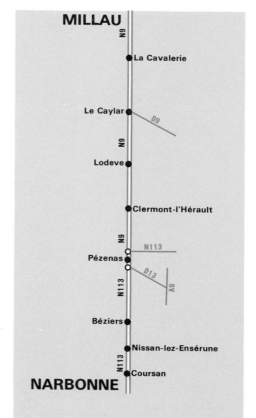

MOULINS

- Bessay-sur-Allier
- Varennes-sur-Allier
- Les Gadons — D907
- Vichy
- Abrest
- Puy-Guillaume
- Pont-de-Dore — Thiers
- Courpière
- Olliergues
- Ambert
- Arlanc
- La Chaise-Dieu
- Bellevue-la-Montagne
- St-Paulien

LE PUY

71 Moulins – Le Puy

(219km = 136 miles)

At first straight and level across the wide cultivated Allier valley with, from Vichy, fine views of the river. Then a pleasant winding ascent towards Thiers. From Pont-de-Dore the windings of R Dore are followed to the open plain around Ambert. After Arlanc a long winding climb through dense pine forests on to the wooded Auvergne plateau. From St-Paulien the road descends with a superb view of the Castle of Polignac and the surrounding volcanic rocks. Finally from the bridge over the R Borne there is a celebrated view of Le Puy.

The route is SP 'Lyon' & 'Vichy' out of Moulins. In the opposite direction SP 'Clermont-Ferrand' out of Le Puy.

N7			Moulins	219
	5.5	5.5	Toulon-sur-Allier	213.5
	14.5	9	Bessay-sur-Allier	204.5
	25	10.5	St-Loup	194
	27.5	2.5	Chazeuil	191.5
	30	2.5	Varennes-sur-Allier	189
N209	32.5	2.5	Junc N7/N209	186.5
	48	15.5	Les Gadons	171
	53.5	5.5	Cusset	165.5
D906	57	3.5	Vichy	162
	60.5	3.5	Abrest	158.5
	64.5	4	St-Yorre	154.5
	77.2	12.7	Puy-Guillaume	141.8
D44e	87.7	10.5	Junc D906/D44e	131.3
			(Thiers 4.5km)	
D44	90.2	2.5	Junc with Autoroute A72	128.8
D906	92.7	2.5	[Pont-de-Dore]	126.3
			(Thiers 5km)	
	102.7	10	Courpière	116.3
	119	16.3	Olliergues	100
	142.5	23.5	Ambert (1,762ft)	76.5
	158.5	16	Arlanc (2,018ft)	60.5
	175.5	17	La Chaise-Dieu (3,550ft)	43.5
	181.5	6	Sembadel-Gare	37.5
	192.7	11.2	[Bellevue-la-Montagne]	26.3
	203.7	11	St-Paulien	15.3
N102	207.7	4	Junc D906/N102	11.3
	219	11.3	Le Puy (2,067ft)	

72 Issoire – Orange

(271.5km = 168.5 miles)

Across the mountains of the Massif Central. The wide valley of the Allier is followed to Vieille-Brioude where the river is crossed. After Le Puy reasonably fast through mountainous country. At first across the Velay plateau, then descends by the beautiful Ardèche Valley. Below Thueyts the Pavédes Géants, a natural 'staircase' of basalt, comes into view. At Labégude is the spa of Vals-les-Bains stretching up the narrow gorge of the Volane; later from a bend on the rise into Aubenas there is a fine view of the Ardèche Valley. After crossing the Ardèche at St-Didier a hilly stretch follows to Viviers on the right bank of the River Rhône. The river is crossed and the trunk road to the south is joined near Pierrelatte. The final section is by part of the fast, but very busy 'Lyon-Avignon' Rhône valley road.

Road	km	int	Place	km
N9			**[Issoire]** (1,266ft)	271.5
	10	10	[St-Germain-Lembron]	261.5
N102	19	9	[Lempdes] (1,440ft)	252.5
	34.1	15.1	Brioude	237.4
	38.7	4.6	Vieille-Brioude	232.8
	56.7	18	St-Georges-d'Aurac	214.8
	69.2	12.5	Fix-St-Geneys (3,626ft)	202.3
	82.2	13	Borne	189.3
	83.2	1	Junc with D906	188.3
N88	94.5	11.3	Le Puy (2,067ft)	177
	97.5	3	Taulhac	174
	108.1	10.6	Bizac	163.4
	114.4	6.3	Costaros	157.1
	119.3	4.9	La Sauvetat	152.2
N102	128.3	9	Junc N88/N102	143.2
	142.3	14	Lanarce	129.2
	147.3	5	Col de la Chavade (4,170ft)	124.2
	157.8	10.5	Mayres (1,887ft)	113.7
	166.9	9.1	Thueyts	104.6
	177.5	10.6	Lalevade	94
	182.5	5	Labégude (Vals les Bains across river)	89
	186.5	4	Aubenas (984ft)	85
	190	3.5	St-Didier	81.5
	197.5	7.5	Lavilledieu	74
	202	4.5	Villeneuve-de-Berg	69.5
D107	212.5	10.5	Junc N102/D107	59
	214.5	2	[Alba]	57
N86	226	11.5	Junc D107/N86	45.5
	227.5	1.5	Viviers	44
N93	232	4.5	Junc N86/N93	39.5
N7	238	6	Junc N93/N7	33.5
	240.5	2.5	[Pierrelatte]	31
	252.5	12	[La Croisière] (Pont-St-Esprit) 4km by D994	19
	256.5	4	[Mondragon]	15
	261	4.5	[Mornas]	10.5
	265	4	Piolenc	6.5
	271.5	6.5	Orange	

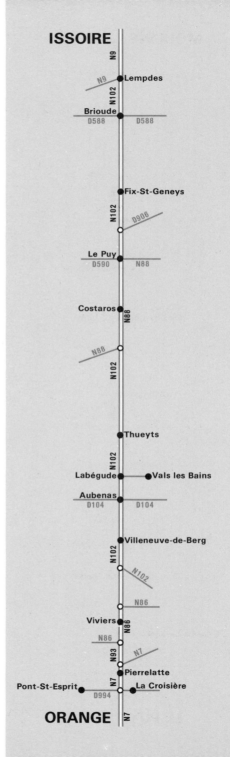

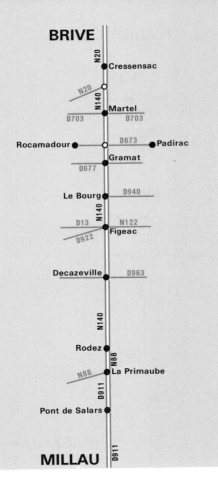

BRIVE
N20
Cressensac
N20
N140
Martel
D703 D703
Rocamadour • D673 • Padirac
Gramat
D677
Le Bourg D940
N140
D13 N122
D922 Figeac
Decazeville D963
N140
Rodez
N88
N88 La Primaube
D911
Pont de Salars
MILLAU D911

73 Brive – Millau

(228.6km = 142 miles)

A pleasant ascent out of the Corrèze valley, then across the cultivated plateau cut by the valley of the River Dordogne, crossed between Martel and Montvalent. Then from Le Bourg a long and finally winding descent through woods to Figeac and beyond to the River Lot at Capdenac. An exceptionally picturesque run follows via Decazeville to Valady, after which the road climbs to the desolate Causse du Comtal before dropping down to the River Aveyron at Rodez. Then from the Aveyron valley onto the moors of the Rouergue Plateau; after Pont de Salars (excursion to reservoir by D523) rather desolate country until the descent into Millau on the River Tarn. Note the excursions to Rocamadour and Padirac. The route is SP 'Cahors' on N20 out of Brive.

Road			Place	Distance
N20			Brive-la-Gaillarde	228.6
	9	9	[Noailles]	219.6
	20	11	Cressensac	208.6
N140	21	1	Junc N20/N140	207.6
	34	13	Martel	194.6
	43	9	Montvalent	185.6
	50	7	Junc with D673	178.6
			Rocamadour 4km west	
			Padirac 9km east	
	58	8	Gramat	170.6
	68	10	[Thémines]	160.6
	75	7	Le Bourg	153.6
	88.5	13.5	Planioles	140.1
	92	3.5	Figeac	136.6
	99	7	[Capdenac]	129.6
	108	9	Bouillac	120.1
	119.5	11.5	Decazeville	109.1
	124.5	5	Firmi	104.1
	138.5	14	[Valady]	90.1
N88	156.5	18	Rodez	72.1
D911	164.8	8.3	La Primaube	63.8
	168.3	3.5	[Flavin]	60.3
	181.8	13.5	Pont de Salars	46.8
	206.8	25	[Bois du Four]	21.8
	228.6	21.8	Millau (1,243ft)	

MILLAU N9
D999 La Cavalerie
N9
La Caylar
D9
Lodève
N9 N9
N109
Gignac
D32 D32
MONTPELLIER N109

74 Millau – Montpellier

(115km = 71.5 miles)

Views over the Tarn and Doubie valleys on the ascent to the vast barren Causse de Larzac. On this plateau graze the herds of sheep, providing the milk for 'Roquefort' cheese. Then down by the impressive Pas de l'Escalette into vine-growing Languedoc and the low rugged hills of Les Garrigues.

Road			Place	Distance
N9			Millau (1,243ft)	115
	19	19	La Cavalerie (2,625ft)	96
	41	22	Le Caylar (2,401ft)	74
	45.5	4.5	Pas de l'Escalette	69.5
			(2,044ft)	
	61	15.5	[Lodève] (531ft)	54
N109	76	15	Junc N9/N109	39
	77	1	St-Félix-de-Lodez	38
	81	4	St-André-de-Sangonis	34
	85	4	Gignac	30
	110.5	25.5	Celleneuve	4.5
	115	4.5	Montpellier	

75 Orange – Marseille

(118km = 73.5 miles by toll motorway)
(125km = 77.5 miles by RN7 & RN113)
Alternative routes, by toll motorway *Autoroute du Soleil,* or
by all-purpose road.
Both routes are fast and straight with easy undulations
passing across the rocky, irrigated countryside of the Plain
of Provence. Later rather hilly. Marseille centre can be
avoided by leaving the A7 at Toulon Junc.

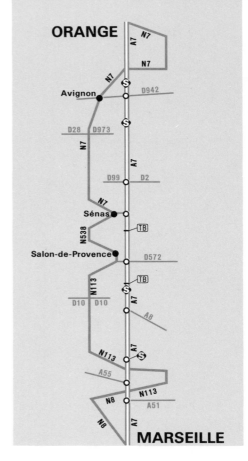

A7				
			Orange motorway fork	118
			(Junc A7/A9)	
17	17		Sorgues service area	101
			(northbound only)	
21	4		Avignon – Nord/	97
			Carpentras-Junc	
28	7		Morières service area	90
			(southbound only)	
31	3		Avignon-Sud Junc	87
44	13		Cavaillon/Nîmes Junc	74
54	10		Sénas Junc	64
59.5	5.5		Toll booths	58.5
61	1.5		Salon Nord Junc	57
			(exit for southbound	
			traffic only)	
68	7		Salon Sud Junc	50
74	6		Toll booths	44
75	1		Lançon service area	43
81	6		Motorway fork	37
			(Junc A7/A8)	
88	7		Rognac/Berre Junc	30
94	6		Vitrolles Junc & service	24
			area	
96	2		Marignane Junc	22
100	4		Junc with A55	18
105	5		Junc with A51	13
108	3		St-Antoine/Hôpital	10
			Nord Junc	
113	5		Arnavaux-Junc	5
115	2		Toulon Junc	3
118	3		Marseille	

**or avoiding toll
motorway**

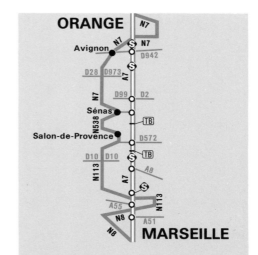

N7				
			Orange	125
	9	9	[Courthezon]	116
	18.5	9.5	Sorgues	106.5
	24.5	6	Le Pontet	100.5
	29	4.5	Avignon	96
	40	11	Junc with D973	85
			(Avignon Sud Junc 1 km)	
	40.5	0.5	R Durance Br	84.5
	52.5	12	Plan d'Orgon	72.5
	56.5	4	Orgon	68.5
N538	62.5	6	Sénas	62.5
	73.5	11	Salon-de-Provence	51.5
N113	76.5	3	Junc N538/N113	48.5
	89	12.5	X-rds with D10	36
	103	14	Vitrolles Junc	22
	105	2	Marignane Junc	20
	111	6	Junc with N368	14
N8	116.5	5.5	St-Antoine	8.5
	125	8.5	Marseille	

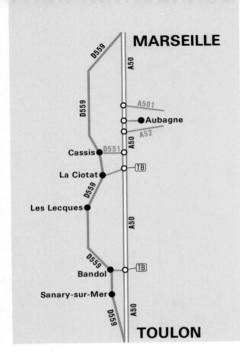

MARSEILLE

D559
A50
D559
A501
●Aubagne
A52
A50
Cassis D551
A50
TB
La Ciotat
D559
Les Lecques●
A50
D559
TB
Bandol
Sanary-sur-Mer●
A50
D559
TOULON

76 Marseille – Toulon

(64km = 40 miles via motorway)
(75km = 46.5 miles via D559)
The recommended route follows Autoroute A50. The alternative is attractive and winding over the hills to La Ciotat, with a view of the bay of Cassis, then through several resorts. Extensively built-up around Toulon. If travelling in the opposite direction Marseille Centre can be avoided by leaving A50 at Aix/Lyon Junc.

A50				
			Marseille	64
	3	3	Aix/Lyon Junc	61
	10	7	La Penne/La Valentine/ St-Menet Junc	54
	16	6	Motorway fork (Junc with A501)	48
	18	2	Aubagne Sud/Toulon par RN Junc	46
	19.5	1.5	Motorway fork (Junc with A52)	44.5
	23	3.5	La Bédoule Junc	41
	26	3	Cassis Junc	38
	28	2	La Ciotat Junc (Toll booth)	36
	37	9	St-Cyr-sur-Mer-Junc	27
	49	12	Bandol Junc (Toll booth)	15
	56.5	7.5	Ollioules/La Seyne Junc	7.5
	60.5	4	Toulon-Ouest Junc	3.5
	64	3.5	Toulon	

alternative route

D559				
			Marseille	75
	8	8	Le Redon	67
	14	6	Col de la Gineste (1,073ft)	61
	23.5	9.5	[Cassis]	51.5
	27.5	4	Pas de Bellefille (646ft)	47.5
	35	7.5	[La Ciotat]	40
	42.5	7.5	[Les Lecques]	32.5
	53	10.5	Bandol	22
	59	6	Sanary-sur-Mer	16
	61	2	Junc with D616 (Le Brusc 4km)	14
	62.8	1.8	Six-Fours les Plages (Les Sablettes 5.5km by D16)	12.2
	68.2	5.4	[La Seyne]	6.8
	75	6.8	Toulon	

MARSEILLE

D559
A50
D559
A501
●Aubagne
A52
A50
Cassis D551
TB
La Ciotat
D559
Les Lecques●
A50
D559
Bandol TB
Sanary-sur-Mer●
A50
D559
TOULON

77 Toulon – Fréjus

(89.5km = 55.5 miles recommended route)
(113km = 70 miles touring route via Corniche des Maures)
(94km = 58 miles via N98)

The first, and recommended route goes inland and follows Autoroute A57, N97 and Autoroute A8. Passing through picturesque Provençal scenery with olive groves, cork forests, and low wooded mountains on either side. The touring routes pass through extensively built-up areas around Toulon and Hyères. The first follows the coast to Hyères, and then from Le Lavandou to Fréjus runs close to the sea with the Maures mountains in the background. The stretch to Cavalaire by the Corniche des Maures is particularly sinuous. The second alternative goes direct to Hyères and then between La Verrerie and Carrefour-de-la-Foux (St 'St-Raphael par Forêt du Dom') avoids the Corniche des Maures and is therefore faster. SP 'Hyères' to leave Toulon.

A57			Toulon	89.5
	2	2	Le Pradet/Carqueiranne Junc	87.5
	3.5	1.5	La Valette-Sud Junc	86
	4.5	1	La Valette-Est Junc	85
	5	0.5	La Valette-Nord/ Hyères Junc	84.5
	9.5	4.5	La Farlède Junc	80
N97	13.5	4	Junc with D554	76
	27.5	14	Puget-Ville	62
	32	4.5	[Carnoules]	57.5
	35.5	3.5	[Pignans]	54
N7	50	14.5	[Le Luc]	39.5
	52	2	Le Cannet-des-Maures	37.5
A8	53.5	1.5	Le Luc/Toulon Junc of Autoroute A8	36
	62.5	9	Vidauban service area	27
	72.5	10	Le Muy/Draguignan Junc	17
	82.5	10	Le Canaver service area (westbound only)	7
N7	84.5	2	Puget-sur-Argens/ Fréjus/St-Raphael Junc	5
	89.5	5	Fréjus	

or by touring route

A57			Toulon	113
D42	1.7	1.7	Junc A57/D42	111.3
	4.7	3	[Cap-Brun]	108.3
D559	7.5	2.8	Pont de la Clue	105.5
	9.5	2	Le Pradet (La Garonne 2.5km by D86)	103.5
	14.5	5	Carqueiranne	98.5
	19.5	5	L'Amanarre (Hyères Plage 2km by D42, Giens and La Tour-Fondues 5km farther on D97)	93.5
	21.5	2	Junc with D97 (Hyères Plage 2.5km)	91.5
N98	24.5	3	Hyères	88.5
	28	3.5	Junc with D12	85
	34	6	[La Londe les Maures]	79
D559	41.5	7.5	Junc N98/D559	71.5
	44.5	3	[Bormes les Mimosas]	68.5
	47.5	3	Le Lavandou	65.5

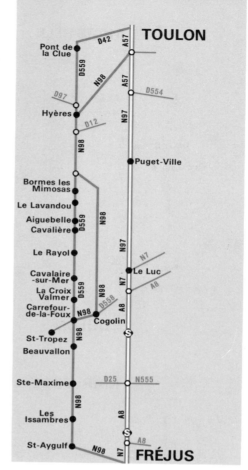

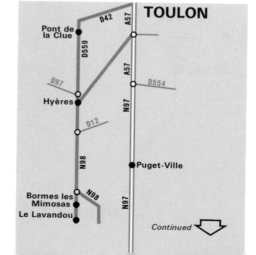

Continued

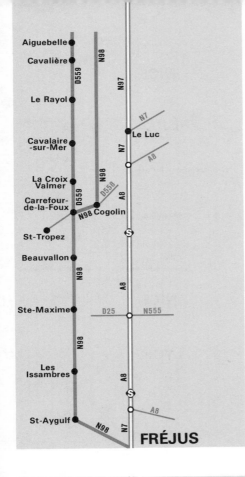

	49.5	2	[St-Clair]	63.5
	51.5	2	Aiguebelle	61.5
	54.2	2.7	Cavalière	58.8
	57.2	3	Pramousquier	55.8
	58.2	1	Canadel-sur-Mer	54.8
	61.2	3	Le Rayol	51.8
	68.5	7.3	Cavalaire-sur-Mer	44.5
	74.5	6	La Croix Valmer	38.5
	78	3.5	Junc with D89	35
			(Gassin 2.5km)	
N98	81.5	3.5	Carrefour-de-la-Foux	31.5
			(St-Tropez 5km)	
	83	1.5	[Port Grimaud]	30
	84	1	St-Pons-les-Mûres	29
	86.5	2.5	Beauvallon	26.5
	90.5	4	Ste-Maxime	22.5
	95	4.5	La Nartelle	18
	97.5	2.5	Val-d'Esquières	15.5
	99	1.5	St-Peire-sur-Mer	14
	100.5	1.5	Les Issambres	12.5
	104	3.5	La Gaillarde	9
	106	2	St-Aygulf	7
	113	7	Fréjus	

or via Forêt du Dom

A57			Toulon	94
	2	2	Le Pradet/Carqueiranne Junc	92
	3.5	1.5	La Valette-Sud Junc	90.5
	4.5	1	La Vallette-Est Junc	89.5
N98	5	0.5	La Valette-Nord/ Hyères Junc	89
	16.5	11.5	Hyères	77.5
	26	9.5	[La Londe-les-Maures]	68
	32.5	6.5	La Verrerie	61.5
	33.5	1	Junc with D559	60.5
	58.5	25	Cogolin	35.5
	62.5	4	Carrefour-de-la-Foux	31.5
			as above	
	94	31.5	Fréjus	

78 Fréjus – Nice

(67km = 41.5 miles via the Esterel Mountains)
(76km = 47 miles via the Corniche d'Or)
The first route crosses the well-wooded Esterel Mountains by a moderately hilly road with easy curves, and is the faster. The second follows the coast along a beautiful corniche road below the Esterel Mountains.
Finally through established resorts of the Riviera to Nice. Between Golfe-Juan and Antibes an alternative would be via D2559 following the coastline round Cap d'Antibes. After Antibes the N98 parallels the N7 on the seaward side of the railway.
For toll motorway route see Iter 4.

N7			Fréjus	67
	16	16	L'Auberge de l'Esterel	51
	25	9	Tremblant	42
	28.5	3.5	[Mandelieu]	38.5
	30	1.5	[Cannes Airport]	37
	35	5	Cannes	32
	41	6	Golfe-Juan	26
	44	3	Juan-les-Pins	23
			(Cap d'Antibes 2.5km)	

95

N98	46	2	Antibes	21
	52.5	6.5	Villeneuve-Loubet Plage	14.5
	57	4.5	Cros de Cagnes	10
	61	4	[Nice Airport]	6
	67	9	Nice	

or via the coast

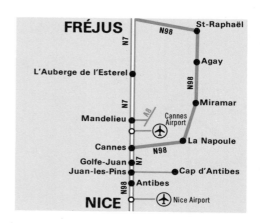

N98			Fréjus	76
	3	3	St-Raphaël	73
			(Valescure 3.5km)	
	8	5	Boulouris	68
	11	3	Le Dramont	65
	12	1	Camp Long	64
	13	1	Agay	63
	18	5	Anthéor	58
	24.2	6.2	Le Trayas	51.8
	27.5	3.3	Miramar	48.5
	33.5	6	Théoule-sur-Mer	42.5
	36	2.5	La Napoule	40
			(Cannes Airport/	
			Mandelieu/La Napoule	
			Junc of Autoroute A8	
			3km; Iter 4)	
N7	44	8	Cannes	32
			as above	
	76	32	Nice	

79 Lyon – Grenoble

(104km = 64.5 miles by toll motorway)
(107km = 66.5 miles by all purpose road)
Alternative routes, by toll motorway or by all purpose road.
Both routes cross a wide cultivated plain to the distant
mountains. More hilly after Bourgoin. Final stretch from
Voreppe follows the intensively cultivated, attractive Isère
valley. The second route is by part of the *Route Napoléon* on, a
straight and fast road which runs more or less parallel to the
motorway. Both routes are SP 'Chambéry' and 'Grenoble'
out of Lyon.

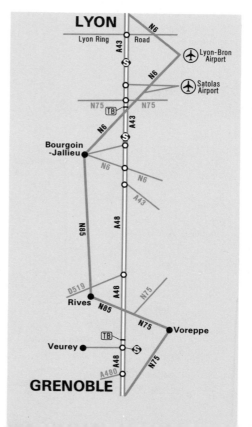

			Lyon	104
A43	6	6	Junc with Lyon ring road	98
	9	3	St-Priest Junc	95
	13.5	4.5	Service area	90.5
	20	6.5	Satolas Airport Junc	84
	24	4	L'Isle d'Abeau Ouest	80
	26	2	Toll booths	78
	34	8	L'Isle d'Abeau service	70
			area	
	36	2	L'Isle d'Abeau-Est/	68
			Bourgoin-Ouest Junc	
	42	6	Bourgoin-Est Junc	62
A48	46	4	Motorway fork	58
			(Junc A43/A48)	
	71	25	Rives Junc	33
	89	18	Toll booths	15
	90	1	Veurey Junc & service	14
			area	
	98	8	Motorway fork	6
			(Junc with A480)	
	104	6	Grenoble	

**or avoiding toll
motorway**

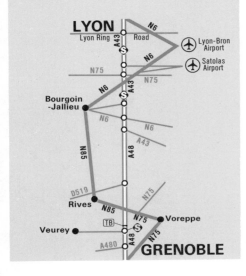

N6			Lyon	107
	8	8	Bron	99
	10	2	[Lyon-Bron Airport]	97
	17	7	St-Bonnet-de-Mure	90
	18	1	St-Laurent-de-Mure	89
	20	2	Junc with rd to Lyon-Satolas Airport	87
	25	5	X-rds with D75	82
	28.5	3.5	La Verpillière	78.5
	36.5	8	La Grive	70.5
	40	3.5	Bourgoin-Jallieu	67
N85	41	1	Junc N6/N85	66
	44.5	3.5	Nivolas-Vermelle	62.5
	47	2.5	La Combe	60
	56	9	Champier	51
	66	10	La Frette	41
	80	14	[Rives]	27
	86.5	6.5	Junc with N92/D592	20.5
N75	91.5	5	Junc N85/N75	15.5
	93	1.5	[Voreppe]	14
	95.5	2.5	Le Chevalon	11.5
	101	5.5	St-Egrève	6
	107	6	Grenoble	

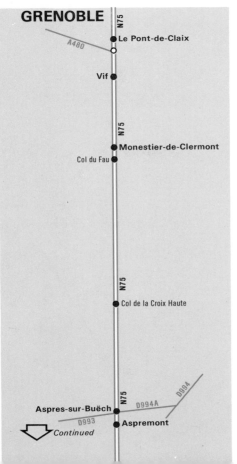

80 Grenoble – Nice
(334km = 207.5 miles)

This route is known as the lower *Route des Alpes,* and also forms part of the *Route Napoléon,* taken by the Emperor on his return from Elba. It is an easily graded road, and is swept in winter, and thus is an alternative to the Rhône valley (Iter 3 and 4) for journeys to the Riviera coast. It begins by following the River Drac and its tributary, the Gresse, then climbs over the beautiful Dauphine Alps into the valley of the River Buech, followed to the River Durance. This is followed, often in view, to its tributary the River Bléone, alongside which the road continues to Digne, and by a series of narrow valleys on to the River Var at Puget-Theniers. The river is closely followed through the very attractive scenery of the Maritime Alps into Nice, the last 30km by a fast straight road.

The route is SP 'Sisteron' and then 'Nice'. In the opposite direction SP 'Digne', then 'Sisteron' and 'Grenoble'.

The first few miles out of Grenoble have been duplicated by Autoroute A480.

N75			Grenoble (689ft)	334
	8	8	Le Pont-de-Claix (801ft)	326
	10.5	2.5	Junc with Autoroute A480	323.5
	13	2.5	Varces	321
	17	4	Vif (1,050ft)	317
	34.5	17.5	Monestier-de-Clermont (2,776ft)	299.5
	36.5	2	Col du Fau (2,986ft)	297.5
	70	33.5	Col de la Croix Haute (3,858ft)	264
	76	6	[Lus-la-Croix-Haute]	258
	83	7	St-Julien-en-Beauchêne (3,021ft)	251
	89.5	6.5	La Faurie (2,756ft)	244.5
	98	8.5	Aspres-sur-Buëch (2,497ft)	236
	101.5	3.5	Aspremont	232.5

	106	4.5	Pont la Barque	228
	109	3	Serres (2,205ft)	225
	125.5	16.5	Laragne-Montéglin	208.5
	139	13.5	Junc with N85	195
N85	143.5	4.5	Sisteron (1,581ft)	190.5
	147	3.5	Junc with D946	187
	157.5	10.5	Château-Arnoux	176.5
	163.5	6	[Malijai]	170.5
	182.5	19	Digne (1,995ft)	151.5
	194.5	12	Châteauredon	139.5
	199.5	5	Chabrières	134.5
N202	212.5	13	Barrême (2,362ft)	121.5
	224.5	12	Col des Robines (3,297ft)	109.5
	226.5	2	[St-André-les-Alpes] (2,936ft)	107.5
	230.5	4	Pont-St-Julien (2,821ft)	103.5
	233.5	3	[St-Julien-du-Verdon] (2,992ft)	100.5
	240	6.5	Col de Toutes Aures (3,691ft)	94
	251	11	Les Scaffarels (2,149ft)	83
	257.5	6.5	Pont-de-Gueydan (1,755ft)	76.5
	263.5	6	Entrevaux (1,591ft)	70.5
	270.5	7	Puget-Théniers (1,329ft)	63.5
	280	9.5	Touët-sur-Var	54
	297	17	Pont de la Mescla	37
	304	7	Plan-du-Var	30
	306.5	2.5	[Pont Charles-Albert]	27.5
	309	2.5	[St-Martin-du-Var]	25
	324	15	Nice-St-Isidore/Digne Junc of Autoroute A8	10
N98	327.8	3.8	Junc N202/N98	6.2
	328	0.2	[Nice Airport]	6
	334	6	Nice	

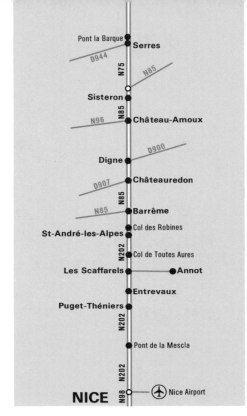

81 Paris – Chartres

(94.5km = 59 miles via A13 & N10)
(93km = 58 miles via N185 & D906)
A faster route by toll motorway is now available. For details see Iter 16.

The first route leaves the city by the toll-free Autoroute (motorway) A13. After the R Seine br and the St-Cloud road tunnel, through wooded country to Versailles. Onwards to Chartres a generally fast and pleasant road, partly through the fine forest of Rambouillet. The alternative passes through the Bois de Boulogne to Longchamps, crossing the R Seine, and then through wooded suburbs. After Rambouillet the alternative route via Maintenon is possibly more interesting, it leaves Rambouillet on the west side and goes past the park and château of the President of France. *In the opposite direction note junction with A12; this motorway can be used to bypass Versailles when bound for Paris or St-Germain.*

unclass			Paris	94.5
A13	7	7	Junc Boulevard Périphérique/A13 (Porte d'Auteuil) (Iter 101)	87.5
D182	15.5	8.5	Versailles-Nord/ Vaucresson Junc	79
N10	19.5	4	Versailles	75
	24.5	5	St-Cyr-l'Ecole	70

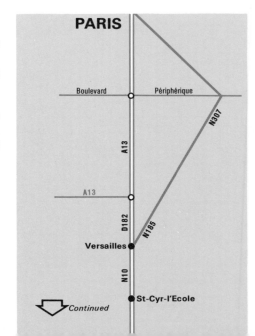

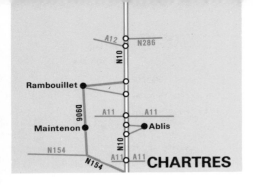

25.5	1	Junc with N286	69
27.5	2	Junc with A12	67
30.5	3	[Trappes]	64
38	7.5	Coignières	56.5
45.5	7.5	[Le Perray-en-Yvelines]	49
52	6.5	[Rambouillet]	42.5
65	13	Rambouillet/Ablis Junc of Autoroute A11 (Iter 16)	29.5
66.5	1.5	[Ablis]	28
90	23.5	Chartres Est Junc of Autoroute A11 (Iter 16)	4.5
94.5	4.5	Chartres	

alternative route

unclass		Paris	93
	4	4	Porte Dauphine (Iter 101)	89
	7	3	[Longchamps Racecourse]	86
N307	10	3	Pont de St-Cloud	83
	10.5	0.5	[Junc with Autoroute A13]	82.5
	11	0.5	St-Cloud	82
N185	12	1	Junc N307/N185	81
N10	20	8	Versailles as above	73
D906	52.5	32.5	Rambouillet	40.5
	57	4.5	Le Buissonnet	36
	61	4	St Hilarion	32
	65	4	Epernon	28
	68	3	Hanches	25
	74	6	Maintenon	19
N154	87	13	Junc D906/N154	6
	89	2	Lèves	4
	93	4	Chartres	

82 Chartres – Tours

(139.5km = 86.5 miles)

A fast, straight road throughout, following the wooded valley of the Loire between Châteaudun and Vendôme, then passing over the open plain of La Beauce to the River Loire. *Note junction with A10; this motorway can be used to bypass Tours when bound for Poitiers. In reverse note junction with A11; this motorway can be used to bypass Chartres when bound for Versailles and Paris.*

N10			Chartres	139.5
	8.5	8.5	Thivars	131
	10	1.5	Thivars/Chartres Sud Junc of Autoroute A11 (Iter 16)	129.5
	20.5	10.5	[Vitray-en-Beauce]	119
	31.5	11	[Bonneval]	108
	36.5	5	Flacey	103
	40.5	4	Marboué	99
	45.5	5	Châteaudun	94
	57.5	12	Cloyes-sur-le-Loir	82
	70.5	12	X-rds with N157	69
	84.5	14	[Vendôme]	55
	110.5	26	[Château-Renault]	29
	124.5	14	Monnaie	15
	131	6.5	Tours Nord/Airport Junc of Autoroute A10 (Iter 7)	8.5
	139.5	8.5	Tours	

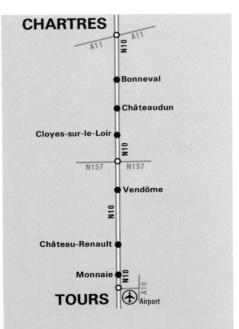

83 Tours – Bordeaux

(331.5km = 206 miles)

The recommended route between Tours and Bordeaux is by toll motorway (Autoroute A10). For details see Iter 7.
This route follows the old 'Bordeaux' road, fast to Montbazon where, in a pleasant setting, the R Indre is crossed, then straight and fast across an open plateau to St-Maure-de-Touraine, and on through the more attractive country of the Vienne and Clain valleys to Poitiers. The road continues to be fast through undulating, usually well-wooded country and concludes with a run across the wine growing district near the rivers Dordogne and Garonne. From St-André-de-Cubzac a choice of routes, by the toll-free section of Autoroute A10 (see Iter 7), or the parallel all-purpose road to Bordeaux.

N10			Tours	331.5
	5.5	5.5	Tours Sud/Montbazon Junc of Autoroute A10	326
	12	6.5	Montbazon	319.5
	34	22	Ste-Maure-de-Touraine	297.5
	44	10	La Celle-St-Avant	287.5
	52.5	8.5	Dangé-St-Romain	279
	60.5	8	Ingrandes	271
	68.5	8	Châtellerault	263
	82.5	14	La Tricherie	249
	89.5	7	Jaunay Clan	242
	98.5	9	[Poitiers Nord Junc of Autoroute A10]	233
	102	3.5	Poitiers (Iter 42)	229.5
	108	6	[Poitiers Sud Junc (no. 20) of Autoroute A10]	223.5
	110	2	Junc with N11	221.5
	121.8	11.8	[Vivonne]	209.7
	138.3	16.5	[Couhé-Verac]	193.2
	156.9	18.6	Les Maisons-Blanches	174.6
	169.5	12.6	[Ruffec]	162
	187.6	18.1	[Mansle]	143.9
	202.8	15.2	La Chignolle	128.7
	215	12.2	[Angoulême]	116.5
	221.8	6.8	[La Couronne]	109.7
	247.5	25.7	Barbezieux	84
	268.7	21.2	Chevanceaux	62.8
	275.5	6.8	Montlieu-la-Garde	56
	281.5	6	Chierzac	50
D911	306.5	25	Junc N10/N137/D911 (Autoroute A10, 1.5km)	25
	308.5	2	St-André-de-Cubzac	23
	314	5.5	St-Vincent-de-Paul	17.5
	317	3	La Grave-d'Ambarès	14.5
	322	5	Carbon-Blanc	9.5
N10	323.5	1.5	Junc with Autoroute A10	8
	331.5	8	Bordeaux	

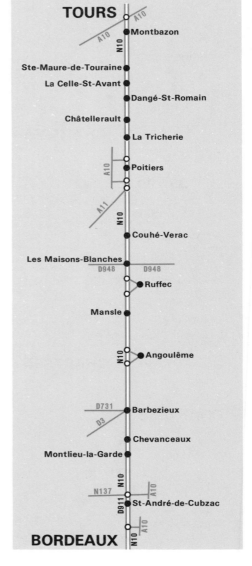

84 Saintes – Royan

(37km = 23 miles)
From the R Charente at Saintes at first undulating and pleasant, then level and featureless to the coast.

N150			Saintes	37
	5	5	Junc with D728	32
	8	3	Pessines	29
	14.5	6.5	Pisany	22.5
	27	12.5	Saujon	10
	32	5	Médis	5
	37	5	Royan	

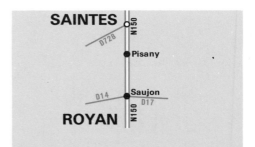

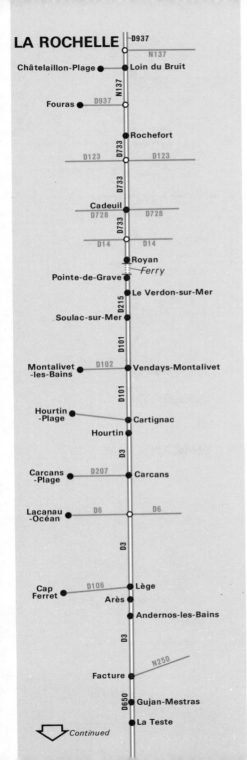

85 La Rochelle – Biarritz (via the coast)

(385.5km = 239.5 miles)

Across level, former marshlands to Rochefort after which the scenery improves as the road rides slightly above the 'flats' offering broad views. After crossing the Gironde Estuary by ferry, the road passes all the way through the pine forests of Les Landes and to reach the coast it is necessary to make the indicated excursions.

Between Arès and Arcachon through a series of small villages along the Bassin d'Arcachon. The section from Facture to Arcachon can be bypassed by the parallel Expressway A66.

Large inland lagoons can be seen by short drives from Biscarrosse, Parentis-en-Born, Aureilhan and Léon.

SP 'Rochefort', 'Saintes', and 'Bordeaux' out of La Rochelle. In the opposite direction SP 'Bayonne' out of Biarritz, then SP 'Bordeaux' on N10.

A parallel toll motorway (Autoroute A63) is available for the final run from Capbreton to Biarritz, see Iter 8.

D937			**La Rochelle**	385.5
N137	5.5	5.5	Junc with La Rochelle bypass	380
	10.5	5	Loin du Bruit (Châtelaillon-Plage 1.5km)	375
	22	11.5	Junc with D937 (Fouras 5km)	363.5
D733	31	9	Rochefort	354.5
	38.5	7.5	Junc with D123 (St-Agnant 0.5km)	347
	42	3.5	Villeneuve	343.5
	53	11	Cadeuil	332.5
	56.5	3.5	Chalons	329
	62.5	6	X-rds with D14	323
	64.5	2	St-Sulpice-de-Royan	321
	71	6.5	Royan (Iter 84)	

Ferry across the Gironde

N215			Pointe-de-Grave	314.5
	75	4	[Le Verdon-sur-Mer]	310.5
D1 E	79	4	Junc N215/D1E	306.5
D101	82	3	Soulac-sur-Mer	303.5
	102	20	Vendays-Montalivet (Montalivet-les-Bains, 8km by D102)	283.5
	119	17	Cartignac (Hourtin-Plage 9km)	266.5
D3	122	3	Hourtin	263.5
	134	12	Carcans (Carcans-Plage 14km)	251.5
	145	11	Junc with D6 (Lacanau-Océan 12km)	240.5
	146	1	Lacanau	239.5
	158	12	Le Porge	227.5
	168	10	Lège (Cap Ferret 24km)	217.5
	171	3	Arès	214.5
	175.5	4.5	Andernos-les-Bains	210
	191	15.5	Biganos	194.5
D650	192	1	Facture (Expressway A66 1.5km by D3)	193.5
	200.5	8.5	Gujan Mestras	185
	204.7	4.2	La Hume	180.8
	207.2	2.5	[La Teste]	178.3

D218	212.5	5.3	Arcachon	173
	216.5	4	Pyla-sur-Mer	169
	219.5	3	Pilat-Plage	166
D83	240.5	21	Road no. change	145
D146	243.5	3	Biscarrosse-Plage	142
D652	251.5	8	Junc D146/D652	134
	253	1.5	Biscarrosse	132.5
	262	9	Parentis-en-Born	123.5
D46	265	3	Junc D652/D46	120.5
D626	275.5	10.5	Pontenx-les-Forges	110
	279	3.5	St-Paul-en-Born	106.5
	283	4	[Aureilhan]	102.5
	286	3	Mimizan (Mimizan Plage 6km)	99.5
D652	293	7	Bias	92.5
	302	9	Junc with D41 (Contis-Plage 7.5km)	83.5
	303.5	1.5	St-Julien-en-Born	82
	307.5	4	Lit-et-Mixe	78
	317.5	10	St-Girons (St-Girons Plage 5km)	68
	326	8.5	Léon	59.5
	332	6	Moliets-et-Maa (Moliets Plage 3km)	53.5
	339.5	7.5	Vieux-Boucau-les-Bains	46
D79	341.5	2	Junc D652/D79	44
D152	351.5	10	Junc D79/D152	34
D652	355	3.5	Junc D152/D652	30.5
	356.5	1.5	[Hossegor]	29
	358	1.5	Capbreton (Junc with Autoroute A63 3km by D28)	27.5
N10	363.5	5.5	Labenne	22
	376.5	13	Bayonne	9
D910	381	4.5	Anglet	4.5
	385.5	4.5	Biarritz	

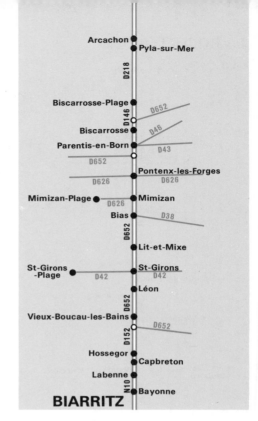

86 Le Mans – Les Sables d'Olonne

(250.7km = 156 miles)

At first generally fast, undulating through beautiful woods and forests, to the flat country around Angers. Leave Angers by the 'Niort' & 'Poitiers' road to the SE, crossing the rivers Authion, the Loire and the Louet, then continue by the 'Cholet' road across La Vendée, fairly fast through pleasantly varied scenery. Particularly attractive crossing the R Layon before St-Lambert-du-Lattay, and the R Sèvre Nantais at Mortagne-sur-Sèvre. The excursion to the Puy-de-la-Garde (700ft) is recommended for a fine view. Approaching La Roche-sur-Yon and on to Les Sables d'Olonne it is less interesting, open countryside.

N23			Le Mans	250.7
	9	9	Arnage	241.7
	16.5	7.5	Guécélard	234.2
	23.5	7	Cérans-Foulletourte	227.2
	42.8	19.3	La Flèche	207.9
	49.8	7	Bazouges-sur-le-Loir	200.9
	55.5	5.7	Durtal	195.2
	70.2	14.7	Seiches-sur-le-Loir	180.5
	78.7	8.5	Pellouailles-les-Vignes	172
N160	88.7	10	Angers	162
N260	92.7	4	Junc N160/N260	158
	99.7	7	Junc with D748	151

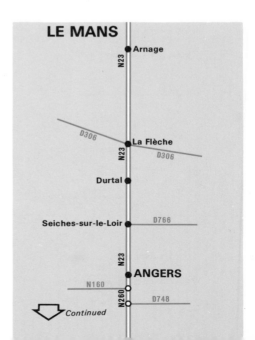

Continued

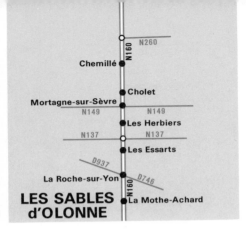

N160	102.2		Junc N260/N160	148.5
	115	12.8	St-Lambert-du-Lattay	135.7
	128.2	13.2	[Chemillé]	122.5
	135.8	7.6	St-Georges-du-Puy-de-	114.9
			la-Garde (Puy-de-la-	
			Garde 2km by D265)	
	142.8	7	Nuallé	107.9
	150.4	7.6	[Cholet]	100.3
	160.4	10	Mortagne-sur-Sèvre	90.3
	176	15.6	Les Herbiers	74.7
	187.5	11.5	X-rds (N137)	63.2
			(Iter 45)	
	195.8	8.3	Les Essarts	54.9
	204.8	9	La Ferrière	45.9
	215.5	10.7	La Roche-sur-Yon	35.2
	233.5	18	La Mothe-Achard	17.2
	241	7.5	St-Mathurin	9.7
	250.7	9.7	Les Sables d'Olonne	

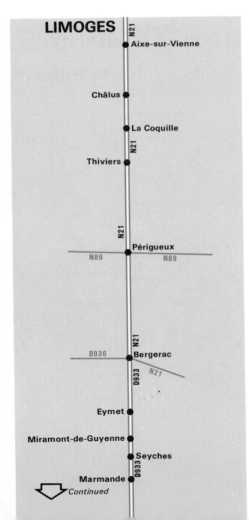

87 Limoges–Biarritz

(418.4km = 260 miles)
Generally very pleasant but, as far as Marmande, fairly winding and somewhat slow. To Aixe-sur-Vienne along a picturesque stretch of the river, then rise and fall through the woods and meadows of Perigord, following the R Isle from Sarliac-sur-l'Isle to Périgueux.
Onwards to Bergerac, on the Dordogne, undulating through forested country, then more open, although still pleasantly wooded and sometimes very winding. After crossing the Garonne at Marmande continuing straight and level through the pine forested region of Les Landes. Beyond Mont-de-Marsan across undulating farming country; later pine woods and moorland. The distant Pyrénées come into view beyond Dax. In the opposite direction SP 'Bayonne' out of Biarritz, then SP 'Bordeaux' on N10.
A parallel toll motorway (Autoroute A63) is available between St-Geours-de-Maremne and Biarritz, see Iter 8.

N21			Limoges	418.4
	12.7	12.7	Aixe-sur-Vienne	405.7
	20.2	7.5	Séreilhac	398.2
	35.4	15.2	Châlus	383
	49.6	14.2	La Coquille	368.8
	64.6	15	[Thiviers]	353.8
	75.6	11	[Négrondes]	342.8
	88.6	13	[Sarliac-sur-l'Isle]	329.8
	90.6	2	Laurière	327.8
	93.3	2.7	Antonne-et-Trigonant	325.1
	103.7	10.4	Périgueux	314.7
	109.2	5.5	Pont-du-Cerf	309.2
	122.6	13.4	Bordas	295.8
	127.8	5.2	Maison-Jeannette	290.6
	138.3	10.5	Campsegret	280.1
	147.1	8.8	[Pombonne]	271.3
D933	150.9	3.8	Bergerac	267.5
	160.4	9.5	Rouffignac-de-Sigoulès	258
	175.9	15.5	Eymet	242.5
	187.2	11.3	Miramont-de-Guyenne	231.2
	195.4	8.2	Seyches	223
	206.4	11	[Virazeil]	212
	210.9	4.5	Marmande	207.5

	214.9	4	[Coussan]	203.5
	219.9	5	[Junc with Autoroute A62]	198.5
	235.5	15.6	Casteljaloux	182.9
	250.5	15	Houeillès	167.9
	267.5	17	Lapeyrade	150.9
	285.5	18	St-Justin	132.9
	293	7.5	Pillelardit	125.4
D932	300.5	7.5	Le Caloy	117.9
N124	310.5	10	[Mont-de-Marsan]	107.9
	323	12.5	Campagne	95.4
	336.4	13.4	Junc with D924	82
	337.4	1	Tartas	81
	349.2	11.8	Pontonx-sur-l'Adour	69.2
	361.9	12.7	St-Paul-les-Dax (for Dax 2km)	56.5
	375.4	13.5	Junc with N124e (Autoroute A63, 2km)	43
N10	377.4	2	St-Geours-de-Maremne	41
	384.4	13	St-Vincent-de-Tyrosse	34
	390.9	6.5	Bénesse-Maremne	27.5
	396.4	5.5	Labenne	22
	409.4	9	Bayonne	9
D910	413.9	4.5	Anglet	4.5
	418.4	4.5	Biarritz	

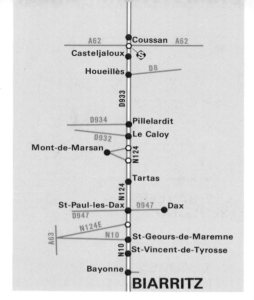

88 Bergerac–Lourdes

(259.8km = 161.5 miles)

Initially easy rise and fall across agricultural and wine-producing country, with extensive views over the valley of the R Lot, crossed at Villeneuve-sur-Lot. After crossing the Garonne at Agen across the old province of Gascogny and the land of the Armagnacs, mainly by the valley of the R Gers to Auch.
Then a pleasant road through wooded country, ascending from Miélan to the viewpoint of Puntous de Laguian. After Rabastens-de-Bigorre straight and level to Tarbes. Finally into the attractive country of the foothills of the Pyrénées.

N21			Bergerac	259.8
	12.2	12.2	Bouniagues	247.6
	26.8	14.6	Castillonnès	233
	35.6	8.8	Lougratte	224.2
	41.3	5.7	Cancon	218.5
	48.5	7.2	Castelnaud-de-Gratecambe	211.3
	61.5	13	Villeneuve-sur-Lot	198.3
	77.7	16.2	La Croix-Blanche	182.1
	91	13.3	Agen	168.8
	102	11	Layrac	157.8
	110.4	8.4	Astaffort	149.4
	129.6	19.2	Lectoure	130.2
	141	11.4	Fleurance	118.8
	148	7	Montestruc-sur-Gers	111.8
	165.8	17.8	Auch	94
	190.8	25	Mirande	69
	204.8	14	Miélan	55
	210.8	6	Puntous de Laguian (1,050ft)	49
	220.5	9.7	Rabastens-de-Bigorre	39.3
	237.4	16.9	Aureilhan	22.4
	240.4	3	Tarbes	19.4
	247.9	7.5	[Tarbes Airport]	11.9
	254.4	6.5	Adé	5.4
	259.8	5.4	[Lourdes] (1,345ft)	

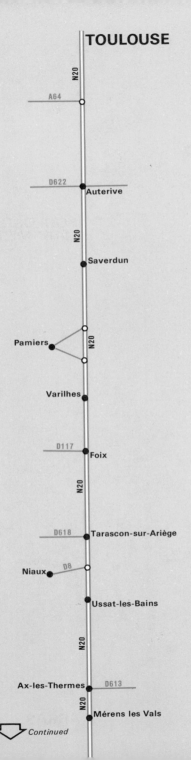

TOULOUSE

N20

A64

D622
Auterive

N20

Saverdun

Pamiers

N20

Varilhes

D117
Foix

N20

D618
Tarascon-sur-Ariège

Niaux
D8

Ussat-les-Bains

N20

Ax-les-Thermes
D613

N20

Mérens les Vals

Continued

89 Toulouse – Ax-les-Thermes – Andorra-la-Vella

(192km = 119.5 miles)

(a) Toulouse–Ax-les-Thermes

(127km = 79 miles)

Very fast for 11km by the wide Garonne valley, then crosses the river to Pinsaguel. From here the R Ariege is followed, the valley being fairly broad at first then progressively narrower as the distant Pyrénées come into view; slow and winding into the thickly-wooded foothills. SP 'Foix' and then 'Ax-les-Thermes'. In the opposite direction SP 'Foix' & 'Toulouse'.
The first few miles of the route out of Toulouse have been duplicated by Autoroute A64 (single carriageway motorway).

N20			Toulouse	127
	11	11	Junc with N117	116
	12	1	Pinsaguel	115
	14	2	Junc with Autoroute A64	113
	22	8	Vernet	105
	33	11	Auterive	94
	49.5	16.5	Saverdun	77.5
	62	12.5	Road Junc (Pamiers 3km)	65
	68	6	Junc with D119 (Pamiers 2km)	59
	71.5	3.5	Junc with D12	55.5
	75.5	4	Varilhes	51.5
	79.5	4	St-Jean-de-Verges	47.5
	85	5.5	Foix (1,247ft)	42
	92	7	Junc with D117	35
	96.5	4.5	Mercus	30.5
	101	4.5	Tarascon-sur-Ariège (1,555ft)	26
	102	1	Junc with D8 (Niaux 3km)	25
	104	2	Ussat-les-Bains	23
	108.5	4.5	Sinsat	18.5
	111.5	3	Les Cabannes	15.5
	115	3.5	La Remise	12
	118.5	3.5	Luzenac	8.5
	124.5	6	Savignac-les-Ormeaux	2.5
	127	2.5	**Ax-les-Thermes** (2,362ft)	

(b) Ax-les-Thermes–Andorra-la-Vella

(65km = 40.5 miles)

Ascent through the Ariège gorges then westward into Andorra; fine mountain views; later by the gorge of the R Valira. On the whole rather slow. Height restriction 3.50 metres near L'Hospitalet. In France the route is signposted 'Andorre' and 'Espagne', later changing to 'Andorra' and 'Espanya'. In the opposite direction SP 'Francia', then 'Ax-les-Thermes' and 'Toulouse'. *The Port d'Envalira has a maximum gradient of The Port d'Envalira has a maximum gradient of 12% and may be obstructed at times between November*

N20			Ax-les-Thermes (2,362ft) (Forge d'Orlu 10.5km by D22)	65
	8.5	8.5	Mérens les Vals (3,461ft)	56.5

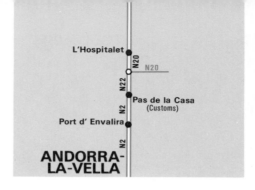

	18	9.5	L'Hospitalet (4,711ft)	47
N22	25	7	Junc N20/N22 (5,700ft)	40
N2	31	6	Pas de la Casa (6,851ft) *(French Customs and Passport Control)*	34
	36	5	Port d'Envalira (7,897ft)	29
	45.5	9.5	Soldeu (6,070ft)	19.5
	53	7.5	Canillo	12
	58.5	5.5	Encamp	6.5
	63.5	5	Les Escaldes	1.5
	65	1.5	Andorra-la-Vella (3,375ft)	

90 Boulogne-sur-Mer–Arras

(117km = 72.5 miles by toll motorway)
(116km = 72 miles by all-purpose road, N1 & N39)
(105.5km = 65.5 miles by touring route, D341)
Three routes are now available. The first route follows the 'Lille' & 'St-Omer' road as far as the Autoroute A26. A generally fast run with sections of dual carriageway and a series of steep hills (max grad 11%) through agricultural country with a few woods. The route then continues by the 'Paris' & 'Reims' toll motorway through gently undulating farming country. The second route is by a fairly fast all-purpose road (N1 & N39), an undulating and hilly route, across typical, fertile farming country of Picardy. Between Montreuil and Hesdin through the pleasant valley of the Canche, with forested country to the north by Hesdin. The touring route follows a quiet secondary road; agricultural country, sometimes wooded, but industrial around Divion.
The first and third routes are SP 'Lille' & 'St-Omer' out of Boulogne; the second is SP 'Paris' & 'Abbeville' to Montreuil, then SP 'Arras' (from port SP 'Sortie/Exit' and then 'Toutes Directions').

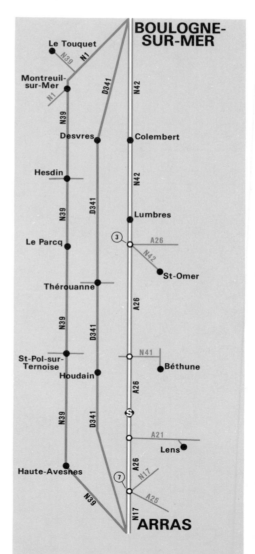

N42			Boulogne-sur-Mer	117
	2	2	St-Martin	115
	7.5	5.5	La Capelle-lès-Boulogne	109.5
	17.2	9.7	Colembert	99.8
	30.2	13	Harlettes	86.8
	39	8.8	Lumbres	78
	41.8	2.8	Setques	75.2
A26	43	1.2	Junc N42/motorway slip road	74
	43.5	0.5	St-Omer Junc (no.3) of Autoroute A26 (Toll booths)	73.5
	74.5	31	Lillers Junc (no.5)	42.5
	86.5	12	Béthune Junc	30.5
	98	11.5	Aix-Noulette Junc (Junc with Autoroute A21, Lens 9km)	19
	102.5	4.5	Service area	14.5
	110.5	8	Arras Nord Junc (no.7) (Iter 1, 25)	6.5
N17	111	0.5	Junc motorway slip road/N17	6
	117	6	Arras	

**or avoiding
toll motorway**

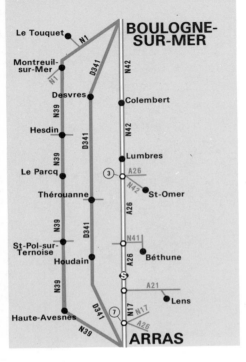

N1		**Boulogne-sur-Mer**	116
	5	5	Pont-de-Briques	111
	15	10	[Samer]	101
	35	20	Junc with N39	81
			(Le Touquet 15km)	
N39	37	2	[Montreuil-sur-Mer]	79
	43	6	Brimeux	73
	61.5	18.5	Hesdin	54.5
	66	4.5	Le Parcq	50
	83	17	St-Pol-sur-Ternoise	33
	87.6	4.6	Roëllecourt	28.4
	105.4	17.8	[Haute-Avesnes]	10.6
	116	10.6	Arras	

touring route

N42		**Boulogne-sur-Mer**	105.5
D341	1	1	Junc N42/D341	104.5
	6	5	Baincthun	99.5
	19	13	Desvres	86.5
	26.5	7.5	Bois-de-Senlecques	79
	41.5	15	Ouve-Wirquin	64
	50.5	9	Thérouanne	55
	57	6.5	Estrée-Blanche	48.5
	62.5	5.5	Auchy-au-Bois	43
	71.5	9	Cauchy-á-la-Tour	34
	74.5	3	Camblain-Châtelain	31
	77.5	3	Divion	28
	80.5	3	Houdain	25
	92	11.5	Camblain-l'Abbé	13.5
	102	10	Anzin	3.5
	105.5	3.5	Arras	

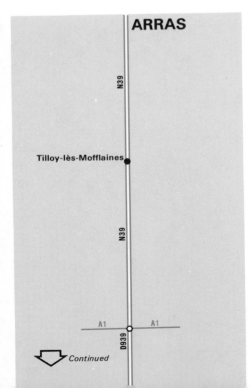

91 Arras–Strasbourg

(486.2km = 302 miles)

The recommended route between Arras and Strasbourg is via Reims and toll motorway A4. For details see Iter 25 and 10.

This route follows mainly all-purpose roads, with a section of motorway after Charleville-Mézières. A straight, fast, monotonous road across the plain of Artois to beyond Cambrai then pleasantly undulating. After Le Nouvion-en-Thiérache there is a stretch of forest and from Hirson the road runs along a high ridge with views across the valleys on either side. After Maubert Fontaine the Ardennes forests are skirted and the Meuse valley is crossed at Charleville-Mézières and again at Sedan. Onwards to Metz, on the Moselle, continuous rise and fall through pleasant, varied scenery of valley and plateau. Then similar scenery of the wide undulating plateau of Lorraine, with views from many hill tops and of Gondrexange Lake before Héming. After Sarrebourg a rather bare plateau on the northern edge of the Vosges Mountains; distant views of the Alsace plain on the descent, through woods, from Phalsbourg. Then skirting the foothills of the Vosges, with vineyards at Wasselonne. From Marlenheim the road runs fast and straight across the plain of Alsace.

N39		Arras	486.2
	4	4	Tilloy-lès-Mofflaines	482.2
D939	7	3	[Arras-Est Junc of	479.2
			Autoroute A1]	
			(Iter 1, 15)	

	13	6	Vis-en-Artois	473.2
	24.3	11.3	Marquion	461.9
	26.8	2.5	[Marquion Junc of Autoroute A26] (Iter 25)	459.4
	30.8	4	Raillencourt	455.4
N30	34.3	3.5	Junc D939/N30	451.9
N43	35.8	1.5	Cambrai	450.4
	47.4	11.6	[Beauvois-en-Cambrésis]	438.8
	50.4	3	[Caudry]	435.8
	58.6	8.2	X-rds with D932	427.6
	60.4	1.8	Le Cateau	425.8
	68.4	8	Catillon	417.8
	71.7	3.3	Chapeau Rouge	414.5
	81	9.3	Le Nouvion-en-Thiérache	405.2
	93	12	La Capelle-en-Thiérache	393.2
	107.5	14.5	Hirson	378.7
	117.7	10.2	Bellevue	368.5
	124	6.3	[Auge]	362.2
	132.4	8.4	Mon Idée (Auvillers-les-Forges 1.5km by D877)	353.8
	136	3.6	Maubert-Fontaine	350.2
	142	6	[Tremblois-lès-Rocroi]	344.2
	143	1	Junc with N51	343.2
	145	2	Rimogne	341.2
	149.7	4.7	Lonny	336.5
A203	160.7	11	Charleville-Mézières	325.5
	165.2	4.5	Junc with N51	321
	167.2	2	Junc with D764	319
N43	180.2	13	Junc A203/N43	306
	183.7	3.5	Sedan	302.5
	185.4	1.7	Balan	300.8
	187.8	2.4	[Bazeilles]	298.4
	192.5	4.7	Douzy	293.7
	205.4	12.9	Carignan	280.8
	214.7	9.3	Margut	271.5
	224.3	9.6	Thonnelle	261.5
	230.3	6	Montmédy	255.9
	236.3	6	Iré-le-Sec	249.9
	242.5	6.2	Marville-St-Jean	243.7
	256.2	13.7	Longuyon (Fermont, 6km NE by D17A)	230
	266.7	10.5	Pierrepont	219.5
	282.2	15.5	[Landres]	204
	294.2	12	Briey	192
	299.7	5.5	Auboué	186.5
	301.2	1.5	Auboué/Briey Junc of Autoroute A4 (Iter 10)	185
	302.7	1.5	Ste-Marie-aux-Chênes	183.5
	305.7	3	St-Privat-la-Montagne	180.5
N3	315.7	10	Junc N43/N3	170.5
	316.7	1	Moulins-lès-Metz	169.5
D955	322.7	6	Metz	163.5
	327.7	5	Grigy	158.5
	340.7	13	X-rds with D910	145.5
	350.2	9.5	Liocourt	136
	354.7	4.5	Delme	131.5
	367.7	13	Château Salins	118.5
	375.7	8	Moyenvic	110.5
	389.7	14	Bourdonnay	96.5
	393.7	4	Maizières-lès-Vic	92.5
N4	410.7	17	Héming	75.5
	418.7	8	Sarrebourg	67.5

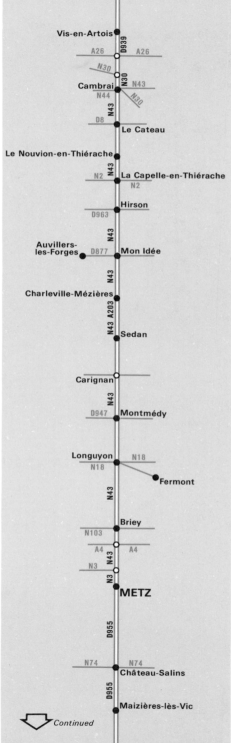

Continued

432.7	14	Mittelbronn	53.5
433.7	1	Phalsbourg/Nancy Junc	52.5
		of A4 Autoroute	
		(Iter 10)	
434.7	1	[Phalsbourg]	51.5
440.2	5.5	Col de Saverne (1,345ft)	46
445.2	5	Saverne	41
448.2	3	[Otterswiller]	38
452.2	4	[Marmoutier]	34
460.2	8	[Wasselonne]	26
464.2	4	Marlenheim	22
470.2	6	Furdenheim	16
473.2	3	Ittenheim	13
486.2	13	Strasbourg	

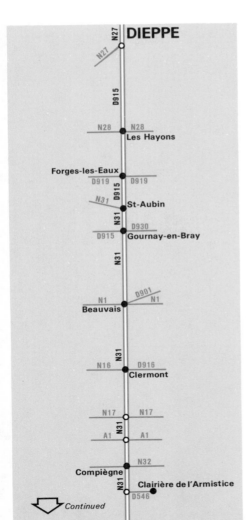

92 Dieppe–Reims

(255.8km = 159 miles)

Leave Dieppe by the 'Paris' road.
A straight road at first, later undulating through the woods and forest of the Norman countryside. After Gournay-en-Bray a generally undulating, fast road across partly cultivated country with several heavily wooded stretches, particularly after Compiègne when passing through the Forêt de Compiègne. Finally a fast and straight road following the cultivated Aisne and Vesle valleys. A stretch of N31 near Reims forms part of the Reims motor-racing circuit.

The route is SP 'Paris' as far as Gournay-en-Bray, then SP 'Beauvais', 'Clermont', 'Soissons' and 'Reims'. In the opposite direction SP 'Rouen' and 'Soissons' out of Reims, and finally SP 'Dieppe' along the D915 beyond Gournay-en-Bray.

N27			**Dieppe**	255.8
D915	3	3	Junc N27/D915	252.8
	16.5	13.5	Torcy-le-Petit	239.3
	30	13.5	Pommeréval	225.8
	37	7	Les Hayons (Iter 58)	218.8
	54	17	Forges-les-Eaux	201.8
N31	72.5	18.5	St-Aubin	183.3
	74	1.5	Gournay-en-Bray	181.8
	80.3	6.3	[St-Germer-de-Fly]	175.5
	90.3	10	Le Vivier Danger	165.5
	92.7	2.4	Le Pont-qui-Penche	163.1
	104	11.3	Beauvais (Iter 22)	151.8
	109.3	5.3	Therdonne	146.5
	116.3	7	[Bresles]	139.5
	121.5	5.2	La Neuville-en-Hez	134.3
	129	7.5	Clermont	126.8
	135	6	Nointel	120.8
	145.8	10.8	X-rds (N17)	110
	149.5	3.7	[Arsy]	106.3
	151.5	2	[Compiègne Junc	104.3
			of Autoroute A1]	
			(Iter 1, 15)	
	154.5	3	Bouquy	101.3
	160.3	5.8	Compiègne	95.5
	164.3	4	Junc with D546	91.5 ·
			(Clairière de	
			l'Armistice 2km)	

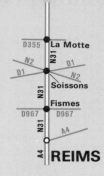

	174.7	10.4	La Motte	81.1
	179.4	4.7	Jaulzy	76.4
	199.3	19.9	Soissons (Iter 94)	56.5
	208.7	9.4	Sermoise	47.1
	216.9	8.2	Braine	38.9
	229.4	12.5	[Fismes]	26.4
	239.8	10.4	Jonchery-sur-Vesle	16
A4	251.8	12	Reims Tinqueux Junc of Autoroute A4 (Iter 10)	4
	254.8	3	Reims Centre Junc	1
	255.8	1	Reims	

93 Reims–Ligny-en-Barrois
(124.2km = 77 miles)

Fast, straight, undulating and very lonely. Little scenic interest except in the later stages beyond Bar-le-Duc, follow the Marne-Rhine canal through wooded country. From La Cheppe to Nettancourt, follows a former Roman road. SP 'Chalons par RN44' out of Reims.

N44			Reims	124.2
	8.5	8.5	[Fort-de-la-Pompelle]	115.7
	10	1.5	Junc with RD31	114.2
	16	6	Beaumont-sur-Vesle	108.2
RD394	24.2	8.2	Junc N44/RD394	100
	28.2	4	Livry-Louvercy	96
	32.7	4.5	Bouy	91.5
	42.2	9.5	X-rds (RD77)	82
	46.2	4	La Cheppe	78
	53.2	7	La Grande-Romanie (Junc with N3)	71
D994	84.2	31	Nettancourt	40
D75	89.2	5	[Brabant-le-Roi]	35
D994	94.2	5	Laimont	30
N135	108.2	14	Bar-le-Duc	16
	124.2	16	Ligny-en-Barrois	

94 Arras – Troyes – Dijon
(426.9km = 265 miles)

(a) Arras–Troyes
(274.6km = 170.5 miles)

The recommended route between Arras and Soissons is by motorway A26 and St-Quentin. For details see Iter 25.

This route follows all-purpose roads. A reasonably fast road with moderate scenery to Ham, where the R Somme is crossed, then hilly and wooded to the Aisne valley at Soissons. The road then climbs on the Plateau de Tardenois and then drops to the River Marne, crossed at Château-Thierry. A winding ascent out of this valley on to the monotonous Brie Champenoise tableland is followed by a fertile stretch of country bordering the R Aube between Anglure and Granges-sur-Aube. From Méry-sur-Seine a practically level road along the broad open valley of the upper Seine.

ARRAS

SP 'Paris' and 'Bapaume' out of Arras, then SP 'Peronne', 'Soissons' and finally 'Troyes'. In the opposite direction SP 'Paris' on N19 out of Troyes, and then SP 'Soissons' on D373.

N17			Arras	274.6
	3	3	Beaurains	271.6
	18.7	15.7	Sapignies	255.9
	22.3	3.6	Bapaume	252.3
			(Bapaume Junc of A1 Autoroute 2km; Iter 1, 15)	
	26.3	4	Beaulencourt	248.3
	37.8	11.5	Bouchavesnes-Bergen	236.8
	41.7	3.9	Mont-St-Quentin	232.9
D937	44.7	3	[Péronne]	229.9
	47.7	3	Junc with D944	226.9
	51.7	4	X-rds with N29	222.9
	55.5	3.8	Athies	219.1
	69.7	14.2	Ham	204.9
	76.9	7.2	Cugny	197.7
	79.4	2.5	Flavy-le-Martel	195.2
	83.4	4	Faillouel	191.2
	91.8	8.4	Chauny	182.8
	104.8	13	[Coucy-le-Château-Auffrique]	169.8
D1	123.8	19	Soissons (Iter 92)	150.8
	136.8	13	Hartennes	137.8
	143.8	7	Oulchy-le-Château	130.8
	145.8	2	Breny	128.8
	150.8	5	Rocourt-St-Martin	123.8
	158.8	8	Château-Thierry Junc A4 (Iter 10)	115.8
	164.8	6	Château-Thierry	109.8
	180.8	16	Fontenelle-en-Brie	93.8
D933	183.6	2.8	Junc D1/D933	91
RD373	189.1	5.5	Montmirail	85.5
	194.1	5	Maclaunay	80.5
	198.1	4	Le Gault-Soigny	76.5
N4	210.6	12.5	Junc RD373/N4	64
RD373	213.6	3	[Sézanne] (Iter 96)	61
	218.6	5	Chichey	56
	232.6	14	Anglure	42
D373	235.6	3	Granges-sur-Aube	39
	243.1	7.5	St-Oulph	31.5
	245.6	2.5	Méry-sur-Seine	29
N19	249.6	4	La Belle Etoile	25
	263.6	14	La Malmaison	11
	274.6	11	Troyes	

(b) Troyes–Dijon

(152.3km = 94.5 miles)
To beyond Châtillon a practically level road following the open valley of the upper Seine, later the route is first well-wooded and then hilly and winding as it crosses the exposed Plateau de Langres, cut by numerous deep river valleys.
SP 'Dijon'. In the opposite direction SP 'Paris par Troyes' and then 'Troyes'.

N71			Troyes	152.3
	5	5	Bréviandes	147.3
	8	3	Maisons-Blanches	144.3
	15	7	Clérey-Sud	137.3
	33.3	18.3	Bar-sur-Seine	119
	42.3	9	[Neuville-sur-Seine]	110
	53	10.7	[Mussy-sur-Seine]	99.3

Continued

60	7	Villers-Patras	92.3
68.8	8.8	Châtillon-sur-Seine	83.5
73.8	5	Buncey	78.5
85.1	11.3	Aisey-sur-Seine	67.2
91.1	6	St-Marc-sur-Seine	61.2
119.3	28.2	Junc with D103 (source of the Seine 2.5km)	33
127.5	8.2	St-Seine-l'Abbaye	24.8
137.7	10.2	Val-Suzon	14.6
152.3	14.6	Dijon	

95 Dijon–Genève

(206km = 128 miles via Faucille Pass)
(208.3km = 129.5 miles via St Cergue Pass)
At first across a vast, undulating plain watered by the R Saône, crossed at Auxonne, the R Doubs, crossed near Dole, and the R Loue, crossed beyond Parcey. The climb over the Jura Mts begins at Poligny, passing through the Culée de Vaux to Monts de Vaux, then, after a wooded plateau, dropping down to the R Ain at Champagnole. Fine gorge scenery to St-Laurent via Pont de la Chaux, from which an excursion can be made to the 'Four Lakes'. Open pastureland again gives way to wooded mountains as the main range is crossed by a modern road over the Faucille Pass (max grad 10%; *possible obstruction in severe weather in winter*), with views on the descent of Lake Geneva and the mountains of Savoy beyond. The alternative route via Nyon avoids the Faucille Pass. SP 'Genève'. In the opposite direction SP 'Paris' and 'Dijon'.

N5		**Dijon**	206
	8.5	8.5	[Neuilly-lès-Dijon]	197.5
	19.6	11.1	Genlis	186.4
	34	14.4	Auxonne	172
	45.5	11.5	Sampans	160.5
N5/ N73	48.5	3	Junc with Dole bypass (Dole 3km; Iter 17)	157.5
N5	55	6.5	Junc N5/N73	151
	57	2	[Gevry]	149
	61	4	Junc with D405 (Dole 7.5km)	145
	62	1	Parcey	144
	63.5	1.5	Junc with D475	142.5
	65.5	2	Nevy-lès-Dole	140.5
	68.5	3	Souvans	137.5
	71	2.5	Junc with D472	135
	80.5	9.5	Aumont	125.5
	87	6.5	Tourmont	119
	90.6	3.6	Poligny (1,073ft)	115.4
	103.4	12.8	Montrond	102.6
	113.6	10.2	Champagnole (1,926ft)	92.4
	123.6	10	La Billaude	82.1
	126.9	3.3	Pont-de-la-Chaux	79.1
	132.9	6	Pont-de-Lemme	73.1
	137.1	4.2	St-Laurent-en-Grandvaux (3,001ft)	68.9
	142.6	5.5	Col de la Savine (3,251ft)	63.4
	146.4	3.8	Morbier	59.6
	149.8	3.4	Morez (2,247ft)	56.2
	159.3	9.5	Les Rousses	46.7

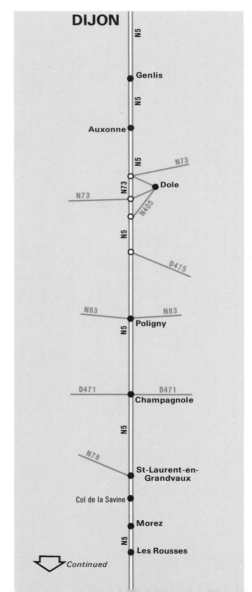

Continued

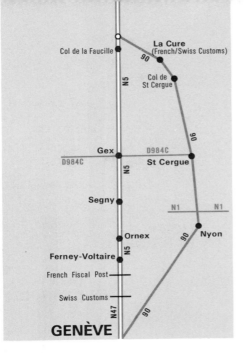

	178.3	19	Col de Faucille (4,341ft)	27.7
	189.5	11.2	Gex (1,985ft)	16.5
	193.7	4.2	Segny	12.3
	197.3	3.6	Ornex	8.7
	199	1.7	Ferney-Voltaire (1,444ft)	7
	200.5	1.5	*French Fiscal Post* of Ferney-Voltaire	5.5
N47	202	1.5	*Swiss Customs* of Saconnex and end of neutral zone	4
	206	4	**Genève** (Geneva) (1,230ft)	

alternative route

			Dijon	208.3
			as above	
N5	159.3	159.3	Les Rousses	49
90	162.3	3	La Cure (3,609ft) *French/Swiss Customs*	46
	164.3	2	Col de St Cergue (La Givrine) (4,051ft)	44
	169.8	5.5	St Cergue (3,422ft)	38.5
	182.3	12.5	Nyon/St Cergue Junc with N1 motorway	26
1	185.3	3	Nyon (1,345ft)	23
	208.3	23	**Genève** (Geneva) (1,230ft)	

96 Paris–Ligny-en-Barrois

(241.2km = 150 miles)

The drab suburbs of Paris are relieved by a run alongside the Bois de Vincennes and a pretty view of the R Marne before crossing at Joinville-le-Pont. Later a fast road across the Brie Plateau and passing through the Forêt d'Armainvilliers, the landscape becoming more open beyond Rozay-en-Brie, but again wooded on the descent to Sézanne. Then follows a monotonous stretch across the Plain of Champagne until the R Marne is crossed at Vitry-le-François. The Marne-Saône canal is followed through good farming country to St-Dizier then the route is hilly, crossing the pleasant valley of the Saulx at Stainville for that of the Ornain at Ligny-en-Barrois.

The route is SP 'Nancy'. In the opposite direction SP 'Paris'.

unclass			Paris	241.2
A4	6	6	Junc A4/Bd Périphérique (Porte de Bercy) (Iter 101)	235.2
	7	1	Ivry s/Seine Junc	234.2
N4	10.5	3.5	Joinville Junc	230.7
	16	5.5	Champigny-sur-Marne	225.2
	20	4	Pincevent (Junc with D185)	221.2
	29.5	9.5	[Ozoir-la-Ferrière]	211.7
	37.2	7.7	[Gretz-Armainvilliers]	204
	40	2.8	[Tournan-en-Brie]	201.2
	49	9	[Fontenay-Trésigny]	192.2
	56	7	[Rozay-en-Brie]	185.2
	65.5	9.5	[Vaudoy-en-Brie]	175.2
	69	3.5	Ouzelle	172.2
	79	10	Beton-Bazoches	162.2

83	4	Courtacon	158.2
90	7	[Sancy-lès-Provins]	151.2
93	3	Montceaux-lès-Provins	148.2
97.5	4.5	Courgivaux	143.7
102	4.5	[Esternay]	139.2
111.5	9.5	Moeurs	129.7
114.7	3.2	[Sézanne] (Iter 94)	126.5
123.7	9	La Raccroche	117.5
135.9	12.2	[Fère-Champenoise]	105.3
152.2	16.3	[Sommesous]	89
160.2	8	Soudé	81
166.2	6	Coole	75
180.2	14	Vitry-le-François	61
183.4	3.2	Marolles	57.8
190.8	7.4	[Thiéblemont-Farémont]	50.4
199.8	9	Perthes	41.4
209.3	9.5	[St-Dizier] (Iter 26)	31.9
215	5.7	Ancerville	26.2
228.7	13.7	Stainville	12.5
234.7	6	Le Petit-Maulan	6.5
241.2	6.5	[Ligny-en-Barrois]	

97 Ligny-en-Barrois–Strasbourg
(222.3km = 138 miles)

A moderately fast, undulating and occasionally hilly route from the Meuse to the Moselle then to the Rhine. The route crosses the Meuse-Moselle watershed before Toul and passes through the dense Forêt de Haye on the way to Nancy. This city and the industrialised Meurthe Valley is avoided by following the Nancy bypass to the south. After Lunéville the route takes a course avoiding the Vosges Mountains, crossing a rather bare plateau after Sarrebourg, but offering distant views of the Alsace plain on the descent, through woods, from Phalsbourg. Then skirting the foothills of the Vosges, with vineyards at Wasselonne. From Marlenheim the road runs fast and straight across the plain of Alsace.

The route is SP 'Nancy' and then 'Strasbourg'. In the opposite direction SP 'Nancy' and later 'Paris'.

An alternative route by toll motorway, Autoroute A4, is available for the final section between Phalsbourg and Strasbourg (see Iter 10).

N4		[Ligny-en-Barrois]	222.3
	10.5	10.5	[St-Aubin-sur-Aire]	211.8
	24.8	14.3	[Void]	197.5
	32.5	7.7	[Pagny-sur-Meuse]	189.8
	44.5	12	Toul Ouest Junc (Toul 3km by D960)	177.8
	45	0.5	Junc with Autoroute A31	177.3
	46	1	Junc with N74	176.3
	49.5	3.5	Junc with N411	172.8
A31	50.5	1	Toul Est Junc (Toul 4km)	171.8
A33	64	13.5	Nancy Ouest Junc of Autoroute A31/A33 (Nancy 5km)	158.3
	70	6	Nancy Sud Ouest Junc	152.3
N4B	74	4	Junc with A330 (Nancy 8km)	148.3
N4	91	17	Junc N4B/N4 (Nancy 20km by N4)	131.3
	101	10	Lunéville	121.3

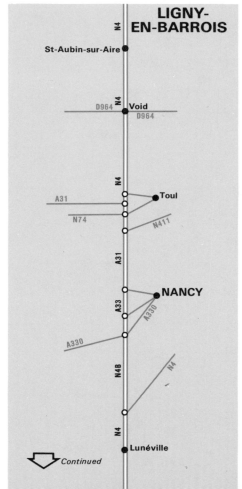

Continued

109.3	8.3	Marainviller	113
120.3	11	Ogéviller	102
120.8	0.5	Junc with D992	101.5
122.8	2	Herbéviller	99.5
126.8	4	Domèvre-sur-Vezouze	95.5
130.8	4	Blâmont	91.5
146.8	16	Héming	75.5
154.8	8	Sarrebourg	67.5
168.8	14	Mittelbronn	53.5
169.8	1	Phalsbourg/Nancy Junc of A4 Autoroute (Iter 10)	52.5
170.8	1	[Phalsbourg]	51.5
176.3	5.5	Col de Saverne (1,345ft)	46
181.3	5	Saverne	41
184.3	3	[Otterswiller]	38
188.3	4	[Marmoutier]	34
196.3	8	[Wasselonne]	26
200.3	4	Marlenheim	22
206.3	6	Furdenheim	16
209.3	3	Ittenheim	13
222.3	13	Strasbourg	

98 Ligny-en-Barrois–Colmar

(208.7km = 129.5 miles)

An undulating and occasionally hilly route, it crosses the Meuse-Moselle watershed before Toul and passes through the dense Forêt de Haye on the way to Nancy. This city and the industrialised section of the Meurthe Valley is avoided by following the Nancy bypass to the south.

After Lunéville, along the broad Meurthe valley to St-Dié, then a winding easy climb over the wooded Vosges Mountains and down through Alsatian vineyards to Colmar at the edge of the broad valley of the R Rhine. *During the winter the Col du Bonhomme is seldom obstructed.*

The route is SP 'Nancy' and then 'Strasbourg' as far as Lunéville, then SP 'St-Dié' and 'Colmar'. In the opposite direction SP 'St-Dié', then 'Nancy' and later 'Paris'.

N4			[Ligny-en-Barrois]	208.7
		10.5	10.5	[St-Aubin-sur-Aire]	198.2
		24.8	14.3	[Void]	183.9
		32.5	7.7	[Pagny-sur-Meuse]	176.2
		44.5	12	Toul Ouest Junc (Toul 3km by D960)	164.2
		45	0.5	Junc with Autoroute A31	163.7
		46	1	Junc with N74	162.7
		49.5	3.5	Junc with N411	159.2
A31		50.5	1	Toul Est Junc (Toul 4km)	158.2
A33		64	13.5	Nancy Ouest Junc of Autoroute A31/A33 (Nancy 5km)	144.7
		70	6	Nancy Sud Ouest Junc	138.7
N4B		74	4	Junc with A330 (Nancy 8km)	134.7
N4		91	17	Junc N4B/N4 (Nancy 20km by N4)	117.7
N59		101	10	Lunéville	107.7
		111.5	10.5	St-Clément	97.2

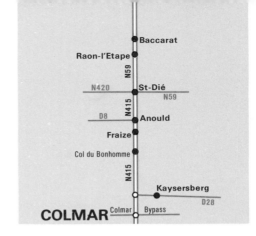

	125.8	14.3	Baccarat	82.9
	135	9.2	Raon-L'Etape	73.7
	140.5	5.5	Etival-Clairefontaine	68.2
			(Etival 1km by D424)	
N415	151.5	11	St-Dié (1,125ft)	57.2
	163.2	11.7	Anould	45.5
	166.7	3.5	Fraize (1,664ft)	42
	168.3	1.6	Plainfaing	40.4
	177	8.7	Col du Bonhomme	31.7
			(3,114ft)	
	182.7	5.7	Le Bonhomme (2,297ft)	26
	188	5.3	[Lapoutroie]	20.7
	197.2	9.2	[Kaysersberg] (974ft)	11.5
	200.7	3.5	Ammerschwihr	8
	204.2	3.5	[Ingersheim]	4.5
			(Les Trois-Epis, 8km by D11)	
	205.7	1.5	Junc with N83	3
			(Colmar bypass)	
	208.7	3	Colmar	

99 Ligny-en-Barrois – Basel

(275.5km = 171 miles)

A pretty, winding road following the Ornain valley to Gondrecourt-le-Château, thence a hilly stretch to Greux; 12% gradients either side of Vouthon-Bas. After Domrémy-la-Pucelle view of the Basilica on the hillside. Beyond Neufchâteau a hilly but fairly fast road across a very pleasant, well wooded countryside. From Épinal to Remiremont, 'built-up' alongside the R Moselle, then a winding climb over the forested Vosges mountains by the Col de Bussang (max grad 10%). *This pass is occasionally obstructed in severe winter weather.* On the far Alsatian hillside a beautiful winding descent with views over the Black Forest across the Rhine valley. Finally a level run through industrial Mulhouse and across the plain to Basel. The route is SP 'Neufchâteau', then 'Épinal', and then 'Mulhouse', and finally 'Bâle'. In St-Louis turn sharp right, SP 'Bâle Tourisme', for entry by Burgfelderstrasse.

In the opposite direction SP 'France' out of Basel by a different frontier crossing then continue by SP 'Mulhouse', then 'Epinal', and later Neufchâteau. In Neufchâteau follow SP 'Nancy' and 'Domrémy' through town, and later SP 'Bar le Duc'.

An alternative route by motorway, Autoroute A36 and A35, is available for the section between Mulhouse and Basel (see Iter 32).

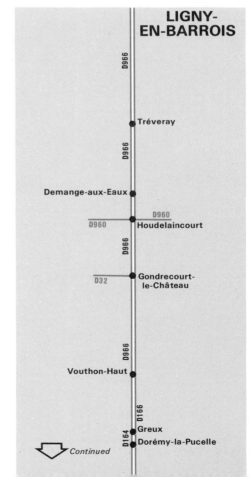

D966			Ligny-en-Barrois	275.5
	9.5	9.5	St-Amand-sur-Ornain	266
	12.5	3	Tréveray	263
	20	7.5	Demange-aux-Eaux	255.5
	23	3	Houdelaincourt	252.5
	28.5	5.5	Gondrecourt-le-Château	247
	38	9.5	Vouthon-Bas	237.5
	39	1	Vouthon-Haut	236.5
D166	42.5	3.5	Road no. change	233
D164	45	2.5	Greux	230.5
	46	1	Domrémy-la-Pucelle	229.5
			(Joan of Arc Basilique 2km)	

	50	4	Coussey	225.5
D166	56.5	6.5	Neufchâteau	219
	66.5	10	Rouvres-la-Chétive	209
	71.5	5	Châtenois	204
	76.5	5	Houécourt	199
	79.5	3	Gironcourt-sur-Vraine	196
	82.5	3	Ménil-en-Xaintois	193
	86.5	4	Rouvres-en-Xaintois	189
	95.7	9.2	[Mirecourt]	179.8
	108.7	13	[Dompaire]	166.8
	119.7	11	Darnieulles	155.8
N57	128.7	8.5	Épinal	147.3
	132.5	4.3	St-Laurent	143
	134	1.5	Dinozé	141.5
	140.3	6.3	Arches	135.2
			(Junc with Épinal eastern bypass)	
	143.8	3.5	Pouxeux	131.7
N66	154.9	11.1	Junc of N57/N66	120.6
	156.9	2	Remiremont	118.6
	168.9	12	Rupt-sur-Moselle	106.6
	179.9	11	Le Thillot (1,640ft)	95.6
	185.9	6	St-Maurice-sur-Moselle (1,800ft)	89.6
	189.9	4	Bussang (1,965ft)	85.6
	193.9	4	Col de Bussang (2,365ft)	81.6
	208.1	14.2	[Malmerspach]	67.4
	209.1	1	Moosch (1,083ft)	66.4
	211.7	2.6	Willer-sur-Thur	63.8
	213.3	1.6	Bitschwiler	62.2
	216.3	3	Thann (1,115ft)	59.2
	221.8	5.5	X-rds with N83	53.7
	229.2	7.4	Road Junc (Thann/Lutterbach Junc of Autoroute A36, 2.5km)	46.3
	231.2	2	Lutterbach	44.3
	237.2	6	Mulhouse	38.3
	243.5	6.3	[Rixheim]	32
	244.5	1	[Rixheim Junc of Autoroute A35]	31
	246	1.5	Habsheim	29.5
	255	9	Sierentz	20.5
	258	3	Bartenheim	17.5
	260	2	St-Louis/Bâle Junc of Autoroute A35	15.5
	261	1	Bartenheim-la-Chaussée	14.5
	264.5	3.5	St-Louis-la-Chaussée	11
	268.5	4	St-Louis	7
	270.5	2	Bourgfelden	5
	271	0.5	French and Swiss Customs	4.5
	275.5	4.5	**Basel (Bâle)** (Basle)	

100 Senlis–Courtenay

(169km = 105 miles)
A byways route, part of the 'Bison-Futé' (Itinéraire Bis) alternative routes network, linking Autoroute A1 and A6, and avoiding the Paris area. Passing through a mixture of pleasant well-preserved forests and open cultivated countryside. This route is well signposted in both directions by the distinctive 'Bison-Futé' signs. Note south of Meaux a short section of motorway is included.

Southbound, follow SP 'Courtenay' and 'Lyon' throughout. In the opposite direction follow SP 'Paris-Est' and 'Lille' to Junction with N4, then 'Senlis' and 'Lille'.

Note: Northbound the route is the same except between Carrefour de Prevers and Obélisque Roundabout when the D231 should be followed (5.7km shorter).

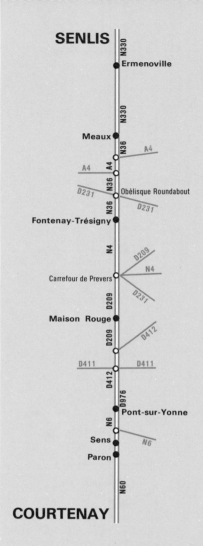

			Senlis/Meaux Junc of Autoroute A1 (Iter 1, 15)	169
N330	0.9	0.9	Roundabout (Junc Motorway slip road/ N330(Senlis 2.9km)	168.1
	12.4	11.5	Ermenonville	156.6
	17.9	5.5	Le Plessis-Belleville	151.1
N36	36.9	19	Meaux	132.1
Motor way spur	38.3	1.4	Motorway terminus	130.7
	39.9	1.6	Nanteuil Junc	129.1
	42.3	2.4	Quincy Junc/exit for southbound traffic only)	126.7
A4	45.1	2.8	Junc Motorway spur/ A4 (Meaux Junc)	123.9
N36	50.6	5.5	Coutevroult Junc (Iter 10)	118.4
	58.5	7.9	Obélisque Roundabout	110.5
D421	68.1	9.6	Fontenay-Trésigny	100.9
N4	69.2	1.1	Junc D421/N4	99.8
	75	5.8	[Rozay-en-Brie]	94
	84	9	[Vaudoy-en-Brie]	85
D209	85.8	1.8	Carrefour de Prevers *(see note)*	83.2
	101.7	15.9	Maison Rouge (X-rds with N19)	67.3
D412	113.7	12	Junc D209/D412	55.3
	119.7	6	Bray-sur-Seine	49.3
	120.6	0.9	Junc with D411	48.4
D976	124.6	4	Road no. change	44.4
N6	134.8	10.2	Pont-sur-Yonne	34.2
N360	142.2	7.4	Junc N6/N360	26.8
N60	145.6	3.4	Sens (Centre 1km)	23.4
	150	4.4	Paron	19
	169	19	**Courtenay**/Sens Junc of Autoroute A6 (Iter 2, 66)	

101 Paris Ring Road (Boulevard Périphérique)

The *Boulevard Périphérique* encircles Paris, and all the routes radiating from central Paris cross the Ring Road at one of the *'Portes'* (gateways).

On approaching the Boulevard Périphérique the following signs are used to divert the traffic streams: 'Paris-Nord', 'Paris-Est', 'Paris-Sud' and 'Paris-Ouest'. Once on the Ring Road, the main direction signs are: 'Lille, Bruxelles' for Autoroute A1; 'Metz, Nancy, Strasbourg' for A4; 'Lyon' for A6; 'Chartres, Orléans' for A10/11; and 'Rouen' for A13.

The itinerary listed below adopts a clockwise order from and to Porte de la Chapelle for convenience only.

PORTE DE LA
CHAPELLE

...

PORTE DE LA
CHAPELLE

The actual route can be used from or to any *'Porte'* and in either direction.

On joining the Ring Road move out of the near-side (right hand) lane as soon as possible.

Signs above the near-side (right hand) lane indicate the next *'Porte'* ahead and it is essential to move into this lane immediately after passing the previous *'Porte'* to leave the Ring Road.

Traffic is usually heavy and is fast-moving except at peak periods when there is considerable congestion.

The AA plan of Paris clearly shows the Ring Road and is available for a small fee from AA Overseas Routes, Fanum House, Basingstoke, RG21 2EA.

	Porte de la Chapelle	1
	(A1) (Iter 1, 15, 22) SP 'Paris-Est'	
1	Porte d'Aubervilliers (N301)	1.5
1.5	Porte de la Villette (N2) (Iter 15)	1.5
1.5	Porte de Pantin (N3)	1.5
1.5	Porte des Lilas (D117)	1
1	Porte de Bagnolet (A3 for A1) (Iter 1, 15)	1.5
1.5	Porte de Montreuil (N302)	0.5
0.5	Porte de Vincennes (N34)	1.5
1.5	Porte de Picpus (Dorée)	1.5
1.5	Porte de Bercy (A4/N4) (Iter 10, 30, 96)	1
1	Quai d'Ivry	1.5
1.5	Porte d'Ivry	1
1	Porte d'Italie (N7) (Iter 23) (Junc with Autoroute du Soleil A6)	1.5
1.5	Porte de Gentilly	0.5
0.5	Junc with Autoroute du Soleil A6	0.5
0.5	Porte d'Orléans (N20) (Iter 2, 7, 16)	1
1	Porte de Châtillon (N306)	0.5
0.5	Porte de Vanves	0.5
0.5	Porte de Brancion	1
1	Porte de la Plaine	1
1	Porte de Sèvres	1
1	Porte de St-Cloud (N10)	1
1	Porte d'Auteuil (A13) (Iter 9, 12, 81)	1
1	Porte de Passy	1.5
1.5	Porte Dauphine (Iter 81)	1
1	Porte Maillot (N13) (Iter 9, 12)	1
1	Porte de Champerret (N308)	1.5
1.5	Porte d'Asnières (N309)	0.5
0.5	Porte de Clichy (N310 for A15)	1.5
1.5	Porte de St-Ouen	1
1	Porte de Clignancourt (N14)	1
1	**Porte de la Chapelle** (A1) (Iter 1, 15, 22)	

How to use the gazetteer

The numbers which appear after the name of the town or place of interest in the gazetteer refer to the itineraries on which that place can be found.

Where to stay

The hotels selected are denoted by their AA classification. Although the system of classification is similar to the AA system in this country, the variations in the traditions and customs of hotel-keeping abroad often make identical grading difficult. The definitions are intended to indicate the type of hotel rather than the degree of merit. Motels, motor hotels and some purpose-built hotels are indicated by white stars (eg ☆☆). The symbol **Lf** against a hotel name indicates the establishment is part of the national chain of family run hotels.

★ Hotels simply furnished but clean and well kept; all bedrooms with hot and cold running water; adequate bath and lavatory facilities.

★★ Hotels offering a higher standard of accommodation: adequate bath and lavatory facilities on all main floors and some private bathrooms and/or showers.

★★★ Well-appointed hotels, with a large number of bedrooms with private bathrooms/showers.

Full details of AA-recommended hotels in France may be obtained from the publications *Travellers' Guide to France* and *Travellers' Guide to Europe*.

Where to eat

Restaurants have been selected on the basis of their location and the price of the meals they provide.

Where to camp

The campsites listed have been recommended to us by our members and/or our associate overseas clubs. Full details of AA-recommended campsites may be obtained from the publication *Camping and Caravanning in Europe*.

Gothic splendour on the Church of St Vulfran, Abbeville

ABBEVILLE 21, 22, 58
Situated on the River Somme, Abbeville was severely damaged during both World Wars; however several old buildings have survived, including the fine Gothic Church of St-Vulfran and an 18th-century château, Bagatelle. The museum contains prehistoric finds and medieval works of art.

Where to stay
★**Conde**, 14 place de la Libération ☎(22)240633
★**Jean Bart**, 5-7 rue Ste-Catherine ☎(22)242171

Where to eat
Auberge de la Corne 32 chaussée du Bois
Au Châteaubriant 1 place Hôtel de Ville
L'Escale en Picardie 15 rue Teinturiers

AGAY 78
A small seaside resort in a sheltered position on a picturesque sandy bay.

Where to eat
Auberge de la Rade, boulevard Bord de Mer

Where to camp
Camping Agay Soleil Route de Cannes
Camping Rives de l'Agay, Avenue due Grataodis
Camping Vallée du Paradis, Route du Grataodis

At Dramont (Le) (2km SW)

Where to stay
★★★**Sol et Mar**, au Dramont ☎(94)952560

Where to camp
Camping International du Dramont

AGEN 19, 88
Lying on the right bank of the River Garonne, Agen is a well known market town specialising in fruit and vegetables. It has a fine museum which boasts the 'Venus-de-Mas', a green marble statue, and several etchings by Goya. At the edge of the town a 19th-century aqueduct takes the canal across the River Garonne.

Where to stay
☆☆**Ibis**, Ilot 5, boulevard Cornot ☎(53)473123
☆☆**Perigord**, 42 place XIV Juillet ☎(53)661001
☆☆**Residence Jacobins,** 1 place Jacobins ☎(53)470331

Where to eat
Bar du pont de la garde, 30 boulevard de la Liberté
Sous les platones, 42 cours du IXe de Ligne

Where to camp
Camping Municipal avenue de G1-Leclerc.

AIGUEBELLE 77
Where to stay
★★★**Roches Fleuries** (4km on N599 to Le Lavondu, ☎(94)710507
★★★**Plage** ☎(94)058074 (no restaurant)

AIGUILLON 19
Where to camp
Camping Municipal Vieu Moulin 500m E of village off D666.

AIRE-SUR-LA-LYS 25
A picturesque little town in northern France with attractive streets, busy markets and several fine monuments.

Where to stay
★**Europ,** 14 Grand place ☎(21)390432 (no restaurant)

Where to eat
Hostellerie Trois Mousquetaires Château de la Redoute

AISEY-SUR-SEINE 94
Where to stay
★**Roy Lf** ☎(80)932163

AIX-EN-PROVENCE, 4
Formerly the capital of Provence, Aix has retained much of its 17th- and 18th-century character, particularly in the area surrounding the Cours Mirabeau, where pavement cafés and shops mingle with elegant mansions. The town has now been developed as a spa. It is noted for its almonds, a speciality being the calisson – an iced, almond-flavoured biscuit. Aix is particularly busy during the summer when several festivals are held, including the International Music Festival during July and August. Places of interest include the Romanesque/Gothic cathedral, the Tapestry Museum in the old Archbishop's Palace and the Cézanne Studis, devoted to the work of artist Paul Cézanne, who was born in Aix in 1839.

Where to stay
★★★**Manoir Lf** rue d'Entrecosteaux 8 ☎(42)262720 (no restaurant)
☆☆☆**Novotel Beaumanoir** Résidence Beaumanoir (A8) ☎(42)274750
☆☆☆**Novotel Sud** Périphérique Sud, Arc de Meyran ☎(42)279049

★★★**Paul Cézanne** 40 avenue V-Hugo ☎(42)263473 (no restaurant)
☆☆**Campanile** ZAC du Jas de Bouffan ☎(42)594073
☆☆**Ibis** Chemin des Infirmeries ☎(42)279820
★★**Renaissance** 4 boulevard de la République ☎(42)260422 (no restaurant)
★★**Residence Rotunde** 15 avenue des Belges ☎(42)262988 (no restaurant)

Where to eat
Abbaye des Cordeliers 21 rue Lieutaud
Le Clams 22 Cours Sextius
Flunchs 2 avenue des Belges

Where to camp
Arc en ciel Au Pont des 3 Sautets
Chantecler Av du Val

ALENÇON 38, 39, 59, 60
An ancient fortress town famous for the manufacture of lace since the 17th century. Examples may be seen in the Art Gallery and Lace Museum. The house where Ste-Thérèse de l'Enfant Jesus was born in 1873 attracts many pilgrims.

Where to stay
☆☆**Campanile**, route de Paris ☎(33)295385
★★**France**, 3 rue St-Blaise ☎(33)262636 (no restaurant)
★★**Gare Lf** 50 avenue Wilson ☎(33)290393
★**Industrie Lf** 20-22 place du G1-de-Gaulle ☎(33)290651
★**Paris**, 26 rue D-Papin ☎(33)250164 (no restaurant)

Where to eat
Le Ralais de l'Étoile, 25 cours Clemenceau

Where to camp
Camping Guéramé, rue de Guéramé

ALTKIRCH 32
An old town in a pleasant situation overlooking the River Ill. There is an interesting church, and the Sundgau Museum, in the Place Hôtel-de-Ville, has exhibits relating to the archaeology and folklore of the region.

Where to stay
★**Sundgovienne Lf** (3.5km W on D419) route de Belfort ☎(89)409718
★**Terrasse Lf**, 44-46 rue du 3e-Zouave ☎(89)409802

AMBERT 71

Where to stay
★★**Livradois**, 1 place du Livradois ☎(73)821001
★**Gare**, 17 avenue de la Gare ☎(73)820022

Where to eat
Le Relais Des Routiers, 4 place du Général-Courtial

AMBOISE 61
A picturesque old town overlooking the River Loire. Amboise's principal attraction is the splendid château, built during the 15th century on the site of a feudal fortress. It contains the beautiful Chapel of St-Hubert, set high on the ramparts, and the Minimes Tower with the unusual feature of a ramp-type stairway which can be mounted by a horseman. The town also has associations with Leonardo da Vinci, who lived at Clos-Lucé from 1516 until his death in 1519. His 15th century house is open to the public and contains models of some of the machines he designed.

AMIENS 22
Set on the banks of the River Somme, this old capital of Picardy provides a pleasant mixture of ancient riverside streets and modern development following extensive war damage. The contrast of old and new is reflected in Amiens' most impressive buildings, the 13th century Gothic cathedral and the modern Perret Tower. Jules Verne, the novelist, spent the last years of his life in the town and this is commemorated in the Centre de Documentation Jules Verne.

Where to stay
★★★**Grand Hôtel de l'Universe**, 2 rue Noyen ☎(22)915251 (no restaurant)
★★**Carlton-Belfort**, 42 rue de Noyon ☎(22)922644
★★**Gritti**, 8 place A-Fiquel ☎(22)913632
☆☆**Ibis**, 'Le Centrum' ☎(22)925733 rue Ml-de-Lattre de Tassigny
★★**Nord-Sud**, 11 rue Gresset ☎(22)915903
★★**Paix**, 8 rue de la République ☎(22)913921 (no restaurant)
★**Normandie**, 1 bis rue Lamartine ☎(22)917499 (no restaurant)

Where to eat
Bonne Auberge, route Nationale
Josephine, 20 rue Sire-Firmin-Leroux
Mermoz, 7 rue J-Mermoz

LES ANDELYS 9, 12
This little town consists of the twin settlements of Grand and Petite Andelys. The former is a shopping centre with a busy market, the latter a charming old town in a beautiful setting beside the River Seine. To the south the imposing clifftop remains of Château Gaillard provide magnificent views over the Seine Valley. The château was a great fortress built by Richard the Lionheart in the late 12th century as a defence against the King of France entering the Seine Valley.

Where to stay
★**Chaine d'Or Lf**, 27 rue Grande, place St-Sauveur ☎(32)540031
★**Normandie**, 1 rue Grande ☎(22)541052

Where to eat
Paris, 10 avenue République

ANDERNOS-LES-BAINS 85

Where to camp
Fontaine-Vielle, 4 boulevard du Cl-Wurtz
Pleine Fôret

ANGERS 41, 42, 62, 63, 86
Spread over both banks of the River Maine, Angers, the ancient capital of Anjou, is an important textile and wine-producing centre. The castle, dating originally from the 9th century, has a superb collection of old tapestries including the famous 'Apocalypse Tapestry', nearly 170 metres long and dating from the late 14th century. The cathedral, built between the 12th and 13th centuries, contains stained glass from several different periods and the former St-Jean Hospital, retaining many 12th century features, is now the home of the Lurçat Museum. The town also features in the Anjou Festival during June and July, and the Anjou Wine Festival, which is held earlier in the year.

Where to stay
★★★**Anjou**, 1 boulevard Ml-Foch ☎(41)882482
☆☆☆**Mercure**, boulevard Carnot ☎(40)437656
★★**Boule d'Or**, 27 boulevard Carnot ☎(41)437656
☆☆**Climat de France**, rue du Château-d'Orgemont
★★**Croix de Guerre**, 23 rue Château-Gontier ☎(41)886659
★★**France**, 8 place de la Gare ☎(41)884942
★★**Progrès**, 26 rue D-Papin ☎(41)881014 (no restaurant)
★★**Univers**, 2 rue de la Gare ☎(41)884358 (no restaurant)

Where to eat
L'Entrecôte, avenue Joxé
La Haute Chaine, 5/7 boulevard
Ayrault
Le Toussaint, 7 rue Toussaint
Le Vert d'Eau, 9 boulevard
G-Dumesnil

Where to camp
**Camping Campexel Lac de
Maine**
Camping Parc de la Haye

ANGOULÊME 83
Overlooking the River Charente is the
old fortified town of Angoulême, which
still retains much of its medieval
charm. The old town walls are now
converted into attractive boulevards
affording fine views of the surrounding
countryside. A notable example of
Romanesque building is the ornate
12th century Cathedral of St-Pierre
which is covered on one side by a
scene of seventy figures depicting
Judgement Day. Other places of
interest are the Chapel of Cordeliers,
Municipal Museum and the Musée de
la Société Archeologique.

Where to stay
★★★**Grand France,** 1 place des
Halles ☎(45)954795
★★**Epi d'Or,** 66 boulevard
R-Chabasse ☎(45)956764
(no restaurant)
★**Flore,** 414 route de Bordeaux
☎(45)928055

Where to eat
Le Chandelier, 7 rue de Saintes à
St-Cybard
Le Palma, 4 rampe d'Aguesseau
Terminus, place Gare

Where to camp
**Camping Municipal de
Bourgines**

ANTIBES 4, 78
In a delightful position between two
bays, Antibes is the centre for the local
flower-growing trade and specialises
in carnations and roses. The 16th
century Grimaldi Château overlooks
the old part of the town and contains a
museum devoted to the work of
Picasso. Nearby is a fort where
Napoleon was once imprisoned.

Where to stay
★★★**First,** 21 avenue des Chênes
☎(93)618737
☆☆**Mercator** chemin des Groules,
quartier de la Brague (4km N via N7)
☎(93)335075 (no restaurant)

At Cap D'Antibes
★★★**Gardiole,** chemin de la
Garoupe ☎(93)613503

★★★**Residence du Cap,** 161
boulevard J.F. Kennedy
☎(93)610944
★★**Beau Site,** 141 boulevard
Kennedy ☎(93)615343
(no restaurant)

Where to eat
L'Armoise, 2 rue Touraque
Auberge Provençale, place
Nationale
La Caléche, 25 rue Vauban
Le Caméo, place Nationale
Du Bastion, 1 avenue Gén-Maizière
L'Ecurie Royale, 33 rue Vauban
Flunchs, Chemin St-Claude
La Marguerite, 11 rue Sadi Carnot
L'Oasis, 35 boulevard Président-
Wilson
L'Oursin, 16 rue République

Where to camp
Logis de la Brague, RN7
Pylône

At Biot (7km N on N7 & A8)
Airotel Parc l'Eden, chemin du Val
de Pome
Embruns
Prés, quartier la Romaine

At Brague (La) (4km N on N7)
Frênés

ARCACHON 85
This popular holiday resort can be
found in the Bassin D'Arcachion, a
natural basin renowned for its oyster
beds and fish farms. The town nestles
amongst dunes and pine woods and
has an aquarium and museum, a bird
sanctuary and various sports facilities.

Where to stay
★★★**Arc,** 89 boulevard Plage
☎(56)830685 (no restaurant)
★★★**Tamarins,** 253 boulevard
Côte d'Argent ☎ (56)225096

Where to eat
Bayonne, 9 cours Lomarque
Chez Boron, 15 rue Prof-Jolyet

Where to camp
**Camping Municipal des
Abatilles,** allées C. Peguy

ARDRES 1, 25
★★★**Grand Clément,** place du
Gl-Leclerc ☎(21)354066
★★**Relais Lf,** boulevard C-Senlecq
☎(21) 354200
★**Chaumière,** 67 avenue de
Rouville ☎(21)354124
(no restaurant)

Where to eat
La Bonne Auberge, à Brêmes

Where to camp
At Autingues (2km S)
St-Louis, 197 rue Leulene

ARÈS 85

Where to camp
Abberts
Canadienne, route du Cap Ferret
Cigale
Camping Municipal Goelands

ARGENTAN 39
This small town on the banks of the
River Orne is famous for needle-point
lace, a craft practised by the nuns of the
Benedictine abbey, where examples
may sometimes be seen (on request).
Much of Argentan has been rebuilt
after suffering severe war damage in
1944 when it was the site of the last
battle of Normandy.

Where to stay
★★★**Renaissance Lf,** avenue de
la 2E D-B ☎(33)671611

Where to eat
Le Normandy, 35 avenue de la 2E
D-B

Where to camp
**At Mauvaisville (2.8km NE off
N158)**
Camping Val de Baize

ARGENTON-SUR-CREUSE 36
On the banks of the River Creuse, this
small, quaint town is interesting for its
old galleried buildings as well as the
Chapel of Notre-Dames-des-Bancs.

Where to stay
★★**Manor de Bolsvilliers,** 11 rue
Moulin de Bord (no restaurant)
★**France Lf,** 8 rue J-J-Rousseau,

Where to eat
Chez Maître Jean, 67 au Rollinat

ARRAS 1, 15, 25, 90, 91, 94
Despite extensive war damage
sustained between 1914 and 1918
the town has managed to preserve
much of its medieval Flemish
character. Most of its buildings have
been restored in their original styles
and there are many arcaded streets
and gabled houses. Places of interest
include the cathedral and Palace of St-
Vaast, dating from the late 18th
century, the fine citadel established by
Vauban in the 17th century, the 18th
century law courts and the 17th
century town hall.

Where to stay
★★★**Univers,** 3 place Croix Rouge
☎(21)213401
★★**Astoria,** 12 place Ml-Foch
☎(21)210814
★★**Commerce,** 24 rue Gambetta
☎(21)211007 (no restaurant)

★★**Moderne,** 1 boulevard
Faidherbe ☎(21)233957
★**Chánzy Lf,** 8 rue Chánzy
☎(21)210202

Where to eat
Grandes Arcades, 8 Grand Place
Au Point du Jour, 13 avenue
Michonneau
La Rapière, 44 Grand Place
Aux Trompettes d'Artillerie, 209
rue de Cambrai
Victor Hugo, 11 place V-Hugo

ARROMANCHES 11
A seaside resort which became
internationally famous as the site for
'Mulberry B', one of the two artificial
harbours which were towed piece by
piece across the Channel and used for
landing troops and supplies during the
Allies during the period following the
D-Day invasion. On 6 June 1984 HM
The Queen took the salute here for ex-
servicemen while attending the 40th
anniversary commemoration along the
Invasion Coast.

ASPRES-SUR-BUËCH 80
An interesting town with natural
mineral springs and a restored
Romanesque church.

AUBAGNE 76
This town has been the home of the
French Foreign Legion since 1962
and has an interesting museum
dealing with the history of the
regiment.

Where to eat
Flunchs, Route de Géménos
Le Relais des Routiers, La
Tourtelle

Where to camp
Claire – Fontaine, route de la
Tuilliere

AUBENAS 72
A small ancient town overlooking the
River Ardèche. There are some
attractive 16th century houses.

Where to eat
Le Fournil, 34 rue 4 Septembre

Where to camp
Camping Municipal Pins

AUCH 88
Leading down the hillside from Auch
to the River Gers below is a 232-step
stairway which has a magnificent
statue of d'Artagnan on one of its
landings. The old quarter of the town
has a folk museum, a fine cathedral
and a 14th century former prison,
reached via the Place Salinis.

Where to stay
★★★**France,** place de la Libération
☎(62)050044
★★**Poste,** 5 rue-C-Desmoulins
☎(62)050236

Where to camp
Camping Municipal, S on N21
(route de Tarbes)

AUVILLERS LES FORGES 91
Where to stay
★★**Lenoir Lf,** ☎(24)543011

Where to eat
Arret des Routiers

AUXERRE 2, 66
A town of distinctly medieval
appearance on the banks of the River
Yonne containing numerous 15th
century Renaissance-style buildings.
The most imposing feature is the
Cathedral of St-Etienne, built between
the 13th and the 16th centuries,
which dominates the riverside area.
Other places of interest include the
Leblanc-Duverny Museum, which
contains some magnificent 18th
century tapestries. Auxerre is
surrounded by vineyards and orchards
and has become a popular touring
centre for the neighbouring region.

Where to stay
★★★**Clairions Lf,** avenue Worms
☎(86)468564
★★★**Maxime,** 2 quai de la Marine
☎(86)521419
★★**Cygne,** 14 rue du 24 Août
☎(86)522651 (no restaurant)
★★**Fontaine,** 12 place C-Lepère
☎(86)524080 (no restaurant)
★★**Normandie,** 41 boulevard
Vauban ☎(86)525780
(no restaurant)
★★**Seignelay,** 2 rue Pont
☎(86)520348

Where to eat
Courte-Paille, N6 – 200m from A6
exit
La Grilladerie, 45 bis boulevard
Vauban
Le Relais le Vaulabelle, 36
boulevard Vaulabelle
La Terrasse de la Nouvelle Gare,
7 rue P-Doumer

AUXONNE 95
A former frontier town which has
retained traces of its ancient
fortifications and is noted for its
beautiful shaded gardens overlooking
the River Saône. Napoleon was
stationed here during the early part of
his military career and there is a section
in the local museum dealing with this
period of his life.

Where to eat
★**Corbeau Lf,** 1 rue de Berbis

Where to camp
Camping Municipal Arquebuse

AVALLON 2, 66
A picturesque old town perched on a
spur overlooking the Cousin Valley.
The medieval ramparts encircling the
town centre have been converted into
a pleasant promenade. Within the
ramparts are a number of interesting
old buildings including the Church of
St-Lazare, dating originally from the
12th century.

Where to stay
★★★**Moulin des Ruats,** Vallée du
Cousin (4.5km W)
☎(86)340714
★★**Relais Fleuri Lf,** (5km E on N6)
☎(86)340285

Where to eat
Les Capucins, 6 avenue D-Doumer
Cheval Blanc, 55 rue Lyon
Le Relais des Minimes, 84 rue de
Lyon

Where to camp
**Camping Municipal Sous
Roche**

AVIGNON 4, 5, 75
The fortified town of Avignon still
retails a medieval appearance since it is
encircled by ramparts and dominated
by the massive Palace of Popes. The
ancient palace stands near to the
Romanesque cathedral and is
overlooked by the Rocher-des-Domes.
Although now incomplete, the famous
Pont d'Avignon remains of interest and
dates back to 1177. The town is host
to the Festival of Dramatic Art and
Dance each year and is a good base for
a touring holiday.

Where to stay
☆☆☆**Mercure Avignon – Sud,**
route Marseille – la Barbière
☎(90)889110
☆☆☆**Novotel Avignon – Sud,**
route de Marseille (N7)
☎(90)876236
★★**Angleterre Lf,** 29 Boulevard de
Raspail ☎(90)863431
(no restaurant)
★★**Midi,** 53 rue de la République
☎(90)821556 (no restaurant)
★**Jaquemart,** 3 rue F-David
☎(90)863471 (no restaurant)
Where to eat
Auberge de France, 28 place
Horloge
Au Pied de Boeuf, 49 route
Marseille
Brunel, 49 rue Balance
Cabaret Neuf, Cantarel – Montfavett

Le Férigoulo, 30 rue J-Vernet
Flunchs, 11 boulevard Raspail
La Fourchette, 7 due Racine
Les Mayenques, 41 bis route Lyon
Le Rallye Bar, 18 boulevard Limbert
St-Didier, 41 rue Saraillerie
Trois Clefs, 26 rue Trois Faucons
Le Vernet, 58 rue J-Vernet

At Avignon – Nord
Flunchs, RN542 – ZAC du Tronquet

Avignon – Sud
Courte – Paille, Autoroute A7

Where to camp
Bagatelle
Camping Municipal St-Bénézet,
lile de la Barthelasse

AVRANCHES 40, 41, 47, 48, 50
Although one of the oldest known
towns in Normandy, Avranches is best
known for its proximity to Mont-St-
Michel. A fine view of this imposing
fortified island is provided from the
Jardin des Plantes (Botanical
Gardens). Early manuscripts relating
mainly to the Abbey of Mont-St-Michel
are contained within the Avranchin
Museum. Henry II did public penance
in Avranches following the murder of
Thomas à Becket and a paving stone
known locally as *La plateforme* on the
site of the former cathedral marks the
spot. A more recent monument in the
town square commemorates the area
where General Patton had his
headquarters while planning his major
offensive in 1944.

Where to stay
★★**Croix d'Or,** 83 rue de la
Constitution ☎(33)580488
★★**St-Michel,** 5 place Gl-Patton
☎(33)580191

Where to eat
Au Rendez-Vous des Routiers,
107 rue de la Liberté
Le Relais des Routiers, 70 rue de
la Constitution
La Source, 25 rue de Cdt-Bindel,
route de Mortain

Where to camp
Camping Mares, 10 rue de Verdun

AX-LES-THERMES 89
An ancient spa town with sulphur and
sodium springs. There is a casino and
good sporting facilities.

Where to stay
★★★**Royal Thermal,** esplanade
de Couloubret ☎(61)642251
★★**Moderne Lf,** 20 avenue du
Dr-Gomma ☎(61)642024
★★**Roy René Lf,** 11 avenue du
Dr-Gomma ☎(61)642228

★**Lauzerale,** promenade du
Couloubret ☎(61)642070

AZAY-LE-RIDEAU 62
The outstanding feature of the town is
its magnificent 16th century
Renaissance château, lying amid
parkland on the bank of the River Indre.
The château contains fine furnishings
and tapestries and has a beautiful main
staircase.

Where to stay
★★**Grand Monarque Lf,**
☎(47)433008

Where to eat
Le Relais de la Gare, 59 avenue de
la Gare

BANDOL 76
An attractive resort, noted for its
equable climate and for its locally
produced red wine. A museum of
wines and spirits is open during the
summer months.

Where to stay
★★**Bale,** 62 rue Marçon
☎(94)294092 (no restaurant)
★**Golf,** Plage de Renécros
☎(94)294583 (no restaurant)
★★**Provençal,** rue des Écoles
☎(94)295211
★★**Resérve,** route de Sanary
☎(94) 294271

Where to eat
Grotte Provençale, 21 rue
Dr-L-Marçon
Le Lotus, place L-Artaud
Réserve, oute de Sanary

Where to camp
Vallongue, 3 km NW on N559.

BARBEZIEUX 83
This small town is perched on a hillside
and has a restored 11th century
church and parts of a 15th century
castle, which now houses the town
museum.

Where to stay
★★**Boule d'Or Lf,** 11 boulevard
Gambetta ☎(45)782272

BARBIZON 23
This well known resort on the edge of
the Forest of Fontainbleu has long
been a favoured haunt of painters.
Millet, Rousseau and others
established the 'Barbizon School' of
painting here in the mid 19th century.

Where to stay
★★**Charmettes,** Grand Rue
☎(6)0664021

Where to eat
Le Relais de Barbizon

BAR-LE-DUC 93
Despite a good deal of
industrialisation, the town has retained
a picturesque old quarter and the fine
Church of St Etienne, dating from the
15th century. The Voie Sacrée (Sacred
Way) runs from Bar to Verdun,
crossing one of the battlefields of
World War I.

BARNEVILLE-CARTERET 40
A small fishing port and marina, this
seaside resort with its broad sandy
beaches faces the Channel Islands.

Where to stay
At Barneville Plage
★★**Isles Lf,** boulevard Maritime
☎(33)549076

Where to camp
Camping Pré Normand

Where to stay
At Carteret
★★**Angleterre,** 4 rue de Paris
☎(33)548604
★★**Marine,** 2 rue de Paris
☎(33)548696
★★**Plage et du Cap,** Le Cap
☎(33)548696

Where to eat
L'Hermitage-Maison Duhamel,
at the port

Where to camp
Camping Airotel du Bocage

BARREME 80

Where to camp
Napoléon

BAR-SUR-AUBE 30
A small market town girdled by
boulevards built on the site of its
medieval ramparts. The church of St-
Pierre contains several 12th-14th
century features

Where to stay
★**Commerce,** 38 rue Nationale
☎(25)270876

Where to camp
Camping Gravière, rue des
Varennes

BAR-SUR-SEINE 94
A small town beside the River Seine
with some picturesque old houses.
The Renaissance-style Church of St-
Etienne is noted for its 16th century
stained glass.

Where to stay
★★**Barséquanais,** 7 avenue
Gl-Leclerc ☎(25)388275

LA BAULE 55, 60
A charming town, amid pine woods,
which has become one of the most
fashionable resorts on the French
Atlantic Coast. La Baule enjoys a mild
climate and its fine beaches and wealth
of sporting and entertainment facilities
have ensured its continuing popularity

Where to stay
★★★**Majestic,** esplanade F-André
☎(40)602486 (no restaurant)
★★**Bellevue Plage,** 27 boulevard
Océan ☎(40)602855
★★**Concorde,** 1 avenue de la
Concorde ☎(40)602309
(no restaurant)
★★**Palmeraie Lf,** 7 allée
Cormorans ☎(40)602441
★★**Rivièra,** 16 avenue des Lilas
☎(40)602897
★★**Welcome,** 7 avenue des
Impairs ☎(40)603025
(no restaurant)

Where to eat
Au St-Christophe, 89 avenue
H-Bertho

Where to camp
Camping Ajoncs d'Or
Camping Municipal, avenue
P-Minot & avenue R-Flandin
Camping Róseraire, 20 avenue
J-Sohier, route du Golf

BAUMES-LES-DAMES 17
A small industrial town noted for the
manufacture of pipes, Baumes-les-
Dames occupies an ideal situation,
nestling in the thickly forested Doubs
Valley. It has become a popular holiday
resort and excursion centre.

Where to stay
At Hyèvre-Paroisse (7km E)
★★**Ziss,** (N83) ☎(81)840788

BAYEUX 11
Founded in the Roman era, Bayeux's
more recent distinction is that it was
the first town in France to be liberated
in 1944, having miraculously suffered
no war damage. The Cathedral of
Notre-Dame dates from 1077 and is
situated in the old quarter of the town
with its distinctly medieval flavour.
Opposite the cathedral, the former
Bishop's Palace contains the world
famous Queen Matilda's Tapestry. A
magnificent 231ft-long creation of
embroidery, believed to have been
worked in Britain, it traces the history
of the Norman Conquest of England in
the manner of a modern strip cartoon.

Where to stay
★★**Lion d'Or Lf,** 71 rue St-Jean
☎(31)920690

Where to eat
La Colombe, 13 route de Caen,
St-Vigor-le-Grand
Gourmets, place St-Patrice

Where to camp
Camping Municipal Calvados,
boulevard d'Eindhoven

BAYONNE 8, 85, 87
Famous for its delicious ham products
and for chocolate, Bayonne is an
important industrial and commercial
centre. The yearly Bayonne Festival
features local history and Basque
folklore, which can also be traced in the
Basque Museum. Nearby, the Bonnat
Museum has many beautiful works of
art, and in the suburb of St-Esprit is the
magnificent Cathedral of Ste-Marie
with its high elegant spires, fine
stained glass and 14th century
cloisters.

Where to stay
★★**Agora,** avenue J-Rostand
☎(59)633090
★★**Capagorry,** 14 rue Thiers
☎(59)254822 (no restaurant)
★**Basses-Pyrénées,** 12 rue Tour
de Sault ☎(59)590029

Where to eat
Auberge Cheval Blanc, 68 rue
Bourgneuf
Beluga, 15 rue Tonneliers
Euzkalduna, 61 rue Pannecau
La Tanière, 53 avenue Cap,
Resplondy par allées Boufflers

Where to camp
Airotel la Chêneraie, 4km NE of
N117 Pau Road

BEAUGENCY 61
A town of distinctly medieval
appearance on the banks of the River
Loire. Fragments of Beaugency's
original fortifications have been
retained, including the massive 11th
century keep, the Tour de l'Horloge
gateway and the Tour du Diable, which
afforded protection for the 14th
century bridge. The 15th century
Château Dunois contains an
interesting regional museum.

Where to stay
★★★**Ecu de Bretagne Lf,** place
du Martroi ☎(38)446760

BEAUMONT-SUR-SARTHE 39
A quiet little town on the right bank of
the river.

Where to stay
★**Barque,** 1 place de la libération
☎(43)970016
★**Chemin de Fer Lf,** La Gare
(1.5km E on D26) ☎(43)970005

Where to camp
**Camping Municipal du Val de
Sarthe,** route de Mamers

BEAUNE 2, 17, 29
A beautiful old city in the heart of the
Burgundy vineyards. Much of
Beaune's medieval splendour has
been retained in the shape of ancient
houses and well-preserved ramparts,
parts of which have now been
converted into wine cellars. One of the
most outstanding buildings is the
Hôtel-Dieu, founded as a hospital for
the poor during the 15th century and
continuing to perform the same
function, with very little structural
alteration, until the 1970s, when it
became a home for the aged. Other
places of interest include the Church of
Notre-Dame, noted for its frescoes and
tapestries and the Burgundy Wine
Museum, housed in the former
residence of the Dukes of Burgundy.

Where to stay
★★★**Cep,** 27 rue Maufoux
☎(80)223548
☆☆☆**PLM,** (A6) ☎(80)214612
★★★**Poste,** 3 boulevard
Clemenceau ☎(80)220811
★★**Bourgogne Lf,** avenue C-de-
Gaulle ☎(80)222200
★★**Central Lf,** 2 rue V-Millot
☎(80)247724
☆☆**Climat de France Lf,** ZA de la
Chartreuse ☎(80)227410
☆☆**Samotel,** route de Pommard
(N74) ☎(80)223555

Where to eat
Auberge Bourguignonne, 4
place Madeleine
Auberge de la Gare, 11 avenue
des Lyonnais
Chez Maxime, 3 place Madeleine
Le Malmedy, 6 rue du Lieut-Dupuis
Le Relais de France, 13 faubourg
Bretonnière

Where to camp
**Camping Municipal Cent
Vignes,** 10 rue A-Dubois

BEAUVAIS 22, 92
The town's most important building,
the Cathedral of St-Pierre, was spared
the destruction that much of the town
experienced during 1940. A fine
example of 13th century architecture,
the cathedral was initially destined to
be one of the most ambitious Gothic
structures ever to be built, but the

original plan was never completed. Nevertheless the cathedral has many outstanding features. Adjoining it, the Galerie Nationale de Tapisserie contains fine displays of Beauvais-famous tapestries.

Where to stay
☆☆☆**Mercure,** ZAC St-Lazare, avenue Montaigne ☎(4)4020336
★**Commérce Lf,** 11 & 13 rue Chambiges ☎(4)4451258
★**Palais,** 9 rue St-Nicholas ☎(4)4451258

Where to eat
Court-Paille, on N1 Beauvais-Paris

Where to camp
Camping Municipal, chemin de Carmard

BEAUVALLON 77

Where to stay
★**Marie Louise,** Guerrevieille (1 km NE) ☎(94)960605

BELFORT 17, 31, 32

A busy industrial centre which has for centuries guarded the Belfort Gap, a pass between the Jura and Vosges mountain ranges, which provided a natural route for invaders. The old quarter, which was turned into a fortified star-shaped town by Vauban during the 17th century, huddles on the left bank of the River Savoureuse, while the modern city spreads itself over the right to a more contemporary design. Both are overlooked by Vauban's citadel and by the 72ft Lion of Belfort, a sandstone sculpture by Bartholdi (the creator of the Statue of Liberty in New York harbour) which commemorates the town's heroic resistance when besieged by the Germans in 1870.

Where to stay
★★★**Grand Lion,** rue G-Clemenceau ☎(84)211700

Where to eat
Le Relais d'Alsace, 5 avenue de la Laurencie
Thiers, 9 rue Thiers

At Danjoutin (3km S)

Where to stay
☆☆☆**Mercure,** rue de Dr-Jacquot ☎(84)215501

BELIN-BÉLIET 8

Where to stay
★**Alienor d'Aquitaine Lf,** ☎(56)880123

BELLAC 42

In a picturesque setting overlooking the River Vincou, Bellac is famous as the birthplace of the dramatist Jean Giraudoux. The house where he was born in 1882 has been preserved as a memorial and another interesting feature of the town is the local church which has two naves, one Romanesque and one Gothic.

Where to eat
La Promenade, 4 rue Denfert-Rochereau

BERGERAC 87, 88

On the banks of the River Dordogne, the premier industry in this town is tobacco growing, with the only Tobacco Museum in France being housed in the Town Hall. Wine producing is also important and the nearby Monbazillac Vineyards can be visited from here.

Where to stay
★★**Bordeaux Lf,** 38 place Gambetta ☎(53)571283

Where to eat
Le Cyrano, 2 boulevard Montaigne

BERGUES 14

A small town which has retained its 17th century Flemish appearance, with old walls and a surrounding moat surviving from Vauban's fortifications.

Where to stay
☆☆**Motel 25,** (2km S at interchange Autoroute Lille-Dunkerque) ☎(28)687900
★**Tonneller,** 4 rue de Mont de Piété ☎(28)687005

Where to eat
Cornet d'Or, 26 rue Espagnole

BERNAY 38, 59

The Basilica Notre-Dame-de-la-Couture, which has a roof composed of wood, is just one of several old churches to be found in this ancient town which developed rapidly around its abbey during the 11th century.

Where to stay
★**Angleterre et Cheval Blanc Lf,** 10 rue Gl-de-Gaulle ☎(32)431259

Where to eat
Le Relais du Chemin de Fer, 29, boulevard Dubus
Trois Vals, route Rouen

Where to camp
Camping Municipal

BESANÇON 17, 27

An ancient town, lying in a loop of the River Doubs, which is the administrative capital of the Franche–Comté region and has also become a popular tourist centre. Besançon has been associated with the manufacture of clocks and watches since the 17th century and a section of the Fine Arts Museum is devoted to the history of this trade. A 19th century astronomical clock with some 30,000 moving parts can also be seen in the town. Besançon's most outstanding feature is the lofty Citadel, established by Vauban in the early 18th century on the site of a medieval fortress. This fortification now encompasses a zoo and several museums, including one devoted to the work of the French Resistance. Other places of interest include the fine 18th century cathedral, the house where Victor Hugo was born at 140 Grande Rue and a number of other attractive old buildings and churches.

Where to stay
☆☆**Novotel,** 22 bis rue de Trey ☎(81)501466 (no restaurant)
☆☆**Ibis,** 4 avenue Carnot ☎(81)803311
★**Family,** 13 rue du Gl-Lecourbe ☎(81)813392 (no restaurant)
★**Gambetta,** 13 rue Gambetta ☎(81)820233

Where to eat
Carnot. 8 avenue Carnot
Tour de la Pelote, 39 quai Strasbourg

Where to camp
At Roche-lez-Beaupré, (NE on N83)
Camping Municipal Plage

BESSINES-SUR-GARTEMPE 36

Where to stay
☆☆☆**Toit de Chaume,** (5km S on Limoges rd) ☎(55)760102
★★**Vallée,** (N20) ☎(55)760166

Where to eat
Bellevue

Where to camp
At Mortetolles-sur-Semme,
(4.5km N on N20)
Camping Municipal

BÉTHUNE 1, 25, 90

An industrial town on the Aire Canal.

Where to stay
★★**Vieux Beffroi,** 48 Grand Place ☎(21)251500
★**Bernard et Gare Lf,** 3 place de la Gare ☎(21)572002

Where to eat
Le Moulin Lille, 710 rue du Pont de Pierce

BÉZIERS 5, 70
This wine-producing town overlooking the River Orb has many tree-lined avenues. There is a statue to Paul-Riquet, who built the Canal du Midi here in the 17th century, linking the Mediterranean and Atlantic oceans. Nearby, there is an excellent open air museum called the Oppidum which has fine views of the surrounding mountains.

Where to stay
★★★**Imperator,** 28 allées P-Riquet ☎(67)490225 (no restaurant)
☆☆**Ibis,** (5km S-exit Béziers Est from A9) ☎(67)625514

Where to eat
Cigale, 60 allées P-Riquet
Ragueneau, 36 allées P-Riquet
Le Relais de la Grande Vitesse, 23 boulevard de Verdun
Le Relais de L'Oppidum, Route de Narbonne

BIARRITZ 8, 85, 87
The golden sandy beaches and brine springs attract thousands of visitors to this fashionable seaside resort, which began as a fishing village. There are many sporting and entertainment facilities, as well as an excellent Maritime Museum. Spectacular views of the town, coastline and lighthouse can be seen, especially from the Rocher-de-la-Vierge, which is linked to the mainland by a narrow footbridge.

Where to stay
★★★**Regina & Golf,** 52 avenue de L'Imperatrice ☎(59)240960 (no restaurant)
★★★**Windsor,** Grande Plage ☎(59)240852
★★**Beau-Lieu,** 3 esplanade du Port-Vieux ☎(59)242359
★**Palacito,** 1 rue Gambetta ☎(59)240489 (no restaurant)

Where to eat
L'Alambic, 5 place Bellevue
Auberge de Chapelet, route d'Arcangues
Auberge de la Négresse, boulevard Aérodrome
Belle Epoque, 10 avenue Victor Hugo
Flunchs, centre Commercial BAB 2
L'Operne, 17 avenue Edouard VII

Where to camp
Biarritz, 28 rue d'Harcet
Splendid, 12 rue d'Harcet

BIAS 85

Where to camp
Camping Municipal Tatiou

BIDART 8
A small resort with a pleasant beach.

Where to stay
★★★**Bidortea,** route d'Espagne (N10) ☎(59)549468

Where to eat
Le Chistera, N10
Elissaldia, place Église
L'Hacienda, route d'Ahetz

The sea and Villa Belza at Biarritz

Where to camp
Airotel Résidence des Pins, route de Biarritz
Berrua, route d'Arbonne
Ferme Oyamburus
Itsasoa-la-Mer
Jean Paris, quartier M-Pierre
Pavillon Royal, avenue Prince de Gaulles
Ruisseau, route d'Arbonne

BISCARROSSE 85

Where to camp
Mayotte
Rive

BISCARROSSE – PLAGE 85

Where to camp
Camping Municipal de la Plage

BLANGY 58

Where to stay
★**Poste,** 44 Grand Rue ☎(35)935020
★**Ville,** 2 rue Notre-Dame ☎(35)935157

Where to camp
Camping Municipal, 14 rue G-Chekroun

BLAYE 46
A busy harbour on the Gironde with many interesting ancient buildings including the ruins of the Roman basilica and the Blayais Museum, once the house of the Master-at-Arms.

Where to stay
★★**Citadelle,** place d'Armes ☎(56)421710

Where to camp
At Mazion, (5.5km NE on RN937)

BLÉRIOT-PLAGE 21

Where to stay
★**Dunes** ☎(21)345430

BLOIS 7, 61

An ancient town in a picturesque location on the River Loire amid rising hills. The surrounding area is predominantly farming country, but Blois' best known industry is the manufacture of chocolate, which has been produced at the local Poulain factory for over a century. Blois' most outstanding building is the château, an interesting mixture of architectural styles ranging from the 13th to the 17th centuries. There are numerous other places of interest, including the 16th century Cathedral of St-Louis and several 16th century mansions in the old quarter, which lies between the château and the cathedral.

Where to stay
☆☆**Campanile,** 15 rue de la Vallée-Maillard ☎(54)744466
☆☆**Ibis,** rue de la Vallée-Maillard ☎(54)746060
★**Bellay Lf,** 12 rue Minimes ☎(54)782362 (no restaurant)
★**Gerbe d'Or,** 1 rue Bourg-Neuf ☎(54)742645
★**St-Jacquest Lf,** place Gare ☎(54)780415
★**Viennois Lf,** 5 quai A-Coutant ☎(54)741280

Where to eat
Noë, 10 bis avenue Vendôme
La Péniche, promenade du Mail
Hôtel St-Lazare, 138 rue du Bourg-Neuf

BOLLENE 3

A little town in the Provençal retaining its ancient ramparts and some old houses, which contrast with the nearby André Blondel Power Station.

Where to stay
☆☆**Campanile,** avenue T-Aubanel ☎(90)300042

Where to eat
Le Relais de la Grande Croisière

BONNEVAL 82

An ancient walled town containing a 13th century Gothic church and a number of old houses. The abbey, around which Bonneval developed, is now in use as a psychiatric hospital.

Where to stay
★★**Bois Guibert,** (N10) ☎(37)472233

BONNY-SUR-LOIRE 23, 66

Where to stay
☆☆**Fimotel-Val de Loire,** (N7) ☎(38)316462

BORDEAUX 7, 8, 19, 46, 83

The industrialised seaport of Bordeaux is the fifth-largest city in France and is noted for its fine wines. Throughout the old part of the town many buildings are of 18th century date, particularly the magnificent colonnaded Grand Theatre (1780), situated in the lively Place de la Comédie. The Esplanade des Quinconces is the largest square in Europe, and the cathedral dates from the 12th century. Close to the beautiful Dordogne Valley, Bordeaux has good sports facilities and interesting museums.

Where to stay
☆☆☆**Mercure Bordeaux de Lac,** quartier du Lac ☎(56)509030
★★★**Normandie,** 7 cours 30 Juillet ☎(56)521680 (no restaurant)
☆☆☆**Novotel Bordeaux le Lac,** quartier du Lac ☎(56)509970
☆☆☆**Sofitel,** Centre Hôtelier ☎(56)509014
☆☆**Arcade,** 60 rue E-le-Roy ☎(56)909240
★★**Bayonne,** 15 cours de L'Intendance ☎(56)480088 (no restaurant)
☆☆**Campanile,** quartier du Lac ☎(56)395454
☆☆**Ibis,** quartier du Lac ☎(56)509650
★★**Sèze,** 23 allées Tourny ☎(56)526554 (no restaurant)
★**Etche-Ona,** 11 rue Mautrec ☎(56)443649 (no restaurant)

At Artigues (7km NE)
☆☆**Campanile,** avenue de la Prairie ☎(56)327332

At Lormont (5km NE)
☆☆**Climat de France,** Carrefour des 4 Pavillons N10 ☎(56)329610

Where to eat
L'Alhambra, 111 bis rue Judaique
Auberge, 3 rue Buffon
Le Bahan, 28 rue Buhan
Le Caihau, 3 place du Palais
Chez le Chef, 57 rue Huguerie
Chez Pierrette, 186 avenue Labarde
Courte-Paille, Bordeaux-Bruges
Flunchs, 4 et 6 cours de L'Intendance
Flunchs, Centre Commercial Auchan – Quartier du Lac
Flunchs, Centre Commercial Mériadeck
La Jabotière, 86 rue Bègles
Le Lac, 163 avenue de Labarde
La Peniche, 8 Quai de la Monnaie
Le Porto, 202 bis Quai de Brazza
Le Relais d'Auvergne, 131 bis, quai des Chartrons

Le Relais de la Cage Aux Rossignals, 206 avenue Thiers
Le Relais du Bon Coin, 142 rue Lucien Faure
Tupina, 6 rue Porte de la Monnaie
Le Vieux Bordeaux, 27 rue Buhan

At Mérignac
Courte-Paille, Route de Cap Ferret – Face à Carrefour
Flunchs, Centre Commercial Carrefour, Chemin de Mirepin

BORMES-LES-MIMOSAS 77

An attractive resort noted for its pleasant climate, situated on a steep incline at the entrance to the Dom Forest. The town contains some old streets so steep and treacherous that one of them is known locally as *rompi-cuou* (neck-breaker), but a climb to the terrace of the Chapel of St-Francis is rewarded by a fine view. Bormes takes its name from the abundance of plants which decorate the streets, notably eucalyptus and mimosas.

Where to stay
★★**Safari,** route Stade ☎(94)710983
★**Belle Vue Lf,** place Gambetta ☎(94)711515

Where to eat
La Cassole, ruelle Moulin
Tonnelle des Delices, place Gambetta

Where to camp
Manjastre, 98 route de Dom
Versoyen, Route des Arcs

BOULOGNE 21, 90

A leading commercial and passenger port as well as the premier fishing port in France. The upper town contains the 13th century castle, the 19th century Cathedral of Notre-Dame, and the remains of the medieval town walls.

Where to stay
★★**Alexandra,** 93 rue Thiers ☎(21)305222 (no restaurant)
★★**Faidherbe,** 12 rue Faidherbe ☎(21)316093 (no restaurant)
☆☆**Ibis,** quartier L-Danremont bd Diderot ☎(21)301240
★★**Lorraine,** 7 place de Lorraine ☎(21)313478 (no restaurant)
★★**Metropole,** 51 rue Thiers ☎(21)315430 (no restaurant)
★**Hamiot,** 1 rue Faidherbe ☎(21)314420
★**Londrés,** 22 place de France ☎(21)313563 (no restaurant)

At Portel (Le) (1 km SW)
★**Beau, Rivage et Armada,** place Mon-Bourgain ☎(21)315982

Where to eat
La Liegeoise, 10 rue A Monsigny
La Matelote, 80 boulevard Ste-Beuve
Plage, 124 boulevard Ste-Beuve
Hostellerie, 17 rue Gare

At Boulogne St Martin
Flunch, (RN42)

Where to camp
Phare

BOURG-EN-BRESSE 18

Between the Massif Central and the Jura mountains, Bourg-en-Bresse is the market for all local farm produce and is noted for poultry. The town has undergone much industrial development, but some old crafts, such as furniture and glazed pottery manufacture, still survive. Within the town are many old buildings, including the Church of Notre-Dame and the local museum, which is housed in the 16th century monastery buildings and has many interesting exhibits.

Where to stay
★★★Logis de Brou, 132 boulevard Brou ☎(74)221155 (no restaurant)
★★Chantecler, 10 route St-Etienne du Bois ☎(74)224488
☆☆Ibis, ZAC de la Croix Blanche, boulevard Ch-de Gaulle ☎(74)225266

Where to eat
Chalet de Brou, 7 avenue Alsace–Lorraine
Courte-Paille, N75 a 2km direction Pont d'Ain
Le Français, 7 avenue Alsace–Lorraine
Eglise de Brou, Face église de Brou
Savoie, 15 rue P-Pioda
Trichard, 4 cour Verdun

Where to camp
Camping Municipal de Challes avenue de Bad Kreuznach

BOURGES 65

A busy commercial and industrial town at the junction of the rivers Auron and Yèvre. Bourges has retained many timber-framed homes and imposing buildings dating back to its rich medieval past when the town grew up around the Cathedral of St-Etienne. The lofty tower of this 12th century building still dominates the town and the whole building, noted especially for its fine stained-glass, is considered to be one of the most beautiful in the country. The 15th century Jacques Coeur Palace, formerly the home of Charles VII's treasurer, built on the remains of the Gallo-Roman town walls, is also well worth a visit.

Where to stay
★★★Angleterre, 1 place des Quatre Piliers ☎(48)246851
★★D'Artagnan, 19 place Séraucourt ☎(48)246751
★★Christina, 5 rue Halle ☎(48)705650 (no restaurant)
★★Poste, 22 rue Moyenne ☎(48)700806 (no restaurant)
★★St-Jean, 23 avenue M-Dormoy ☎(48)241348 (no restaurant)

Where to eat
Auberge Val d'Auron, 170 rue Lazency
Courte-Paille, route d'Orléans–Carrefour de Verdun
Ile d'or, 39 boulevard Juranville
Le Relais des Ailes, 147 avenue M-Haegelen

LE BOURGET 1, 15

Where to stay
☆☆☆Novotel, rue le Pont Yblon (N2) ☎(1)8674888

BOURGOIN-JALLIEU 79

Where to stay
☆☆Campanile, Zac de St-Hubert l'Isle d'Abeau Est ☎(74)935063
☆☆Climat de France, 15 rue E-Branly Zac de la Maladière ☎(6)4460123

Where to eat
Petit Auberge N6
Le Relais de la Maison Blanche Route Nivolas-Vermelle
Les Trois Faisons

BOURGTHEROULDE-INFREVILLE 59

Where to stay
★Corne d'Abondance Lf, pl de la Mairie ☎(35)876008

BREST 49

Long established as a naval port with one of the finest natural harbours in the world, the town underwent a great deal of rebuilding after suffering extensive damage during World War II, making Brest the most modern town in Brittany. A large portion of the town's waterfront is covered by the naval base and dockyard; the 12th century castle is also the property of the Admiralty. The Cours Dajot is a fine, extensive promenade laid out during the 18th century on the site of the old town wall.

Where to stay
☆☆☆Novotel de Brest, Zac de Kergaradec, route du Gouesnon ☎(98)023283
★★★Sofitel Océania, 82 rue de Siam ☎(98)806666

Where to eat
Au Relais, 3 rue Kléber
Flunch, 20 rue J-Jaurès
Flunch, 11 boulevard de Plymouth

BRIARE 23

An industrial town situated at the point where the Briare Canal crosses the River Loire. Briare is well known for the manufacture of porcelain and there is a museum of historic cars on the southern outskirts of the town.

Where to stay
★Cerf, 22 boulevard Buyser ☎(38)370080

Where to eat
Le Carrefour Briare, RN7

BRIGNOLES 4

The old town, with its narrow, twisting streets, clings to the slopes of a low hill, while the new development has spread over the verdant plain below. Once famous for its plums, Brignoles is now an important bauxite and marble-working centre and is also the focal point for the local wine trade.

BRIONNE 59

Now involved in the textile trade, Brionne was originally built as a strongpoint to command the Risle Valley. From the base of the 12th century castle ruins there is an attractive view of the town and surrounding countryside.

Where to stay
★Logis de Brionne Lf, 1 place St-Denis ☎(32)448173
★Vieux Donjon, 19 rue de la Soie ☎(32)448062

Where to eat
Le Relais du Lac, 29 rue de la Cabotière

BRIOUDE 72

A market town and salmon-fishing centre on the River Allier, with a 12th century church.

Where to stay
★★Briva Lf, route Puy ☎(71)501049
★★Moderne Lf, 12 avenue V-Hugo ☎(71)500730

Where to eat
Julien, 7 rue Assas
Le Relais Des Sports, Route de Clermont

BRIVE-LA-GAILLARDE 73

On the banks of the River Corèze lies this important fruit and vegetable-producing town. Dominating the centre is the 12th century Church of

St-Martin, surrounded by handsome, ornamental buildings. South of Brive-la-Gaillarde are the famous Grottes de St-Antoine and Grottes des Larnouroux, used as hiding places and chapels in the Middle Ages.

Where to stay
★★**Cremaillère Lf,** 53 avenue de Paris ☎(55)743247
★★**Truffe Noir,** 22 boulevard A-France ☎(55)743532
★**Montauban Lf,** 6 avenue E-Herriot ☎(55)240038

Where to eat
La Belle Epoque, 27 avenue J-Jaurès
Chez Monique, Varetz
La Crémaillère, 53 avenue Paris
L'Ermitage, 25 boulevard Koenig
Nouvel Hotel, 2 avenue Desgenettes
La Périgourdine, 15 avenue Alsace-Lorraine
Regent, 3 place W-Churchill

Where to camp
Camping Municipal des Iles, boulevard Michelet

CAEN 11, 12, 39, 47
An industrial port and university city on the River Orne, Caen has many beautiful buildings and ancient houses. William the Conqueror built the Abbaye aux Hommes, which now houses the town hall, and the 11th century castle which is now the fine arts museum. The Abbaye aux Dames was founded by his queen, Matilda, and the crypt in which she was buried has been retained.

Where to stay
★★★**Malherbe,** place Ml-Foch ☎(31)844006
★★★**Moderne,** 116 boulevard Gl-Leclerc ☎(31)860423
☆☆☆**Novotel,** avenue de la Côte de Nacre ☎(31)930588
★★**Bristol,** 31 rue du XI Novembre ☎(31)845976 (no restaurant)
★★**Château,** 5 avenue du 6-Juin ☎(31)861537 (no restaurant)
★★**Métropole,** 16 place de la Gare ☎(31)822676 (no restaurant)
★**Bernières,** 50 rue Bernières ☎(31)860126 (no restaurant)
★**St-Jean,** 20 rue des Martyrs ☎(31)862335

Where to eat
Alcide, 1 place Courtonne
Le Chalut, 3 rue Vaucelles

Poêle d'Or, 7 rue Laplace
Pub William's, place Courtonne

Where to camp
Camping Municipal, route de Louvigny

Where to stay
At Hérouville-St-Cast
☆☆**Campanile,** Parc Tertaire, boulevard du Bois ☎(31)952924
☆☆**Ibis Caen,** 4 quartier Savary ☎(31)935446

Where to eat
Flunch, quartier du Val, Centre Commercial

CAGNES 4
This old fortified town is spread among hills dotted with groves of oranges and olives, and along the coast at Cros-de-Cagnes. The medieval castle in the old town attracts many artists and there is an excellent museum of 20th century artists' work as well as a museum devoted to Renoir who spent the last twelve years of his life here.

Where to stay
★★★**Cagnard,** rue Ponhs Long ☎(93)207322
★★★**Tierce,** boulevard de la Plage/boulevard Kennedy ☎(93)200209

Where to eat
Josy-Jo, 2 rue Planastel
Le Neptune, boulevard Plage
Peintres, 71 Montée Bourgade au Haut de Cagnes

CAHORS 37
Lying in a bend on the River Lot, this medieval town is noted for its magnificent 14th century fortified Valentré Bridge, which stretches the length of the town and has three towers. Within the town, the cathedral has a beautiful carved Romanesque north door and the Municipal Museum gives an insight into local history.

Where to stay
★★★**Wilson,** 72 rue Prés Wilson ☎(65)354180 (no restaurant)
★★**France Lf,** 252 avenue J-Jaurès ☎(65)351676 (no restaurant)
★★**Terminus Lf,** 5 avenue C-de-Freycinet ☎(65)352450 (no restaurant)

At Laroque-Des-Arcs (5km N)
★**Beau Rivage** ☎(65)353058

Where to eat
Préfecture, 64 rue Préfecture
Le Relais de la Bourse, 7 place Rousseau
La Chartreuse, faubourg St-Georges

La Taverne, 41 rue J-B Delpech

Where to camp
Camping Municipal St-Georges

CALAIS 1, 13, 21, 25
A popular seaside resort which is also one of the leading Channel ports. Although Calais suffered severe war damage, some medieval defences have remained, despite extensive restoration.

Where to stay
★★★**Meurice,** 5 E-Roche ☎(21)345703 (no restaurant)
★★**Bellevue,** 25 place d'Armes ☎(21)345375 (no restaurant)
★★**Capitainerie,** quai du Danube ☎(21)961010
★★**George V,** 36 rue Royale ☎(21)344029 (no restaurant)
☆☆**Ibis,** rue Greuze, zup de Beau-Marais ☎(21)966969
★★**Pacific,** 40 rue de Duc de Guise ☎(21)345024
★**Beffroi,** 10 rue A-Gerschel ☎(21)344751 (no restaurant)
★**Sole Meunière,** 53 rue de la Mar ☎(20)343608 (no restaurant)

Where to eat
Le Channel, 3 boulevard Résistance
Côte d'Argent, Plage de Calais
La Diligence, 5 rue E-Roche
Moulin à Poivre, 10 rue E-Neuve
Relais de la Muraille

CAMBRAI 25, 91
An historic old town famous for its fine linen known as 'cambric'. Its most important building is the 18th century Church of St-Géry.

Where to stay
★★★**Beatus,** 38 route de Paris ☎(27)814570 (no restaurant)
★★★**Château de la Motte Fenelon,** Square du Château ☎(27)836138
☆☆**Ibis rte de Bapaume,** Fontaine Notre Dame ☎(27)835454
★★**Mounton Blanc,** 33 rue Alsace-Lorraine ☎(27)813016
★★**Poste,** 58-60 avenue de la Victoire ☎(27)813469 (no restaurant)
★**France,** 37 rue Lille ☎(27)813880 (no restaurant)

Where to eat
Les Arcades, 12 Mar-de-Lattre-de-Tassigny
L'Escargot, 10 Gen-De-Gaulle
Chez Francis, 10 rue des Docks
La Gargotte-Chez Jacky, 136 boulevard Jean-Bart
Le Relais Dupleix, 1 boulevard Dupleix

Le Relais des Routiers, 224 rue du Cateau

CANNES 4, 78
Once a small fishing village, Cannes has become a popular resort due to its delightful location below the Esterel mountain range and its exceptionally mild climate. The internationally famous film festival held here every year brings the starstruck in droves to its bars and beaches. The seafront promenade is bordered by palm trees and contrasts sharply with the narrow streets of the old town, where the 12th century Suquet Tower and museum can be found. The Super-Cannes Observatory just outside the town has spectacular views of the coast and countryside.

Where to stay
★★★**Embassy,** 6 rue de Bone ☎(93)387902
★★★**Frantel Beach,** 13 rue du Canada ☎(93)382232
★★★**Savoy,** 5 rue F-Einsey ☎(93)381774
☆☆**Campanile,** Aérodrome de Cannes – Mandelieu ☎(93)486941
★★**France,** 85 rue d'Antibes ☎(93)392334 (no restaurant)
★★**Roches Fleuries,** 92 rue G-Clemenceau ☎(93)392878 (no restaurant)

Where to eat
Au Mal Assis, 15 quai St-Pierre
Aux Bons Enfants, 80 rue Meynodier
Caveau Provençal, 45 rue Felix-Faure
La Cigale, 1 rue Florian
La Coquille, 65 rue Felix-Faure
La Croisette, 15 rue Commandant-André
Le Croquant, 18 boulevard J-Hibert
Gaston-Gastounette, 7 quai St-Pierre
Gilbert de Cassis, 17 rue G-Monod
Lamour, 45 boulevard Groisette
Mère Besson, 13 rue Frères-Pradignac
Le Monaco, 15 rue 24-août
Monsieur Madeleine, 12 boulevard Jean-Hibert
L'Olivier, 9 rue Rouguiere
Poêle D'Or, 23 rue États-Unis
Poivre Vert, 11 rue L-Blanc

Where to eat
Taverna Romana, 10 place Suquet
Voile au Vent, 17 quai St-Pierre

At Bocca (5km W)

Where to camp
Cerisiers

At Cannet (Le)
Grand Saule, boulevard de la Frayère

CAPBRETON 8, 85
Once an important port, Capbreton is now a popular seaside resort.

Where to stay
★★**Océan Lf,** avenue de la plage ☎(58)721022

Where to eat
Mille Sabords, GU port de Plaisance La Sardinière, 87 avenue G-Pompidou

Where to camp
Camping Municipal Civelle Pointe

CAP D'ANTIBES 78
An attractive peninsula that has a museum, a lighthouse and many gardens including the beautiful Thurret Garden.

CARANTEC 56
A family-orientated seaside resort on a peninsular.

Where to stay
★**Falaise,** Plage du Kelenn ☎(98)670053

CARCASSONNE 20
Carcassonne lies in the foothills of the Pyrenees and is famous for its well-preserved medieval fortifications. The double towered ramparts of La Cité overlook the River Aude below, and make a spectacular scene at night when floodlit. The lower part of the town, beside the river, has many winding lanes and narrow streets steeped in history, with buildings and museums such as the Cathedral of St-Michel and the Musée des Beaux Arts.

Where to stay
★★★**Cité,** place St-Nazaire ☎(68)250334
★★★**Donjon Lf,** 2 rue Comte Roger ☎(68)710880 (no restaurant)
★★★**Terminus,** 2 avenue Ml –Joffre ☎(68)252500 (no restaurant)
★★**Aragon,** 15 Montée Cormbéléran ☎(68)471631 (no restaurant)
☆☆**Croque Sel,** route Narbonne (N113) ☎(68)251415
☆☆**Ibis,** route de Berriac ☎(68)479835
★★**Logis de Trencavel Lf,** 286 avenue du Gl-Leclerc ☎(68)710953
★★**Montségur,** 27 allée d'Léna ☎(68)253141 (no restaurant)

Where to eat
La Crémade, 1 rue Plo
Languedoc, 32 allée d'Léna
Le Relais de l'avenir, 93 avenue Franklin-Roosevelt

At Pennautier (4km NW of N113)

Where to camp
Lavandières, N113

CARENTAN 11
An important milk and butter marketing centre. The octagonal spire of the 12th century Church of Notre-Dame is a well known local landmark.

Where to stay
★**Auberge Normande Lf,** boulevard Verdun ☎(33) 420299

Where to eat
Le Derby, 21 rue de la 101 Airborn
Marché et des Herbagers, place Valnoble

Where to camp
Camping Municipale le Haut Dyck

CARHAIX-PLOUGUER 56
A former Roman settlement in the heart of Brittany, where Breton is spoken. Carhaix-Plouguer is now a milk-producing centre and is at the centre of a cattle-breeding area.

Where to stay
★★**Gradlon,** 12 boulevard de la République ☎(98)931522

Where to eat
Au Cheval Breton, 2 boulevard de la République

CASSIS 76
A busy fishing port, well known for its seafood, which has become a popular resort. Its position makes it an ideal centre for visiting the famous Calanques, a series of deep, natural harbours which run inland between towering cliffs along the coast south-east of Marseilles.

Where to stay
★★★**Plage,** place Bestovan ☎(42)010570

Where to eat
Le Flibustier, impasse Gd Carnot
L'Oustau de la Mar, quai Baux

CASTELJALOUX 87

Where to stay
★**Grand Cadets de Gascogne Lf,** place Gambetta ☎(53)930059

Where to eat
Vieille Auberge, rue Posterne

Romanesque features and there is an interesting synagogue, dating from the late 18th century. The museum, housed in the buildings of the old hospital, has a fine archaeological collection.

Where to stay
★★★**Christel Boscodomini**
☎(90)710779

Where to eat
L'Assiette au Beurie, 353 avenue Verdun
Bar du Marché, 86 place du Clos
Fin de Siècle, 46 place du Clos
Nicolet, 13 place Gombetta
Le Relais Saint-Jacques, 649 avenue de la Libération
Les Routiers, 21 avenue de Verdun

Where to camp
Camping Municipal l'Hippodrome

CAVALIÈRE 77

Where to stay
★★★**Surplage** ☎(94)058419
★★**Cap Nègre** ☎(94)058046

Where to eat
Le Café du Larzac, La Baraque des Infruts

Where to camp
Mimosas, route du Lavandou
Parc de Pramousquier

CAVALAIRE-SUR-MER 77

Where to stay
★★**Bonne Auberge,** 400 avenue des Alliés route Nationale
☎(94)640296

Where to camp
Bonporteau
Canissons, route des Canissons
Cros de Mouton
Pinède, route du Lavandou

CHABLIS 2, 66
A small town on the River Serein, known as the 'Porte d'Or' (Golden Gate) of Burgundy. Chablis has been an important wine producing centre for many years and has given its name to the famous white wine. An annual wine festival is held here on the last Sunday in November.

LA CHAISE-DIEU 71
La Chaise-Dieu lies at the heart of a great expanse of forest and has a magnificent church of St Peter which contains many beautiful works of art.

Where to camp
Camping Municipal de la Piscine
Camping Municipal Lac de Clarens

CASTELNAUDARY 20

Where to stay
★★**Palmes,** 10 rue Ml-Foch
☎(68)230310
★**Fourcade,** 14 rue des Carmes
☎(68)230208

Where to eat
L'Auberge, 22 cours République
La Belle Époque, 55 rue Gén-Dejean

CASTELSARRASIN 19

Where to stay
★**Modern,** 54 rue de l'Égalite
☎(68)323010 (no restaurant)

LE CATEAU 91
Birthplace of artist Henri Matisse and once the seat of the Bishops of Cambrai, the former palace of the Archbishops is now a museum containing works by Matisse.

CAUSSADE 37

Where to stay
★★**Dupont,** 12 rue Recollets
☎(63)930502
★★**Larrogue,** avenue de la Gare
☎(63)931014

Where to eat
Le Relais D'Auvergne

Where to camp
Piboulette, route de Carjac

CAVAILLON 4, 75
A small Provençal market town famous for its melons and early vegetables. The cathedral has some

Where to stay
★★**Tremblant Lf**, (D906)
☎(71)000185

CHALONNES-SUR-LOIRE 63

Where to camp
Camping Municipal Candals

CHÂLONS-SUR-MARNE 10, 26

Several old bridges, 17th and 18th century mansions, half-timbered houses and beautiful trees along the bank of the Marne give Châlon considerable character. A pre-Roman settlement that prospered in the Middle Ages, the town is now a centre for the local wine trade. The Gothic Church of Notre-Dame-en-Vaux is considered to be one of the most beautiful in the area. Other notable buildings are the 17th century Hotel des Gouverneurs de Châlons and Hôtel d'Intendence de Champagne, now the Préfecture. One of the three museums has a section devoted to Goethe and Schiller.

Where to stay
★★**Angleterre**, 19 place Mgr-Tissier ☎(26)682151
★★**Bristol**, 77 avenue P-Sémard ☎(26)682463 (no restaurant)
☆☆**Ibis**, route de Sédan, Complexe Agricole ☎(26)651665
★★**Mont des Logès**, La Veuve ☎(26)673343
★★**Pasteur**, 46 rue Pasteur ☎(26)681000 (no restaurant)

Where to eat
Au Mont St-Michel-Chez Claudine, 31 route de Troyes
Le Delko, rue des Douanes, La Veuve
Flunch, avenue du Prés-Roosevelt

Where to camp
Camping Municipal, 51 route de Sarry

CHALON-SUR-SAÔNE 2

Chalon sur Saône has developed from a major Roman settlement into a busy commercial centre and inland port. Buildings of interest include the former hospital, which dates back to the 16th century and the 15th century Tour deDoyenné. Also of interest are the Musée Nicéphore Niepce, which is devoted to the life of Joseph Nicéphore Niepce, and the Musée Denon.

Where to stay
☆☆☆**Mercure**, Centre Commercial de la Thalie, av de l'Europe ☎(85)465189

★★★**Royal**, 8 rue du Port Villiers ☎(85)481586
★★★**St-Georges et Terminus**, 32 avenue J-Jaurès ☎(85)482705
★★★**St-Regis**, 22 boulevard de la République ☎(85)480728
☆☆**Ibis**, Carrefour des Moirots ☎(85)466462 (no restaurant)
★**Rotonde** ☎(85)483593 (no restaurant)
★★**St-Jean**, 24 Quai Gambetta ☎(85)484565 (no restaurant)
★★**St-Remy Lf**, Place Pont Paron, ☎(85)483804 (no restaurant)

Where to eat
Le Bourgogne, 28 rue Strasbourg
Centre Routier Rive Gauche, avenue de Verdun
Courte Paille, N6 Face Centre Commercial
Le Provençal, 22 place Beaune
La Réale, 8 place Gen-de-Gaulle

CHALUS 87

A small hilltop town surrounded by densely wooded granite hills and dominated by the ruined but massive tower of its 11th century castle. It was while attacking the castle that Richard the Lionheart was hit by a bolt from a crossbow; he died at Chinon from his wounds.

CHAMBORD 61

The largest château in the Loire Valley stands here on the banks of the River Cosson, in the midst of an extensive wooded park which has been a rich hunting reserve since it was built in the 16th century. Chambord was a favourite retreat for French Royalty, particularly Louis XIV, whose protégé Molière wrote *Le Bourgeois Gentilhomme* and *Monsieur de Pourceaugnac* at the château. Chambord's outstanding feature is the staircase in the guardroom, composed of two ornately decorated spirals which never actually meet.

CHAMONIX-MONT-BLANC 18

Lying at the foot of Mont Blanc in an attractive Alpine valley, Chamonix has become one of the largest winter sport resorts in France, with a multitude of facilities for visitors. Gazing up to the highest peak in the French Alps is the Saussure Monument, which commemorates the first scientific ascent of the mountain by Saussure and Balmat in 1787. The first Winter Olympic Games was held here in 1924.

Where to stay
★★★**Mont Blanc**, place d'Église ☎(50)530564

★★★**Richemond**, 228 rue Dr-Paccard ☎(50)530885
★★★**Sapinière-Montana**,102 rue Mummery ☎(50)530763

Where to camp
Mer de Glace
Rosierès, 1km NE on N506

CHAMPAGNOLE 95

At the foot of Mont Rivel, overlooking the beautiful Ain Valley, lies this prosperous town reliant on its steel, iron and cement industries as well as furniture-making and toy-making factories. Champagnole is also popular as a holiday destination, with those who enjoy winter sports.

Where to stay
★★★**Ripotot**, 54 rue Ml-Foch ☎(84)521545

Where to eat
Auberge des Gourmets
Belle Époque, 54 rue Mar-Foch

Where to camp
Camping Municipal Boyse, route de Voiteur

CHAMPTOCEAUX 63

A small town in a picturesque setting, on a terrace overlooking the River Loire. Champtoceaux is noted for its locally-produced white wine and for the Promenade de Champalud, a balcony behind the church which provides spectacular views over the surrounding countryside.

Where to stay
★★**Côte Lf**, 2 rue du Dr-Giffard ☎(40)835039

Where to eat
Auberge de la Forge, 1 bis place des Piliers

CHANTONNAY 45

Where to stay
★★**Moulin Neuf Lf**, ☎(51)943027
★**Mouton Lf**, 31 rue Nationale ☎(51)943022

CHARLEVILLE-MÉZIÈRES 91

Although these two towns, on either bank of the River Meuse, have been amalgamated, each retains its individuality. Charleville, with its 17th century chequerboard town planning is today a commercial area. The town's association with the poet Arthur Rimbaud, who was born here in the mid 19th century, is reflected in the Vieux Moulin which houses a museum containing some of his possessions. Mézières, an old settlement, is the administrative centre and its buildings include the Préfecture.

At Villers-Semeuse (5km E)
Where to stay
☆☆☆**Mercure**, rue L-Michel
☎(24)570529
Where to eat
Auberge de la Forest
La Cigogne, 40 rue Dubois-Crance
Mont Olympe, rue Paquis
Where to camp
Camping Municipal Mont Olympe

CHARTRES 16, 34, 35, 81, 82
Standing on a hill above the River Eure, Chartres is a pleasant mixture of old gabled houses, cobbled streets and church spires. The majestic 12th century Gothic cathedral, referred to by Rodin as the 'Acropolis of France' contains the largest display of medieval stained glass in the country.
Where to stay
★★★**Grand Monarque**, 22 place des Épars ☎(37)210072
☆☆☆**Novotel**, avenue M-Proust, le Madeleine ☎(37)348030
★★**Capitainerie**, 5 avenue M-Proust ☎(37)359111
★★**Poste**, 3 rue du Gl-König ☎(37)210427
★**Ouest**, 3 place Sémard ☎(37)214327 (no restaurant)
Where to eat
Auberge St-Maurice, 20 rue St-Maurice
Chez Francine, 59 rue Grand-Faubourg
Normand, 24 place Épars
Le Relais des Beaumonts, Rocade sud de Chartres
Le Relais la Couronne, 27 boulevard C-Péguy

CHÂTEAU-ARNOUX 80
An attractive town overlooked by a 15th century castle.
Where to stay
★★★**Bonne Étape**, (N85) ☎(92)640009
Where to camp
Camping Municipal Salettes

CHÂTEAUBOURG 16
Where to stay
★★★**Ar Milin**, ☎(99)003091
Where to eat
Le Bon Accueil, lieu-dit les Fossés

CHÂTEAUBRIANT 60
An old fortified town which lies on the borders of Brittany and Anjou, within an area of woodlands and ponds in the pretty Chère Valley. The town has a fine 11th century castle with additions made as recently as the 19th century.
Where to stay
★★★**Hostellerie de la Ferrière**, route de Nantes ☎(40)280028
★**Armor**, 19 place Motte ☎(40)811119 (no restaurant)
Where to eat
Le Relais Paris-Océan, 25-29 rue d'Ancenis

CHÂTEAU-DU-LOIR 39
Where to camp
Camping Municipal Coëmont

CHÂTEAU-DE-SERRANT 63
An impressive château, designed by Philibert Delorme, the architect of the Tuileries in Paris and Fountainebleu, and constructed between the 16th and the 18th centuries. The interior is richly furnished and contains many fine objects d'art.

CHÂTEAUDUN 82
A busy market centre overlooking the River Loir. The château, dating originally from the 12th century, has one of the most impressive round keeps in the country. Later additions include the 15th century Sainte-Chapelle, noted for its statues and two Gothic wings which contained the living quarters. Some fine 16th century homes can be seen in the old town, and the local museum has a splendid ornithological collection.
Where to stay
★★**Amorial**, 59 rue Gambetta ☎(37)451957
★★**Beauce**, 50 rue de Jallans ☎(37)451475 (no restaurant)
★**Rose Lf**, 12 rue L-Licors ☎(37)452183
★**Trois Pastoureaux**, 31 rue A-Guillet ☎(37)450162
Where to eat
Caveau des Fouleurs, 33 rue Fouleries
La Licorne, 6 place 18-Octobre
Le Saint-Jean, 1 route de Brou

CHÂTEAU-GONTIER 41
An attractive town with narrow streets and old houses, important for its calf sales.
Where to stay
★★**Mirwault**, ☎(43)071317

CHÂTEAULIN 54
Standing on a bend in the canalised River Aulne, just above the tidal reaches, this small town is one of the major salmon-fishing centres in the area. Overlooking the town is the Chapel of Our Lady, which provides fine views of the deep Aulne Valley.

CHÂTEAUNEUF-SUR-LOIRE 66
Where to stay
★**Nouvel du Loiret Lf**, 4 place A-Briand ☎(38)584228

CHÂTEAUROUX 36, 67
The 15th century Château Raoul overlooks this industrial town, and just to the north are the remains of the former abbey at Déols. Also of interest is the museum which contains exhibits of the Napoleonic period, and from here a picturesque route leads to the Châteauroux Forest.
Where to stay
★★★**France**, 16 rue V-Hugo ☎(54)270080
★**Central**, 19 avenue de la Gare ☎(54)220100 (no restaurant)
Where to eat
Bar De L'Avenue, 1 avenue de la Manufacture
l'Escale
l'Escargot, 7 rue J-Jaurès
Jean Bardet, 1 rue J J-Rousseau
La Rallye, 9 rue Bourdion
Les Routiers, 199 avenue des Marins
Where to camp
Camping Municipal Rochet

CHÂTEAU-THIERRY 94
A much-invaded town famous for the 1918 battle when French and American forces halted the German advance on Paris. A memorial on the heights above the town commemorates this event. The author Jean de la Fontaine was born here in 1621 and his former home is now a museum.
Where to stay
★**Girafe**, place A-Briand ☎(23)830206 (no restaurant)
Where to eat
St-Éloi, 27 avenue Soissons

CHÂTELAILLON-PLAGE 46, 85
Where to stay
★★**Grand**, 13 avenue Gl-Leclerc ☎(46)562097
★★**Hostellerie Select**, 1 rue G-Musset ☎(46)562431
★**Majestic**, place de St-Marsault ☎(46)562053

Château de Chenonceaux spans the River Cher

Where to eat
Armor, au port de Plaisance
Chez Yannik, 23 boulevard
Libération

Where to camp
Clos des Rivages, avenue des
Boucholeurs

CHÂTELGUYON 67, 68

Where to stay
★★★**International,** rue A-Punnet
☎(73)860672
★★★**Splendid,** 5-7 rue
d'Angleterre ☎(73)860480

Where to eat
La Grilloute, avenue Baraduc

CHÂTELLERAULT 7, 83
Found at the confluence of the rivers
Clain and Vienne amid undulating
wooded countryside. There are many
old houses; the most famous is the
16th century Maison de Descartes,
home to the philosopher René
Descartes during his early life and now
a museum.

Where to stay
★★★**Moderne,** 74 boulevard
Blossac ☎(49)213011
★★**Croissant,** 19 avenue J-F
Kennedy ☎(49)210177
☆☆**Ibis,** avenue Camille Plage,
quartier de la Forêt ☎(49)217577
★★**Univers,** 4 avenue G-
Clemenceau ☎(49)212353

CHÂTILLON-SUR-INDRE 67
A small market town above the River
Indre, full of winding streets, alleys and
stairways which give access to many
ancient houses. There is a fine
Romanesque church, and the remains
of the château include a 13th century
round keep from which there is a fine
view over the Indre Valley.

Where to stay
★**Auberge de la Tour Lf,**
☎(54)387217

Where to eat
Promenade, place Champ de Foire
Le Relais du Mail, boulevard du Gl-
Leclerc

CHÂTILLON-SUR-SEINE 94
An ancient town on the banks of the
River Seine which has been
extensively rebuilt following damage
during World War II. The local
museum, in the Maison Philandrier,
contains the Treasure of Vix, the
personal belongings of a 6th century
Gaulish nobleman, which was
discovered at Vix, some 7km away, in
1953.

Where to stay
★★**Côte d'Or,** rue C-Ronot
☎(80)911329
★★**Sylvia,** 9 avenue de la Gare
☎(80)910244 (no restaurant)
★**Jura,** 19 rue Dr-Robert
☎(80)912696 (no restaurant)

Where to eat
Europa, place Résistance

Where to camp
Camping Municipal, esplanade St-
Vorles

CHAUMONT 26, 27, 28, 30, 31
An old town situated on an escarpment
between the valleys of the rivers Suize
and Marne. Chaumont contains a
number of elegant houses dating from
the 17th and 18th centuries and some
medieval buildings which retain corner
staircase turrets. The most
outstanding feature of the town,
however, is the magnificent 50-arched
viaduct which spans the Suize Valley.

Where to stay
★★★**Terminus Reine,** place de la
Gare ☎(25)0366666
☆☆**Etoile d'Or,** route de Langres
☎(25)030223
★★**Grand Val,** route de Langres
☎(25)039035
★**France,** 25 rue Toupot de Beveaux
☎(25)030111

Where to eat
Auberge Alsacienne – Le Bar des
Ailes, route de Neuilly
Chez Jean, 29 avenue Carnot

CHAUMONT-SUR-LOIRE 61
The little town of Chaumont stands
high above the River Loire. Its most
outstanding feature is the imposing
15th century Gothic château. It is
approached through a beautiful park
planted with cedar trees and has an
elegant interior containing fine
tapestries and furniture. The stables,
complete with saddle-room and
carriages, are also well worth a visit.

Where to stay
★★★**Château Lf,** ☎(54)469804

Where to camp
Camping Grosse Grève

CHENONCEAUX 65

Said to be one of the most beautiful châteaux of the region, Chenonceaux was built during the 16th century. It stands on two piers in the River Cher and is approached through some beautiful formal gardens. The interior is noted for its works of art, and a Waxworks Museum can be visited in the grounds.

Where to stay
★★**Bon Laboureur et Château** (N75) ☎(47)299002
★**Roy,** 9 rue Dr-Brenneau ☎(47)299017

Where to eat
Gâteau Breton

CHERBOURG 11, 40

A port which has become important in the handling of trans-Atlantic and cross-Channel traffic. The 15th century Church of La Trinité is virtually the only ancient building to survive the destruction of World War II. The Museum of Second World War and Liberation is within the Fort-du-Roul, which also offers extensive views over the town and harbour.

Where to stay
☆☆☆**Mercure,** Gare Maritime ☎(33)440111
★★**Beauséjour,** 26 rue Grande Vallée ☎(33)531030 (no restaurant)
★★**France,** 41 rue Ml-Foch ☎(33)531024
★★**Louvre,** 28 rue de la Paix ☎(33)530228 (no restaurant)
★**Rennaissance,** 4 rue de l'Église ☎(33)432390 (no restaurant)
★**Torgistorps,** 14 place de la République ☎(33)433232 (no restaurant)

Where to eat
Cafeteria Terre Plein Maritime, quai de Normandie
Le Clos Normand, Le Mont-á-la-Quesne par Brix
A L'Horizon, 24 rue Surconf
Le Relais des Routiers, 10 rue l'Onglet

Where to camp
Camping Pins

At La Glacerie (6km SE via N13)
Where to stay
☆☆**Campanile,** rue Montmartre ☎(1) 757111

CHINON 62

Standing on the banks of the River Vienne, Chinon has retained much of its medieval appearance. It is famous for its ruined château, composed of three moated fortresses. These are the Fort St-Georges, built by King Henry II of England and reputedly the scene of his death in 1189; the Château du Milieu where Joan of Arc was received by the Dauphin in 1429; and the Château du Coudray where she slept during her stay. Many picturesque old houses can be seen in the town. The House of the States-General, where Richard the Lionheart died in 1199, has been converted into a local museum.

Where to stay
★**Boule d'Or Lf,** 66 quai J-d'Arc ☎(47)930313
★**Gargantua,** 73 rue Voltaire ☎(47)930471

Where to eat
La Relais de la Forêt, 37 route de Tours

Where to camp
Camping Municipal

CHOLET 86

An industrial town, noted for the manufacture of handkerchiefs and table linen. The development of this trade is traced in the History Museum, which also recalls Cholet's involvement in the bloody Vendéen war of the 18th century.

Where to stay
★★★**Fimotel,** avenue Sables d'Olonne (2kms S) ☎(41)624545
☆☆**Campanile,** Parc de Carteron, square de la Nouvelle France ☎(1) 7571111

Where to eat
La Petite Fourchette, 70 boulevard de Strasbourg
Le Relais des Routiers, 8 place de la République

Where to camp
Camping Lac de Ribou, avenue du Lac

LA CIOTAT 76

An ancient port with a modern resort area created at La Ciotat-Plage. The Church of Notre-Dame-de-l'Assomption is notable for its wall paintings.

Where to stay
★★★**Rose Thè,** 4 boulevard Beau Rivage ☎(42)830923 (no restaurant)
★★**Rotonde,** 44 boulevard de la République ☎(42)086750

Where to eat
Golfe, 14 boulevard A – France
At Auberge la Ciotat – Plage NE 1,5 km par D 559
Le Revestel (Chez Gève)

CLAIRIÈRE DE L'ARMISTICE 92

A replica of the railway carriage in which the armistice to end World War I was signed on 11 November 1918 stands in a wooded glade. Inside are exhibits and a display of slides relating to this event.

CLAMECY 66

An ancient town, full of old houses and narrow winding streets, standing at the confluence of the Rivers Beuvron and Yonne. Clamecy was once famous for its 'Flotteurs' who floated rafts of locally-cut logs down the river to Paris. A section of the local museum is devoted to the history of this trade which died out in the early part of the present century.

CLÉRES 33

This is one of Normandy's most popular towns. The park surrounding the much-restored 14th century château contains an interesting zoo, specialising mainly in birds, although some species of animals are also on display. Cléres is also the home of the Normandy Car Museum, which has a fine collection of vintage vehicles and bicycles, some of them more than a century old.

CLERMONT-FERRAND 67, 68, 69

Known as the capital of the Auvergne, Clermont-Ferrand lies on sloping ground overlooking a valley to the east and Monts Dômes to the west. Many buildings in the old town, including the 13th century Cathedral of Notre Dame, are built of distinctive black volcanic rock contrasting sharply with the modern suburbs. The Musée du Bargoin, which contains Roman and prehistoric remains, and the Musée du Ranguet, are also of historical interest.

Where to stay
★★★**Colbert,** 19 rue Colbert ☎(73)932566 (no restaurant)
★★★**Gallceni,** 51 rue Bonnaboud ☎(73)935969
★★★**PLM Arveine,** 16 place Delille ☎(73)919206
☆☆**Campanile,** rue C-Guichard ☎(77)918891
★★**Minimes,** 10 rue des Minimes ☎(73)933149 (no restaurant)
★**Foch,** 22 rue Ml-Foch ☎(73)934840 (no restaurant)
★**Ravel,** 8 rue de Maringues ☎(73)915133 (no restaurant)

Where to eat
Auvergne Pyrénées les Routiers, 12 bis place Corne-Deschaut
Le Brezou, 51 rue St-Dominique
Buffet Gare Routiere, 69 boulevard Gergovia
Clavé, 10-12 rue St Augustin
Courte-Paille, N9 (route de Kiom. Boulevard Clementel)
Le Domino, 60 avenue Edouard-Michelin
Le Machon, 26 place St Pierre
Le Relais des Carmes, 44 rue des Jacobins
Le Relais de Strasbourg, 59 avenue de l'Union
Truffe d'Argent, 17 rue Lamartine

CLOYES-SUR-LE-LOIR 82
A small town, with several ancient buildings. Émile Zola, the 19th-century novelist, lived here for a time while researching his novel *Earth*.

Where to stay
★★**St-Jacques,** 35 rue Nationale ☎(37)984008
★**St-Georges Lf,** 13 rue du Temple ☎(37)985436

Where to eat
Dauphin, rue J-Chauveau

COGOLIN 77
A small industrial town noted for the manufacture of carpets and the production of wine. The local carpet factory (Les Tapis et Tissus de Cogolin) is open to visitors on most weekday afternoons.

Where to eat
Lou Capoun, rue Marceau

Where to camp
Argentière

COLMAR 98
A picturesque city lying on the perimeter of the Vosges foothills on the banks of the River Lauch. Colmar's charm lies mainly in its medieval appearance, with an abundance of half-timbered, gabled houses, many of which date from the 16th century. The old tanners' quarter (Quartier des Tanneurs) has recently been tastefully restored to provide the inhabitants with modern facilities whilst leaving the exterior of the buildings to appear virtually untouched by time. Colmar is also famous for its art treasures, and the Unterlinden Museum contains many examples of the work of Mathias Grünewald and Martin Schongauer, both natives of the town. Another museum is devoted to the work of Bartholdi, the sculptor of the Statue of Liberty in New York and the Lion of Belfort, who was also born in Colmar and designed a number of its attractive fountains.

Where to stay
★★★**Champs de Mars,** 2 avenue de la Marne ☎(89)41545 (no restaurant)
☆☆**Novotel,** 49 route de Strasbourg ☎(89)414914
★★★**Terminus Bristol,** 7 place de la Gare ☎(89)235959
☆☆**Campanile,** rue des Frères Lumière 21 Nord ☎(89)241818
★★**Turenne,** 10 route Bâle ☎(89)411226 (no restaurant)

Where to eat
Colmar Sud, 88 avenue route de Bâle
Flunch, 8 avenue de la République
Trois Poissons, 15 quai Poissonnerie

Where to camp
Camping Intercommunal de l'III

COLOMBEY-LES-DEUX-ÉGLISES, 30
This village was the home of General Charles de Gaulle, the leader of the Free French during World War II and President of France, from 1933 until his death in 1970. His house, La Boisserie, is open to the public and his grave may be seen in the village churchyard. A pink granite cross of Lorraine has been erected in the General's honour on a neighbouring hilltop.

Where to stay
★★★**Dhuits,** N19, ☎(25)015010

COMBEAUFONTAINE 31

Where to stay
★**Balcon Lf,** route de Paris ☎(84)786234

COMBRONDE 67

Where to stay
★**Family,** ☎(73)971001

COMPIÈGNE 1, 15, 92
Lying in the Oise Valley at the edge of one of the most beautiful forests in France is Compiègne, where Joan of Arc was finally captured in 1430. The magnificent Royal Palace, dating from the 14th century, was rebuilt and enlarged by Louis XV and became a favourite residence of Napoleon. Within the palace is a museum devoted to the second empire of Napoleon III, and an Automobile Museum. The early 16th century town hall has a unique belfry where wooden figures known as 'Picantins', strike the quarter hour.

Where to stay
☆☆**Campanile,** avenue de Huy ☎(4)4204235
★★**Harlay,** 3 rue Harlay ☎(4)4230150 (no restaurant)
☆☆**Ibis,** 18 rue E-Branly, quartier de l'Université ☎(4)4231627

Where to eat
Flunch, Venette N31
La Royale Pinte, 41 rue de Soissons

CONCARNEAU 51
A busy fishing port which has become a popular tourist resort. Concarneau's principal attraction is the fascinating walled town (Ville Close), which stands on an island and is linked to the mainland by two bridges. Surrounded by medieval ramparts, the town is a jumble of narrow alleys and contains the Fishing Museum, located in the former arsenal, and the shellwork display centre. An interesting sea-world exhibition can be visited on the mainland at the Marinaview on the Quai de la Croix.

LA COQUILLE 87

Where to stay
★**Voyogeurs Lf,** rue de la République (N21) ☎(53)528013

Where to eat
Les Portes du Perigord Vert, les Communaux

CORBEIL-ESSONNES 2, 23

Where to eat
Aux Armes de France, 1 boulevard J-Jaures ☎(6)4962404
L'Ermitage, 137 boulevard de Fontainebleau ☎(6)4962942
L'Escale, 10 rue de Seine ☎(6)4962658
La Nancelle, 31 rue de la Papeterie ☎(6)4962117

At Le Plessis-Chenet (4km S)
Where to stay
☆☆**Climat de France,** 2 rue Panhard ☎(6)4938536

COSNE-SUR-LOIRE 23
A small industrial centre at the mouth of the Nohain Valley. There is an interesting museum dealing with the history of the River Loire.

Where to stay
★★**Grand Cerf,** 43 rue St-Jaques ☎(86)280446
★**Vieux Relais Lf,** 11 rue St-Agnan ☎(86)282021

Where to eat
La Panetière, 18 place Pêcherie
Le Relais des Trois Couleurs, 21 rue St-Agnan
Sévigné, 16 rue du 14 Juillet

Where to camp
Camping Municipal L'Ile, route de Bourges

COUCY-LE-CHÂTEAU-AUFFRIQUE 94
Despite extensive damage during World War I, the town has retained portions of its 13th century fortifications, including an imposing keep and fragments of the ramparts. The 13th century Porte de Soissons contains an interesting history museum.

COURTENAY 2, 66

Where to eat
Le Rabolit, place Marché ☎(38)974452
Le Relais, 26 rue Nationale ☎(38)974160
Le Relais des Sports, 38 rue de Villeneuve

COUTAINVILLE 40
A seaside resort built among sand dunes.

Where to stay
★Hardy Lf, place 28 Juillet ☎(33)470411

Where to camp
Camping Martinet
Camping Moueltes, rue du Dr-Viaud le Passous

COUTANCES 40
This town, known as the religious centre of the Cotentin Peninsula, is perched on a hill crowned by the magnificent Cathedral of Notre-Dame, built during the 13th century.

Where to stay
★Moderne, 25 boulevard Alsace-Lorraine ☎(33)451377 (no restaurant)

Where to eat
Au P'tit Home, 4 rue Harcourt
Le Relais 50, 76 avenue Division Leclerc
Le Relais du Viaduc, 25 avenue de Verdun

CRESSENSAC 37, 73

Where to stay
★Chez Gilles Lf, (N20) ☎(65)377006

LA CROIX VALMER 77
A small health resort, noted for its locally produced wine. A stone cross marks the spot where the Emperor Constantine is said to have seen a vision on his way to Rome.

Where to stay
★★★Mer, 2.5km SE on N559 ☎(94)796061

Where to eat
La Cigale, Route Nle 559
Esquinade, domaine de Barbigoua 50
St-Laurent, Odyssée 80

Where to camp
Sélection

DAX 87
This famous health resort lies below the pine forests of Les Landes on the banks of the River Adour and is noted for its hot water spring. Some ancient ruins can be found in the Théodore-Denis Park and a Roman mosaic is preserved in the Church of St-Vincent-de-Younte's. Also of interest is the cathedral, which contains some interesting 17th century paintings.

Where to eat
Aub des Pins, 86 avenue F-Planté
Auberge de la Chalosse, 157 avenue Georges – Clemenceau
Bois de Boulogne, 1km par allée des Baignots
Fin Gourmet, 3 rue Pénitents
Richelieu, 13 avenue V-Hugo
Sarres Batuze "chez pepe", 19 avenue G-Clemenceau

Where to camp
Chênes, Bois de Boulogne

DIEPPE 33, 92
Considered to be France's oldest seaside resort, Dieppe has retained many of its old alleys and interesting areas, in spite of its prominent position as a major passenger and commercial port. It was the scene of an exploratory landing by Canadian commandos in August 1942, which suffered heavy losses but provided valuable information for the subsequent allied invasion. There is a plaque commemorating the raid, along with a monument to Dieppe men who explored Canada between the 16th century and 18th century, in the Square du Canada, which is situated below Dieppe Castle.

Where to stay
★★★Aguado, 30 boulevard de Verdun ☎(35)842700 (no restaurant)
☆☆Ibis Dieppe, le Val Druel, ☎(35)826530
★★Select, 1 rue Toustain, ☎(35)841466
★★Windsor Lf, 18 boulevard de Verdun ☎(35)841523

Where to eat
Armorique, 17 quai Henri-IV
L'Avenir, 10 Cours de Dakar, Port de Commerce
Marmite Dieppoise, 8 rue St-Jean Port, 99 quai Henri-IV
Le Sully, 97 quai Henri-IV

DIGNE 80
Digne enjoys a beautiful climate surrounded by lavender fields, beside the River Bléone. There is an interesting museum containing natural history and the works of two 19th century painters, and the Romanesque Cathedral of Notre-Dame-du-Bourg, which can be found in the old quarter.

Where to stay
★★★Ermitage Napoléon, boulevard Gambetta ☎(92)310109
★★Algion Lf, 1 rue de Provence ☎(92)310270
★★Mistre, 65 boulevard Gassendi ☎(92)310016

Where to camp
Camping Municipal, Bourg route de la Javie

DIJON 28, 29, 66, 94, 95
The capital of old Burgundy, Dijon is, in many ways, one of the most interesting towns in the country. A wealth of magnificent old buildings has been preserved, notably the former residence of the Dukes of Burgundy, which contains the town's Fine Arts Museum and the Gothic Church of Notre-Dame, where a unique Flemish chiming clock is struck by models of a blacksmith and his family. The church also contains an 11th century Black Virgin, believed to be one of the oldest surviving examples of French wood sculpture.

Where to stay
★★★Chapeau Rouge, 5 rue Michelet ☎(80)302810
★★★Frantel, 22 boulevard de la Marne ☎(80)723113
★★★Ibis Central, 3 place Grangier ☎(80)304400
★★Hostellerie du Sauvage, 64 rue Monge ☎(80)413121
★★Jura, 14 avenue MI-Foch ☎(80)416112 (no restaurant)
★Nord, 2 rue Liberté ☎(80)305858

Where to eat
Court-Paille, N74
Flunch, 24 boulevard de Brosses
Pierre Fillion, 39 rue Buffon
Le Rallye, 39 rue Chabot-Charny
Le Vinarium, 23 place Bossuet

Where to camp
Camping Municipal Lac, 43 avenue Albert – 1er

Where to stay
At Perrigny-les-Dijon (9km S on N74)
☆☆☆ **Novotel Dijon Sud,** route de Beaune ☎(80)521422
☆☆ **Ibis,** route de Lyon – Beaune ☎(80)528645

DINAN 48
Overlooking the River Rance, the most impressive approach to the town is on the Rennes to Dol road. Dinan is a very attractive town with a great deal to interest the tourist. It is surrounded by impressive ramparts and dominated by a 14th century castle. The old quarter of the town is full of picturesque narrow streets, quaint houses and pleasant gardens.

Where to stay
★★ **Avaugour Lf,** 1 place du champs Clos ☎(96)390749

Where to eat
Caravelle, 14 place Duclos
La Marmite, 91 rue de Brest

Where to camp
Camping Châteaubriand, 103 rue Châteaubriand

DINARD 52
On the Rance estuary opposite St Malo, Dinard became an elegant and exclusive seaside holiday resort for British and American travellers in the 19th century. Although still elegant the resort is less exclusive today, and owes much of its popularity to its entertainment facilities, two large beaches and the splendid views of the adjacent coast.

Where to stay
★★ **Bains,** 38 Avenue George-V ☎(99)461371
★★ **Dunes Lf,** 5 rue G-Clemenceau ☎(99)461272
★★ **Emeraude Plage,** 1 boulevard Albert 1er ☎(99)461579
★★ **Printania,** 5 avenue George-V ☎(99)461307

Where to eat
Prieuré, 1 place Gl-de-Gaulle
Le Relais de la Gare, 28 rue de la Corbinais

Where to camp
Camping Mauny
Camping Municipal Port Blanc, rue du Sgt-Boulanger
Camping Prieuré

DOL-DE-BRETAGNE 48, 64
A small town perched on the edge of a high cliff, Dol-de-Bretagne has a splendid Gothic Cathedral, a number of old houses, and the Guillotière Museum, which illustrates the history of the area.

Where to stay
★★ **Bresche Arthur Lf,** boulevard Deminiac ☎(99)480144
★★ **Bretagne Lf,** 17 place Châteaubriand ☎(99)480203

Where to eat
Le Relais des Sports et du Bon Accueil, 23 bis rue de Rennes
Les Routiers, 46 rue des Ponts

Where to camp
Camping Municipal
At Baguer-Pican (4km E on N176)
Camping Ferme-Camping du Vieux Chêne

DOLE 17, 95
Although the town has now become a busy industrial and commercial centre on the River Doubs, it has retained a picturesque old quarter where gabled, turreted buildings cluster around the lofty bell tower of the 16th century Church of Notre Dame. A fine view

Dole and its 16th century church of Notre Dame

over this area can be obtained from the Place aux Fleurs. Louis Pasteur was born in Dole in 1822 and his home in the Rue Pasteur has been converted into a museum containing a number of mementoes of his life and work. Dole also has an interesting museum with sections devoted to local archaeology and 16th and 17th century art.

Where to stay
★★★ **Chandioux,** place Grévy ☎(84)790066

Where to camp
Camping Pasquier

DOMPAIRE 99

Where to stay
★★ **Commerce Lf,** place MI – Leclerc ☎(29)365028

DOMRÉMY-LA-PUCELLE 99
Joan of Arc was born in this small village beside the River Meuse in 1412. Her birthplace (Maison Natale de Jeanne d'Arc) has been preserved, and adjacent to it is a small museum containing mementoes of her life. One mile to the south of Domrémy-la-Pucelle is the Basilique du Boise-Chenu, which marks the spot where Joan of Arc first heard the voices summoning her to fight for France.

DONZANAC 37
A pretty country town on the River Maumont.

DORDIVES 23

Where to stay
★**César Lf,** 8 rue de la République
☎(38)927320 (no restaurant)

Where to eat
Le Relais Routier, RN7

DOUÉ-LA-FONTAINE 42

One of the oldest towns in the area, Doué-la-Fontaine is noted for its rose growing, and for the number of troglodyte dwellings in the vicinity. The town itself contains an arena which was hewn out of a local quarry during the 15th century and is now used for theatrical performances and flower shows. An extensive zoo is located on the outskirts.

Where to stay
★**Dagobert,** 14 place Champ-de-Foire ☎(41)591444

Where to eat
le Nord, 18 place du Champ-de-Foire

DRAGUIGNAN 4

A former Roman settlement which has retained a medieval appearance and become a busy market centre. The Tour de l'Horloge (clock tower) marks the spot where a Roman fort and a feudal castle once stood. To the east of the town, on the D59, lies an Allied Military Cemetary containing the graves of British and American troops who died during the airborne invasion in August 1944.

Where to stay
★★**Col de l'Ange,** route de Lorgues ☎(94)682301

Where to eat
La Calèche, 7 boulevard G-Péri

DREUX 34

A lively town in the pleasantly wooded Blaise Valley which evolved from an ancient Gallic settlement into a thriving commercial and tourist centre. The Chapelle Royale St-Louis, the only remaining portion of Dreux's ducal fortress, contains the tombs of the Orléans family.

Where to stay
At Montreuil (8km NE)
★★**Auberge Gué des Grues**
☎(37)435025

Where to eat
Le Marceau, 40-42 boulevard Marceau
Le Relais de la Poste, 2 rue Gl-de-Gaulle
Le Relais des Rochelles, 13 rue des Rochelles

DUNKERQUE (DUNKIRK) 13, 14

The northern-most town and one of the principal seaports of France, Dunkirk was the scene of the historic withdrawal of the British Expeditionary Force in May-June 1940. Much of the town was destroyed at the time but the 16th century Church of St-Eloi and the restored Renaissance-style town hall are still intact. The Chapel of Notre-Dame-les-Dunes is one of the chief pilgrimage centres of northern France.

Where to stay
★★★**Europ,** 13 rue de Levghenaer ☎(28)662907
★★★**Frantel,** rue J-Jaurès ☎(28)665180 (no restaurant)
★★**Borel,** 6 rue l'Hermitte ☎(28)665180 (no restaurant)

At Armbouts Cappel
☆☆☆**Novotel,** Voie Express – Bordure du Lac (7kms) ☎(28)659733

Where to eat
Courte-Paille, ZAC Saint-Pol-Jardin, Saint-Pol-sur-Mer
Aux Ducs de Bourgogne, 29 rue Bourgogne
Metropole, 28 rue Thiers
Victoire, 35 avenue Bains

ÉCOMMOY 39

Where to stay
★**Commerce Lf,** 19 place République ☎(43)271034

Where to eat
Le Relais du Midi, 2 place Foch

ENTREVAUX 80

An ancient fortified town overlooking the River Var with a fine 17th century cathedral. There are beautiful views of the valley below from the Citadel.

EPINAL 99

Famous for coloured prints (Images d'Epinal) which were produced during the 18th century, Epinal is now an industrial town in a pleasant situation on the banks of the River Moselle. A number of picturesque old buildings can be seen in the town, particularly around the Place des Vosges, and Epinal's two museums deal exclusively with paintings; the Imagerie Pellerin featuring examples of the Images d'Epinal. A colourful carnival and folklore festival is held here each year during the week before Easter.

Where to stay
★★**Résidence,** 39 avenue des Templiers ☎(29)824564 (no restaurant)
★★**Vosges et Terminus,** 16 place de la Gare ☎(29)823578 (no restaurant)
★**Azus,** 54 quai des Bons Enfants ☎(29)822915 (no restaurant)

Where to eat
Restaurant de l'Abbattoir, 63 rue de Nancy

ERQUY 52

Where to stay
★**Beauregard Lf,** boulevard de la Mer ☎(96)723003

Where to camp
Pins, route du Guen
Roches
St-Pabu, W on D786
Vieux Moulin, on D783

EVREUX 12, 34

An ancient town in the Iton Valley, Evreux has suffered repeated war damage over the last fifteen centuries but has been well repaired and emerged as a pleasant market town retaining some of its historical buildings. The cathedral, a mixture of many architectural styles, is still undergoing restoration; but some early features have been preserved, notably the nave arches, which date from the 12th century.

Where to stay
★★**France Lf,** 29 rue St-Thomas ☎(32)390925
★★**Grenoble,** 17 rue St-Pierre ☎(32)330731 (no restaurant)
☆☆**Ibis,** avenue W-Churchill ☎(32)381636
★★**Normandy,** 37 rue R-Féray ☎(32)331440
★★**Orme Lf,** 13 rue Lombards ☎(32)393412 (no restaurant)

Where to eat
Le Kélan, 87 rue Joséphine
Le Relais de l'Ouest, 45 boulevard Gambetta
Vielle Gabelle, 3 rue Vielle-Gabelle

Where to camp
Camping Municipal No 2, route de Conches

EVRY 2, 23

Where to stay
☆☆**Novotel Paris Evry,** (A6) ☎(6)0778270
★★**Arcade,** cours B-Pascal, Butte Creuse ☎(6)0782990

Where to eat
Courte-Paille, A6, (opposite the Novotel)

FALAISE 39
An attractive town in the Ante Valley, Falaise suffered severe war damage during the German retreat in 1944. The town has been extensively rebuilt, but its most prominent feature remains the huge ruined castle where William the Conqueror, the illegitimate son of Robert, Duke of Normandy and Arlette, a Falaise tanner's daughter, was born in 1027.

Where to stay
★★**Normandie,** 4 rue Al-Courbet
☎(31)901826
★★**Poste Lf,** 38 rue G-Clemenceau
☎(31)901314

Where to eat
La Fine Fourchettes, 52 rue G-Clemenceau
Le Marianne, 9 rue du Ml-Foch
Le Relais Chez Durand, 33 avenue d'Hastings

Where to camp
Camping Municipal Château

LE FAOU 54
An ancient port in an attractive situation at the head of the Faou estuary. A number of corbelled houses may be seen in the main street, giving the town an old-fashioned appearance.

LA FÈRE 25
A riverside town with a 12th-15th century church and a museum containing numerous works of art.

Where to stay
★**Tourelles,** 51 rue de la République ☎(23)563166

FERMONT 91
Fort Fermont is one of the largest fortifications of the Maginot Line.

LA FERTÉ-ST-AUBIN 36
A small town with a charming old quarter dominated by the moated 17th century château.

Where to stay
★★**Perron,** 9 rue du Gl-Leclerc
☎(38)765336

Where to eat
Auberge de l'Ecu de France,
6 rue Gl-Leclerc

FIGEAC 73
Figeac lies on the River Céle and has a very interesting museum, housed in the former Mint. Split into two sections, the Lapidary Museum and the Champollion Museum, it contains various artifacts including a cast of the Rosetta Stone.

Where to stay
★★**Carmes Lf,** 18 place XII Mai
☎(65)342078

Where to eat
Le Relais des Chasseurs, La Vayssière

Where to camp
Carmes, chemin de la Curie

LA FLÈCHE 86

Where to eat
Le Relais des Routiers, 65 rue St-Jacques
Vert Galant, 70 Grande-Rue

Where to camp
Camping Route d'Or, allée de la Porvidence

FLEURANCE 88

Where to stay
★★**Fleurance,** route d'Agen
☎(62)061485

Where to eat
Du Stade, place de l'Église

FOIX 89
An ancient town with fine, old timbered houses in a picturesque setting beneath the 11th century castle.

Where to stay
★★★**Barbacane,** 1 avenue de Lérida ☎(61)655044 (no restaurant)
★★★**Tourisme,** 2 cours l-Cros
☎(61)655121

Where to eat
Le Charmille
Le Relaise du Soleil d'Or, 57 avenue du Ml-Leclerc
XIX Siècle, 2 rue Delcassé

Where to camp
Camping Municipal Lac de Labarre, route de Pamiers

FONTAINEBLEAU 2, 23
A royal hunting lodge was established here in the 12th century. The palace was extensively enlarged between the 16th and 18th centuries and now covers a considerable area. Much of the sumptuous internal decoration was commissioned by Napoleon, who lived here during the upheaval of his abdication. The Palace is surrounded by fine gardens and the grounds are surrounded by the huge Forest of Fountainebleau.

Where to stay
★★★**Aigle Noir,** 27 place N-Bonaparte ☎(6)4223265
★★**Ile de France Lf,** 128 rue de France ☎(6)4222117
★★**Londres,** 1 place du Gl-de-Gaulle ☎(6)4222021I
★★**Toulouse,** 183 rue Grande
☎(6)4222273 (no restaurant)
★**Forêt,** 79 avenue Prés-Roosevelt
☎(6)4223926 (no restaurant)
★**Neuville,** 196 rue Grande
☎(6)4222339

Where to eat
Bistro St-Antoine, 26 rue Ferrare
Filet de Sole, 5 rue Coq-Gris
Le Grillardin, 12 rue Pins

FONTEVRAUD-L'ABBAYE 62
Founded in 1099, the abbey has retained some fine medieval features, notably the 12th century church which contains the tombs of Henry II of England, his wife Eleanor of Aquitaine, and their son Richard the Lionheart. The large octagonal kitchen is one of the few Romanesque kitchens in existence.

FORGES-LES-EAUX 92
A pleasant spa once famous for its metalwork.

Where to eat
Paix, 17 rue Neufchâtel
Les Routiers de la Gare, 57 rue du Gl-Leclerc

Where to camp
Camping Municipal Minière, boulevard N-Thiesse

FOUGÈRES 41, 64
Connected with the manufacture of footwear since 1832, Fourgères is a picturesque old town beside a forest, overlooking the Nançon Valley. The outstanding feature of the town is the heavily fortified castle, a fine example of medieval military architecture. This vast fortress with its thirteen towers rates among the largest in Europe.

Where to stay
★★**Voyageurs,** 10 place Gambetta
☎(99)990820 (no restaurant)
★**Moderne Lf,** 15 rue Tribunal
☎(99)990024

Where to eat
Aux Amis de la Route, 6 boulevard St-Germain

Where to camp
Camping Municipal Paron

FOULAIN 28, 31

Where to stay
★**Chalet** (N19) ☎(25)311111

FOURAS 46, 85

Fouras is a small coastal town situated at the mouth of the River Charente. This small resort enjoys views across to Ile d'Oléron and coastline either side of the town, best seen from the Pointe-de-la-Fumée. The nearby Ile d'Aix can be reached by boat from Fouras.

Where to stay
★★**Grand Hotel les Bains,** 15 rue Gl-Burncher ☎(46)840344

FRAYSSINNET 37

Where to stay
★**Bonne Auberge Lf,**
☎(65)310002
☆**Escale** ☎(65)310001

At Pont-de-Rhodes (1 km N on N20)
★**Relais,** ☎(65)310016

Where to camp
Tirelire

At Pont-de-Rhodes
Plage du Relais

FRÉJUS 4, 77, 78

Fréjus was founded in 49BC by Julius Caesar and is famous for its Roman ruins, which include an amphitheatre, an aqueduct and a gateway. Parts of the cathedral date from the 10th century and the 13th century cloister now houses an excellent museum. Set amongst vineyards and orchards, the town is also near a zoo and a safari park.

Where to stay
☆☆☆**St Augul,** 214 route nationale 98 ☎(94)810123

Where to eat
Lou Calen, 9 rue Desaugiers
La Pinède, route de Bagnols
Les Potiers, 135 rue Potiers
Le Relais des Trois Chênes,
route de Cannes
Oasis, boulevard Alger

Where to camp
Acacias, NE on N7
Baune, route de Bagnols-en-Forêt
Bellevue, route de Bozon
Colombier
Fréjus, route de Bagnols-en-Forêt
Holiday Green, route de Bagnols-en-Forêt
Pierre Vert, 4 route de Bagnols-en-Forêt
Pins Parasols

At Tour-de-Mare (4km NE)
International Europe, 7 route Nationale
Motel Camping Kangourou,
route de Valescure

GACÉ 38, 59

Where to stay
★★★**Champs Lf,** route d'Alençon-Rouen ☎(33)355145
★**Étoile d'Or,** 60 Grande Rue
☎(33)355003

Where to eat
L'Étape, 31 route de Rouen

GENNES 62

Where to stay
★★**Loire Lf,** ☎(41)518103
★★**Naulets d'Anjou,** rue Croix de Mission ☎(41)518188

Where to camp
Camping Districal du Bord de l'Eau

GEX 95

Close to the Swiss border, Gex is a popular tourist resort 12km below the Col de la Faucille, near to the mountains and Geneva.

Where to stay
★**Bellevue,** avenue de la Gare
☎(50)415540

Where to eat
Auberge des Chasseurs,
Echenevex
Le Florimont, 6km par N5

GIEN 66

A pleasant little town, situated on the River Loire and famous for its decorated pottery, or 'faience'. Gien suffered bomb damage during World War II, but has been tastefully restored to blend with the architecture of its 15th century château, which contains a museum of hunting and falconry. The Faience Factory, also containing a museum, lies to the west of the town.

Where to stay
★★**Rivage Lf,** 1 quai de Nice
☎(38)672053

Where to eat
Auberge de la Croix-Blanche,
17 route de Bourges
La Marmite, route de Paris

GOLFE-JUAN 78

Set amongst orange and mimosa trees, this attractive resort was once a landing point for Napoleon following his return from Elba in 1815.

GOURNAY-EN-BRAY 92

A busy dairy centre in the Epte Valley which is famous for its cream cheese, in particular the well-known 'Petit Suisse'. The Church of St-Hildevert, dating from the 11th century, contains some interesting carvings.

Where to eat
Le Relais Paris/Dieppe

GRAMAT 73

Where to stay
★★★**Château de Roumégouse,** 4.5km NW on N140 ☎(65)336381
★★**Centre Lf,** place République
☎(65)387337
★**Lion d'Or Lf,** place République
☎(65)387318

Where to eat
Le Relais Du Centre, place de la République
Le Relais De L'Europe, 8 avenue Louis Mazet
Le Relais Gourmand, 2 avenue Gare

GRANVILLE 40

A seaside resort and commercial port, the town is divided into upper and lower Granville, each significantly different from the other. Upper Town, founded by the English in 1439 is still enclosed by ancient fortifications; within its walls there are numerous exhibits depicting Granville's military and religious past. Lower Town is more modern, dominated by business and tourist trade.

Where to stay
★★**Bains,** 19 rue G-Clemenceau
☎(33)501731

Where to eat
Chez Mathias, 184 avenue de la Libération
Normandy-Chaumière, 20 rue Dr-P-Poirier
Le Phare, 11 rue Port

GRASSE 4

Famous for its perfumes made from locally-grown flowers, Grasse lies on a pleasant hillside and enjoys a gentle climate. The old quarter has many narrow winding streets and tall old buildings as well as a cathedral and two interesting museums.

Where to stay
★★**Aromes Lf**, (N85)
☎(93)704201

Where to eat
Amphitryon, 16 boulevard V-Hugo
Chez Pierre, 3 avenue Thiers
Maître Boscq, 13 rue Fontette

Where to camp
Camping Municipal, boulevard A-de-Rothschild

At Opio (8km E by D2085 & D3)
Caravan Inn, 1.5km S of Opio on D3

GRENOBLE 79, 80
Grenoble is renowned for its beautiful location on the banks of the River Isère, with the Grande-Chartreuse Mountains providing an awesome backdrop. Once the setting for the Winter Olympics (1968), it is a popular holiday resort with many facilities including a Palais-de-Sport. Grenoble has many old buildings such as the Fort-de-la-Bastille, which affords a glorious view of the town and surrounding countryside. Also of interest are the Palais-de-Justice, the Musée Dauphinois and the Cathedral of Notre-Dame, to name but a few.

Where to stay
★★★**Angleterre**, 5 place V-Hugo
☎(76)873721 (no restaurant)
★★★**Grand**, 5 rue de la République
☎(76)444936
★★★**Terminus**, 10 place Gare
☎(76)872433 (no restaurant)
★★**Alpazur**, 59 avenue Alsace-Lorraine ☎(76)464280
(no restaurant)
☆☆**Flimotel**, 20 avenue J-Jaurès
☎(76)242312
★★**Gallia**, 7 boulevard MI-Joffre
☎(76)873921 (no restaurant)
☆☆**Ibis**, Centre Commercial des Trois Dauphins, rue F-Poulat
☎(76)474849
★★**Paris Nice**, 61 boulevard J-Vallier ☎(76)963618 (no restaurant)
At Clais (10.5km S on N75 & D269)
★★★**Oiseaux** ☎(76)980774
At Pont-de-Claix (8km S on N75)
★★**Villancourt**, Cours St-André
☎(76) 981854

At Voreppe (12km NW by A48)
☆☆☆**Novotel**, Autoroute de Lyon
☎(76)508144

Where to eat
A ma table, 92 cours J-Jaurès
Auberge Bressane, 38 1er Impasse Beaublache
Auberge L'Echaillon, St-Quentin-Sur-Isère, Tullins

Le Café des Tourists, 153 Cours Berriat
Le Café du Nord, 44 Grand rue Monestier de Clermont
Chaumière Savoyarde, 27 rue G-Péri
Concorde, 9 boulevard Gambetta
Le Cyrano, 3 place Firmin Gauthier
Le Pommeroise, 1 place Herbes
Poularde Bressane, 12 place P-Mistral
Rabelais, 55 avenue Alsace-Lorraine

Grenoble-Echirolles
Courte-Paille, 175 cours Jean-Jaurès

Grenoble-Voreppe
Courte-Paille, route de Lyon Vers Grenoble, A48

GRISOLLES 19, 37

Where to stay
★★**Relais des Garrigues**, N20
☎(63)303159

Where to eat
Le Relais de la Gare, Nationale 20

Where to camp
Aquitaine, route de Montauban

GUÉTHARY
This pretty little town is a popular bathing and health resort and has retained much of its Basque character.

Where to stay
★★**Mariéna**, avenue Mon-Mugabure ☎(59)265104
(no restaurant)

Where to eat
Madrid

GUINGAMP 49
An industrialised market town which has retained a number of medieval features. Several ancient houses can be seen in the main square and the Basilica of Notre-Dame-de-Bon-Sécours, originally dating from the 14th century, is an imposing mixture of Gothic and Renaissance styles. A 'Pardon' takes place here each July, centred upon the statue of the Black Virgin which stands in a chapel near the entrance to the church.

HAM 94
A port on the River Somme with an interesting Romanesque and Gothic church, a 16th century abbey and an ancient ruined castle.

Where to stay
★**France**, 5 place Hôtel-de-Ville
☎(22)810022

Where to eat
Valet, 58 rue Noyon

LE HAVRE 9, 38
On the right bank of the Seine estuary, Le Havre is a relatively modern port and the second largest in France after Marseille. The old 16th century town was redesigned after World War II, mainly in reinforced concrete. One of the largest squares in Europe, the Place-de-l'Hôtel-de-Ville with a public garden at its centre, can be found in Le Havre. Places of interest include the Fine Arts Museum with its splendid galleries and Old Havre Museum dealing with local history.

Where to stay
★★★**Bordeaux**, 147 rue L-Brindeau ☎(35)226944
(no restaurant)
★★★**Marley**, 121 rue de Paris
☎(35)417248 (no restaurant)
☆☆☆**Mercure**, chaussée de Angoulême ☎(35)212345
★★**Foch**, 4 rue Caligny
☎(35)425069 (no restaurant)
★★**Grand Parisien**, 1 cours de la République ☎(35)252383
(no restaurant)
★★**Ile de France**, 104 rue A-France ☎(35)424929
(no restaurant)
★★**Monaco**, 16 rue de Paris
☎(35)422101
★★**Petit Vatel**, 86 rue L-Brindeau
☎(35)417207 (no restaurant)
★**Voltaire**, 14 rue Voltaire
☎(35)413091 (no restaurant)

Where to eat
L'Athanor, 120 rue Guillemard
Cambridge, 90 rue Voltaire
Guimbarde, 61 rue L-Brindeau
La Petit Bedon, 39 rue L-Brindeau
A la Pipe, 128 boulevard de Graville
Le P'lit Comptoir, 31 rue du GI-Faidherbe
La Rascasse, 2 rue Gustave Nicolle
Le Relais, quai Georges-V
Le Relais des Routiers, 57 rue Marceau
Le Rescator, 47 rue E-Lang
Au Téléphone, 173 boulevard Admiral Mouchez

LE HAYE-DU-PUITS 40

Where to stay
★**Gare Lf**, ☎(33)460422

Where to eat
Le Relais des Amis, 16 rue du Château

Where to camp
Camping Etang des Haizes,
St-Symphorien-le-Valois

HÉDÉ 43
An old city perched on a hill
overlooking the canal locks.

Where to stay
★★**Hostellerie du Vieux Moulin
Lf,** (N137) ☎(99)454570

Where to eat
Vielle Auberge, N137

HENNEBONT 51
An ancient town beside the River
Blavet which has retained portions of
its medieval fortifications. The steeple
of the 16th century church of Notre-
Dame-du-Paradis is a well-known
landmark and the remains of the
former abbey are preserved in the
grounds of the local stud farm.

HESDIN 90
An ancient town with a fine 17th
century town hall.

Where to stay
★**Flanders Lf,** 22 rue d'Arras
☎(21)868021

Where to eat
La Choppe, 47-49 rue d'Arras

HOSSEGOR 8, 85
A well-populated seaside resort on the
west coast of France.

Where to stay
★★**Beauséjour,** avenue Genêts
par avenue Tour du Lac
☎(58)435107
★★**Ermitage Lf,** allées des Pins
Tranquilles ☎(58)435222

Where to eat
L'Amiral, avenue P-Lahary
Huitrères du Lac, avenue Touring
Club

Where to camp
Rey

LES HOUCHES 18
A small village which bursts into
activity during the winter season in an
attractive location near to Mont Blanc.

Where to stay
★★**Piste Bleue,** route les Chavants
☎(50)544066

Where to camp
Airhôtel du Bourgeat, 1.5km NE
Petit Pont, 2km E on N506, 120m
above N506

HOURTIN 85
Where to camp
Mauriflaude, route de Pauillac

HYÈRES 77
The oldest of the Riviera resorts,
Hyères lies on a hillside in a sheltered
position and is noted for the growth of
early fruit and vegetables. The wide,
tree-lined streets of the modern town
contrast pleasantly with the ancient
buildings and gateways of the old
quarter, which stands below the ruins
of a feudal castle. Of special interest in
this area are the church of St-Paul,
dating originally from the 12th
century, and the Renaissance and
Romanesque buildings which
surround it. The harbour is filled with
pleasure craft and passenger ferries
serving the Hyères Islands which lie a
short distance from the shore.

Where to eat
Asia, 28 boulevard A-Denis
Comme chez Sol, boulevard de la
Marine
Le Delfins, place Clemenceau
Relais du Gros Pins, 15 avenue
Paul-Renaudel
Le Tison d'Or, 1 rue Gallieni

ISIGNY 11
Isigny lies on the edge of rich dairy
farming country.

Where to stay
☆☆**France Lf,** 17 rue Demagny
☎(31)220033

L'ISLE-SUR-LE-DOUBS 17
Where to eat
Le Palais de la Biere, 15 rue de-
Lattre-de-Tassigny

Where to camp
Camping Municipal Lumes

ISSOIRE 69, 72
Where to stay
★★**Parlou Lf,** 18 avenue Kennedy
☎(73)892211

Where to eat
Le Bergerie
Le Chapeau Rouge, route de St-
Germain
Les Chevaliers de la Route, 1 rue
du Mas
Hostellerie les Vigneaux, N9
Le Relais, 1 avenue Gare

IVRY-LA-BATAILLE 34
Where to stay
★★**Grand St-Martin Lf,** 9 rue Erzy
☎(32)364139

JAVRON 60
Where to eat
La Terrasse

Where to camp
Camping Municipal, route de
Mayenne

JOINVILLE 26
A small town beside the River Marne,
Joinville is famous as the home of
Jean-de-Joinville, the 13th century
chronicler. The town's principal
building is the 16th century Château-
du-Grand-Jardin, set in a park stocked
with exotic plants, which was once the
seat of the Dukes of Guise.

Where to stay
★**Poste Lf,** place Grève
☎(25)961263
★**Soleil d'Or,** 7 rue des Capucins
☎(25)961566

JOSSELIN 51
A small town on the River Oust
containing the most famous château
in Brittany. Built between the 15th
*The castle at Josselin is one of
the most romantic
buildings in
Brittany*

and 16th century the château, which overlooks the river, has several old slate-roofed houses behind it, and nearby is the Basilica of Notre-Dame du Roncier.

Where to stay
★★**Château,** 1 rue Gl-de-Gaulle ☎(97)222011

Where to eat
La Rochette, 128 rue Glatinier

JOUGNE 27

Where to stay
★**Deux Saisons** ☎(81) 490004

JUAN-LES PINS 4, 78

A popular holiday resort with a lovely sandy beach set against a backdrop of pine trees.

Where to stay
★★★**Apparthotel Astor,** 61 chemin Fournel Badine ☎(93)610738
★★★**Hellos,** 3 avenue Dautheville ☎(93)615525
★★★**Juana,** avenue G-Gallice, la Pinèda ☎(93)610870
★★**Alexandra,** rue Pauline ☎(93)610136
★★**Cyrano,** avenue L-Gallet ☎(93)610483 (no restaurant)
★★**Emeraude,** 11 avenue Saramartel ☎(93)610967
★★**Noailles,** avenue Gallice ☎(93)611170
★**Midi,** 93 boulevard Poincaré ☎(93)613516

Where to eat
Bijou Plage, route Bord-de-Mer
Le Perroquet, avenue G-Gallice

JULLOUVILLE 40

A collection of houses scattered among pine trees.

Where to stay
★★**Casino Lf,** rue de la Mer ☎(33)618282

Where to eat
Le Village, Edenville (1km S on D911)

Where to camp
Camping Chaussée, avenue de la Libération
Camping Dr-Lemmonier

KAYSERSBERG 98

A small wine-growing centre lying below the hill-top ruins of a medieval castle. Kaysersberg has retained much of its 16th-17th century character in the shape of numerous half-timbered buildings and a picturesque fortified bridge which spans the River Weiss. The town is famous for its associations with Dr Albert Schweitzer who was born here in 1875. His home is still standing at 124 Rue du Gl-de-Gaulle, and contains a museum devoted to his life and work.

LAMBALLE 48, 49, 52

A charming market town with much character, on a hill overlooking the River Gouessant. The Church of Notre-Dame stands on a terrace which provides panoramic views of the valley.

Juan Les Pins – fashionable resort

Where to stay
★★**Angleterre Lf,** 29 boulevard Jobert ☎(96)310016
★★**Auberge du Manoir des Portes,** La Poterie ☎(96)311362
★**Tour d'Argent Lf,** 2 rue du Dr-Lavergne ☎(96)310137

LANDERNEAU 49

An ancient port on the River Elorn, well known for salmon fishing and locally-grown spring vegetables. Landerneau is popular with tourists on account of its quaint old buildings and churches. Its location makes it an ideal centre for excursions.

Where to stay
☆☆**Ibis** ☎(98)213132

LANGON 19

Where to eat
Grangousier, 2 chemin du Peyrot
Le Relais Laharanne, 10 rue Dotézac

Where to camp
Camping Municipal Allées Marine, 2 avenue de l'Hippodrome

LANGRES 27, 28, 31

An old fortified town standing on a high plateau above the Marne Valley. Langres presents the visitor with an attractive mixture of cobbled streets and old houses and the ramparts, with their original towers and gateways, have been turned into a pleasant walking area providing fine views. The town has a fine cathedral, dating from the 12th century, and a section of the Breuil de St-Germain Museum is devoted to the philosopher Diderot who was born in Langres in 1713.

Where to stay
★★**Europe,** 23 rue Diderot
☎(25)851088
★★**Lion d'Or,** route de Vesoul
☎(25)850330
★**Cheval Blanc,** 4 rue de l'Estres
☎(25)850700

Where to eat
Auberge Jeanne d'Arc, 26 rue Gambetta
La Bonne Auberge, faubourg de la Collinière
Le Relais des Routiers, faubourg de la Collinière

LAON 25
An ancient town set on a scarped hill and dominated by an imposing 12th century cathedral. The old town, on the upper slopes, retains many historic buildings and remnants of the old ramparts, and the museum has a 12th century Knights Templar chapel in its courtyard.

Where to stay
★★**Angleterre,** 10 boulevard de Lyon ☎(23)230462
☆☆**Finotel,** Zac Ile de France (N2)
☎(23)210811
★**Bannière de France,** 11 rue de F-Roosevelt ☎(23)232144
★**Chevaliers,** 3 rue Serurier
☎(23)234378

Where to eat
Chenizelles, 1 rue Bourg
Le Vertefeuille, RN 44 – Le Verte Feuille

Where to camp
Camping Municipal, 22 rue J-P-Timbaud

LARAGNE-MONTÉGLIN 80
Where to stay
★**Terrasses Lf,** avenue Provence
☎(92)650854

LAVAL 16, 41, 60
A busy industrial and market centre, the town has retained its attractive old quarter, the best view of which may be obtained from the Pont A-Briand and the 13th century Pont Vieux, which cross the River Mayenne in the town centre. Pleasantly decorated 16th century houses are grouped around the castle and cathedral. The castle has two distinct parts; a new Renaissance building converted into Law Courts in the 19th century and the old castle dating from the 12th century, its main feature the impressive three-storey keep, now a museum.

Where to stay
☆☆**Ibis,** route de Mayenne
☎(43)538182

Where to eat
A la Bonne Auberge, 168 rue de Bretagne
Le Relais de Niafles, Niafles-Changé-les-Lavel
La Rousine, route Tours

LE LAVANDOU 77
An attractive resort and fishing port, Le Lavendou is a departure point for ferries to the Hyères Islands.

Where to stay
★★★**Calanque,** 62 avenue Gl-de-Gaulle ☎(94)710596
★★★**California,** route de St-Tropez ☎(94)710263
★★★**Résidence-Beach,** boulevard Front-de-Mer
☎(94)710066
★**Petite Bohème,** avenue F-Roosevelt ☎(94)711030

Where to eat
La Bouée, 2 avenue Ch-Cazin
Denise et Michel, 8 rue Patron-Ravello
Le Grill, 22 rue Patron-Ravello

Where to camp
Minosas
St-Pons, 1km SW

LES LECQUES 76
Where to stay
★★★**Grand,** ☎(94)262301

LECTOURE 88
On a hill overlooking the River Gens, Lectoure has several old buildings of interest. The former Bishops Palace now houses the town hall, law courts, art gallery and museum.

Where to eat
Bouviers, 8 rue Montebello
Le Gascogne, route Agen

Where to camp
Lac des Trois Vahées, 3km SE on N21

LENS 1, 15, 25, 90
Where to eat
El Caballero, 28 avenue du 4 Septembre

LÉON 85
Where to camp
Lou Puntaou

LÉZIGNAN-CORBIÈRES 20
Where to stay
★**Tassigny,** Rond Point de Lattre
☎(68)271151

Where to camp
Camping Municipal Pinéda

LIGNY-EN-BARROIS 93, 96, 97, 98, 99
In a picturesque setting between the River Ornain and the Marne/Rhine canal, Ligny-en-Barrois is an old town with narrow winding streets and a number of old houses.

LILLE 14, 15
A highly industrialised town, Lille is one of the foremost textile centres in the world. Despite a great deal of modernisation the older part has retained a distinctly Flemish appearance. The town is overlooked by Vauban's imposing 17th century citadel, surrounded by pleasant gardens.

Where to stay
★★★**Bellevue,** 5 rue J-Roisin
☎(20)574586
★★★**Carlton,** 3 rue de Paris
☎(20)552411
★★★**Royal,** 2 boulevard Carnot
☎(20)510511 (no restaurant)

Where to eat
Ala Bascule, 12 rue Cambrai
Le Calamity, 37 rue des Postes
Chez Alcide, 5 rue Debris St-Étienne
Chez Bernard, 65 rue de la Barre
Le Compostelle, 4 rue St-Étienne
Flunch, 57 rue de Béthune
Flunch, 33 avenue Charles St-Venant
Flunch, (RN352)
Paris, 52 bis rue Esquermoise
Le Relais du Port, 17 boulevard de la Lorraine
Le Restaurant, 1 place Sebastopol
Rot le Féguide, place Gare

LIMOGES 36, 37, 42, 87
On a ford across the River Vienne is the ancient town of Limoges, famous for its 200-year old porcelain manufacturing industry and the brightly coloured Limoges enamels, connected with the town since the 12th century. Examples of the craft can be found in the Adrien-Dubouché National Museum and the Municipal Museum. The town has several buildings of historical note such as the Gothic cathedral and 12th century Church of St-Pierre.

Where to stay
★★★**Luk,** 29 place Jourdan
☎(55)334400

★★**Caravelle,** 21 rue A-Barbès
☎(55)777529 (no restaurant)
☆☆**Ibis,** rue F-Bastiat ZAC
industrielle Nord 2 ☎(55)375014
★★**Jourdan,** 2 avenue du Gl-de-
Gaulle ☎(55)774962
★**Relais Lamartine Lf,** 10 rue des
Cooperateurs ☎(55)775339

Where to eat
Au Petit Bor, 'Chez Bichon' 68
avenue de Lattre-de-Tassigny
Buffet Gare Bénédictins
Le Chambord, 3 avenue Gen-de-
Gaulle
Le Fontenoy, 246 bis, avenue du
Général Leclerc
Lou Galetou, 26 rue Boucherie
Maracana, 100 rue Armand Dutreix
Petits Ventres, 20 rue Boucherie
Pré St-Germain, 26 rue de la Loi
Versailles, 20 place Aine

At Limoges Nord
Courte-Paille, N20 à 2km direction
Paris

Where to camp
**Camping Municipal de la Vallée
de l'Aurence**

LE LION D'ANGERS 41
A small town in a picturesque setting
on the banks of the Oudon.

Where to stay
★**Voyageurs,** 2 rue Gl-Leclerc, quai
Oudon ☎(41)913008

Where to camp
Camping Municipal Frénes

LISEUX 12
A thriving industrial and commercial
centre with the oldest Gothic cathedral
in Normandy. Liseux has become a
place of pilgrimage since Ste-Thérèse
was canonised in 1925, a basilica to
her memory was consecrated in
1954.

Where to stay
★★★**Grand Normandie Lf,** 11
bis rue au Char ☎(31)621605
★★★**Place,** 67 rue H-Chéron
☎(31)311744 (no restaurant)
★★**Lourdes,** 4 rue au Char
☎(31)311948
★**Coupe d'Or Lf,** 49 rue Pont-
Mortain ☎(31)311684

Where to eat
Acacias, 13 rue Résistance
Pileou Face, 68 boulevard H-
Fournet
Le Relais Fleuri, 75 rue Fournet
Relais Paris-Cherbourg, 113
avenue du Six-Juin

Where to camp
Camping Municipal, rue de la
Vallée

LIT-ET-MIXE 85
Where to camp
Camping Municipal, Cap de
l'Hormy
Camping Municipal Univers,
route des Lacs

LOCHES 67
A beautiful town on the banks of the
River Indre with a picturesque walled
medieval quarter at its centre. Many
fine old buildings are located in this
area including the imposing château
and the ancient keep, dating originally
from the 11th century, which has
some well preserved dungeons. The
château was the home of Agnès Sorel,
Charles VIII's favourite, during the
15th century, and her recumbent
figure is on display in the Charles VIII
room.

Where to stay
★**France,** 6 rue Picois
☎(47)590032

Where to camp
Camping Municipal, route de
Châteauroux

LODÈVE 70, 74
An old town standing at the confluence
of the Rivers Lergue and Soulondres.
In former years, Lodève was an
important textile centre, but this trade
has now declined, although rugs are
still manufactured here. Places of
interest include the 13th century
cathedral of St-Fulcran and the
Jacques Audibert Museum which
deals with geology and pre-history.

Where to stay
★★**Croix Blanche,** 6 avenue de
Fumel (N9) ☎(67)441087

Where to eat
Le Relais Croix de Cartels
**Le Relais de la Fontaine
D'Amour,** Route Nationale 9
Le Relais de l'Escalette, Route
Nationale 9
Le Relais des Sports, 11 avenue
Jean-Jaurès

LONGUYON 91
The town stands in pleasant wooded
surroundings at the confluence of
Rivers Chiers and Crusne. There are
French and German military
cemeteries in the neighbourhood.

Where to stay
★★**Lorraine,** Face Gare
☎(8)2395007

LORIENT 51
One of the foremost French naval
ports.

Where to stay
★★★**Richelieu,** 31 place J-Ferry
☎(97)213573

Where to eat
Cornouaille, 13 boulevard Ml-
Franchet-d'Esperey
Flunch, Centre Commercial K2

At Lanester (5km NE)
Where to stay
☆☆**Novotel,** Zone Commercial de
Bellevue ☎(97)760216
☆☆**Ibis,** Zone Commerciale de
Bellevue ☎(97)764022

LOUDUN 42
A pleasant town with many old houses,
encircled by a boulevard following the
line of the former ramparts. There are
several interesting churches and a
notable landmark is the Tour Carrée,
dating from the 11th century, from
which there is a fine view.

Where to stay
☆☆☆**Mercure,** 40 avenue Leuze
☎(49)981922 (no restaurant)
★**Roue d'Or Lf,** 1 avenue d'Anjou
☎(49)980123

LOURDES 88
In a beautiful Pyrenean setting,
Lourdes is one of the most famous
places of pilgrimage in the world. The
Cité Religieuse contains the Grotte
Massabielle where Ste-Bernadette
saw the visions of the Virgin in 1858
and the pools where invalids and the
infirm bathe. In 1958 an enormous
underground basilica was built to
celebrate the centenary of the visions.
Throughout the town are many
interesting buildings and churches
including the Basilica du Rosaire, the
Soubirous family home and the
Pavillon Notre Dame.

Where to stay
★★★**Grotte,** 66 rue de la Grotte
☎(62)945887
★★**Provençale,** 4 rue Baron Duprat
☎(62)943134
★★**St-Roche,** 6 place J-d'Arc
☎(62)940214

Where to eat
L'Ermitage, place Mgr-Laurence
Gave, 17 quai St-Jean

Where to camp
Arrouach, quartier Biscaye
Belle-Vue, 45 avenue A-Marqui
Domec, route de Julos
Prat, 22 avenue A-Béguère
Sarsan
Sclerie, 64 avenue A-Marqui
Theil No 23

LOUVIERS 9, 12, 34
A small, attractive town in the Eure Valley near the forest. Since the establishment of contemporary light industries, the town's former long-standing connection with wool and textiles has been broken.

Where to eat
Au Rendez-vous des Sportifs, 27 avenue W-Churchill
Le Relais des Routiers, 13 rue de Paris
La Truite, 56 rue du Quai

Where to camp
Camping Bel Air, St-Lubin

Where to stay
At St-Pierre-du-Vauvray (8km E)
★★★**Hostellerie de St-Pierre** ☎(32)599329

At Vironvay (4km SE on N182A)
Where to stay
★★**Saisons** ☎(32)400256

LE LUC 4

Where to stay
★**Hostellerie du Parc,** 1 rue J-Jaurès ☎(94)607001

Where to eat
Relais la Provence, Route Nationale 7

LUNEL 5

Where to stay
★**Palais,** 12 avenue de Lattre de Tassigny ☎(67)711139

Where to camp
Bon Port, Access via D24

LUNÉVILLE 97, 98
A spacious town in forested surroundings with a fine 18th century château which earned Lunéville the title of 'Little Versailles'. The château stands in the landscaped Parc des Bosquets where *son et lumière* performances are held during the summer. The château also contains a museum devoted to the pottery for which Lunéville is famous and a motorcycle museum is located nearby.

LUS-LA-CROIX-HAUTE 80

Where to stay
★**Chamousset Lf,** ☎(92)585112
★**Touring,** 75 route Nationale ☎(92)585001

LYON 2, 3, 24, 79
Between the River Saône and River Rhône, France's third largest city is renowned for the manufacture of silk. Throughout Lyon are many beautiful parks and historic buildings, including the Place Bellecour, dominated by a statue of Louis XIV and the Place Terreux where many people were guillotined during the French Revolution. From the Basilique de Notre-Dame-Fourvière there is a magnificent view of the city.

Where to stay
★★★**Beaux Arts,** 75 route Prés-Herriot ☎(7)8380950 (no restaurant)
★★★**Bordeaux et du Parc** 2 rue du Bêlier ☎(7)8375873 (no restaurant)
★★★**Carlton,** 4 rue Jussieu ☎(7)8425651 (no restaurant)
★★**Globe & Cecil,** 21 Gasparin ☎(7)8425895 (no restaurant)
☆☆**Ibis Lyon la Port Dieu Sud,** place Renaudel ☎(7)895421
★★**Moderne,** 15 rue Dubois ☎(7)8422183 (no restaurant)

At Bron (10km SE)
☆☆☆**Novotel Lyon Aeroport,** rue L-Terray ☎(7)8269748
☆☆**Campanile,** quartier Rebufer, rue Maryse-Bostie ☎(7)8364540
☆☆**Climat de France,** (7)8265076
☆☆**Ibis,** 36 avenue du Doyen J-Lepine ☎(7)8543134

At Charbonnières-les-Bains (8km NW on N7)
☆☆☆**Mecure,** 78 bis route de Paris (N7) ☎(7)8347279

At Ecully (7.5km NW)
☆☆**Campanile,** route de Dardilly ☎(7)8331693

Where to eat
L'Alsacienne, 20 place Carnot
Argenson, 90 avenue Tony Garnier
Aub de l'Ile, quartier St-Rambart, Ile Ste Barbe
Au Petit Col, 68 rue Charité
Aux Amis de la Route, 71 avenue Leclerc
Beluga, Centre Commercial
La Blandon, 28 rue Sergent Blandon
Le Bistrot de Lyon, 64 rue Merciére
Boeuf d'Argent, 29 rue Boeuf
La Bonne Auberge 'Chez Jo', 48 avenue Felix-Faure
Bourillot, 8 place Célestins
Cazenove, 75 rue Boileau
Chevallier, 40 rue du Sergent Blandon
Chez Jean-Francois, 2 place Célestins
Chez Rose, 4 rue Rabelais
Christian Grisard, 158 rue Cuvier
Cortassa, 20 rue Sully
Les Fantasques, 47 rue Bourse
Garioud, 14 rue Palais Grillet

La Gerlande, 9 rue de Gerlande
La Grand Camp, place Colt-Rivière
Les Grillons, 18 rue D'Vincent à Champagne-au-Mont-d'Or-par
Le Gourmandin, 156 rue P-Bert
Henry, 27 rue Martinière
Mère Brazier, 12 rue Royale
La Mère Vittet, 26 cours Verdun
Orsi, 3 place Kleber
Pastourelle, 51 rue Tête-d'Or
Pied de Chochon, 9 rue St-Polycorpe
La Pinte à Gones, 59 rue Ney
Les Routiers, 21 quai Perrache
Tante Alice, 22 rue Remparts-d'Ainay
La Tassée, 20 rue Charité
La Voûte, 11 place A-Gourju

At Lyon Bron
Courte-Paille, N6 Près Aèroport

At Lyon Ecully
Courte-Paille, Autoroute A6 exit Ecully direction Champagne
Flunchs, Centre Commercial le Pèrollier

At Lyon Pierre-Benite
Courte-Paille, Autoroute A7 a 200m exit Pierre-Benite Nord

MÂCON 2, 18
Set in the heart of the wine-growing country, Mâcon thrives as a commercial centre and river port. Many of the buildings were destroyed during the Revolution although the twin towers and narthex of the old Cathedrale St-Vincent still stand. The town is recognised by the French as the birthplace of the poet Lamartine and there is a museum dedicated to him. Other places of interest include the Musée Municipal des Ursulines which contains some African instruments and the 14th century restored Pont St-Laurent.

Where to stay
☆☆**Novotel Mâcon Nord,** ☎(85)360080
★★**Bellevue,** 416-420 quai Lammartine ☎(85)380507
★★**Champs Elysées,** 92-109 quai J-Jaurès ☎(85)382794 (no restaurant)
★★**Genève Lf,** 1 rue Bigonnet ☎(85)381810
★★**Terminus Lf,** 91 rue V-Hugo ☎(85)391711

At Saint Albain (10km N)
☆☆☆☆**Sofitel,** (A6) ☎(85)381617

In the Old Port at Marseille

At Sancé-les-Mâcon (4km N)
☆☆☆**Vielle Ferme (FAH),** N6
☎(85)384693
☆☆**Climat de France,** ZAC des
Platières, rue du 19 Mars 1962
☎(85)392133

Where to eat
Auberge Bressane, 14 rue 28
Juin 1944
Courte-Paille, Autoroute A6 exit
Mâcon-Sud
Pierre, 7 rue Dufour
Rocher de Cancale, 393 quai J-
Jaurès

Where to camp
Camping Municipal

MAGESCQ 8

Where to stay
★★**Relais de la Poste Lf,**
☎(58)577025

MAINTENON 34, 81
A town celebrated for the 15th century
castle with its lovely park.

Where to stay
★**Aqueduc Lf,** place Gare
☎(37)276005

LA MALÈNE 69

Where to stay
★★★**Manoir de Montesquiou,**
☎(66)485112

MALMAISON 9, 12
The château of Malmaison was home
to Napoleon for a short time. It was
Josephine Bonaparte's favourite
house and she lived there after their
divorce in 1809. The château is now a
fine museum of the Napoleonic era.

MANDELIEU 4, 78

Where to stay
☆**Esterel,** 1625 avenue de Fréjus
☎(93)499220

★**Matringe,** route de Fréjus
☎(93)495086 (no restaurant)

Where to eat
L'Etrier, route de Fréjus
Les Ormes, 320 avenue Cannes

Where to camp
Cigales, boulevard de la Mer
Plateau des Chasses
Roc Fleuri, route de Pégomas

LE MANS 16, 39, 86
At the confluence of the Rivers Sarthe
and Huisine, Le Mans is a busy
industrial and commercial centre with
new estates around a medieval town,
partly enclose by 4th century ramparts.
Features of the town are the
impressive 11th century cathedral and
the late 15th century Maison de la
Reine-Bérengère which now contains
the Museum of History and
Ethnography. Le Mans is perhaps
most famous for its association with
the motor car; early automobiles were
developed here in the late 19th
century. Louis Renault established his
first decentralised factory close by, and
south of the town lies the famous
circuit where the twenty four hour race
takes place each year. The same
complex contains the Bugatti testing
and training circuit and automobile
museum.

Where to stay
★★★**Moderne,** 14 rue Bourg-Belé
☎(43)247920
☆☆☆**Novotel le Mans Est,** ZAC
les Sabions, boulevard R-Schumann
☎(43)852680
★★**Central,** 5 boulevard
R-Levasseur ☎(43)240893
(no restaurant)
★★**Chantecler,** 50 rue Pelouse
☎(43)245853
☆☆**Ibis,** rue C-Marot
☎(43)861414

Where to eat
Le Relais Droguet, 114 rue F-
Geneslay

Le Relais Fleury, 10 place de
l'Eperon
Renaissance, 114 avenue Gl-
Leclerc
Le Séquoia, 2 rue V-Bonhommet

Where to stay
At Arnage (9km S via N23)
☆☆**Campanile,** La Gêmerie
boulevard P-Le-Faucheux
☎(43)218121

MANSLE 83

Where to stay
★★**Beaurivage,** Près du Pont
☎(45)203126

MANTES 9, 12
On the left bank of the River Seine,
Mantes is noted for its vast 12th-14th
century Church of Notre Dame.

Where to stay
☆☆**Ibis,** allée des Martinets, ZAC
des Brosses, Magnanville
☎(3)0926565

Where to eat
Le Novelty, 47 rue de la Papeterie
Le Relais Chez Marcel, 88 rue
Pierre-Sémart
Le Relais de la Cure d'Air, 161
boulevard du Ml-Juin

MARANS 45

Where to eat
Le Relais du Point du Jour, 2 rue du Moulin

Where to camp
CM Bois Dinot, route de Nantes

MARLENHEIM 91, 97

Where to stay
★★**Cerf Lf,** 30 rue du Gl-de-Gaulle
☎(88)877373
★★**Hostellerie Reeb Lf,** (N4)
☎(88)875270

Where to eat
Auberge du Kronthal, carrefour
N4-D422

MARMOUTIER 91, 97

The outstanding feature of the town is the red sandstone church of St-Maur, considered to be one of the most beautiful churches in the region.

MARSEILLE 75, 76

One of the largest cities in France, Marseille is a major port and also a busy industrial centre. The old harbour, guarded by two forts, has been retained, linked to the modern town by the famous La Canebière, a thoroughfare crowded with shops, cafés and hotels. Marseille has a number of interesting churches including the Basilica Notre-Dame-de-la-Garde, which towers above the city, providing excellent views from the terrace. There are many museums, covering most aspects of the city's history, notably the Maritime Museum, the Roman Docks Museum and the Museum of Old Marseille. A short boat ride from the harbour will bring the visitor to the legendary Château d'If, the fortified island prison which was the setting for Alexandra Dumas' novel *The Count of Monte Cristo.*

Where to stay
★★★**St-George,** 10 rue du
Commandant Dessemond
☎(91)525692 (no restaurant)
☆☆**Ibis,** 6 rue de Cassis
☎(91)785925

Where to eat
Au Pescadou, 19 place Castellane
Aux Delices de Mourepiane,
578 chemin de Littoral
Béarnais, 16 rue S-Torrents
Le Bellecour, 26 cours Julien
La Charpenterie, 22 rue Paix
Chez Antoine, 35 rue Musée
Chez Caruso, 158 quai Port
Flunchs, 8-10 rue St Férréol

Grand Bar, Dégustation du Port, 2 quai de la Joliette
Max Caizergues, 11 rue G-Ricard
Piment Rouge, 20 rue Beauvou
Le Relais, 40 quai de Lazaret
Le Relais de l'Independence,
234 boulevard de Paris
Le Relais de Amis, 181 avenue
Roger Salengro
Le Relais des Amis, 188 boulevard
de Paris
Le Relais International, 68 rue
Pierre Albrand

At Marseille Nord
Flunchs, chemin de la Palaud

At Marseille Vitrolles
Courte-Paille, ZAC du Griffon
N113 Vitrolles. Near Centre
Commercial Carrefour
Flunchs, quartier de Griffon RN 113

MARTEL 73

This charming market town is situated on the Quercy Causse, a high limestone plateau, and was named after the 8th century local hero Charles Martel. Historic buildings include the 12th century Maison-Fabri and the 15th century church of St-Maur.

At Gluges (5km SE on N681)
Where to stay
★**Falaises,** ☎(65)373359

MARVEJOLS 69

An old fortress town retaining three of its ancient gates and some interesting 17th century houses.

Where to stay
★**Paix Lf,** 2 avenue de Brazza
☎(66)321017

Where to eat
A la Bete du Gevaudan, 1
boulevard de Chambrun

MASSIAC 69

A pleasant country holiday town with a pretty 15th century church.

Where to stay
★★**Poste,** avenue de C-Ferrand
(N9) ☎(71)230201

Where to camp
Camping Municipal Alagnon,
avenue de Courcelles

MAYENNE 60

The town stands on two hills sloping down to the Mayenne River, the two halves still linked by the old bridge. The walls of the 11th century castle afford excellent views of Mayenne.

Where to stay
★★**Grand Lf,** 2 rue Ambroise-de-
Loré ☎(43)043735 (no restaurant)

★**Croix Couverte Lf,** route de Paris
☎(43)043248

Where to eat
Le Relais des Routiers, 3 rue de la
Madeline
Le Relais l'Escale, route du Mans,
2 rue Colbert

Where to camp
Camping Municipal Piscine, de
St-Léonard

MEAUX 10, 100

This old established town on the River Marne is now a thriving agricultural centre, well known for its manufacture of cheese. Meaux's main places of interest are to be found around the 13th century cathedral and include the 12th century chapter house and the 12th-17th century Bishops Palace which now houses the Museum of Local History.

Where to stay
★★**Siréne,** 33 rue Gl-Leclerc
☎(6)4340780

Where to eat
Au Petit Nain, 7 rue Orsoy
Brasserie Meldoise, 13 avenue F-
Roosevelt

MEHUN-SUR-YÈVRE

A charming old town on the River Yèvre and the Berry Canal. Places of interest include the old château and the Rue Jeanne-d'Arc where Joan of Arc once lodged. The Church of Notre-Dame dates mainly from the 15th century.

Where to stay
★**Croix Blanche,** 164 rue J-d'Arc
☎(48)573001

Where to eat
Relais de l'Esperance, 10 place
du 14 Juillet

MENDE 69

The ancient town of Mende overlooking the River Lot, which is crossed by the 14th century Pont-Notre-Dame-de-Peyrenc. There are many quaint streets and a 14th century cathedral which contains an impressive set of Aubusson tapestries.

Where to stay
★★**Lion d'Or,** 12 boulevard Britexte
☎(66)650646
★★**Paris,** 2 boulevard du Soubeyran
☎(66)650003

Where to eat
La Gogaille, 5 rue Notre-Dame

Where to camp
Sirvens, route du Puy
Tivoli

METZ 10, 91
Deep in the fertile Moselle Valley the ancient town of Metz was founded in the Gallo-Roman era. The attractive 'old quarter' centred round the Place d'Armes where the 13th century cathedral of St-Étienne stands high above the surrounding narrow streets and old houses.

Where to stay
★★★Royal Concorde, 23 avenue Foch ☎(8)7668111 (no restaurant)
★★★Sofitel, Centre St-Jaques, place des Paraîges ☎(8)7745727
★★Central, 3 bis rue Vauban ☎(8)7755343 (no restaurant)
☆☆Ibis, quartier du Pontiffroy, rue Chambière ☎(8)7310173
★Lutèce Lf, 11 rue de Paris ☎(8)7302725

Where to eat
Ville de Lyon, 7 rue Piques

Where to camp
Camping Metz-Plage

MIÉLAN 88

Where to camp
Lac, 2.5km NE via N21 route d'Auch

MILLAU 69, 70, 73, 74
Since the 12th century, the premiere industry in Millau has been glove-making. The town has many old buildings dating from the 12th-15th century and is dominated by the 14th century belfry and church of Notre-Dame.

Where to stay
★★★International, 1 place de la Tine ☎(65)602066
★Causses Lf, 56 avenue J-Jaurès ☎(65)600319
★Paris & Poste, 10 avenue A-Merle ☎(65)600052

Where to eat
La Braconne, 7 place Ml-Foch
Buffet de France, place Gare
Capion, 3 rue J-F-Alméras
Le Relais de L'Avenue, 33 avenue Gambetta
Le Relais des Deux Tilleuls, 17 avenue Martel

Where to camp
Millau-Cureplats, on E bank of river near Pont de Cureplats
Millau Graufesenque, route de Nant
Millau-plage

MIMIZAN 85
During the Middle Ages Mimizan was an important harbour but it silted up in the 18th century. Close by is the seaside resort of Mimizan-Plage.

Where to stay
At Mimizan-Plage
★★Côte d'Argent, 4 avenue M-Martin ☎(58)091522

Where to camp
Camping Municipal Lac, avenue de Woolsack

At Mimizan-Plage
Airotel Marina
Camping Municipal, boulevard de l'Atlantique

MIRAMBEAU 7, 46

Where to stay
★Union, rue Principal ☎(46)496164

MIRECOURT 99
An industrial centre noted particularly for the manufacture of musical instruments. Mirecourt has retained several 17th century buildings and the covered market also dates from this period. A museum devoted to musical instruments is located in the town hall.

MOISSAC 19
In the depths of the countryside, beside the River Tarn and surrounded by vineyards, lies the pretty town of Moissac. It has several interesting buildings, which include the intricately decorated church of St-Pierre and the adjoining beautiful 11th century Cloisters.

Where to stay
★★★Moulin, 1 place du Moulin ☎(63)040355
★Pont Napoléon, 2 allées Montebello ☎(63)040155

Where to eat
Pont-Napoleon, au pont

Where to camp
Camping Municipal, l'Ile de Bidounet

MONTARGIS 23, 66
An attractive town bisected by the Briare Canal and branches of the River Loing. Montargis is famous for the manufacture of sweets, usually almond-flavoured, and also has a museum dealing with the work of the local artist Girodet.

Where to stay
★★★Grand Post, 2 place V-Hugo ☎(38)980068
★Tour d'Auvergne Lf, 20 rue J-Jaurès ☎(38)850116

Where to eat
Coche de Briare, 72 place République

Chez Pierre, 57 rue J-Jaurès
Pais Montargis, 221 rue E-Mengin

MONTAUBAN 19, 37
This pretty market town lies on both sides of the River Tarn and has many 17th century buildings, mostly collected around the arcaded Place National. The 14th century Pont Vieux, with its seven arches, spans the river and is close to the Ingres Museum which is housed in a former Bishops Palace.

Where to stay
★★Midi Lf, 12 rue Notre-Dame ☎(63)631723
★Orsay (opposite station) ☎(63)630057

At Montbeton (3km W)
★★★Coulandrières, route de Castelsarrasin ☎(63)031809

Where to eat
Chapon Fin, 1 place St-Orens
Delmas, 10 rue Michelet
Le Relais de Fonneuve, Lieu-dit Fonneuve
Stop Bar les Routiers, 5 faubourg Toulousain

Where to camp
Alsace, route de Paris

MONTBAZON 7

Where to eat
La Chancelière, 1 place Marronniers ☎(47)260067

MONTBÉLIARD 17
An ancient town which, despite some industrialisation, including the establishment of a Peugeot car factory at nearby Sochaux, has retained a number of interesting old buildings. Pride of place must go to the fine fortified château which dates from the 15th century. It contains a museum with exhibits relating to the work of Georges Cuvier, the 18th century naturalist, and Étienne Oehmichen who invented the helicopter in 1924, both of whom were born in Montbéliard.

Where to stay
☆☆Ibis, rue J-Foillet, ZAC du Pied d'Egouttes ☎(81)971920

Where to eat
Bistro au Boeuf, 1 rue Gl-Leclerc
Le Comté, 18 rue Belfort

MONT DE MARSAN 87
Noted for its gastronomic delights, this market town enjoys a mild climate, encouraging the growth of palms, magnolias and other flowers. The Hippodrome stages bullfighting as

well as horse-riding events, and there are two museums, both housed in 14th century buildings.

Where to stay
★★★**Richelieu Lf,** 3 rue Wlerick
☎(58)061020

Where to eat
Bar des Sports, place des Arènes
Le Midou, 12 place Porte-Campet
Zanchettin, St-Médard

Where to camp
Camping Municipal, 2.5km E on D1

MONT DOL 64
A granite mound which commands fine views over the surrounding marshes and coastline. A chapel stands on the summit near the spot where St-Michael is said to have fought with Satan.

MONTÉLIMAR 3
The ruins of a castle dating back to the 12th century may still be seen at Montélimar, made famous by its white nougat confectionary.

Where to stay
★★★**Relais de l'Empereur,** place M-Dormoy ☎(75)012900
★★**Sphinx,** 19 boulevard Desmarais ☎(75)018664 (no restaurant)
★**Beausoleil Lf,** 14 boulevard Pêcher, place d'Armes
☎(75)011980 (no restaurant)

Where to eat
Court-Paille – A 200m exit Autoroute A7, N7 direction Valence
Le Grillon, 40 rue Cuiraterie
Sodexas Relais PLM, Aire de Service de Montélimar

Where to camp
Deux Saisons

MONTLUÇON 67
The oldest part of this industrial town surrounds a 15th century castle which houses two interesting museums; a Museum of Folklore and the Musée International de la Vielle.

Where to stay
★★★**Terminus,** 47 avenue M-Dormoy ☎(70)052893
★★**Château St-Jean,** Parc St-Jean ☎(70)050465

Where to eat
Aux Ducs de Bourbon, 47 avenue Marx Dormoy
Grenier à Sel, 10 rue Notre-Dame
La Caravelle, 17 quai Louis Blanc
Le Relais des Marronniers, Lamaids

Les Routiers, Altées des Soupirs
Lion d'Or

Where to camp
Mas, 4.5km W of town on N145 on banks of Etang de Sault.

MONTMIRAIL 94
An old-established town overlooking the Petit Morin Valley. It is noted mainly for its 17th century château where Paul de Gondi, later to become Cardinal de Retz, was born.

Where to stay
★**Vert Galant,** 2 place Vert Galant
☎(26)422017

Where to eat
Rallÿe-Routier, 4 avenue Ch-de-Gaulle

MONTPELLIER 5, 74
A busy town in an agricultural area which has been the seat of a university and a medical school since the 13th century. Montpellier contains a number of elegant 17th century mansions and a fine view of both the town and the surrounding countryside can be obtained from the terraced Promenade du Peysou. Places of interest include the Fabre Museum with 19th century paintings covering most European schools and the fine Botanical Gardens, founded at the end of the 16th century.

Where to stay
★★★**Frantel,** 218 rue de Bastion-Ventadour, quartier le polygone
☎(67)646566
☆☆☆**Mercure Montpellier Est,** 662 avenue de Pompignane
☎(67)655024
☆☆☆**Novotel,** 125 bis avenue de Palavas ☎(67)640404
☆☆**Climat de France,** rue de Caducée ☎(67)524333
☆☆**Ibis,** route de Palavas
☎(67)588230

At Pérols (8km S at Montpellier Airport)
★★★**PLM Fréjorgues,** route de Carnon ☎(67)500304

Where to eat
Chandelier, 3 rue Leenhardt
Flunchs, Centre Commercial Avenue de Montmorency
Logis des Trois Rois, 12 rue Trésoriers-de-la-Bourse
Le Louvre, 2 rue Vieille
L'Olivier, 12 rue A-Ollivier
Réserve St-Firmin, 10 rue St-Firmin
Table de la Reine, 8 rue Bras-de-Fer
Montpellier Sud:
Courte-Paille, Autoroute A9 near hotel Ibis

Where to camp
Camping Municipal Reclusages, avenue des Reclusages

MONTREUIL 21, 90

Where to stay
★★★**Château de Montreuil,** 4 Chaussée des Capucins
☎(21)815304
★**Central,** 7-9 rue du Change
☎(21)061033

Where to eat
Auberge La Grenouillère

Where to camp
Camping Municipal

MONTREUIL-BELLAY
An attractive town on the River Thouet, partly surrounded by medieval fortifications. The dominating feature is the château, dating mainly from the 15th century and containing well-preserved kitchens and living quarters.

Where to stay
★**Splendid Lf,** rue Dr-Gaudrez
☎(41)523021

Where to eat
Hostellerie Porte St-Jean, 432 rue Nationale

Where to camp
Camping Airotel Nobis

MONTRICHARD 65
An interesting town with a number of 15th-16th century buildings overlooked by the remains of a feudal castle. Wine cellars have been established in the cliffs along the River Cher and some troglodyte dwellings may also be found.

Where to stay
★★**Bellevue Lf,** quai du Cher
☎(54)320617
★★**Tête Noire Lf,** route de Tours
☎(54)320555

MONTSOREAU 62
An attractive village downstream from the confluence of the Rivers Loire and Vienne. The 15th century château contains the Goums Museum dealing with French military activities in Morocco.

Where to eat
Loire

Where to camp
Camping Isle Verte

LE MONT-ST-MICHEL 48, 50
One of the chief natural curiosities and ancient monuments of France, Mont-St-Michel stands on the site of an

153

oratory founded in the 8th century. It is composed of a 260ft rock, encircled at its base by medieval walls and towers with buildings of various architectural styles rising irregularly from its side, and surmounted by an historic 10th-16th century abbey. A causeway connects the island to the mainland about ½ mile offshore and twice a month, following a new or full moon, there is a remarkable bore.

Where to stay
★★**Digue Lf,** La Digue (2km S on D976) ☎(33)601402
☆☆**K,** La Digue ☎(33)601418
★★**Mère Poulard,** ☎(33)601401

Where to eat
Terrasses Poulard

Where to camp
Camping Gué de Beauvoir
Camping Mont-St-Michel

MOREZ 95
Nestling in the wooded valley of the River Bienne is the small light-industrial town and resort of Morez. Within the town there are a variety of flourishing trades ranging from saw-mills to watchmaking. Spectacle-making has continued here since the 18th century and Morez is now the home of the National Centre for Optical Research. Magnificent views of the valley and the old viaducts can be seen from the viewpoints at La Roche au Dade or the Belvédère de la Garde.

Where to stay
★★**Central Modern,** 106 rue de la République ☎(84)330307

MORLAIX 49, 56
The town is dominated by an impressive feat of 19th century civil engineering, a large two-storey viaduct, striding the deep valley into which flows the river of Morlaix. This is a town with character, a 14th century Dominican convent is now the

museum, there are pleasant riverside walks and some charming old houses, one of the most attractive being the 16th century Duchess Anne's House.

Where to stay
★★★**Grand Hôtel d'Europe,** 1 rue d'Aiguillon ☎(98)621199

Where to eat
Auberge des Gourmets, 90 rue Gambetta
Marée Bleue, 3 Rampe St-Mélaine

MORTAGNE-SUR-SÈVRE 86

Where to stay
★★★**France Lf,** 4 place du Dr-Pichat ☎(51)676337

Where to eat
Le Relais de la Gare, 52 route de Cholet
Le Relais des Routiers, 7 rue Nationale

MOULINS 23, 24, 65, 68, 71
Situated on the River Allier, Moulins has a wealth of historical and interesting buildings, one of which is the impressive Cathedral of Notre-Dame, built in the flamboyant Gothic style. Another notable building is the unusual 'Le Jacquemart' clock tower which has the animated figures of a

Mont St Michel

17th century family that strike the clock bells at intervals. Also within the town are several 15th century mansions which are now museums.

Where to stay
★★★**Paris,** 21 rue de Paris ☎(70)440058
★★**Dauphin,** 59 place Allier ☎(70)443305
☆☆**Ibis,** Angle de la route de Lyon ☎(70)46712
★★**Moderne,** 9 place J-Moulin ☎(70)440506
★**Parc Lf,** 31 avenue Gl-Leclerc ☎(70)441225

Where to eat
Des Cours, 36 cours J-Jaurès

Le Relais des Trois Rubans, 1 route de Paris

MULHOUSE 32, 99
Despite a good deal of industrialisation this former textile-producing town on the Rhone-Rhine Canal retains traces of its medieval fortifications and a number of interesting old buildings. Of special note are the fine Renaissance town hall and the Musée de l'Impression sur Étoffes (Museum of Printed Fabrics) which contains examples of this craft from all over the world. Other places of interest include the Musée Français du Chemin de Fer (French National Railway Museum) and the town zoo, which lies to the south-east near a viewpoint. From here there is a magnificent panorama of Mulhouse, the Black Forest, the Jura mountains, and on a clear day, the Bernese Alps.

Where to eat
Auberge Lefèvre, 82 rue Lefèvre
Châtaigneraie, 109 avenue 1er Division-Blindée
Flunch, 14 boulevard de l'Europe

Where to camp
Camping Municipal, avenue P-de-Coubertin

At Sausheim (6km NE on D422)
Where to stay
☆☆☆**Mercure**, rue Ille Napoléon
☎(89)445440
☆☆☆**Novotel**, rue Ille Napoléon
☎(89)4444444
☆☆**Ibis**, route de Sausheim
☎(89)543233

LE MUY 4

Where to eat
Le Relais de la Chaumière

Where to camp
Cigales
Sellig, route d'Aix-en-Provence

NANCY 97, 98
Formerly the capital of the ancient
Duchy of Lorraine, Nancy is a busy
university town well known for its
wealth of fine 18th century Baroque
buildings. Most of the town's
magnificent architecture was
commissioned by Stanislaus
Leszcýnski, the dethroned King of
Poland, and several outstanding
examples can be seen in the Place
Stanislas, where his statue has been
erected. Other places of interest
include the old Ducal Palace,
containing a local history museum, the
church of Notre-Dame-de-Bon-
Secours, where Stanislaus and his wife
Catherine Opalinska are buried,
numerous museums and Pépinière
Park which includes a zoo.

Where to stay
★★★**Frantel**, 11 rue R-Poincaré
☎(8)3356101
★★★**Grand Concorde**, 2 place
Stanislas ☎(8)3350301
★★**Albert 1er/Astoria**, 3 rue
Armée-Patton ☎(8)3403126
★**Américain**, 3 place A-Maginot
☎(9)3322853 (no restaurant)
★**Poincaré**, 81 rue R-Poincaré
☎(8)3402599 (no restaurant)

Where to eat
Le Relais du Port, 5 rue H-Bazin

At Laxou (3km SW A33)
Where to stay
☆☆☆**Mercure**, 2 rue de la Saône
☎(8)3964221

NANTES 44, 45, 57, 63
A modern industrial town and busy
seaport at the mouth of the River Loire,
with maritime traditions stretching
back to the Gallo-Roman era. Although
best known today for its shipyards and
refineries, Nantes has preserved an
attractive old quarter around the Place
Royale and the Island of Feydeau,
where a number of 18th century
buildings may be seen. There is a fine
cathedral, sadly damaged by fire in
1972, which contains the famous
Renaissance tomb of François II,
dating from the early 16th century, and
several museums including the Fine
Arts Museum with a splendid
collection of Renaissance and 20th
century paintings and a museum
devoted to the life and work of the
writer Jules Verne.

Where to stay
★★★**Central**, 4 rue du Couédic
☎(40)200935
★★★**Frantel**, 3 rue Dr-Zamenhof
☎(49)471058
★★**Astoria**, 11 rue Richebourg
☎(40)743990 (no restaurant)
★★**Bourgogne**, 9 allée du Cdt-
Charcot ☎(40)40334
(no restaurant)
★★**Graslin**, 1 rue Prion
☎(40)891609 (no restaurant)

Where to eat
L'Ancre d'Or, 55 boulevard G-Roch
La Bougrière, rue J-Verne
Flunchs, 4 & 6 rue de Feltre
La Tour D'Auvergne, 17 rue La
Tour d'Auvergne

Where to camp
**Camping Municipal Val du
Cens**, boulevard du Petit Pont 21

**At Carquefou (4km NE on D337,
off N23)**
Where to stay
☆☆☆**Novotel Nantes
Carquefou**, allée des Sapins
☎(40)492184
☆☆☆**PLM Carquefou**, route de
Paris, Le Petit Bel Air (N23 exit A1)
☎(40)302924
☆☆**Campanile**, boulevard des
Pastureaux ☎(40)490182
☆☆**Climat de France**, CD337,
Petit Bel Air

Where to eat
Courte-Paille, route de Paris

NANTUA 18
This popular holiday resort on the side
of Lake Nantua backs on to wooded
hills and was once an important
religious centre. The original 12th
century Benedictine Abbey was
destroyed during the French
Revolution, but still of interest is the
Church of St-Michel with its beautiful
doorway.

LA NAPOULE-PLAGE 78
Overlooked by a 14th century castle,
the town has a fine sandy beach and
harbour.

Where to stay
★★★★**Ermitage du Riou**,
boulevard de Mer ☎(93)499566

Where to eat
Brocherie 11, au port
Lou Castéou
Marin

Where to camp
Azur-Vacances

NARBONNE 5, 6, 20, 70
This former port, now connected to the
sea by a canal, is an important wine
centre. It has an unusual 13th century
cathedral which was never fully
completed, and old houses contain
museums devoted to archaeology, art
and pottery.
★★★**Midi Lf**, avenue de Toulouse
☎(68)410462
☆☆☆**Novotel Narbonne Sud**,
quartier Plaisance, route d'Espagne
☎(68)415952
★★**Dorade**, 44 rue J-Jaurès
☎(68)326595 (no restaurant)
☆☆**Ibis**, quartier Plaisance (N9)
☎(68)411441
★★**Languedoc**, 22 boulevard
Gambetta ☎(68)651474
★★**Résidence**, 6 rue Premier-Mai
☎(68)321941 (no restaurant)
★**Lion d'Or**, 39 avenue P-Sémard
☎(68)320692

Where to eat
Alsace, 2 avenue P-Sémard
Le Floride, 66 boulevard F-Mistral
Le Novelty, 33 avenue des Pyrénées
**Le Pavillon Bleu 'Chez Michel et
Patrice'**, Route de Béziers
Le Relais des 2 Mers Narbonne
Réverbère (Giraud), 4 place
Jacobins
Au Signal D'Arret, 40 avenue de
Bordeaux

Where to camp
Relais de la Nautique, Anse des
Galères

NEMOURS 2, 23
A popular tourist centre in the Loing
Valley with a 15th century château.
There is an interesting museum of
prehistory on the eastern outskirts and
to the west lies the Rochers Gréau
Park, encompassing many acres of
rocky forest.

Where to stay
☆☆☆**Euromotel**, l'Aire de Service
(2km SE on A6) ☎(6)572810
(no restaurant)

★★**Ecu de France,** 3 rue de Paris
☎(6)4281154
★**Roches,** avenue d'Ormesson, St-
Pierre ☎(6)4280143
★**St-Pierre,** 12 avenue Carnot
☎(6)4280157

Where to eat
Le Petit Casino, 7 rue Thiers
Vieux Moulin, 5 avenue Lyon

Where to camp
Camping ACCCF

NEUFCHÂTEAU 99
An important town during the Middle
Ages on account of its location at the
junction of several main routes. Places
of interest include the church of St-
Nicholas, which has a number of 12th
and 13th century features, and the
16th century Renaissance town hall,
noted for its fine staircase.

Where to eat
La Boulangerie, 1 place J-d'Arc

NEUFCHÂTEL-EN-BRAY 58
Famous for its local cheeses, this town
has been extensively rebuilt since
1940.

Where to stay
★★**Grand Cerf,** 9 Grande Rue
☎(35)930002

Where to eat
Le Relais d'Eawy
Le Relais des Sports, 3 rue Carnot
Le Relais du Marche Neuf, 8
Grande Rue St-Jacques

NEVERS 23
An interesting old town situated on the
River Loire near its confluence with the
Allier. Nevers is famous for the
manufacture of pottery and glassware,
trades which have flourished here
since the 16th century and the local
museum traces the history of Nevers'
pottery or 'faience'. The town contains
many medieval buildings including the
impressive Romanesque and Gothic
cathedral, dating from the 14th
century, the 15th century Ducal Palace
and the Porte du Croux, a 14th century
tower which formed part of the
medieval defences and now contains a
museum of archaeology. The Convent
of St-Gildard is notable as the last
resting place of the embalmed body of
Ste-Bernadette.

Where to stay
★★★**Diane,** 38 rue du Midi
☎(86)572810
★★**Folle Lf,** route les Saulaies
☎(86)570531
★★**Molière,** 25 rue Molière
☎(86)572996 (no restaurant)

★**Morvan,** 28 rue Mouësse
☎(86)611416
★**Ste-Marie,** 25 rue Petit-Mouësse
☎(86)611002

Where to eat
Hotel Nivernais, 106 route de
Lyon-Plegny
Le Relais du Lion d'Or, 13
faubourg de Lyon
Le Relais la Cremaillere, Grande-
Rue Rouy

NIAUX 89
The wall paintings in this prehistoric
cave, including bison, horses and
reindeer, are considered to be among
the finest examples of Magdalenian
art.

NICE 4, 78, 80
Lying in the sheltered Baie des Anges,
protected by a backdrop of hills,
France's most popular resort enjoys a
beautiful year-round climate which
attracts many to the luxurious hotels
and mansions that line the elegant
seafront promenade. Several
museums devoted to artists and
maritime history can be found, and
nearby at Nice-Cimiez there is a 3rd
century arena and Roman Baths.

Where to stay
★★★**Bedford,** 45 rue du Ml-Joffre
☎(93)821836 (no restaurant)
★★★**Brice,** 44 Ml-Joffre
☎(93)881444
★★★**Gounod,** 3 rue Gounod
☎(93)882620 (no restaurant)
★★★**Locarno,** 4 rue avenue des
Baumettes ☎(93)962800
(no restaurant)
★★★**Malmaison,** 48 boulevard V-
Hugo ☎(93)876256
☆☆☆**Massenet,** 11 rue Massenet
☎(93)871131
☆☆☆**Mecure,** 2 rue Halevy
☎(93)823088 (no restaurant)
★★★**Napoléon,** 6 rue Grimaldi
☎(93)877007 (no restaurant)
★★★**Windsor,** 11 rue Dalpozzo
☎(93)885935 (no restaurant)
★★★**Continental Massena,** 58
rue Groffredo ☎(93)854925
(no restaurant)

Where to eat
Aux Gourmets,. 12 rue Dante
Bon Coin Breton, 5 rue Blacas
La Casbah, 3 rue Dr-Balestre
Chez Les Pêcheurs, 18 quai des
Docks
Chez Rolando, 3 rue Desboutins
Don Camillo, 5 rue Ponchettes
Florian, 22 rue A-Karr
Gourmet Lorrain, 7 avenue Santa-
Fior

Le Grand Pavois "Chez Michel",
11 rue Meyerbeer
Los Caracolès, 5 rue St Francois-
de-Paule
La Madrague, 13 bis cours Saleya
La Merenda, 4 rue Terrasse
La Nissarda, 17 rue Gubernatis
La Poularde chez Lucullus, 9 rue
Deloye
Le Relais Provencal, 87 boulevard
René-Cassin
Le Rive Droite, 22 avenue St-Jean
Baptiste
Rivoli, 9 rue Rivoli
Le St-Laurent, 12 rue Paganini
St-Moritz, 5 rue Cangres
Venga Venga da Mireille, 11
boulevard Pierre Seriord

At the Airport (7km)
Ciel d'Azur
Grill Soleil d'Or

At the Station
Flunchs, Avenue Thiers

At Halevy
Flunchs, 7 rue Halevy

At Lingestière
Flunchs, RN 202

NÎMES 5
A busy city with a thriving trade in
locally-produced wine and a growing
reputation as a tourist centre. Nîmes
contains some of the best-preserved
Roman remains in the region,
including the 1st century arena,
seating up to 20,000 spectators, and
the Maison Carrée, formerly a temple
dating from the same period, which
has been restored and now houses a
fascinating Museum of Antiquities.
Other Roman edifices such as the
baths and the Temple of Diana have
been incorporated into the 18th
century landscaped Jardin de la
Fontaine. Apart from its Roman relics,
Nîmes has a rebuilt 11th century
cathedral and a museum dedicated to
the later life of the town.

Where to stay
★★★**Cheval Blanc et des
Arènes,** 1 place des Arènes
☎(66)672003
☆☆☆**Novotel Nîmes Ouest,** 124
chemin de l'Hostellerie
☎(66)846020
★★**Carrière,** 6 rue Grizot
☎(66)672489
☆☆**Ibis,** Chemin de l'Hostellerie
☎(66)380065
☆☆**Louvre,** 2 Square de la
Couronne ☎(66)672275

**At Marguerittes (7km NE via
N86)**
☆☆**Marguerittes,** route d'Avignon
☎(66)260123

Where to eat
Au Chapon Fin, 3 rue Château-Fadaise
Flunchs, 10 boulevard Amiral Courbet
Le Lisita, 2 boulevard Arènes

At Nîmes-Ouest
Courte paille, Centre Hôtelier Autoroute A9

Where to camp
Domaine de la Bastide, route de Générac

NIORT 7
Niort's most unusual industry is the making of preserves and liquers from Angelica. One of the town's many museums is housed in the old castle keep and another, the Musée du Pilon, can be found in the 16th century former Town Hall. Also of interest are the church of Notre-Dame and the Musée des Beaux-Arts.

Where to stay
★★★**Brèche,** 8 avenue Bujauit ☎(49)244178
★★**Grand,** 32 avenue Paris ☎(49)242221 (no restaurant)
☆☆**Ibis,** avenue de la Rochelle ☎(49)735454
★★★**Terminus Lf,** 82 rue de la Gare ☎(49)240038

Where to eat
Au Rendez-vous des Bretons, 195 avenue de la Rochelle
Belle Étoile, 115 quai M-Métayer
Le Bon Accueil, 424 avenue St Jean-d'Angely
Charly's, 5 avenue Paris
Cloche d'Or, 7 rue Brisson

NOEUX-LES-MINES 25

Where to stay
★★**Tourterelles,** 374 route Nationale ☎(21)669075

Where to eat
Chez Francine et Patrick, 94 route Nationale
Le Relais des Routiers, 415 bis, rue Nationale
Paix, 115 rue Nationale

NONANCOURT 34
The town grew up around an 11th century castle. In the late 12th century Richard the Lionheart and Phillip Augustus signed a treaty here defining their part in the Third Crusade.

Where to stay
★**Grand Cerf Lf,** 17 Grande Rue ☎(32)581527

Where to eat
Rest du Cinema Bourvil, 67 Grande Rue

NOUAN-LE-FUZELIER 36

Where to stay
★**Moulin de Villiers Lf,** (3km N by D44), route Chaon ☎(54)887227

Where to eat
Le Dahu, 14 rue de la Mare

LE NOUVION-EN-THIÈRACHE 91

Where to stay
★**Paix,** 37 rue V-Vicary ☎(23)970455

NOZAY 44, 60

Where to stay
★**Gergaud Lf,** 12 rue Nantes ☎(40)794754

NUITS-ST-GEORGE 29
An important wine-producing centre in the Côtes-de-Nuits. The local museum has many exhibits dating back to the villages Gallo-Roman origins.

Where to stay
☆☆**Ibis,** 1 avenue Chambolland ☎(80)611717

Where to eat
Le Relais des Cultivateurs, 12 rue du Gl-de-Gaulle

OLIVET 36
In a pleasant rural setting beside the River Loiret, Olivet has a number of old houses and riverside windmills. To the south-east lies the Floral Park of the Source, covering some 74 acres, where the source of the Loiret can be seen.

Where to stay
★★★**Frantel la Reine Blanche,** rue de la Reine Blanche ☎(38)664051
☆☆**Climat de France,** ZAC de la route de Bourges ☎(38)692055
★★**Rivage,** 635 rue de la Reine Blanche ☎(38)660293

Where to eat
Courte-Paille, route de Vierzon
Flunchs, avenue de Verdun
Manderley, 117 sentier des Prés

Where to camp
Camping Municipal Olivet, rue du Pont Bouchet

ORANGE 3, 4, 5, 72, 75
Orange has many examples of Roman architecture, in particular the well-preserved theatre and remains of a temple, as well as a beautifully decorated 1st-century Triumphal Arch.

Where to stay
☆☆☆**Euromotel Orange,** route de Caderousse ☎(90)342410
★★**Boscotel,** route de Caderousse ☎(90)344750
★★**Louvre & Terminus,** 89 avenue F-Mistral ☎(90)341008 (no restaurant)

Where to eat
Le Forum, 3 rue Mazeau
Le Moulin à Vent, Pont de l'Aigue
Le Pigraillet, chemin colline St-Eutrope
Le Sanglier, 50 cours Aristide-Briand
Lou Coudoulet, RN7 exit Sud

ORGEVAL 9, 12

Where to stay
☆☆☆**Novotel,** (N13) ☎(3)9759760
★★**Moulin d'Orgeval** ☎(3)9759574

Where to eat
Courte-Paille, N13 (Autoroute exit Poissy)

ORLÉANS 7, 35, 36, 61, 66
A busy market and industrial town standing at the most northerly point of the River Loire. Orléans suffered damage during World War II but its subsequent restoration has been carefully carried out to blend with its historical attractions. Joan of Arc, an adopted daughter of the town following her deliverance of Orléans from the English, is commemorated in a variety of places. A section of stained glass window in the imposing 13th century cathedral traces the history of her life, and the Centre Jeanne d'Arc contains vivid audio-visual displays relating to the battle for Orléans. Other places of interest include the Fine Arts Museum and the Centre Charles Péguy devoted to the life and work of the late 19th century poet and philosopher.

Where to stay
★★★**Cedres,** 17 rue du Ml-Foch ☎(38)622292 (no restaurant)
☆☆**Arcade,** 4 rue Ml-Foch ☎(38)542311

★★**Marguerite Lf,** 14 place Vieux-Marché ☎(38)537432 (no restaurant)
★★**Terminus,** 40 rue de la République ☎(38)532464 (no restaurant)

Where to eat
Jean, 64 rue Ste-Catherine
Étoile d'Or, 25 place Vieux-Marché
Le Relais des Quatre Marches, 163 route de St-Mesmin
Le Relais du Parc, 45 rue du Parc
Le Relais Péguy, 47 faubourg Bourgogne

At La Source (10km S off N20)
Where to stay
☆☆☆**Novotel,** 2 rue H-de-Balzac ☎(38)630428
☆☆**Campanile,** 326 rue Châteaubriand ☎(38)635820

Where to eat
At St-Jean-de-la-Ruelle
Flunchs, rue de la Mouchetière

Where to camp
Camping Municipal Gaston-Marchand, route de Blois

ORLY 23

Where to stay
☆☆**Arcade,** esplanade Aérogare Sud ☎(1)2682345

At Morangis (2.5km SE)
☆☆**Campanile,** 34 avenue F-de-Lesseps ☎(6)4486130
☆☆**Climat de France,** ZI des Sables, rue Lavoisier ☎(1)4483155

PACY-SUR-EURE 34

Where to stay
★★**Etape,** 1 rue Isambard ☎(32)361277

PADIRAC 73
Here, at the Padirac Chasm, is the entrance to an underground river which has carved vast galleries and caves in the limestone rock of the Gramat Causse. The Chasm can be explored, under supervision, during the summer months.

PAMIERS 89
A major commercial and industrial centre.

Where to stay
★★**Parc Lf,** 12 Piconnières ☎(61)670258

Where to camp
Camping Municipal, NW on D119 beside river

PARENTIS-EN-BORN 85

Where to eat
Poste

Where to camp
Arbre d'Or, route du Lac
SI, route de l'Etang

PARIS 1, 2, 7, 9, 10, 12, 15, 16, 22, 23, 30, 81, 96
The third largest capital city in Europe, Paris has an international reputation as the world's most attractive city. A truly cosmopolitan centre which retains an essential Frenchness; it is a city of wide avenues, squares, and parks, of bridges across the Seine and cafés on every corner. Rich in history and culture, some of its best-known features include the 12th-13th century Cathedral of Notre-Dame, the Louvre with its unrivalled collection of paintings and the 19th century Basilica of Sacré-Coeur which stands in a commanding position on the Butte Montmartre. The Place de la Concorde recalls the reign of the guillotine and the Place de la Bastille marks the site of the notorious prison. Built for the Exhibition of 1889 the Eiffel Tower is an instantly recognisable landmark to the many visitors who keep this famous city crowded at most times of the year.

Where to stay
1st Arrondissement
★★★**Duminy – Vendôme,** 3 rue Mont-Thabor ☎(1)2603280 (no restaurant)
★★**Family,** 35 rue Cambon ☎(1)2615484 (no restaurant)
★★**Montana-Tuileries,** 21 rue St-Roch ☎(1)2603510

2nd Arrondissement
★★★**Horset Opéra d'Antin,** 18 rue d'Antin ☎(1)742301 (no restaurant)
★★**France,** 4 rue du Carre ☎(1)2333098 (no restaurant)

5th Arrondissement
★★**Collège de France,** 7 rue Thénard ☎(1)3267836 (no restaurant)

6th Arrondissement
★★★**Madison,** 143 boulevard St-Germain ☎(1)3297250 (no restaurant)
★★★**Senat,** 22 rue St-Sulpice ☎(1)3254230 (no restaurant)
★★**Angleterre,** 44 rue Jacob ☎(1)2603472 (no restaurant)

7th Arrondissement
★★★**Cayré,** 4 boulevard Raspail ☎(1)5443888 (no restaurant)
★★**Splendid,** 29 avenue de Tourville ☎(1)5515598 (no restaurant)

8th Arrondissement
★★★**Élysées Ponthieu,** 24 rue de Ponthieu ☎(1)2256870 (no restaurant)
★★**Elysée,** 12 rue Saussaies ☎(1)2652925 (no restaurant)
★★**Europe,** 15 rue Constantinople ☎(1)5228080 (no restaurant)
★★**Ministère,** 31 rue de Surène ☎(1)2662143 (no restaurant)
★**Brescia,** 16 rue d'Edimbourg ☎(1)5221431 (no restaurant)

9th Arrondissement
★★★**Blanche Fontaine,** 34 rue Fontaine ☎(1)5267232 (no restaurant)
★★★**Caumartin,** 27 rue Caumartin ☎(1)7429595 (no restaurant)
★★★**Excelsior Opéra,** 5 rue La Fayette ☎(1)8749930 (no restaurant)
★★★**Franklin,** 19 rue Buffault ☎(1)2802727 (no restaurant)
★★★**Havane,** 44 rue de Trévise ☎(1)7707912 (no restaurant)
★★★**Hélios,** 75 rue de la Victoire ☎(1)8742864 (no restaurant)
★★**Lorette,** 36 rue Notre-Dame de Lorette ☎(1)2851881
★**Palmon,** 30 rue Maubeuge ☎(1)2850761 (no restaurant)
★**Laffon,** 25 rue Buffault ☎(1)8784991 (no restaurant)

10th Arrondissement
★★★**Horset Pavillon,** 38 rue de l'Echiquier ☎(1)2469275
★★★**Terminus Nord,** 12 boulevard Denain ☎(1)2802000 (no restaurant)
★★**Altona,** 166 rue du Faubourg Poissonière ☎(1)8786824 (no restaurant)
★★**Modern Est,** 91 boulevard de Strasbourg ☎(1)6072472 (no restaurant)

13th Arrondissement
★★**Timhotel Italie,** 22 rue Barrault ☎(1)5806767
★★**Timhotel Tolbiac,** 35 rue de Tolbiac ☎(1)5837494 (no restaurant)
★**Arts,** 8 rue Coypel ☎(1)7077632 (no restaurant)

15th Arrondissement

☆☆**Arcade,** 2 rue Cambronne
☎(1)5673520
★★**Pacific,** 11 rue Fondray
☎(1)5752049 (no restaurant)
★★**Timhotel Montparnasse,** 22 rue de l'Arrivée ☎(1)5489662 (no restaurant)

16th Arrondissement

★★★**Élysées Bassano,** 24 rue de Bassano ☎(1)7204903 (no restaurant)
★★★**Frémiet,** 6 avenue Frémiet ☎(1)5245206 (no restaurant)
★★★**Horset St-Cloud,** 21 rue Gudin ☎(1)6519922 (no restaurant)
★★★**Massenet,** 5 bis rue Massenet ☎(1)5244303 (no restaurant)
★★★**Sevigné,** 6 rue de Belloy ☎(1)7208890 (no restaurant)
★★**Farnese,** 32 rue Hamelin ☎(1)7205666 (no restaurant)
★★**Keppler,** 12 rue Keppler ☎(1)7206505 (no restaurant)
★★**Rond Point de Longchamp,** 86 rue de Longchamp ☎(1)5051363
★★**Vermont,** 11 bis rue Bois-de-Boulogne ☎(1)5000497 (no restaurant)

17th Arrondissement

★**Verniquet,** 3 rue Verniquet ☎(1)3802630 (no restaurant)

18th Arrondissement

☆☆**Ibis Paris Montmartre,** 5 rue Caulaincourt ☎(1)2941818
☆☆**Pigalle Urbis Paris,** 100 boulevard Rochechouart ☎(1)6069917 (no restaurant)
★★**Timhotel Montmartre,** 11 place E-Goudeau ☎(1)2557479 (no restaurant)

Where to eat

1st Arrondissement

Baumann Balford, 9 rue Coquillière
Chez Gabriel, 123 rue St-Honoré
Pasadena, 7 rue du 29-Juillet
Pied de Cochon, 6 rue Coquillière
Pierre Traiteur, 10 rue Richelieu
Saudade, 34 rue Bourdonnois
La Soufflé, 36 rue Mt-Thabor

2nd Arrondissement

Brasserie Gus, 157 rue Montmartre
Chez Georges, 1 rue Mail
La Corbeille, 154 rue Montmartre
La Petit Coin de la Bourse, 16 rue Feydeau
'Pierre' A La Fontaine Gaillon, place Gaillon
La Tour Hassan, 27 rue Turbigo

3rd Arrondissement

Ambassade d'Auverge, 22 rue Grenier St-Lazare
Taverne des Templiers, 106 rue Vieille du Temple

4th Arrondissement

Au Gourmet de l'Isle, 42 rue St-Louis-en-l'Île
Bofinger, 5 rue Bastille
Galon, 36 boulevard Henri-IV
Guirlande de Julie, 25 place des Vosages
Wally, 16 rue le Regrattier

5th Arrondissement

Atelier Maître Albert, 1 rue Maître-Albert
Balzar, 49 rue Écoles
Coupe-Chou, 11 rue Lanneau
Dodin-Bouffant, 25 rue F-Sauton
Moissonnier, 28 rue Fossées-St-Bernard
La Truffière, 4 rue Blainville

6th Arrondissement

Au Grilladin, 13 rue Mézières
Dominique, 19 rue Bréa
Le Foux, 2 rue Clément
Le Pralognan, 3 rue Houtefeuille
Taverne Basque, 45 rue Cherche-Midi

7th Arrondissement

La Chaumière et le Potager, 35 rue Beaune
Chez Françoise, Aérogare des Invalides
Ferme St-Simon, 6 rue St-Simon
Le Petit Laurent, 38 rue Varenne
Tan Dinh, 60 rue Verneuil
Vert Bocage, 96 boulevard Latour-Moubourg

8th Arrondissement

André, 12 rue Marbeuf
Au Vieux Berlin, 32 avenue George-V
La Capricorne, 81 rue Rocher
Courte-Paille, Angle rues Ponthieu
Flunchs, 5 rue de Berri
Indra, 10 rue Commandant-Rivière
Tong Yen, 1 bis rue Jean-Mermoz

9th Arrondissement

Mövenpick, 12 boulevard Madeleine
Pagoda, 50 rue Provence
Le Saintongeais, 62 rue faubourg Montmartre

10th Arrondissement

Brasserie Flo, 7 cour Petites-Ecuries
Julien, 16 rue faubourg St-Denis
Nicolas, 12 rue Fidélité

11th Arrondissement

Chordenoux, 1 rue J-Vallés
Pyrénées Cévennes, 106 rue Folie-Méricourt
Repaire de Cartouche, 8 boulevard Filles-du-Calvaire

Paris would be incomplete without its street cafés

12th Arrondissement
Sologne, 164 avenue Daumesnil
Le Traversière, 40 rue Traversière

13th Arrondissement
Etchegorry, 41 rue Croulebarbe
Rhône, 40 boulevard Arago

14th Arrondissement
Le Bonne Table, 42 rue Friant
Mon Pays, 49 avenue Jean-Moulin
Pinocchino, 124 avenue Maine

15th Arrondissement
Bocage Fleuri, 19 rue Duranton
Le Chaumière, 54 avenue F-Faure
Le Cour, 12 rue Cepré
La Giberne, 42 bis avenue Suffren

16th Arrondissement
Al Mounia, 16 rue Magdebourg
Le Moi, 7 rue G-Courbet
Morens, 10 avenue New-York
Tse-Yang, 25 avenue Pierre 1er de
Serbie

17th Arrondissement
Baumann, 64 avenue Ternes
Ma Cuisine, 18 rue Boyen
Le Santenay, 75 avenue Niel
Timgad, 21 rue Brunel
La Toque, 16 rue Tocqueville

18th Arrondissement
Chez Frézet, 181 rue Ordener
Flunchs, 1 et 3 rue Caulaincourt
La Manna, 148 avenue St-Ouen
Marie-Louise, 52 rue Championnet
Le Pichet, 174 rue Ordener
Sanglier Bleu, 102 boulevard
Clichy

19th Arrondissement
Dagorno, 190 avenue J-Jaurès
Deux Taureaur, 206 avenue J-
Jaurès
Le Sancerre, 13 avenue Corentin
Cariou

Where to camp
Paris-Ouest-Bois-de-Boulogne,
allée du Bord de l'Eau

PAYRAC 37

Where to stay
★★**Hostellerie de la Paix Lf,**
☎(65)379515

Where to camp
Panoramic
Pina, route de Cahors

PÉRIGUEUX 87
This ancient town beside the River Isle
is internationally famous for its
regional cookery, specialising in
truffles and *pâté de foie gras*.
Representing parts of the town's long
history are the Arena and Tour de
Vésone, the only surviving part of a
2nd century temple, and the medieval

Cathedral of St-Font with its five
domes. Other ancient buildings
include the remains of the Château
Barrière which has an unusual
staircase and old keep.

Where to stay
★★★**Domino,** 21 place
Francheville ☎(53)082580
☆☆**Ibis,** 8 boulevard Saumonde
☎(53)536458

Where to eat
Relais Biby, 202 bis, route
d'Angoulême
Le Relais des Arènes, 1 rue de
Chonzy
Relais Napoléon, Route de Paris

Where to camp
Barnabe-Plage

PÉRONNE 15, 25, 94
A medieval stronghold at the
confluence of two rivers, the town's
16th century Church of St-Jean and
town hall were re-built after the 1914-
18 war.

Where to stay
★★**St-Claude Lf,** 42 place L-
Dandré ☎(22)844600
★**Remparts Lf,** 21 rue Beaubois
☎(22)840122

**At Asservillers (adj to autoroute
A1)**
☆☆☆**Mercure,** (A1)
☎(22)841276

Where to eat
L'Auberge des Etangs, 14
faubourg de Paris
Chez Pierre, 61 route de Paris
Le Quenouille, 4 avenue
Australiens
Relais du Mont St-Quentin,
avenue des Australiens

PERPIGNAN 6
This busy university and market town
over the River Têt was the seat of the
kingdom of Majorca in the Middle
Ages. A palace still stands as a
monument to these times. Among the
many impressive buildings here is the
14th century Castillet which houses a
craft museum, the Loge-de-Mer and
the Hyacinthe Rigaud Museum where
the work of this famous 17th century
painter is exhibited.

Where to stay
★★★**Mondial,** 40 boulevard
Clemenceau ☎(68)342345
(no restaurant)
★★★**Windsor,** 8 boulevard Wilson
☎(68)511865 (no restaurant)
☆☆**Campanile,** Lotissement Porte
d'Espagne, rue A-Leverman, route du
Perthus ☎(68)567575

★★**Christina,** 50 cours de Lassus
☎(68)352461 (no restaurant)

Where to eat
Le Bourgogne, 63 avenue Gén-
Leclerc
Festin de Pierre, 7 rue Théâtre
Flunchs, Mas Golte RN9
Le Lido, 31 avenue Julien-Pancho
Relais St-Jean, 1 Cité Bartissol
Rest le Helder, 1 rue Courteline
La Serre, 2 bis rue Dagobert
Le Supion, 71 avenue Gén-Leclerc

PÉZENAS 70
An attractive town surrounded by
vineyards and containing many 16th
and 17th century buildings, many of
them in Renaissance style, with fine
courtyards and staircases. The Vulliod-
St-Germain Museum is full of local
history and has a section devoted to
Molière who was a frequent visitor to
the town.

PHALSBOURG 91, 97
A small town which was fortified by
Vauban during the 17th century. The
ornate Porte de France and Porte
d'Allemagne were originally part of
Vauban's defences and the local
museum traces the history of the town.

Where to eat
Au Soldat de l'An 11, 1 route de
Saverne

Where to camp
**Camping Municipal Vieux
Château,** rue de la Manutention

PIERRE-BUFFIÈRE 37

Where to stay
★**Providence,** 20 rue Nationale
☎(55)006016

PIERRELATTE 3, 72

Where to stay
★★**Hostellerie Tom II Lf,** 5
avenue Gl-de-Gaulle (N7)
☎(75)040035

Where to eat
Le Ratelier
Les Recollets, 6 place Église

PLOËRMEL 51
This small, ancient town with much
character is typically Breton. Its most
prominent building is the 16th century
church of St-Armel. Dr Guérin, a citizen
of Ploërmel, invented lint surgical
dressing which proved invaluable to
the wounded during the Franco-
Prussian War of 1870.

Where to stay
★**Commerce-Reberminard,** 70
rue de la Gare ☎(97)740532

Where to eat
Aux Amis de la Route, route de
Rennes
Le Moderne, 10 rue des Forges

Where to camp
Camping Belles Rives, route de
Taupont

POITIERS 7, 42, 83
On a rocky plateau where the Rivers
Clain and Boivre meet lies the
university town and bishopric of
Poitiers. A leading art centre, the town
has a wealth of historic buildings. The
churches mainly represent the
Romanesque style, the most
renowned of which is the church of
Notre-Dame-la-Grande. Probably the
oldest Christian building in France,
dating back to the 14th century, is the
Bapistry of St-Jean, now a museum
and situated to the south of the
imposing cathedral of St-Pierre.

Where to stay
★★★**France,** 28 rue Carnot
☎(49)413201
★★★**Royal Poitou,** route de Paris
(3km N on N10)☎(49)017286
★★**Europe,** 39 rue Carnot
☎(49)881200 (no restaurant)
☆☆**Ibis Poitiers Sud,** avenue du 8
Mai 1945 ☎(49)531313
★★**Ibis,** ZAC de Beaulieu 'Les
Maches'
☎(49)611102
★★**Relais du Stade,** 84-86 rue J-
Coeur ☎(49)462512 (no restaurant)

**At Chasseneuil-du-Poitou (8km
N by N10)**
☆☆☆**Novotel Poitiers Nord,**
(N10) ☎(49)527878
☆☆☆**Relais de Poitiers,** (N10)
☎(49)529041
☆☆**Campanile,** ZI de Chasseneuil-
du-Poitou, Voie Ouest ☎(49)528540

Where to eat
Armes d'Obernai, 19 rue A-Ranc
Auberge de la Cigogne, 20 rue
Planty
Delamé, 10 rue P-Guillon
Maxime, 4 rue St-Nicholas
Le Poitevin, 76 rue Carnot
Les Relais des Douves, 2 av de la
Libération

POIX 22
A small tourist centre with the ruins of
an ancient castle, a 16th century
church and an impressive viaduct.

Where to stay
★**Poste,** 13 place de la République
☎(22)900033

POLIGNY 95
The small town of Poligny, famed for

its wine and Gruyère cheese, lies near
the foot of the mountains Grimont and
Croix du Dan. Within the town is the
17th century Hôtel-Dieu which
contains an interesting pharmacy and
the church of St-Hippolyte, notable for
its fine statues of the 15th century
Burgundian school.

PONS 7, 46
Where to stay
★★**Auberge Pontoise,** rue
Gambetta ☎(46)940099

Where to eat
Resto Grill 'Charentotel',
Autoroute A10 Aire de Saint-Léger

At St-Léger
Le Rustica

Where to camp
Chardon

PONTARLIER 27
A commercial centre which has
become increasingly popular as a base
from which to explore the attractive
surrounding countryside. A feature of
the town is the triumphal arch built in
honour of Louis XV during the 18th
century.

Where to stay
★★**Poste,** 55 rue de la République
☎(81)391812
★★**Terrassa,** 1 rue de la République
☎(81)390515

Where to camp
Camping Municipal

PONTAUBAULT 41, 48, 50
Where to stay
☆☆☆**13 Assiettes Lf,** (1km N on
N175) ☎(33)581403

Where to eat
Le Relais du Mouton Blanc, rue
Patton

PONT-AUDEMER 12, 38
The River Risle divides the town into a
number of arms, where several
waterside buildings provide
picturesque vistas, particularly the half-
timbered houses along the 'Cour
Canel'. The Church of St-Ouen has
some fine stained glass windows.

Where to stay
★★★**Vieux Puits,** 6 rue Notre-
Dame du Pré ☎(32)410148
★**Palais & Poste,** 8 rue Stanislas
☎(32)415074
★**Risle,** 16 quai R-Lablanc
☎(32)411457

Where to eat
La Bonne Bouffe, route de St-Paul,
Les Saulniers
**Au Rendez-Vous des
Chauffeurs,** 4 rue Notre-Dame du
Pré

PONT-DU-GARD 5
This town is famous for its spectacular
three-tier Roman aqueduct which
spans the River Gardon and once
carried the water supply from Uzès to
Nîmes. Modern traffic can cross on the
third tier which was adapted in the
18th century.

Where to stay
★★**Vieux Moulin,** rive Gauche
☎(66)371435

At Remoulins (4km E)
★★**Moderne,** place des Grands-
Jours ☎(66)372013

Where to camp
**International les Gorges du
Gardon,** route de Uzès
Pont-du-Gard, route de Uzès
Sousta
Valive

PONTIVY 56
An attractive town on the River Blavet.
The old quarter of the town, with its
ancient overhanging houses around
the Place-du-Martray, is offset by the
'new' quarter planned by Napoleon.

Where to stay
★★**Porhoët,** 41 avenue Gl-de-
Gaulle ☎(97)253488 (no restaurant)

PONT-L'ÉVÊQUE 12
With its Gothic Church of St-Michel
and half-timbered houses, Pont-
l'Évêque has been famous for its
cheese since the 13th century.

Where to stay
★**Lion d'Or Lf,** place Calvaire
☎(31)640038

Where to eat
Auberge de la Touques, place
Église
Le Station, 9 place de la Gare

Where to camp
Camping Municipal, rue de
Beaumont
Camping Cour de France

PONTORSON 48, 50
Where to stay
★★**Montgomery Lf,** 13 rue
Couesnon ☎(33)600009

Where to eat
Le Family, 4 rue de Rennes

LES PONTS-DE-CÉ 63

Where to stay
☆☆**Campanile,** chemin de Moulin-Marcille ☎(41)683459

PONT-SUR-YONNE 100

Where to stay
★★**Ecu Lf,** 3 rue Carnot ☎(86)670100

Where to eat
Le Relais Tourtel, 5 avenue du Gl-Leclerc

POUANCÉ 60

Where to camp
Camping Municipal Roche Martin, rue des Étangs

POUGES-LES-EAUX 23

A small town near the River Loire, Pouges-les-Eaux is noted for the health-giving properties of its mineral springs, which are particularly beneficial to sufferers from diabetes and nutritional disorders.

Where to eat
Courte Paille, 2km N

Where to camp
Camping Municipal Chanternes

POUILLY-SUR-LOIRE 23

Where to stay
★★**Boutelle d'Or Lf,** 13 bis route de Paris ☎(86)391384
★**Relais Fleuri Lf,** (0.5km SE on N7) ☎(86)391399

PUGET-THÉNIERS 80

A charming little town at the meeting point of the River Roudoule and the River Var, with many picturesque houses retaining a medieval appearance. The 13th century church was built by the Templars and has some beautiful 15th century wood carvings.

LE PUY 71, 72

A massive 12th century cathedral lies at the centre of this remarkable town, which is renowned for its lace making. Two gigantic volcanic rock cones rise above the houses; the Rocher Corneille acts as a pedestal for an immense statue of the Virgin and a picturesque 12th century chapel crowns Rocher St-Michel. This pretty town also has a lace making museum and other interesting churches.

Where to stay
★★★**Christel,** 15 boulevard A-Clair ☎(71)022444

Where to eat
Bateau Ivre, 5 rue Portail d'Avignon
Poste, 53 boulevard St-Louis
Sarda, 12 rue Chênebouterie
La Taverne, 50 boulevard Carnot

Where to camp
Camping Municipal Bouthezard, place de l'Hôtel-de-Ville

PYLA SUR MER 85

A pleasant seaside town located close to the mouth of the Bassin d'Arcachon.

Where to stay
★★★**Guitoune,** 95 boulevard de l'Océan ☎(56)227010
★★**Beau Rivage,** 10 boulevard de l'Océan ☎(56)220182

Where to camp
Dune, route de Biscarosse
Petit Nice, route de Biscarosse Pyla

QUIMPER 51, 53, 54

Traditional costume often seen on Quimper's streets adds to the atmosphere of old 'Breton' reflected in this fascinating town. Threaded with narrow cobbled streets and quaint old buildings the town is dominated by its fine 13th-18th century cathedral, and the River Odet flows through its centre. Pottery has been a local industry since the late 17th century and a section devoted to it can be seen in the Brittany Museum, where the Breton costume is exhibited.

Where to stay
★★★**Griffon,** 131 route de Bénodet ☎(98)903333
★★**Gradlon Lf,** 30 rue Brest ☎(98)950439 (no restaurant)
☆☆**Ibis Quimper,** rue G-Eiffel, ZI de l'Hippodrome Sectour Ouest ☎(98)905380
☆☆**Ibis Quimper Nord,** le Gourvily, route de Brest ☎(98)957764
★★**Tour d'Auvergne Lf,** 11-13 rue des Réguaires ☎(98)950870

Where to eat
Le Relais Chez Michele, 96 avenue de la Libération
Le Relais Routiers de l'Eau Blanche, 148 avenue de la Libération
La Rotonde, 36 avenue France Libre

Where to camp
Camping Orangerie de Lanniron

QUIMPERLÉ 51

A small town in an attractive setting at the confluence of the Rivers Ellé and Isole. The lower town contains a number of interesting old houses, particularly in the Rue Dom-Morice, where they are grouped around the former abbey church of Ste-Croix, dating from the 12th century.

QUINTIN 53

Built on terraces above the River Gouët, the town has retained a number of interesting old buildings and traces of its medieval fortifications. The Basilica contains several religious relics, among them a piece of the Virgins' girdle which was brought to Quintin from Jerusalem in the 13th century.

LE RABOT 36

Where to stay
☆**Bruyères** (N20) ☎(21)880570

RAMBOUILLET 16, 81

A pleasant town in the attractive surroundings of the Forest of Rambouillet. Its 16th-17th century château is the summer residence of the President of France.

Where to stay
★**St-Charles,** 1 rue de Groussay ☎(3)4830634 (no restaurant)

Where to camp
Camping Municipal Etang d'Or
Camping Port Hardy, 76 rue de Petit Parc

LE RAYOL 77

A small town set on terraces in delightful wooded surroundings. The sheltered beach is reached via a pleasant woodland walk.

RECOLOGNE 27

Where to stay
★**Escale Lf,** ☎(81)863213

REIMS 10, 25, 26, 92, 93

Coronation place of early French kings, the historic city of Reims takes its name from the Remi, a Celtic tribe which settled here. During World War I the city was extensively damaged and

agricultural centre with the largest cider-apple market in the world. The old quarter, which escaped the devastating fire in 1720 and damage during World War II, has picturesque streets lined with 15th and 16th century half-timbered houses. Close by are the Cathedral of St-Pierre and the Basilica of St-Sauveur. The cathedral contains a famous 15th century Flemish altarpiece carved in wood depicting the life of the Virgin.

Where to stay
★★★**Frantel,** place du Colombier ☎(99)795454
★★★**Guesclin,** 5 place de la Gare ☎(99)314747
☆☆☆**Novotel Rennes Alma,** avenue du Canada ☎(99)506132
★★★**Président,** 27 avenue Janvier ☎(99)654222 (no restaurant)
☆☆**Climat de France,** ZAC de Beauregard Sud ☎(99)541203

Where to eat
Baron, 26 rue St Georges
L'Ouvrée, 18 place Lices
La Pastorelle, 18 rue Penhoët

Where to camp
Camping Municipal Gayeulles

At Cesson-Sévigné (6km E on N157)
Where to stay
☆☆**Ibis Rennes,** La Perrière ☎(99)629393
☆☆**Ibis Rennes Cesson,** route de Paris ☎(99)002172

RIOM 67, 68
An attractive town noted for its well-preserved, ornate old buildings such as the Palais de Justice (Law Courts) where a 14th century chapel, the last remaining trace of the castle of the Dukes of Berry, may be seen. There are two museums and the church of Notre-Dame-du-Marthuret contains a fine 16th century statue, the 'Virgin and Bird'.

ROANNE 24
This busy port on the Roanne to Digoin Canal was founded in Roman times and has an interesting museum containing pieces from the Roman and medieval era. The 17th century Lycée and the 14th-16th century castle remains are also of interest.

Where to stay
☆☆☆**Ibis,** 21 du Côteau, le Côteau ☎(77)683622

---

again to a lesser extent during World War II. The cathedral still dominates the city and remains one of the most inspired masterpieces of Gothic art. Reims is now a prominent champagne-producing city and the extensive cellars beneath the streets may be visited on application.

Where to stay
☆☆☆**Mercure Reims Est,** ZISE les Essillards, route de Châlons ☎(26)050008
★★★**Paixe,** 9 rue Buirette ☎(26)400408
☆☆**Campanile,** Val de Murigny 11 ☎(26)366694
☆☆**Climat de France,** rue B-Russel, ZAC de la Neuvillette ☎(26)096273
★★**Continental,** 93 place Drouet d'Erlon ☎(26)403935 (no restaurant)
★★**Europa,** 8 boulevard Joffre ☎(26)403620 (no restaurant)
★★**Grand du Nord,** 75 place Drouet-d'Erlon ☎(26)470782 (no restaurant)
★★**Univers,** 41 boulevard Foch ☎(26)886808 (no restaurant)
★★**Welcome,** 29 rue Buirette ☎(26)880639 (no restaurant)

Where to eat
Courte-Paille, A4 exit 'Cormontreuil'
Flunchs Continent, Centre Commercial Continent

Restrop de Reims, A4 (Aire de Service de Reims Champagne les Petites Loges par Mourmelon-le-Grand)

Where to camp
Camping Airotel de Champagne, avenue Hoche

At Tinqueux (4km W of N31)
Where to stay
☆☆☆**Novotel,** route de Soisson ☎(26)081161

REMIREMONT 99
An old town on the banks of the Moselle which grew around an ancient convent. Parts of the abbey have been preserved, notably the Ancien Palais Abbatial which is now the Palais de Justice. One of the most attractive parts of the town is the rue Charles-de-Gaulle which contains a number of picturesque arcaded houses and there are two interesting museums, the Charles-Friry Museum, dealing with the history of the abbey and Charles de Bruyère Museum, devoted to local history.

Where to eat
Étoile d'Or, 4 impasse Halles

RENNES 16, 43, 44, 49, 50, 51, 55
On the rivers Ille and Vilaine and known as the capital of Brittany, Rennes is a thriving industrial and

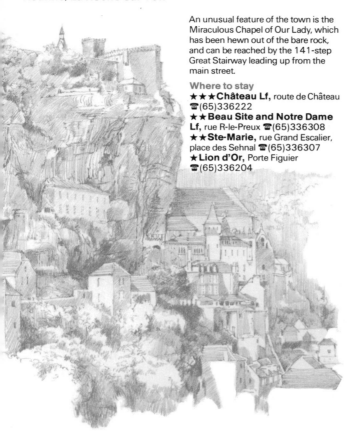

An unusual feature of the town is the Miraculous Chapel of Our Lady, which has been hewn out of the bare rock, and can be reached by the 141-step Great Stairway leading up from the main street.

Where to stay
★★★**Château Lf,** route de Château ☎(65)336222
★★**Beau Site and Notre Dame Lf,** rue R-le-Preux ☎(65)336308
★★**Ste-Marie,** rue Grand Escalier, place des Sehnal ☎(65)336307
★**Lion d'Or,** Porte Figuier ☎(65)336204

★★**Troisgros,** 22 cours de la République ☎(77)716697

At St-Germain-Lespinasse (10km NW on N7)
★★★**Relais de Roanne** ☎(77)719735

Where to eat
Bonnin, 48 rue Ch-de-Gaulle
Côté Jardin, 10 rue Benoît Malon
Don Camillo, 6 rue P-Brossolette
Le Relais Des Buttes, 10 rue Alfred de Musset

Where to camp
Camping Municipal

ROCAMADOUR 37, 73
A 14th century castle towers above the remarkable town of Rocamadour, carved into the harsh rock face below. Seven churches can be found in the square known as Parvis-des-Églises; of particular note are the Basilica of St-Sauveur and the Chapel of St-Michel.

Rocamadour – with houses built into the rock

LA ROCHE-BERNARD 57
A pleasant town overlooking the River Vilaine. Formerly a port, its harbour is now used exclusively by pleasure craft, but La Roche-Bernard has retained an attractive old quarter containing some picturesque old houses dating from the 15th and 16th century.

Where to camp
Camping Municipal

ROCHEFORT 46, 85
The port of Rochefort, at the mouth of the River Charente, was founded in 1666 by Colbert. Pierre Loti, the famous author, lived and died here, and his home is now a museum containing souvenirs from many of his voyages. The Naval Museum and Municipal Museum occupy the Hôtel des Cheusses, and the Town Hall and church of St-Louis can be found in the Place Colbert, near a beautiful fountain.

Where to stay
★★★**Remparts,** 43 rue C-Pelletan ☎(46)871244

Where to eat
Le Marais, 10 rue Lesson

LA ROCHELLE 45, 46, 85
This picturesque established sea port has become a popular resort with lovely beaches and a yachting centre. There are many interesting buildings throughout the town including the Cathedral of St-Louis, the Musée Lafaille and the Musée d'Orbigny. Overlooking the pretty harbour are two 14th century towers, namely the Tour St-Nicholas and the Tour de la Chaine which stand guard together with the Tour de la Lanterne, which was once the town prison.

Where to stay
★★★**Brises,** chemin Digue Richellieu ☎(46)438937 (no restaurant)
★★★**France et d'Angleterre,** 22 rue Gargoulleau ☎(46)413466
☆☆**Campanile,** route de Paris ☎(46)340729
☆☆**Ibis,** place du Cdt-de-la-Motte Rouge ☎(46)416022
★★**St-Nicholas,** 13 rue Sardinerie ☎(46)417155 (no restaurant)
★**Trianon et Plage,** 6 rue de la Monnaie ☎(46)412135

Where to eat
Le Claridge, 1 rue Admyrauld
La Closerie, 20 rue Verdière
Delmas Bar, 32 boulevard Emile-Delmas
Parc, 38 rue Th-Renaudot
Quatre Sergents, 49 rue St-Jean du Parot
Serge, 46 cours des Dames

Where to camp
Camping Municipal Port Neuf, boulevard A-Rondeau

LA ROCHE-SUR-YON 86
Capital of the department of Vendée, the town was laid out in its present pattern by Napoleon. A fine equestrian statue of the founder stands in the Place Napoleon. Places of interest include the museum of local history and archaeology and one of the largest stud farms (haras) in France, renowned for breeding trotting horses, is located here and visits can be arranged at most times of the year.

Where to stay
☆☆**Campanile,** les Bazinières route de Nantes ☎(51)372786

Where to eat
Le Bon Accueil, route de la Tranche
sur Mer

ROC TRÉVEZEL 56
A rock escarpment rising to 1228ft,
which provides spectacular views over
a wide area.

RODEZ 73
Set on a hill over 2000 feet high, the
most prominent feature of Rodez is the
cathedral, which is built of rose-
coloured stone and has a six-storey
high belfry. Around the Place-de-la-
Cité several old buildings can be found,
one of which houses the Musée
Fenaille.

Where to stay
★★★**Broussy,** 1 avenue V-Hugo
☎(65)681871
★★★**Tour Majie,** boulevard Gally
☎(65)683468 (no restaurant)
★**Poste,** 2 rue Beteille
☎(65)680147

Where to stay
Regent, 11 avenue Durand-des-
Gros
Le Relais Mon Bar, 19 avenue
Victor-Hugo
Le Rocade, La Roquette
St-Amans, 12 rue Madeleine
Les Trois Mulets, 31 rue St-Cyrice

Where to camp
Camping Municipal Layoule,
route d'Espalion

ROMILLY-SUR-SEINE 30
Where to stay
☆☆**Climat de France,** avenue
Diderot ☎(25)249240

Where to eat
Le Relais Champenois, 85 rue P-
Sémart

RONCHAMP 31
A small industrial town set in a
charming valley, Ronchamp is famous
for the Chapel of Notre-Dame-du-Haut
which stands on a hilltop above the
town. The chapel was designed in
1955 by the architect Le Corbusier
and is a truly impressive sight with its
wing-shaped roof and stark white
walls silhouetted against a backdrop of
rolling green hills.

ROSCOFF 54, 56
In addition to being a cross-channel
ferry terminal and lobster fishing port
Roscoff is a popular seaside resort with
its own form of spa, a seawater therapy
centre. Of interest is the 16th century
church of Notre-Dame-de-Croaz-Boz,

decorated with sculpted cannons and
ships. A fig tree planted here by the
monks in 1625 can produce as much
as 800lbs of figs a year.

Where to stay
★★★**Gulf Stream Lf,** rue
Marquise de Kergariou
☎(98)697319
★**Bains,** place Église
☎(98)612065

LES ROSIERS 62
Where to stay
★★**Jeanne de Laval,** (N152)
☎(41)518017
Where to eat
La Toque Blanche, 0.5km W via
N152

ROUEN 9, 12, 33, 34, 58, 59
Fourth-most important port in France,
Rouen is sometimes referred to as Ville
Musée (Museum Town). The old town
on the right bank of the Seine, is a
masterpiece of medieval architecture;
its famous landmarks and monuments
have been skillfully restored and the
town is almost completely re-
established to its pre-war state. Rouen
also boasts the largest and grandest
church in France; the Cathedral of
Notre-Dame. An impressive view of
the city can be gained from the belfry
next to the Gros-Horloge, the famous
great clock above the street of the
same name. Rouen is the scene of the
Martyrdom of Joan of Arc, and a
museum portraying her life is in the
Place du Vieux Marche, the old market
square where she was burnt at the
stake.

Where to stay
★★★**Dieppe,** place B-Tissot
☎(35)980698
☆☆**Arcade,** 20 place de l'Église St-
Sever ☎(35)628182
★★**Cardinal,** place de la Cathédral
☎(35)702442 (no restaurant)
★★**Cathédrale,** 12 rue St-Romain
☎(35)715795 (no restaurant)
★★**Europe,** 87 aux Ours
☎(35)708330 (no restaurant)
★★**Nord,** 91 rue Gros-Horloge
☎(35)704141 (no restaurant)
★★**Paris,** 12-14 rue de la
Champmeslé ☎(35)700926
(no restaurant)
★★**Québec,** 18-24 rue Québec
☎(35)700938 (no restaurant)
★★**Viking,** 21 quai du Havre
☎(35)703495 (no restaurant)
★**Arcades,** 52 rue des Carmes
☎(35)701030 (no restaurant)
★**Normandie,** 19 & 21 rue de Bec
☎(35)715577 (no restaurant)
★**Vielle Tour,** 42 place Haute Vielle
Tour ☎(35)700327 (no restaurant)

At Barentin (17km NW)
Where to stay
☆☆**Ibis,** ☎(35)910123

At Le Petit-Quevilly
☆☆**Fimotel,** 122 avenue J-Jaurès
☎(35)623850

At St-Étienne-du-Rouvray (2km S off N138)
☆☆**Novotel Rouen Sud Le
Madrillet** ☎(35)665850
☆☆**Ibis Rouen-Sud,** avenue M-
Bastie ☎(35)660363

Where to eat
Chez Hélène et Pierrot, 65 Quai
G-Boulet
Flunchs, 60 rue des Carmes
London Bar, 55 quai Cavelier-de-la-
Salle
Les Plantanes, 57 avenue du Mont
Riboudet
Le Relais 207, 44 quai Cavelier-de-
la-Salle
Relais d'Orléans, 32 quai Cavelier-
de-la-Salle

ROYAN 84, 85
This coastal town was badly damaged
during World War II but has since
developed into a pleasant resort and
popular conference centre. The
sheltered sandy beaches, enhanced by
a backdrop of pine wooded slopes,
now attract many holidaymakers.

Where to stay
★★**Grand de Pontaillac,** 195
avenue de Pontaillac ☎(46)380044
(no restaurant)

Where to eat
Le Chalet, 6 boulevard La Grandière
L'Esperance, 72 avenue
d'Aquitaine
Le Relais de l'Aéroport, route de
Saintes, Aérodrome de Royan
Le Squale, 102 avenue Semis

At Pontaillac (2km NE on D25)
Where to camp
Clairfontaine, allées des Peupliers
Source, Vaux-sur-Mer

LE ROZIER 69
One of the principal tourist centres for
visiting the gorges of the Tarn and the
Jonte.

RUFFEC 83
Where to stay
★**Toque Blanche,** 16 rue du Gl-
Leclerc ☎(45)310016

Where to eat
Au Rendez-vous des Routiers,
34 avenue Célestin

ST-AIGNAN 65
A picturesque town on the River Cher with a number of interesting 15th century houses and a 16th century château. The 11th-12th century church is noted for the murals in its crypt.

Where to stay
★★**St-Aignan Lf,** 7-9 quai J-J Delorme ☎(54)751804

ST-BRIEUC 48, 49, 52, 53
On a plateau above the deep valleys of the Gouëdic and the Gouet which are both crossed by impressive viaducts, St-Brieuc is an important administration, commercial and industrial centre. Some of the narrow streets around the fortified 13th century cathedral have some interesting old buildings.

Where to stay
★★★**Alexandre 1er,** 19 place du Guesclin ☎(96)337945
★★★**Griffon,** rue de Guernsey ☎(96)945762

Where to eat
Au Beaufeuillage, 2 rue de Paris

ST-CAST-LE-GUILDO 52
Where to stay
★**Angleterre & Panorama Lf,** rue Fosserole ☎(96)419144

Where to camp
Camping Municipal Mielles, 500m NE on coast

ST-DIE 98
A cathedral town standing on the River Meurthe amid attractive wooded scenery. St-Die's main claim to fame is that the first book using the name 'America' for the land discovered by Colombus was published here in 1507. A copy of this publication is on display at the local history library and other places of interest include the imposing 14th century cathedral and the neighbouring Gothic cloisters.

ST-DIZIER 26, 96
An industrial town which has retained one or two interesting buildings. Its main tourist attraction is the Motor Museum of France which lies 6km to the north-west at Villers-en-Lieu.

Where to stay
★★★**Gambetta,** 62 rue Gambetta ☎(25)052210

★**Auberge la Bobotte,** (3km W on N4) ☎(25)562003
★**Soleil d'Or,** 64 rue Gambetta ☎(25)056822

Where to eat
Bar de l'Est, 56 avenue Alsace Lorraine
Chez Marina, 152 avenue de Joinville
François 1er, 64 rue François 1er

ST-FLORENT-LE-VIEIL 63
Where to camp
Camping Municipal

ST-FLOUR 69
This pretty hilltop town overlooking the River Lander is popular as a base from which to tour the Haute Auvergne area. Surrounding the cathedral are several old buildings, including the 17th century Hôtel-de-Ville.

ST-GERMAIN-DE-JOUX 18
Where to stay
★**Reygrobellet Lf,** ☎(50)598113

ST-GERMAIN-EN-LAYE 9, 12
An elegant town surrounded by forest, famous for its Renaissance château. Formerly a royal summer residence, it is now home to the Museum of National Antiquities.

Where to stay
★★★**Ermitage des Loges,** 11 avenue des Loges ☎(3)4518886
☆☆**Campanile,** route de Mantes, Maison Forestière ☎(93)515959

Where to eat
Petite Auberge, 119 bis rue L-Desoyer

ST-JEAN-DE-LUZ 8
Situated at the mouth of the River Nivelle and still retaining much of its Basque charm, this attractive old fishing port is now a fashionable holiday resort, although the fishing industry still flourishes. The town was host to the royal wedding which took place in 1660 between Louis XIV and Infanta Maria-Therésa, daughter of King Philip IV of Spain.

Where to stay
★★★**Chantaco,** route d'Ascain ☎(59)261476
★★★**Poste,** 83 rue Gambetta ☎(59)260453 (no restaurant)
★★**Paris,** 1 boulevard Passicot ☎(59)260062
★**Continental,** 15 avenue Verdun ☎(59)260123

Where to eat
Auberge Kaiku, 17 rue République
Chipiron, 4 rue Etchegaray
Léonie, 4 rue Garat
Ostatua, 25 rue Église
Petit Grill Basque, 4 rue St-Jacques
Ramuntcho, 24 rue Garat
Restaurant 4, 4 rue Ondicola
Taverne Basque, 5 rue République

Where to camp
Camping Municipal Chibaou Berria, 2km SW of Guèthary
International d'Erromardie Iratzia, 1km NE off N10
Itsas Mendi, 5km NE on N10
Tamaris Plage, quatier d'Acotz

ST-JEAN-LE-THOMAS 40
Where to stay
★★**Bains,** (opp Post Office) ☎(33)488420

ST-JULIEN-EN-BEAUCHÊNE 80
Where to stay
★★**Bermond-Gauthier,** (N75) ☎(92)580352

Where to eat
Au Refuge des Amis

ST-JULIEN-EN-GENEVOIS 18
A small frontier town. The ruins of the castle of Ternier lie to the south east.

Where to stay
★**Savoyarde,** 15 route de Lyon ☎(50)492579

ST-LOUIS 99
Where to stay
★★**Pfiffer,** 77 rue Mulhouse ☎(89)697444 (no restaurant)

ST-LUNAIRE 52
Where to camp
Camping Far West, route du St-Briac-sur-Mer
Camping Longchamp, route de St-Briac-sur-Mer

ST-MALO 43, 52, 64
On the Rance estuary, St-Malo is a tourist resort and an important channel port. Although it suffered damage in World War II the town has been restored to its former character. The 12th century cathedral is at the heart of the town whose maze of houses and narrow streets are surrounded by majestic ramparts.

Where to stay
★★★**Central,** 6 Grande Rue ☎(99)408770

★★★**Duguesclin,** 8 place
Duguesclin ☎(99)560130
(no restaurant)
☆☆☆**Mercure,** chaussée du Sillon
☎(99)568484 (no restaurant)
★★**Louvre,** 2-4 rue de Marins
☎(99)408662 (no restaurant)
★**Noguette,** 9 rue de la Fosse
☎(99)408357

Where to eat
A L'Abordge, 5 place Poissonnerie
**Les Écluses, gare maritime de
la Bourse**
Grilles, 2 rue Pie qui Boît

**At La Gouesnière (12km SE on
D4)**

Where to stay
★★**Gare,** (1.5km N on D76)
☎(99)891046
At Paramé (1km E)
★★**Rochebonne,** 15 bd
Châteaubriand ☎(99)560172

At St-Servan-sur-Mer (3km S)
Where to eat
L'Arrivée, 83 rue Villep-Pépin

Where to camp
Camping Cité d'Aleth

**ST-MAURICE-SUR-MOSELLE
99**

Where to stay
★★**Relais des Ballons Lf,** route
Bénélux-Bâle (N66) ☎(29)251109
★**Bonséjour Lf** ☎(29)251233

Where to camp
Camping Deux Ballons

ST-MAXIMIN-LA-STE-BAUME 4
Tradition has it that Mary Magdalene
was buried here in the crypt of an
ancient church. It is believed that her
tomb, along with that of St-Maximin,
was discovered in the 13th century,
shortly before the construction of the
abbey was begun. The abbey is a fine
example of Gothic architecture and
contains a number of interesting
features, including one of the finest
18th century organs in France and a
wealth of beautifully carved
woodwork.

Where to stay
★**Chez Nous,** 3 boulevard J-Jaurès
☎(94)780257

Where to eat
Le Relais du Carillon, 5 rue de la
République

ST-NAZAIRE 55, 60
Lying on the Loire estuary, St-
Nazaire's growth since the early 19th
century has been due to its port

facilities and shipbuilding industry.
Three points of major interest are the
entrance lock, scene of the famous
Canadian-British commando raid in
1942, the submarine pens built by the
Germans during the war, which are
now the sites of various industries, and
the covered submarine exit from which
there is a good view of the town and
the port installations.

Where to stay
★★**Dauphin,** 33 rue J-Jaurès
☎(40)665961 (no restaurant)

Where to eat
Le Lafayette, avenue de Penhoët
Moderne, 46 rue Anjou
Le Relais les Goelands, 12
boulevard de la Fraternité
Trou Normand, 60 rue Paix

ST-OMER 1, 25, 90
A busy town on the River Aa,
surrounded by many canals and
waterways. During both World Wars
the town was badly damaged but
some interesting old buildings remain
intact, among them the Basilica of
Notre-Dame and a school which was
the former 17th century Jesuit chapel.

Where to stay
☆☆**Ibis,** rue H-Dupuis
☎(21)931111
★★**St-Louis,** 28 rue d'Arras
☎(21)383521 (no restaurant)

At Tilques (4km NW on N43)
★★**Vert Mesnil,** (1.5km E of N43)
☎(21)932899

Where to eat
Crémaillère, 12 boulevard
Strasbourg
Le Cygne, 8 rue Caventou
Le Relais de la Renaissance, 38
rue François-Ringat
La Truye qui File, 8 rue Bleuets

ST-POL-DE-LÉON 54, 56
An important market town with two of
the finest buildings in Brittany. They
are the former 13th-16th century
cathedral and the 14th-15th century
Kreisker Chapel and belfry.

Where to eat
Chez Danny, 13 rue du Colombier

ST-POL-SUR-TERNOISE 90
Where to stay
★**Lion d'Or Lf,** 68 rue Hesdin
☎(21)031293

ST-POURCAIN 68
Where to stay
★**Chêne Vert Lf,** 35 boulevard
Ledru-Rollin ☎(70)454065

★**Deux Ponts Lf,** Ilot de Tivoli
☎(70)454114

Where to eat
Hostellerie des Cours, boulevard
Ledru-Rollin
Hôtel du Centre les Routiers, 53
boulevard Ledru-Rollin

ST-QUENTIN 25
St-Quentin's foundations date back to
Roman times and despite the scars
inflicted by both World Wars some
ancient buildings have survived. Two
of these are the 16th century town hall
with its Gothic façade and the 13th
century church of St-Quentin. A
notable collection of European
butterflies can be seen in the
Entomological Museum, and the
Children's Museum is said to be the
only one of its kind in the country. An
ideal centre for visiting World War I
battlefields.

Where to stay
★★**Grand,** 6 rue Dachery
☎(23)626977 (no restaurant)
★★**Paix Albert 1er,** 3 place du 8
Octobre ☎(23)627762

Where to eat
Chez Lina, route de la Fère
Le Pichet, 6 boulevard Gambetta
Le Riche, 10 rue Toiles
Univers, 11 place H-de-Ville

ST-RAMBERT-D'ABLON 3
Where to stay
☆☆**Ibis,** La Champagnière (RN7)
☎(75)030400

ST-RAPHAEL 4, 78
A busy port and holiday resort situated
on the attractive bay of Fréjus. There is
an excellent Museum of Underwater
Archaeology, and an interesting
Templars Church near to a milestone
from the Roman Aurelian Way.

Where to stay
★★★**Continental,** 25 boulevard
de la Libération ☎(94)950014
(no restaurant)
★★**Beau-Séjour,** prom Prés-Coty
☎(94)950375
★★**Provencal If,** 197 rue de la
Garonne ☎(94)950152
(no restaurant)
★**Vieux Port,** 109 avenue
Commandant-Guilbaud
☎(94)952312

Where to eat
Le Relais Bel Azur, 247 boulevard
de Provence
Le Tisonnier, 70 rue Garonne
La Voile d'Or, 1 boulevard Gén-de-
Gaulle

Where to camp
Beauséjour-les-Tasses
Douce Quietude, 3435 boulevard J-Baudino
Royal

ST-TROPEZ 77
One of the best known resorts on the Riviera, St-Tropez owes much of its popularity to its superb position on a peninsula. Its sheltered harbour and yacht marina are a great attraction to sailors. The 16th century citadel, overlooking the town from the east, contains a maritime museum and fine views of the bay and its surroundings can be obtained from its ramparts. The Annonciade Museum, in a converted chapel, has an exceptionally fine collection of works of art.

Boats in the harbour at St Tropez

Where to stay
★★★Coste, Port du Pilon
☎(94)970064
★★★Ermitage, avenue P-Signac
☎(94)975233 (no restaurant)

Where to eat
L'Escale, quai J-Jaurès
Le Girelier, au Port
Laetitia-la Frégate, 52 rue Allard
Les Lices, 3 place des Lices

STE-ENIMIE 69
This small town on the River Tarn has many interesting features including the Fountain of Burle whose waters were reputed to have healing powers. Also, from the Chapel of Ste-Enimie, just north of the town, there are beautiful views of the town and countryside.

Where to stay
★★Commerce, (N586) route de Meyrueis ☎(66)485001

ST-MAXIME 77
A popular resort in an attractive, sheltered setting, with a yacht marina and a fine beach. The town centre is closed to traffic during the summer.

Where to stay
★★Beausite, 6 boulevard des Cistes ☎(94)961953
★★★Belle Aurore, 3 la Croisette
☎(94)960245

LES SABLES D'OLONNE 86
A very popular, family-orientated seaside resort with a magnificent sandy beach and a pretty fishing harbour.

Where to stay
★★Résidence, 36 prom Clemenceau ☎(51)320666 (no restaurant)

Where to eat
Au Coq Hardi, 7 avenue Alaide-Gabaret
Le Relais Chez Dany, 17 rue de la Bauduère
Les Becs Fins, 84 avenue Alcide Gabaret
Loulou, route Bleue
Paix, 20 quai George V
Thèâtre, 20 boulevard F-Roosevelt

Where to camp
Baie de Cayola, route de la Corniche
CM Roses, rue des Roses
Fosses Rouges
Trianon

SABLES-D'OR-LES-PINS 52

Where to stay
★★★Bon Accueil Lf, allée des Acacis ☎(96)414219
★★★Diane Lf, avenue Brouard'
☎(96)414207 (no restaurant)
★★Ajoncs d'Or, allée des Acacis
☎(96)414212
★★Dunes d'Armor & Mouettes,
☎(96)414206
★★Volle d'Or, rue des Acacis
☎(96)414249

SAINTES 7, 46, 84
Built on the River Charente, Saintes has a long history. The Roman influence on this ancient town is evident today by the arch of Germanicus and the amphitheatre, which is still used during the summer months. There are many other fine examples of Romanesque architecture and also the 15th century Cathedral of St-Pierre, built in Gothic style, around which are remains of the old town. Near to the river is an attractive public garden, where many different breeds of horses may be seen from mid July to February.

Where to stay
★★★**Commerce Mancini,** rue des Messageries ☎(46)930661
★★★**Relais du Bois-St-George,** rue des Royan ☎(46)935099
★★**Terminus,** esplanade de la Gare ☎(46)743503 (no restaurant)
★**Messageries,** rue des Messageries ☎(46)936499 (no restaurant)

Where to eat
A l'Arret des Routiers, 44 cours Reverseaux
Auberge de la Boiserie, Maine Allain Chaniers, on the RN 141
Brasserie Louis, 116 avenue Gambetta
Le Relais de l'Oasis, route de Rochefort

Where to camp
Camping Municipal, 1 km on N128

SALBRIS 36

Where to stay
★★★**Parc Lf,** 10 avenue d'Orléans ☎(54)971853
★**Dauphin Lf,** 57 boulevard de la République ☎(54)970483

Where to eat
Le Clé des Champs, 52 avenue Orléans

SALLANCHES 18
This attractive little town has become a popular summer resort. It is surrounded by magnificent mountain scenery.

Where to stay
☆☆**Ibis,** avenue de Genève ☎(50)581442

Where to eat
La Chaumière, route de Megève

Where to camp
Mont Blanc Village, (2km SE off D13)

SALON-DE-PROVENCE 4, 75
A busy market town where an ancient gateway gives access to narrow, winding streets lined with plane trees. The Château de l'Empéri contains a military museum and the restored house of Michel de Nostradamus, the 16th century visionary, is open to the public.

Where to stay
★**Grand Poste,** 1 rue Prés-Kennedy ☎(90)560194

At Barben (La) (8km SE)
★**Touloubre Lf,** ☎(90)551685

At Lançon-Provence (9km SE on A7)
☆☆☆**Mercure,** A7 ☎(90)539070

Where to eat
Craponne, 146 allées Craponne
Le Poêlon, 71 allées Craponne
Pont Restaurant Jacques Borel, Aire de Service de Lançon-de-Provence
Le Touring, 20 place Crouillat

SALSES 6
A pleasant town with a picturesque red brick 15th century castle.

Where to stay
☆☆☆**Relais Rousillon,** (N9) ☎(68)386067

Where to camp
International de Roussillon, Route de Narbonne

SANARY-SUR-MER 76

Where to stay
★★**Tour,** quai Gl-de-Gaulle ☎(94)741010

Where to eat
La Calèche, place Poste

Where to camp
Mogador
Val d'Aran

SARREBOURG 91, 97
An ancient town retaining remnants of its medieval walls. The museum is devoted to regional archaeology and contains many Gallo-Roman relics.

SAUJON 84

Where to eat
Auberge du Moulin
Le Relais de la Gare, 2 rue Clemenceau

Where to camp
Chênes, Medis

SAUMUR 62
A pleasant, compact town known for its mushrooms, sparkling wines and the manufacture of carnival masks. The dominant feature is the 14th century château, which contains two museums. There are some fine old houses in the area around the 12th century Church of St-Pierre and Saumur is also famous for its National Riding School and for the Cavalry and Armoured Corps Academy which dates from the mid 18th century.

Where to stay
★★★**Budan,** 3 quai Carnot ☎(41)512876
★**Croix-Verte,** 49 rue de Rouen ☎(41)673931

Where to eat
L'Escargot, 30 rue Ml-Leclerc
L'Hôtel de la Gare, 16 avenue David d'Angers

Where to camp
Camping Municipal, Ile d'Offard

SAVERNE 10, 91, 97
An ancient town, noted for the cultivation of roses, in a pleasant wooded setting beside the River Zorn. Saverne contains many fine old buildings, but pride of place must go to the 18th century château which was once the residence of the Bishops of Strasbourg. The north façade of the building is particularly striking and the château also contains a fascinating museum of regional archaeology and history. A beautiful rose garden, with more than 1000 different varieties lies on the western outskirts on the banks of the Zorn.

Where to stay
★★**Geisswiller,** 17 rue Côte ☎(88)911851
★**Boeuf-Noir,** 22 Grand Rue ☎(88)911053
★**Chez Jean Lf,** 3 rue de la Gare ☎(88)911019

SEDAN 91
On the River Meuse at the foot of the Ardennes, this industrial town is dominated by its extensive Château-Fort - the largest of its kind in Europe. The French army surrendered at Sedan in 1870 during the Franco-Prussian war.

SÉES 38, 39, 59
A quiet town on the River Orne. Several ecclesiastical buildings surround the magnificent 13th-14th century Norman cathedral.

Where to stay
★**Cheval Blanc Lf,** 1 place St-Pierre ☎(33)278048
★**Dauphin Lf,** 31 place Halls ☎(33)278007

Where to eat
Normandy, 20 place Gl-de-Gaulle
Le Trotteur, 9 rue Billy

SÉNAS 4, 75

Where to stay
★**Luberon,** 17 avenue A-Aune (N7) ☎(90)572010

Where to eat
L'Etape, Route d'Aix
Luberon, N7
Terminus, N7

SENLIS 1, 15, 100

Seat of a bishopric between the 3rd and the 17th century; the 12th century former cathedral is the most outstanding building in the town. The remains of the Gallo-Roman town wall are some of the best-preserved in France.

Where to stay
★★**Nord Lf,** 110 rue de la République ☎(4)4530122

Where to eat
Rôtisserie de Formanoir, 17 rue Châtel

SENS 2, 100

An ancient town retaining a number of interesting old buildings and encircled by pleasant boulevards, laid out on the site of the medieval ramparts. Sens' most prominent building is the Cathedral of St-Étienne, one of the earliest of the large Gothic cathedrals to be built in France. It is chiefly famous for its magnificent treasury which contains one of the richest collections of vestments and religious objects in the country. The adjoining Palais Synodal has an exhibition of Gallo-Roman and medieval works of art and the Municipal Museum deals with local archaeology and also has souvenirs from the Napoleonic era.

Where to stay
★★★**Paris & Poste,** 97 rue de la République ☎(86)651743

Where to eat
Auberge de la Vanne, route Lyon
Hotel des Trois Gares, 29 avenue Vauban
Palais, 18 place République
Soleil Levant, 51 rue E-Zola

SERRES 80

Serres lies above the River Beüch and its many old buildings give it a medieval appearance.

Where to stay
★**Alpes,** avenue Grenoble ☎(92)670018

Where to eat
Au Pont de la Barque, Pont-la-Barque, Signottier

Where to camp
Barillons
Domaine des 2 Soleils

SÈTE 5

Linked to the sea in the south and the Bassin de Thau in the north by a series of canals, Sète is France's second largest Mediterranean port, handling the larger part of the region's extensive export of wine. The city is also famous for its 'Joutes Nautiques', aquatic jousting between combatants in specially-constructed boats. These contests have been held each August for more than 300 years. Places of interest include the Paul Valéry Museum, which has a section devoted to the poetical and philosophical works of Valéry who was born in Sète in 1871.

Where to stay
★★★**Grand,** 17 quai Ml-Lattre-de-Tassigny ☎(67)747177
★★★**Imperial,** place E-Herriot ☎(67)532832 (no restaurant)

Where to eat
Le Chalut, 38 quai Gén-Durand
Jacques Coeur, 17 rue P-Valéry
La Madrague, 16 quai Gén-Durand
La Palangrotte, Rampe P-Valéry
Le Pavillon, 23 route de Montpellier
Le Regence, 1 place Delille
Rest Alsacien, 25 rue P-Sémard
Resto Routier la Peniche, 1 quai des Moulins
La Rotonde, 17 quai Ml-de-Lattre-de-Tassigny

Where to camp
Castellas

SÉZANNE 94, 96

A small industrial town and market centre, noted for the manufacture of spectacle lenses. The most prominent building is the Church of St-Denis, which contains a number of interesting sculptures. An attractive promenade, the Mail des Cordeliers, occupies the site of the town's former fortifications.

Where to stay
★★**Croix d'Or Lf,** 53 rue Notre-Dame ☎(26)806110
★★**France,** 25 rue L-Jolly ☎(26)805252

Where to camp
Camping Municipal

SIGEAN 6

Where to camp
Camping Municipal

SISTERON 80

On a steep hill above the River Durance, the stepped groups of old houses in Sisteron rise up towards the ancient citadel where there is an open air theatre. Nearby, a tunnel through the hillside takes traffic away from the town, leaving the narrow streets free from congestion.

Where to stay
★★★**Grand du Cours,** avenue de la Libération, place de l'Eglise ☎(92)610451 (no restaurant)

Where to camp
Camping Municipal de la Baume

SOISSONS 92, 94

Although Soissons suffered extensive war damage some interesting old buildings have remained. These include the 13th century Cathedral of St-Gervais, the 13th century Abbey of St-Léger where Thomas-à-Becket spent some time, and the even older Abbey of St-Médard, the ruins of which date from around the 18th century.

Where to stay
☆☆**Lions,** route de Reims, ZI Soissons (3km E via N31) ☎(23)593060
★★**Picardie,** 6 rue Neuve St-Martin ☎(23)532193
★**Rallye,** 10 boulevard de Strasbourg ☎(23)530047 (no restaurant)

Where to eat
Grenadin, 19 route de Fère-en-Tardenois

SOUILLAC 37

A popular base from which to tour the surrounding area of the Dordogne, this small town first grew up around a 13th century abbey. Now, the parish church has a beautifully carved door-frame from the original abbey, which was destroyed during the Revolution.

Where to stay
★★**Ambassadeurs Lf,** 7-12 avenue Gl-de-Gaulle ☎(65)327836
★★**Périgord Lf,** 31 avenue Gl-de-Gaulle ☎(65)327828
★★**Renaissance Lf,** 2 avenue J-Jaurès ☎(65)327804
★★**Roseraie Lf,** 42 avenue de Toulosse ☎(65)378269
★**Auberge du Puits Lf,** 5 place Puits ☎(65)378032
★**Nouvel Lf,** 21 avenue Gl-de-Gaulle ☎(65)327958

Where to eat
Le Relais de L'Escale, 41 avenue Louis-Jean Walvy
Vieille Auberge, place Minoterie

SOULAC-SUR-MER 85

Where to camp
Airotel Place, route de l'Amélie
Arros, rue V-Hugo
Genêts
Océan, 3.5km S
Sables d'Argent, route de l'Amélie

Timber framed buildings on one of Strasbourg's waterways

interior. The château is noted for its connections with Joan of Arc, Sully (Henri IV's minister) and the young Voltaire.

Where to stay
★★**Grand Sully Lf,** 10 boulevard Champ de Foire ☎(38)362756
★★**Poste,** 11 rue faubourg St-Germain ☎(38)352622

Where to eat
Le Cercle d'Or, 2 place St-Germain
Esplanade, place Pilier

Where to camp
Camping ESSI

TAIN L'HERMITAGE 3
A wine centre on the east bank of the River Rhône which has an ancient sacrificial altar dating from AD184.

Where to stay
★★★**Commerce,** 69 avenue J-Jaurès ☎(75)086500

Where to eat
Grappe d'Or, 13 avenue Jean-Jaurès

Where to camp
Camping Municipal Lucs, route de Valence

TARARE 24
Nestling in a narrow valley, close to a range of mountains, Tarare thrives from the production of curtain materials and synthetics. In the 18th century the town's most prominent industry was the manufacture of muslin. There is a 17th century Friary and just outside the town, the Chapel of Notre-Dame-de-Bel-Air affords commanding views of the surrounding countryside.

Where to stay
★**Mère Paul,** 2km on N7 ☎(74)631457

Where to eat
Bar Provençal, 8 rue Edouard-Herriot
Le Relais Champetre, le pied de la Montagne

Where to camp
Camping Municipal, route de Lyon

At Amélie-sur-Mer (L') (4.5km S)
Amélie-Plage, 3km S on Soulac road

At Lilian (4.5km S)
Pins, on D101

SOUPPES-SUR-LOING 23

Where to camp
Camping Municipal, chemin des Mariniers

STAINVILLE 96

Where to stay
★★★**Grange Lf,** ☎(29)786015

Where to eat
La Petite Auberge

STRASBOURG 10, 91, 97
Situated on the River Rhine and honeycombed by its tributary the Ill, Strasbourg has been a city of strategic importance since pre-Roman times. The Middle Ages saw it become a thriving industrial port and university centre and the present century has seen Strasbourg named as the seat of the Council of Europe. The magnificent cathedral, founded during the 11th century, towers above the old quarter with its 16th century timbered buildings, covered bridges and museums vividly recalling the city's glorious past. Strasbourg's modern entertainment and sporting facilities have made it a popular tourist and conference centre.

Where to stay
★★★**France,** 20 rue du Jeu des Enfants ☎(88)323712 (no restaurant)

★★★**Grand,** 12 place de la Gare ☎(88)324690 (no restaurant)
★★★**Hannong,** 15 rue du 22 Novembre ☎(88)321622 (no restaurant)
★★★**Monopole-Métropole,** 16 rue Kuhn ☎(88)321194 (no restaurant)
☆☆☆**Novotel Centre Halles,** quai Kléber ☎(88)221099
☆☆☆**PLM Pont de l'Europe,** Parc du Rhin ☎(88)610323
☆☆**Arcade,** 7 rue de Molsheim ☎(88)223000
☆☆**Climat de France,** place A-Maurois Maille Iréne, ZUP Hautepierre ☎(88)285923
☆☆**Ibis,** 1 rue Sebastopol, quai Kléber ☎(88)221499
★★**Vendôme,** 9 place de la Gare ☎(88)324523 (no restaurant)

Where to eat
Au Coin du Pêcheur, 1 rue Migneret
Au Petit Rhin, 4 rue du Port-du-Rhin
Au Rhin Français, 83 route du Rhin
Flunchs Centre, 16 rue du Vieux Marché aux Grains
Flunchs Hautepierre, ZUP de Hautepierre
Le Relais du Port du Rhin, 59 route du Rhin

Where to camp
Camping Montagne-Verte, 2 rue R-Forrer

SULLY-SUR-LOIRE 66
The main attraction of this town is the 14th century Château de Sully, a medieval fortress, surrounded by a moat, with a charming Renaissance

TARASCON-SUR-ARIÈGE 89

Where to stay
★★**Poste Lf**, 16 avenue V-Pilhès
☎(61)646041

Where to eat
Le Castella, place Sainte-Quitterie

TARBES 88
Tarbes was the birthplace of the famous poet Gautier and also the distinguished war marshal Ferdinand Foch, whose house is now a museum. On the northern outskirts of the town lies the beautiful Jardin Massey park which has an observation tower affording lovely views. Tarbes is also noted for its National Stud Farm, which specialises in Anglo/Arab cavalry horses.

Where to stay
★★★**Président**, 1 rue G-Faure
☎(62)939840
☆☆**Campanile**, Lotissement Longchamp, route de Lourdes
☎(62)930854
★**Henri IV**, 7 boulevard B-Barère
☎(67)340168 (no restaurant)

Where to eat
Le Clauzier, 2 place Germain Claverie
La Crémaillère, 32 place du Foirail
L'Isard, 70 avenue Mar-Joffre
Le Relais Chez Lazare, 24 rue Alsace-Lorraine
Tour 'Ty, 86 avenue B-Barère
Le Victor Hugo, 52 rue Victor-Hugo

THANN 99
A small town on the River Thur in a wine-producing area. Thann has a number of picturesque half-timbered buildings and is particularly noted for its collegiate Church of St-Thiebaut, one of the finest examples of Gothic architecture in the region.

THIÉBLEMONT-FAREMONT 26, 96

Where to camp
Camping Charmilles, route de Vitré-le-François

THIERS 71
Thiers is set into the steep hillside close to the River Duronne and is noted for its cutlery-manufacturing industry which has existed within the town for hundreds of years. A few old buildings still stand, including the 15th century Maison du Pirou, a half-timbered mansion, and the Musée Fontenille-Mondière.

Where to stay
☆☆**Fimotel**, route de Clermont-Ferrand ☎(73)806440

TONNEINS 19

Where to eat
Le Robinsons, route d'Agen

Where to camp
Camping Municipal Robinson

TOULON 76, 77
An important naval and commercial port, Toulon suffered damage during World War II, but has since been carefully restored to preserve its original character. The old town is a jumble of narrow streets clustered around the busy covered fish market, and also contains the Naval Museum and the 12th century Cathedral of Ste-Marie-de-la-Seds. The best view of the town and its surroundings can be obtained from Corniche du Mont Faron which climbs into the mountains above the harbour.

Where to stay
★★★**Frantel Tour Blanche**, boulevard Ami-Vence ☎(94)244157

At Farlède (La) (8.5km NE)
☆☆**Climate de France**, quartier de l'Auberte ☎(94)487427

Where to eat
Au Sourd, 10 rue Molière
Calanque, 25 rue Denfert-Rochereau
La Dauphin, 21 bis rue Jean-Jaurès
La Fringale 'chez jo', 522 avenue de la République
Madeleine, 7 rue Tombades
Melodia, 12 rue Molière
Pascal, square L-Verane
Le Relais de l'Escaillon, 1 rue Châteaubriand
Le Relais des Amoureux, 36 avenue du Gl-Pruneau
Le Sporting Bar, 676 Boulevard du Ml-Foch

TOULOUSE 19, 20, 37, 89
The university town of Toulouse is the fourth-largest city in France and has a wealth of art and architecture, most notably the well preserved Basilica of St-Sernin, built of the local red-brick. As well as having many buildings and museums of historical interest, Toulouse is a thriving commercial and industrial centre and has become the cultural centre of southern France.

Where to stay
★★★**Caravelle**, 62 rue Raymond IV ☎(61)627065 (no restaurant)
★★★**Compagnie du Midi**, Gare Matabiau ☎(61)628493
★★★**Concorde**, 16 boulevard Bonrepos ☎(61)624860 (no restaurant)
★★★**Diane**, 3 route de St-Simon ☎(61)075922
☆☆**Ibis les Raisons**, 27 boulevard des Minimes ☎(61)226060
★★**Voyageurs**, 11 boulevard Bonrepos ☎(61)628979 (no restaurant)

Toulouse Airport
★★★**Frantel Wilson**, 7 rue de Labéda ☎(61)212175 (no restaurant)
☆☆☆**Novotel Toulouse Purpon**, 23 rue de Maubec ☎(61)493410

Where to eat
Belvédère, 8e étage 11 boulevard Recollets
Le Cassoulet, 40 rue Peyrolieres
Chez Emile, 13 place St-Georges
Flunchs, 28 allées Jean-Jaurès
Fournil, 36 allées J-Jaurès
La Frégate, 16 place Wilson
Grand-Café de France, 9 impasse des États, Unis
Orsi Bouchon Lyonnais, 13 rue Industrie
Le Paysan, 9 rue G-Péri
Le Rotelou, 61 route de Launaguet
Rôtisserie des Carmes, 11 place Carmes

At Toulouse Fenourlet
Courte-Paille, N20 near Casino

At Toulouse Labège
Flunchs, ZAC de la Grand Borde

At Toulouse Mirail
Courte-Paille, Rocade Ouest, Le Mirail near hotel Ibis

At Toulouse Portet sur Garonne
Flunchs, Centre Commercial Carrefour BP3

Where to camp
Camping Municipal Rupé, chemin du Pont de Rupé

LE TOUQUET 21, 90
Home to a busy airport, Le Touquet is an attractive seaside resort at the mouth of the River Canche.

Where to stay
★★★**Côte d'Opale**, 99 boulevard Dr J-Pouget ☎(21)050811
☆☆☆**Novotel-Thalamer**, La Plage ☎(21)052400
★★★**Westminster**, avenue Verger ☎(21)051966 (no restaurant)
★★**Forêt**, 73 rue de Moscou ☎(21)050988 (no restaurant)
☆☆**Ibis**, Front de Mer ☎(21)053690

★★**Plage,** 13 boulevard de la Mer
☎(21)050322 (no restaurant)
★★**Windsor-Artois,** 7 rue St-
Georges (off rue de la Paix)
☎(21)050544
★**Chalet,** 15 rue de la Paix
☎(21)051299
★**Robertis,** 66 rue de la Londrés
☎(21)051198
★**Touquet,** 17 rue de Paris
☎(21)052254 (no restaurant)

Where to eat
Chalut, 7 boulevard J-Pouget
Diamant Rose, 110 rue Paris
Flavio-Club de la Forêt, avenue
Verger
Georges II

TOURNUS 2
In a beautiful setting beside the River
Saône, Tournus is famous for its well-
preserved abbey buildings. The abbey
Church of Saint-Philibert is one of the
finest examples of the Romanesque
style in France, with parts which date
from the 10th century. Also of interest
is the Musée Perrin de Puycousin and
the Musée Greuze which contains
works of art by Jean-Baptiste Greuze.

Where to stay
★★★**Rempart,** 2 & 4 rue Gambetta
☎(85)511056
★★★**Sauvage,** place du Champ de
Mars ☎(85)511445
★**Terrasses Lf,** 18 avenue du 23
Janvier ☎(85)510174

Where to eat
Nouvel H, 1 bis avenue Alpes
Relais de Martailly
Relais Top les Routiers, route
Nationale 6

**TOURS 7, 39, 61, 62, 65, 67, 82,
83**
A busy wine-producing university
town near the confluence of the Rivers
Loire and Cher. The historical
importance of Tours is vividly recalled
by its wealth of picturesque old
buildings, ranging from the 15th
century houses which line the Place
Plumereau to the stately Renaissance
Hôtel Gouin which now serves as a
museum and art gallery. The shrine of
St-Martin still attracts pilgrims to the
19th century Basilica which bears his
name and portions of the 13th century
church which preceded it can also be
seen nearby. The Cathedral of St-
Gatien, built between the 13th and the
16th centuries, contains some fine
medieval stained-glass and the 12th
century Tour de Guise stands as a
remnant of the castle Henry II of
England established here to guard the
Loire Valley.

Where to stay
★★★**Bordeaux Lf,** 3 place du Ml-
Leclerc ☎(47)054032
★★★**Château de la Loire,** 12 rue
Gambetta ☎(47)051005
(no restaurant)
☆☆**Arcade,** 1 rue G-Claude
☎(47)614444
☆☆**Climat de France,** ZI les
Granges Galand (N76), St-Avertin
☎(47)277117
☆☆**Ibis,** la Petitite Arche, avenue A-
Maginot ☎(47)543220
★**Balzac,** 47 rue de la Scellerie
☎(47)054087 (no restaurant)
★**Foch,** 20 rue Ml-foch
☎(47)057059 (no restaurant)

Where to eat
Flunchs, Galerie Métropole, 14
place J-Jaurès
La Poivrière, 13 rue du Change
Le Relais de l'Aviation, 285
avenue Maginot
Le Strasbourg, 76 boulevard Thiers

TROYES 30, 94
The ancient capital of Champagne,
Troyes achieved great prosperity
during the Middle Ages and its hosiery
and cotton trade has been in existence
since the 16th century. The town has
retained a wealth of timber-framed,
turreted Renaissance houses and
public buildings and is remarkable for
the number of old churches that have
survived, many of them containing
outstanding works of sculpture and
stained glass. The Cathedral of St-
Pierre and St-Paul is particularly
impressive and has a fine medieval
treasury.

Where to stay
★★★**Grand,** 4 avenue Ml-Joffre
☎(25)799090
★★**Paris,** 54 rue R-Salengro
☎(25)433713 (no restaurant)

Where to eat
Café du Midi, 2 avenue Chaumedey
Maisonneuve
Grand Café, 4 rue Champeaux
Restaurant Splendid, 44
boulevard Carnot

USSAT-LES-BAINS 89
A small spa in the Pyrénées noted for
its huge cave, the Grotte de Lombrive.

UZERCHE 37
Perched on a hillside overlooking the
River Vezère, this pleasant town has

many 15th-16th century mansions.
There is also a fortified Church of St-
Pierre and a 14th century gateway.

Where to stay
★★**Ambroise,** avenue de Paris
☎(55)731008
★★**Teyssler,** rue Pont-Turgot
☎(55)731005

VALENCE 3, 19
Founded by the Romans in 123BC,
Valence's narrow streets thread
through the older part of the town,
dominated by the awesome Cathedral
of St-Appollinaire. Within the cathedral
is a monument to Pope Pius VI who
died here in exile. A museum full of
beautiful 18th century works of art is
now housed in the former Bishop's
Palace.

Where to stay
☆☆☆**Novotel Valence Sud,** 217
avenue de Provence (N7)
☎(75)422015
☆☆**Ibis,** 355 avenue de Provence
☎(75)444254
★★**Pic,** 285 avenue V-Hugo
☎(75)441532

At Bourg-lès-Valence
☆☆**Climat de France,** route de
Châteauneuf-sur-Isère
☎(75)427746
★★**Seyvet Lf,** 24 avenue M-Urtin
☎(75)432651

Where to eat
Courte-Paille, route de Grenoble,
near Centre Commercial Valence
La Licorne, 13 rue Chalomet
La Petite Auberge, 1 rue Athènes
Rabelais, 3 place Clercs

Where to camp
Camping Municipal, Centre de
l'Epervière

VALOGNES 11, 40
Valognes is an ancient Roman town.
Although much of it was destroyed in
the last war, some old buildings have
survived, including the remains of
Roman Baths, the 18th century
Benedictine Abbey (now an
almshouse), the ruins of an old castle
and the 18th century Hôtel de
Beaumont.

Where to stay
★**Louvre,** 28 rue Réligieuses
☎(33)400007

Valognes

Where to eat
Au Petit Montrouge, 104 rue des Réligieuses
Le Relais des Routiers, 40 rue des Réligieuses

At St-Sauveur-le-Vicomte (15km S)
Where to eat
Auberge Vieux Château

Where to camp
Camping Municipal Vieux Château

VALS-LES-BAINS 72
In the beautiful valley of the Volane, the town's famed waters have been exported since the 17th century.

Where to stay
★★★Vivorals, 5 rue C-Expilly
☎(75)374263
★★Europe Lf, 86 rue J-Jaurès
☎(75)374394

VANNES 56, 57
An important agricultural centre on the Gulf of Morbihan, Vannes is noted for its 'old quarter', full of narrow alleyways and squares lined with gabled 16th century houses. The whole of this area, a pedestrianised zone, is surrounded by the town's restored 13th century ramparts and is best viewed from the Promenade de la Garenne which was once the park belonging to the ducal castle. Buildings of especial interest include the cathedral, dating originally from the 13th century and the 19th century Renaissance-style town hall.

Where to stay
★★★Marebaudière, 4 rue A-Briand ☎(97)473429
☆☆Ibis, rue E-Jourdan, ZI de Ménimur Est, ☎(97)636111
★Image Ste-Anne, 8 place de la Libération ☎(97)632736
★Marée Bleue, 8 place Bir-Hakeim ☎(97)472429

Where to eat
Le Lys, 51 rue Ml-Leclerc

VARCES 80

Where to stay
★Escale, place de la République
☎(76)728019

VARENNES-SUR-ALLIER 24, 71

Where to eat
Central, place de la Mairie
Dauphin, rue Hôtel-de-Ville
La Locaterie, (1km on N7)
Le Relais des Touristes-Rest de France, 1 rue des Halles

Where to camp
Château de Chezeuil
Plans d'Eau

VARILHES 89

Where to camp
Camping Municipal Parc du Château, route de Pamiers

VATAN 36

Where to eat
Aux Amis de la Route, 5 rue des Récollets France
Le Relais du Chêne Vert, 13 avenue de Paris

VENDÔME 82
In spite of modern industrial development, Vendôme has retained an attractive old quarter, spread over several branches of the River Loire. The town's most impressive building is the church, which was originally part of the 11th century Benedictine abbey. The neighbouring Monks' Building contains a museum dealing with local religious art and archaeology. The château, on a hill overlooking the river, has retained some 13th and 14th century features.

Where to stay
★Vendôme Lf, 15 faubourg Chartrain ☎(54)770288

Where to eat
Chez Annette, 194 bis faubourg Chartrain
Le Daumier, 17 place République
Le Paris, 1 rue Darreau
Le Relais d'Armor, 127 faubourg Chartrain

Where to camp
Camping Grand Prés, rue G-Martel

VERDUN 10
Strategically situated on the River Meuse, Verdun dates from Roman times. Heavy fortification in the 17th century enabled the town to withstand the concentrated assault by German forces during World War I. The town is a centre for touring World War I battlefields and the large military cemetery at Douaumont. Places of interest within the town include the Romanesque Cathedral with its 16th century cloisters, several museums and the impressive Citadel with its famous underground passages.

Where to eat
Accor l'Arche, Aire de Service de St-Nicholas

VERSAILLES 9, 12, 81
Versailles is internationally famous. Standing in beautiful gardens which extend over 250 acres, the Palace of Versailles is one of the most popular attractions in France. Built by Louis XIII and enlarged on a massive scale by Louis XIV it became the chief royal residence of France and has been the scene of many historic events.

Where to stay
★★Clagny, 6 Impasse Clagny
☎(3)9501809 (no restaurant)
★★St-Louis, 28 rue St-Louis
☎(3)9502355 (no restaurant)
★Cheval Rouge, 18 rue A-Chenier
☎(3)9500303

Where to eat
Boule d'Or, 25 rue Ml-Foch
Flunchs, Plaisir-les-Clayes, D161
Potager du Roy, 1 rue Ml-Joffre

VESOUL 31
An industrial town lying at the foot of the imposing hill of La Motte, beside the River Durgeon. Despite an influx of modern factories, Vesoul has retained a number of interesting old buildings including the 18th century Church of St-George.

Where to stay
★★Nord, 7 rue Aigle Noir
☎(84)750256
★★Relais N19, route de Paris
☎(84)764242

VÉZELAY 66
A picturesque town filled with winding streets and old houses, some with carved doors, mullioned windows and staircase turrets. The most outstanding building is the Basilica of Ste-Madeleine, founded during the 9th century, a fine example of French monastic architecture. Good views may be obtained from the top of the tower.

VICHY 71
Lying on the River Allier, Vichy is one of the most famous spas in France. Its waters are still used today, as in Roman times, to treat various complaints and digestive disorders. Now a major tourist centre, the town has a sports complex by the Lac d'Allier together with interesting museums, buildings and parks.

Where to stay
★★★★Pavillion Sévigné, 10 place Sévigné ☎(70)321622
★★★Albert-1er, avenue P-Doumer
☎(70)318110 (no restaurant)

Where to eat
Escargot qui tète, 84 rue Paris
La Grillade Strauss, 5 place
Joseph-Aletti
Nièvre, 17 avenue Gramont
La Rotonde de Lac, boulevard de-
Lattre-de-Tassigny au 'Yacht Club'

Where to camp
At Bellerive (3km W)
Acacias, rue C-Decloître
Beau Rivage, rue C-Decloître
Camping Municipal, 61 av
d'Hauterive

VIENNE 3
Set in the lower Rhône Valley, Vienne
has a well-preserved Gallo-Roman city
with paved streets, villas and shops.
There are also the Roman remains of a
theatre, and the Temple of Augustus
and Livia.

Where to stay
★★Nord, 11 place Miremont
☎(74)857711

Where to eat
Bec Fin, 7 place St-Maurice
Magnard, 45 cours Brillier
La Relais des Routiers, 32 avenue
Berthelot

VILLANDRY 62
Here stands one of the most unusual
châteaux in the area, built during the
16th century to incorporate the keep of
the original fortress. Villandry is
remarkable for its formal gardens
which were redesigned in the 19th
century to provide a geometric mixture
of terraces, moats and canals.

VILLEDIEU-LES-POËLES 47

Where to stay
★★St-Pierre & St-Michel Lf, 12
place de la République
☎(33)610011

Where to eat
Le Relais de l'Agriculture, 57 rue
du Gl-Huard
Le Relais des Routiers, 50 rue du
Bourg l'Abbesse
Le Relais des Voyageurs, gare de
Villedieu

Where to camp
**Camping Municipal Pré de la
Rose,** rue des Costils

VILLEFRANCHE-SUR-SAÔNE 2
An important wine centre and
industrial town with interesting 16th
century houses.

VILLENEUVE-SUR-LOT 88
This thriving market town beside the
River Lot was founded in the 13th
century. Of historical interest are the
two remaining Town Gateways and
the Church of Ste-Catherine as well as
the Pont Vieux which has
commanding views of the River Lot
and countryside.

Where to stay
★★★Parc Lf, 13 boulevard de la
Marine ☎(53)700106
★★Prune d'Or, place de la gare
☎(53)700095

The Château des Rochers at Vitré

Where to eat
Auberge Lou Calel
Hostellerie du Rooy, chemin de
Labourdette
Normandy, 5 place Marine
Le Routier, 31 avenue du Gl-Leclerc
La Toque Blanche

VIMY RIDGE 15
The scene of bitter fighting during
World War I. There is an impressive
monument to the memory of the many
Canadians who gave their lives.

VITRÉ 16
On a steep slope above the Villaine
Valley, Vitré is the best-preserved
walled town in Brittany. The 14th-
15th century castle, which has been
restored and is now the local museum,
dominates the network of old streets
with their gabled medieval houses.

Where to stay
★Chêne Vert, 2 place du Gl-de-
Gaulle ☎(99)750058

VITRY-LE-FRANÇOIS 26, 96
Important during the Middle Ages on account of its strategic location beside the River Marne, Vitry-le-François was virtually destroyed during World War II. A few 17th century buildings survived, including the Church of Notre-Dame, but the remainder of the town has been reconstructed to its original 16th century plan.

Where to stay
★Cloche, 34 rue A-Briand
☎(26)740384
★Nancy, 22 Grand Rue de Vaux
☎(26)740937

Where to eat
Le Relais de la Renaissance, 8 Faubourg de Châlons
Le Rond Point, 28 avenue de la République

VITTEAUX 66
An attractive town containing a number of fine old houses and a 13th century church.

VIVIERS 72
An ancient town with many old buildings including the Maison des Chevaliers and the Romanesque Cathedral of St-Vincent.

Where to eat
Chez Esperandieu – Le Relais Du Vivarais, Route National 86 Lieu-dit Les Sautelles

Where to camp
Rochecondrie Loisirs

VOUGEOT 29
One of the largest vineyards of the Côte d'Or, founded by the Cistercian monks of nearby Citeaux Abbey. The 16th century château has some ancient wine presses on display.

VOUVRAY 61
Set among vineyards, Vouvray is noted for its sparkling wine and visitors are normally welcome to visit the cellars of local merchants and grocers.

Where to stay
★Grand Vatel Lf, avenue Brûlé
☎(47)527032

Where to eat
Le Vouvrillon, 14 avenue Brûlé

WIMEREUX 21
A popular resort with a long sandy beach.

Where to stay
★★Atlantic, Digne de Mer
☎(21)324101
★Centre, 78 rue Carnot
☎(21)324108